CRESCENT BETWEEN CROSS AND STAR

Muslims and the West after 9/11

CRESCENT BETWEEN
CROSS AND STAR

Muslims and the West after 9/11

IFTIKHAR H. MALIK

13th Dec. 06

OXFORD
UNIVERSITY PRESS

OXFORD
UNIVERSITY PRESS

Great Clarendon Street, Oxford OX2 6DP

Oxford University Press is a department of the University of Oxford.
It furthers the University's objective of excellence in research, scholarship,
and education by publishing worldwide in

Oxford New York

Auckland Cape Town Dar es Salaam Hong Kong Karachi
Kuala Lumpur Madrid Melbourne Mexico City Nairobi
New Delhi Shanghai Taipei Toronto

with offices in

Argentina Austria Brazil Chile Czech Republic France Greece
Guatemala Hungary Italy Japan South Korea Poland Portugal
Singapore Switzerland Turkey Ukraine Vietnam

Oxford is a registered trade mark of Oxford University Press
in the UK and in certain other countries

ISBN-13: 978-0-19-547286-8
ISBN-10: 0-19-547286-1

Typeset in Adobe Garamond Pro
Printed in Pakistan by
New Sketch Graphics, Karachi.
Published by
Ameena Saiyid, Oxford University Press
No. 38, Sector 15, Korangi Industrial Area, PO Box 8214
Karachi-74900, Pakistan.

CONTENTS

ACKNOWLEDGEMENTS

Undoubtedly, 9/11 falls within the series of several large-scale tragedies that have so often characterised human history, especially in recent centuries. A hegemonic use of religion and moral uprighteousness for political and such other narrow interests has been with us for quite some time. Uneven polices pursued by Western governments in the Afro-Asian world, especially in the Muslim regions, geared for discretionary economic and geopolitical interests, have only exacerbated mutual schisms. These dichotomies received a fillip and even justification from an enduring academic discourse of Orientalising Islam whereas in the past few decades similar and even more powerful trajectories such as the mass media and influential ideological groups have joined the foray making it into a more pervasive and dangerous preoccupation. In the wake of 9/11, the multi-disciplinary exceptionalisation of Islam by these powerful official and private establishments, instead of auguring a fresher and no less objective perspective, only re-energised the favourite pursuit of *othering* Muslims. As if the Euro-centric modernity was not enough itself, the North Atlantic outreach has discovered a new catechism in the guise of globalization, where diverse societies and their heritage are perceived totally alien, abysmally change-resistant and even outright hostile. Being 'with us' as a fog of war on terror certainly does not help a plural, interdependent and equally uneven world that has yet to whole-heartedly confront serious challenges such as institutional racism, economic marginalisation, collective dispossession, arbitrary invasions, perpetual surrogacy and profiling of selected diaspora communities. Our world requires an honest and more dispassionate understanding of the acrimonious past and an abrasive present if we are to augur a meaningful future for all. This volume is aimed towards that critical thinking which is certainly a prerequisite for a fresher and judicious dialogue on inter-cultural, ideological and international issues. It has benefited from a wide variety of published material without always necessarily agreeing to it. However, appreciation is due to those who helped sustain this effort through their written or spoken words and they are too numerous to be thanked individually. In addition, the print media, numerous web sites and a significant number of seminars and conferences decisively helped formulate this review of several important commentaries. My colleagues and students at Bath Spa University, friends in Oxford and certainly a large number of ordinary people deserve sincere thanks for providing hospitality and sustenance. My family, as ever, stood in good stead when commuting, teaching and numerous media and public engagements turned my life into a whirlwind of activities and globe trotting. The encouragement from Ameena Saiyid has always kept this volume for Oxford University Press on its course, while Rehana Khandwalla, in her own polite but persistent way, remained unrelenting. In addition to my two anonymous readers, my acknowledgements are due for Aquila Ismail, as her pertinent queries and minute observations helped me further clarify my arguments. Certainly, I am responsible for whatever has been observed in these pages and leave the judgement on this effort to its readers.

Oxford
18 May 2006

ACRONYMS

ASSP	Anjuman-i-Sipah-i-Sahabah, Pakistan
BJP	Bharatiya Janata Party
BNP	British National Party
DFID	(British) Department for International Development
EU	European Union
ICRC	International Committee of the Red Cross
ISI	Inter-Services Intelligence (Pakistani intelligence agency)
JI	Jama'at-i-Islami
LFO	Legal Framework Order (General Pervez Musharraf's unilateral amendments [2002] in the Constitution of 1973)
KKK	Ku Klux Klan
MMA	Muttahida Majlis-i-Amal
ML	Muslim League
MNA	Member, Pakistan's National Assembly
MPA	Member, Provincial Assembly
NGO	Non-Government Organization
NWFP	North-West Frontier Province
OIC	Organization of the Islamic Conference
OSP	Office of Special Plans in the Pentagon
PCA	Provisional Control Authority in Iraq
PPP	Pakistan People's Party
RAWA	Revolutionary Association of Women of Afghanistan
RSSS	Rashtriya Swayam Sevak Sangh (Hindutva organization)
SAARC	South Asian Association for Regional Cooperation
USAID	United States Agency for International Development
WMDs	Weapons of Mass Destruction (presumably of Iraq)

INTRODUCTION

The events of 9/11 have certainly unleashed powerful forces which have radically redesigned the politico-ideological contours of contemporary world politics besides ushering an immensely significant new phase in the relationship between Muslims and the West, though it cannot be characterized as a clash of cultures. While to some, the terrorist attacks and the subsequent US-led campaign on terror overwhelmingly focusing on Muslims everywhere, may be symptomatic of an enduring tradition of antagonism, to others, the cataclysmic events have generated a medley of diverse forces including military invasions and rolling back of civil liberties. Whether as a tip of a larger iceberg or merely an instrument for several accompanying trajectories, the dramatic events since September 2001 have laid bare serious anxieties and dilemmas on all sides, which, in several cases, preceded them.[1]

Political and territorial disputes such as in Palestine, Afghanistan, Iraq, Chechnya and Kashmir have assumed new religio-ideological dispensations reviving the old memories among Muslims of the Crusades, expulsions, Inquisitions, colonization, and such events which in the least have revived Orientalist attitudes with dire consequences. The war on terror, from a pervasive Muslim viewpoint, has already become a multi-dimensional anti-Islam campaign with the Neoconservatives, Likudists, Hindutva proponents and several other ultra-right majoritarian forces uniquely converging to deny Muslim communities their due space within the larger plural context. Professor Bernard Lewis, 'the guru of the neocons' is the intellectual mentor of such powerful elements across the North Atlantic regions whose books, especially his recent ones, find only negative aspects in the entire Muslim experience.[2] His enduring apologia for Israel has already turned into a fully-fledged propaganda for war on Iraq and Iran besides reviving the Orientalist discourse.

Lewis's campaign of objectification of Muslim history and cultures is further articulated by ideologues such as Daniel Pipes, Paul Berman, V.S. Naipaul, Ann Coulter, Patrick Buchanan, Bernard-Henri Levy, Ian Buruma, Christopher Hitchens, David Selbourne, Oriana Fallaci, Gilles Kepel and several Neoconservatives who have overnight become specialists on Islam. Several evangelical groups, media conglomerates and influential think tanks also enthusiastically subscribe to a pervasive denigration of Islam whereas policy makers at the Pentagon and other important official establishments, identified as 'Vulcans' by James Mann, have vigorously implemented it using various pretexts and praxis.[3]

In their book, *America Alone*, Stefan Halper and Jonathan Clarke have warned against a pervasive tunnel view of global politics with its negative and belligerent focus on Muslims. To them, the roots of the contemporary Neoconservatives can be traced to the post-Second World War decades in the ideological groundwork owing to 'radical intellectuals' such as Leo Strauss, Nathan Glazer, Daniel P. Moynihan and Irving Kristol, whose successors are imbued with a stronger sense of urgency to reorder the world under an American dictum. In an idealistic yet reductionist view shared by these elements, the world is simply divided between good and evil where the US leads the forces of goodness. Secondly, these elements also mandate that the US can and must apply military means as a fundamental determinant to ensure a pliant world order, without any hesitation in undertaking unilateral actions even if other allies might not be forthcoming. Additionally, Washington should avoid kowtowing to global institutions like the UN. The US is also to primarily focus on the Middle East and global Islam—synonymous with terror—which pose the most serious threat to US primacy in the world. To these Neo-Orientalists, Muslims in Diaspora are an important section of this global Islamic threat and have to be reined in through assertive policy mechanisms, even if it compromises their human rights and citizenship.[4] In other words, security imperatives may definitely supersede the civic prerogatives of a plural coexistence. Following the bomb blasts in London on 7 July

2005, similar attitudes have been variably reverberating at several forums across several North Atlantic regions.

The Neoconservatives share a deeply ingrained disdain for populist democracy and diplomacy in furthering their agendas across the Muslim regions and are equally averse to 'Old Europe', the UN and other multilateral legal and judicial institutions.[5] In fact, Neo-conservatism is intrinsically a phobic ideology featuring exclusivist, racist and imperialist ingredients. In its early years, it operated as a major component of McCarthyism, playing on common American susceptibilities while pronouncing a hyped-up altruism. It began as a major ideological pursuit on the East Coast among analysts such as Irving Kristol, Norman Podhoretz, Daniel P. Moynihan, Michael Novak, Seymour Martin Lipset, Peter Berger, Nathan Glazer and William F. Buckley Jr., who would mostly assemble in the cafeteria of the City College of New York to debate national and international issues. In Chicago, Leo Strauss, Wohlstetter and Allan Bloom were the early Neoconservative proponents who prepared a whole group of like-minded disciples including Richard Perle, Paul Wolfowitz, Alan Keys, Francis Fukuyama and Gary Schmitt.[6] Leo Strauss (1899–1973), a sociologist of German origin, who subsequently migrated to the United States, is retrospectively seen as the philosophical architect of Neo-conservatism.[7] Discomfited with individualism owing to an unhindered modernity and mass-based democracy, Strauss turned towards the classical Greek precept of *eudaimonia* and sought moral bearings anchoring the political alternatives. Seeking out tensions between reason and revelation, defined by him as 'Athens and Jerusalem', Strauss rejected the transcendence of historicism, which sought human thoughts and actions strictly within specific historical contexts.[8] To him, historicism only engendered relativism and a nihilist dictum, and instead turned to the concept of 'natural right' that existed beyond human desire and would arbitrate among humans.[9] To Strauss, *eudaimonia* meaning universal welfare and flourishing of human societies through a good life, was the essence of the ancient Greek tradition and had emanated from Aristotle and Plato, which closely bound humans into a sharing and caring community—now being undermined by the individualistic and hedonistic modernity. Mindful of the American economic and military power, he believed that democracy in the US was not only irreproachable; it was essentially based on moral principles. These traits in an otherwise Hobbesian world had led to American exceptionalism, anchored upon the Declaration of Independence and the Constitution. Such self-congratulatory ideas were promptly welcomed by a generation of American historians, who sought laudatory interpretations of their past. Accordingly, enjoying a superior form of government, Americans were urged to shun finding faults with their country and its past[10] and were exhorted to undertake the prevalence of such noble and moralist virtues in other areas of the world.[11]

The early Neoconservative ideologues mostly published their articles in magazines such as *Commentary* and *Public Interest,* whereas their disciples have been able to acquire important positions within successive American administrations and other important establishments. Their systemic penetration began in the 1970s and serious reversals on Vietnam and the Oil embargo of 1973 added not only to their fury but gained them more listening ears. The American Enterprise Institute (AEI), itself established in 1943, began to co-opt Neoconservative analysts and likewise foundations such as the Heritage, the Georgetown Center for Strategic Studies, the Aspen Institute, the Hudson Institute, Project for New American Century and Freedom House opened their doors to these ideologues. A major breakthrough came with the appointment of Jean Kirkpatrick as the US representative to the UN under President Reagan and the emergence of Donald Rumsfeld as the Defense Secretary. Not only did the Republican Administration become a haven for Neoconservative elements, its war against 'the evil empire' offered them a formidable platform to spearhead multi-dimensional initiatives against the former Soviet Union and other critical liberal opinion groups.

Fukuyamian ebullience and Huntingtonian hypothesis of clash of cultures reflect concurrent views of two leading conservative Straussian scholars. Francis Fukuyama, in fact, in his well known article in *National Interest* in 1989, borrowed his oft-quoted term from his teacher, who had pioneered the idea in his book.[12] In the same vein, Samuel Huntington had borrowed his dialectical term from Bernard Lewis, who had published a piece on a similar theme earlier in *Foreign Affairs*. Their unremitting criticism of the liberal groups in America received a major impetus amidst the Clinton–Lewinsky affair as they used powerful media channels, ethnic lobbies and specific pressure groups to denigrate the latter. The ascendancy of George W. Bush offered them a sought-after opportunity to implement their discretionary policies especially in the Middle East, where, soon after 9/11, the war on terror began to zero in on Afghanistan, Iraq, Syria and Iran while simultaneously allowing Ariel Sharon a free hand in using brute force against the Palestinians. Whereas academics such as Bernard Lewis and an influential section of the Iranian Diaspora persistently urged for a regime change in Iran, most of the Neoconservatives resolved to deal with Saddam Hussein first. To them, Saddam Hussein's rhetoric of socialism and Pan Arab nationalism was equivalent to Hitler's fascism and hence a clear face of evil that had to be eradicated through a regime change.[13] It is interesting to note that the American Neoconservatives, other than influencing the White House and Pentagon, even undertook to articulate Republican foreign policies. To them, the Bush Doctrine was a radical departure from the earlier policies of deterrence, multilateralism and containment as it stood for pre-emption, regime change and a commitment to the American pre-eminence. The United States could not shirk back from its moral and political imperative of reordering of regions such as the Middle East as it could not 'escape its responsibility for maintaining a decent world order. The answer to this challenge is the American idea itself, and behind it the unparalleled military and economic strength of its custodian. Duly armed, the United States can act to secure its safety and to advance the cause of liberty—in Baghdad and beyond.'[14]

Following the re-election of President Bush, the war on terror had already become a war on tyranny and the erstwhile justification for the invasion of Iraq such as the alleged weapons of mass destruction and Baghdad's linkages with global terrorism, were overshadowed by a re-energized campaign against Iran and Syria. A rather simplistic but equally dangerous moralism was disallowing a review of the accruing gruesome human loss, stupendous economic costs, persistent global rebuke and intense regional instability in West Asia, already marooned by internal autocracies and external interventions.

It is true that several Muslim militant groups have owed their promotion if not their formation to those very citadels of powers, which are now intent upon their decimation. Surely, a grave politico-economic disempowerment, disillusionment with the ruling elite due to their coercion and corruption, and a wider ideological vacuum across the Muslim regions have collectively spawned Political Islam as a perceived panacea for a multiple marginalization. But, not long ago, during the Cold War, many of these holy warriors had been fellow travellers—even highly esteemed such as in the case of the precursors of the Taliban—along with the surrogate rulers. Many of these Sunni and Shia radicals have been steadfast beneficiaries of the largesse received owing to geo-political imperatives, until friends turned into foes. The CIA, enjoying active support from the White House and Capitol Hill, mounted the largest covert programme in US history by assisting and training the Afghan Mujahideen.[15] Weapons worth billions of dollars were funnelled into Pakistani tribal areas under the auspices of General Ziaul Haq's Inter-Services Intelligence (ISI), which not only caused the Soviet retreat in 1989, it cost more than one million Afghan and several thousand Pakistani lives. No one was concerned that the Afghans, after all these sacrifices, were left high and dry the way Pakistan's democratic prerogatives had been sidelined by the overriding US security concerns. Concurrently, the Saudis and the Americans had been arming Saddam Hussein to weaken Khomeini's revolutionary Iran, and as a consequence, the Gulf War claimed millions of innocent lives on both sides.

Israel was certainly happy with its two Muslim foes fighting a drawn and costly war during the 1980s, and similarly, the West and the ruling Arab elite ensured further neutralization of both

Baghdad and Tehran by their endlessly locking horns with each other. The Iraq–Iran War certainly weakened Hussein but for Iranians it had been a lonely endeavour. The Soviet Union, one of the two global 'Great Satans'—as Imam Khomeini put it—had finally retreated from Afghanistan in 1989 following a humiliating reversal and now lay shorn of most of its colonial possessions. According to the Islamists, the remaining and still bigger 'Satan'— the United States—had to be confronted, as it had been bankrolling the Zionist expansionists while simultaneously controlling and exploiting Muslim lands and resources though their corrupt, coercive and inefficient surrogates. By this time, the Saudi– American alliance and likewise the Israeli–American interdependence had been fully consolidated with hundreds of billions of petrodollars finding their way into the US, especially in Texas with the houses of Saud and Bush establishing closer personal and economic ventures. For instance, during 2001–2, Saudi royals and their business associates had already pumped $860 billion into the American economy, with Israel fully benefiting from the recycling of this expatriate wealth. It is a different thing that for fellow Muslims, the Saudi dynasty and its kowtowing clerics will recommend a rather obscurantist version of Islam whereas their own national wealth lay in the Western institutions—a fact not lost on several critics of the monarchy. The downfall of the Shah in 1979 and collaboration on Afghanistan and the Iraq–Iran war had greatly assisted the US–Saudi commonalities followed by shared economic interests of the ruling elite on both sides, fully facilitated through Prince Bandar bin Sultan, the long-time Saudi Ambassador in Washington.[16]

During the Iraqi invasion of Kuwait in 1990, Riyadh and Washington became closest allies with the former providing its soil, money and vast resources to the US-led coalition in expelling Hussein's occupying forces from Kuwait. Following the humbling and encircling of Hussein, the US presence on the Arabian Peninsula during the 1990s became a volatile issue for Islamists like Osama bin Laden, who wanted to transform their own corrupt and surrogate regimes into a strict Islamist mould. The Soviet Union had been dissolved but the US was not to be allowed an unchecked role in West Asia, since its former comrades—the war-hardy *Afghan Arabs*—were now determined to defeat the second and bigger 'Satan'.

The Russian withdrawal from Afghanistan led to similar dramatic and no less significant retreats from Eastern Europe and Central Asia, ending the five-decade long Cold War. The Neoconservatives perceived it as the greatest victory of their agenda affirming the righteousness of their mission and possibility of similar achievements elsewhere, including the vital Middle East. By the time Clinton came into power on the aura of a post-Cold War optimism and greater role for the American official and private trajectories, both the Islamists and the Neoconservatives had speeded up their reorganization efforts.[17] The pervasive Muslim dismay over festering anguish in Bosnia, Chechnya, Kashmir, Palestine, Abkhazia and Ngorno Karabakh within the larger context of a wider politico-economic disempowerment, offered these Islamists centre stage.[18] Whereas the Clinton–Lewinsky affair proved a godsend for the Neoconservatives, the Islamists were resuscitated by the continuing hold of West-dependent and abrasively corrupt elite across the Muslim regions. Recruits for both the fundamentalist constellations—Neoconservatives and *jihadis*—came aplenty converging sectional interests with regional agendas, and the Huntingtonian thesis, despite its serious flaws, became a reference point until 9/11 proved a watershed.

Under George W. Bush, Vice-President Dick Cheney assumed the role of the leading patron of the Neoconservatives whereas at the Pentagon, Donald Rumsfeld led foreign as well as defense policies, and powerful ideologues such as Richard Perle, Paul Wolfowitz, Douglas Feith and Elliot Abrams were able to implement their agenda. The Neoconservatives had their colleagues in the State Department including John R. Bolton, David Wurmser and Eliot Cohen offering a helping hand to their colleagues at the Pentagon.[19] The CIA, itself trying to recover from public scrutiny and identity crisis in the post-Cold War years, aligned itself with the neoconservative agenda and directors like James Woolsey advocated a more forward policy in the Middle East. Israel, through its unrestrained support from various American establishments, has been a beneficiary of intimate information on Washington's policies towards the Middle East.[20] Concurrently, ambitious individuals such as Zalmay Khalilzad—a former lecturer at Columbia University and an intermediary between the Unocal and Taliban—who had been close, junior confidants, were duly rewarded with special posts.[21] High-profile Iraqi exiles such as Ahmed Chalabi, Ayad Allawi, Ibrahim al-Jaafari, some known Shia clerics and Kurdish leaders had already been co-opted to build a second-tier of support against Saddam Hussein. The invasion of Iraq, lacking moral, legal or international justification, mostly sought its validity from a variety of shifting and unsubstantiated claims, and was seen as a dress rehearsal for more such campaigns to come. The hardliners at the Washington Project for the New American Century, who had constantly espoused the doctrine of pre-emptive strikes against unfriendly states like Iraq, soon began to urge attacks on Iran and Syria by using pre-emption and prevention interchangeably.

From amongst the academia, the American Neoconservatives have received guidance as well as support from a number of professors such as Aaron Friedberg, James Q. Wilson, Daniel Pipes and Donald Kagan, all led by a re-energised Bernard Lewis. On the West Coast, Stanford University's Hoover Institution had evolved into a Neoconservative outpost and ran several programmes for civil and military personnel from South-west Asia. It is interesting to note that Irving Kristol, one of the early Neoconservative ideologues, was against co-opting intellectuals, though he fully welcomed evangelical elements. Powerful organs of the media such as Fox highlighted Neoconservative views to the extent of turning them into sheer propaganda, especially after 9/11, where syndicated columnists including Charles Krauthammer, Judith Miller, Lawrence Kaplan and several others devoted column after column to the Islamic terrorist threat and linkages between Al-Qaeda and Iraq. Long before 9/11, the Neoconservatives had propounded a militarist interventionism in the Middle East by focusing on the removal of Saddam Hussein and the invasion of Iran, as they exuberantly piloted the idea of the US as the global sheriff.[22] They felt constrained by international treaties and other such instruments, which to them, operated as unnecessary curbs on US power and global imperatives.[23] 9/11 came as a blessing from the blue as the Neoconservatives aggregated their efforts to reorganise the Middle Eastern political map by espousing the invasions of Iraq and Iran besides supporting Israel in its own untiring campaign of Palestinian dispossession.[24] Even in the wake of pervasive defiance and instability in Iraq following the invasion, the Neoconservatives, egged on by pro-Israeli lobbies, were espousing an attack on Iran. Norman Podhoretz, 'the arch-conservative' editor of *Commentary*, opined in August 2004: 'I am not advocating the invasion of Iran at this moment, although I wouldn't be heartbroken if it happened.'[25]

The Fukuyamian ebullience and Huntingtonian premise of the clash of cultures have, in their own powerful way, celebrated Westernism by positing it as the only reference point besides *othering* non-Western communities, especially Muslims. Accordingly, the latter are not only different from the Judeo-Christian West, they are equally antagonistic and the reification of the West rests upon a self-avowed sense of superiority. Such arguments remind one of the colonial and Orientalist self-righteousness. Michael Ignatieff—often referred to as a liberal hawk—went a step further when he exhorted Western powers such as the United States to embark on a benevolent imperial venture not only to neutralize the oppositional forces but also to undertake the socio-political overhaul of non-Western societies. His prescription for an 'empire-lite' hinges on an altruist view of Western polities such as the United States, which could operate globally in the name of a larger good.[26] In the same vein, Fareed Zakaria has not been content with mere control of the non-West including the Muslim world, but instead has advised the instilling of Western liberalism even before the induction of democracy. His writings suggest official support for moderate and modernist forces in the Muslim world including military dictators and unelected monarchs.[27] The British polemicist,

Christopher Hitchens, undertook the advocacy of President Bush in his weekly columns and used familiar official arguments for pre-emptive strikes and regime change in Iraq.[28]

As pointed out by several writers, the problems with such arguments are manifold: firstly, they condone hegemony and conquest without any reservations; secondly, they believe the West–non-West relationship to be totally between two unequals where the West is certainly superior to the rest, and thirdly, they consider Western mores to be the only panacea for human problems without acknowledging that many of those in recent centuries have largely been rooted in the Euro–Atlantic trajectories. Such opinions highlight the continuity of Orientalist typologies based on self-righteous and hierarchical differentiation of human communities.[29] The support for yet another reordering of West Asia without any reference to the past or fear of any serious repercussions, only smacks of a superficial understanding of recent history. Recourse to strong-arm tactics seen since 9/11, has been adopted by such powerful opinion groups as an ethical and overdue pursuit, irrespective of its dire consequences. Such a moral crusade is not merely confined to a few powerful ideologues; it enjoys the consensual support of weighty groups from within the church, media, academia and other establishments and has become a dominant Western discourse.[30] This mistaken celebration of an irredentist modernity, anchored upon partisan forces such as Orientalism, collective violence, environmental degradation and neo-racism, is itself causing serious dilemmas within the North Atlantic societies. However, there are scholars who problematize modernity in a global as well as Western context and refuse to consider religio–political forces in non-Western societies to be anti-modern.[31] To others, Eurocentric views of a celebratory modernity are flawed since they underwrite Western dominance of the rest while overlooking serious contradictions within the Western experience. For many observers, the US projection, especially after the dissolution of the Cold War, is based on erroneous and often exaggerated assumptions and the entire empire-building project, as propounded by the Neoconservatives and an overambitious Pentagon, is inimical to global peace.[32]

The reinforcement of the dictum of differentiation and *othering* of a caricatured East is a potentially dangerous mode of thinking which is gradually turning into a 'moral Waterloo' of Western values.[33] However, the pervasive trend to excepionalize Islam through a regimented attribution of some inherent negativity, inferiority and rigidity to its creed is an age-old Western pursuit, which has never been forsaken. Instead, over the last two decades, it has been reinvigorated, and following 9/11 it has assumed even more dangerous proportions.[34] Strangely enough, several Muslim and non-Muslim opinion groups keep adhering to an assumed myth of Islam being the fastest growing religion in the world. Such a premise is certainly dangerous, firstly because it is mere hearsay, and secondly, it does not take into account vast echelons of Muslim groups, especially in the Diaspora, who have become indifferent towards their Muslimness. In fact, conversions to Buddhism may outnumber every other tradition, though Christianity has certainly been gaining more adherents in the Afro–Asian regions. However, the mythification of Islam as the fastest growing creed allows disillusioned Muslims a needed sense of self-assurance while to antagonists it provides a useful tool to further posit Islam as a growing threat.

In its present context, Orientalism combines historic anomalies and contemporary geo-political ingredients and is joined by a strong ingredient of Islamophobia. It occupies a self-construed moral upper ground and is immensely partisan if not openly racist in its exposition. It is certainly sexist and grows on a strictly hierarchical view of Muslim societies, which pose multiple threats justifying their control through sheer force. The invasions of Afghanistan and Iraq, and Israelis[35] and Russians pursuing multiple campaigns against their underprivileged Muslim populace have occurred simultaneously with several democracies promulgating discretionary policies on travel, immigration and pluralism. While Muslims are overwhelmingly aggrieved over the destruction and denigration of their communities and heritage, their mundane problems of poverty, universal disempowerment and alienation remain unattended both by their rulers and their backers in the West, who prioritize perpetuation of their own discretionary interests. Western espousal of democracy, human rights, inter-gender equality, secular education and economic progress is sceptically viewed as an empty smoke-screen given the past experience of Western regimes only fielding their own partisan interests while occasionally and rather ceremoniously moralizing on higher ideals. These serious contradictions have often been flagged by several Western commentators, as was observed by Terry Waite, when the former hostage noted in November 2005: 'What is the essential difference in the methods deployed by my captors, who were labelled terrorists, and those of the authorities that detain in Guantanamo Bay and elsewhere? They have been detained on suspicion and treated in a way that no civilised nation ought to condone'. As a close associate of the former Archbishop of Canterbury, Waite even criticised several Church leaders for not taking a moral stance on such serious moral issues, and observed: 'As a member of the church I am obliged to say that, although some have spoken out against the matters to which I have referred, the church as a body has hardly been vociferous about them'.[36]

The exposure of torture and brutalization of Muslim internees at Guantanamo Bay, Abu Ghraib Jail, Bagram Air Base and Israel's Facility 1391, and the massacres at Mazar-i-Sharif, Kandahar, Jenin, Rafah, Grozny, Falluja, Karbala, Qaim and Najaf have been justified through a pervasive moralist and racist argument, itself rooted in Orientalism and an enduring denigration of Muslims. Not only have brutal practices such as hooding, rape and sodomy gone on in the full knowledge of many, senior officials in many cases have even sanctioned them. Humiliation of denuded Muslim men both by soldiers and private contractors, the rape of Iraqi women, formation of pyramids of nude bodies and posing with corpses certainly proved to be 'an institutionalized feature of America's war on terror.'[37] The well-known Arab writer, Ahdaf Soueif, while commenting on the psychological and sexual dehumanisation of the Iraqi prisoners by the Coalition troops, alerted everyone to the Western moral dilemma by noting: 'The acts in the photos being flashed across the networks would not have taken place but for the profound racism that infects the American and British establishments.' The intermittent references to liberation of Iraqis from Saddam Hussein's regime (or the Taliban's stronghold) aimed at diluting the resentment where 'Hussein is now [seen as] the moral compass of the west.' On the contrary, these pictures confirmed that both the US and Britain were 'not in Iraq as an act of goodwill' but simply for their own specific interests.[38] This dehumanization reminded another former internee, Haifa Zangana, of her own persistent trauma and that of her people, as she commented: 'Iraqis did not struggle for decades to replace one torturer with another.' Echoing the Pushtuns, Palestinians, Kashmiris, Chechens, Malays and Moros, she further observed: 'We are a proud people welcoming to guests but unforgiving of those who tread with heavy boots across privacy, integrity and history.'[39] Such strong words do not reflect any jubilation over being liberated by some benevolent friends; rather they transmit sheer anger and defiance.

In 2005, there were reports that such human rights abuses were quite widespread rather than being confined to a few known cases. Violence in Iraq multiplied amidst American claims of having an upper hand though the press reports only negated such assertions. More than 400 people lost their lives in less than two weeks in early May 2005 with eighty well-orchestrated suicide attacks, which simultaneously caused grievous injuries to numerous citizens. Iraq appeared ungovernable with the Baghdad regime and the Occupation forces apportioning the blame on an unending supply of 'foreign insurgents'.[40] The legal and moral justification for the invasion of Iraq has remained disputatious despite the January 2005 elections in Iraq and a posthumous emphasis on democracy.[41] The unjustified invasion of Iraq by Western allies without any legal and international backing confronted Tony Blair all through the election campaign in 2005 as he faced accusations of being a 'liar' and 'untrustworthy' from several quarters. Despite putting up a brave face, the British Prime Minister was persistently heckled on not intimating his cabinet and the country on the complete details of the legal advice given by Lord Goldsmith, the British Attorney-General, who himself was influenced by the Americans during his visit in February 2003. Despite initially raising some issues on the legality of the invasion, Lord Goldsmith subsequently changed his evidence.[42] The full contents of his two divergent summaries and Blair's withholding of the vital feedback from his cabinet emerged as the thorniest issues on the eve of the elections when the Labour Party prepared for a third consecutive term in office. Countrywide support for the party decreased due to Blair's controversial war on Iraq with the Labour Party losing a hundred seats and the 'protest vote' going in favour of the Liberal Democrats. Even on the eve of the May elections, leading Iraqi academics and writers in the United Kingdom reminded British voters of the pervasive devastation of their country owing to the invasion.[43] Soon after the elections, pressures on a battered Blair to cede authority to someone else in the Labour Party began to mount, making his position further uncertain and vulnerable. The daily exposé of secret developments leading to the invasion of Iraq often occurred from very close quarters, much to the embarrassment of the Blair government. During the autumn of 2005, amidst bloodletting in Iraq, Christopher Meyer, the former British Ambassador to the US, serialised his memoirs, *DC Confidential* in the *Daily Mail* and *Guardian*. As an insider to the crucial Anglo–American parleys leading to the controversial invasion, Meyer portrayed Blair as a weak leader, who was unduly overawed by the superior American military might and hastily agreed to support the ill-fated military campaign.[44] Meyer's well-publicised accounts were soon followed by the publication in the British press of a secret White House memo based on a Bush–Blair exchange on the possibility of bombing the Qatar-based Al-Jazeera television headquarters so as to stop the telecasts of this Arab channel.[45]

The destruction of Afghanistan, first by the Russians and then by the Anglo–American alliance, despite promises of reconstruction and a curiously shared underlying abhorrence of Islam, completely reflected pervasive Orientalist views and hegemonic undercurrents.

The Taliban came to personify typified Muslims *per se* with their barbaric, uncouth, emotional, irrational, sexist policies. The West had to come in from its upper moral pedestal to rescue yet another trapped Muslim society where *burqa*-clad women symbolized oppression within the context of Islam's supposed penchant for unbridled violence. The civilizing mission had to be ushered in through military means by using cluster bombs, decimation of the few remaining intact hamlets and a vengeful operation against the Islamists sheltering in this country. Osama bin Laden and Mullah Omar came to typify the 'mad Mullahs' who had to be reined in through a larger Western intervention. Hamid Karzai, like other pliant Muslim rulers, was the intermediary to lead Afghanistan towards modernity, though it is a different matter that he himself remained solely dependent upon American security personnel. The deaths of thousands of Afghans, the imprisonment of hundreds of other Muslims at Camp X-Ray, Bagram airbase and elsewhere across the world in secret CIA-run facilities without any recourse to judicial defence, paralleled the promises of democracy and reconstruction, while the country was dished out to avaricious warlords and drug barons. The Pushtun marginalization from the political spectrum through bundling the eastern and southern regions as the hotbeds of Al-Qaeda and Taliban continues amidst numerous military operations undertaken by the US, Pakistani and British special troops. Even after years of targeted operations, the country was less than pacified, with a growing support for the deposed Taliban, as the battle for hearts and minds seems to have been lost. While talking to Christina Lamb, an Afghan might have spoken on behalf of many of his fellow citizens when he observed: 'America has got watches, but the Taliban has the time.'[46]

The vulnerability of the Karzai regime became more evident when, in early May 2005, anti-American demonstrations shook cities like Kabul, Jalalabad and Khost with Afghans ransacking foreign missions and burning American flags. Similar violent demonstrations took place in non-Pushtun regions of Badakhshan, Mazar-i-Sharif and Herat, making it a country-wide protest costing several lives.[47] The underlying anti-Americanism in the country came to the fore owing to a report in *Newsweek* of the desecration of the Quran mainly to coerce the Guantanamo internees into confession. According to reports, the 'interrogators, in an attempt to rattle suspects, placed Qur'ans on toilets and, in at least one case, flushed a holy book down the toilet.'[48] Following the deaths of several and injuries to many more across the Muslim world, the editor of the American weekly tendered an apology in the wake of a 'humiliating retraction'.[49]

Like elsewhere in West Asia, hopes for peace in the Holy Land engendered by the Oslo Accords were equally dashed, largely due to a fall-out from 9/11 and the resultant anti-Muslim idiom in numerous metropolises. Washington's support for the brutal Israeli expansion became unilateral even to the discomfort of several of its former diplomats, though many powerful sections in the Western media including the BBC would gloss over the historical details, and subtly underplay Arab grievances.[50] Target killings, massive retaliation against suicide bombings, large-scale demolition of houses and the construction of a parameter wall dividing Palestinian communities into several disconnected Bantustans not only vetoed the two-state formula as laid down in several international commitments, but also pushed the region into complete chaos and lawlessness. Israel, as claimed by Amnesty International, was pursuing ethnic cleansing and other serious war crimes, which urgently needed to be taken notice of.[51] Ariel Sharon was steadily and vocally helped by Bush, and in 2004 even Tony Blair during his visit to Washington, supported the Israeli annexation of the West Bank. The joint press conference of the three leaders in the White House not only negated the UN resolutions but also froze Washington's own 'Road Map for Peace'. While many concerned quarters in Europe and within Britain, including former diplomats, expressed their unease over the Sharon–Bush–Blair unilateralism, Sharon—defiant of global public opinion—continued with his 'politicide' of the Palestinians. The ultra right sections from amongst the Christians and Jews, while being led by self-professed practising leadership in Tel Aviv, Washington and London, were further invigorated by the fall-out from 9/11. While responsible elements urged for dialogue on the basis of the UN resolutions within the context of two-state formula and equal citizenry for Arabs in Israel,[52] Sharon pursued his own expansionist and annihilative campaigns based on Palestinian dislocation and genocide.

Israel's policy hinged on a few known premises: no right of return for Palestinian refugees; no dissolution of settlements built after 1967; no complete return of the territory captured in 1967 and since; and, no equal citizenry rights for Israeli Arabs. Moreover, it supported expulsions, selected killings and decimation of the Palestinian infrastructure while keeping hundreds of Palestinians in its Facility 1391—the equivalent of Camp Delta at Guantanamo Bay. Using the convenient pretext of the war on terror, it did not shirk from decimating countless refugee settlements in the Occupied Territories. Israel's seasoned campaign received impetus from 9/11 and its inquisitional methods of torture were enthusiastically shared by London, Washington and Delhi, dangerously expanding the parameters of its campaign to a wider Muslim world. Concurrently, Israel's own worries about its demographic smallness versus desire to capture more territory—all within the context of its boastful claims of being the *only* democracy in the region—created a serious moral dilemma for its own dissenting voices. One of its leading intellectuals, Baruch Kimmerling, introduced the term 'politicide', which is certainly more than genocide of a people. He noted:

> By *politicide* I mean a process that has, as its ultimate goal, the dissolution of the Palestinian people's existence as a legitimate social, political, and economic entity. The process may also but not necessarily include their partial or complete cleansing from the territory known as the Land of Israel. This policy will inevitably rot the internal fabric of Israeli society and undermine the moral foundation of the Jewish state in the Middle East. From this perspective, the result will be double politicide—that of the Palestinian entity, and in the long run, that of the Jewish entity as well.[53]

Even the Israeli military strategists were warning against post-1967 occupation and expansions, as the economic and psychological costs besides the strategic overstretch were only exacerbating the country's security dilemma.[54] The death of Yasser Arafat in 2004 and the election of Mahmud Abbas as the President of the Palestinian Authority were perceived as a new opening for peace, though Israel continued with its policy of consolidation of settlements in the West Bank and the Wall. The withdrawal from the Gaza settlements accompanied a greater insistence on holding on to the West Bank and Jerusalem while refusing to accept the right of return for Palestinian refugees. Israel did not participate in the London conference on 1 March 2005 as if the solution to the imbroglio had to come about only from the Palestinians.

While the Western official and other related powerful establishments and their allies elsewhere seek civilizational and geo-political justifications in pursuing arbitrary policies and gigantic military campaigns vis-à-vis the West Asian regions, Muslim regimes have equally been instrumental in aggravating common agony.[55] The inefficient, dictatorial and often oppressive leaders have not shirked from using Islam and narrowly defined nationalism for legitimacy purposes besides keeping their populace completely disempowered. Despite their opportunistic as well as apologetic relationship with the Western regimes, these Muslim governments do not earn any laurels from the latter. Several from among the fifty-four Muslim countries, mostly ruled by pro-Western dictatorships and monarchs, routinely incur Western wrath for hoarding weapons of mass destruction whereas countries such as Israel with proven stocks stay beyond any global or moral reproach. In addition, these regimes keep on endlessly buying weapons from the Western markets while denying basic amenities and rights to their own people. No wonder, the Muslim world is collectively the largest buyer of weaponry and is also home to gnawing forces of poverty, illiteracy, malnourishment and oppression. At another level, the ritualistic and clericalized versions of a humane heritage like Islam have further compounded the pervasive malaise. Political Islam, both at the state and institutional levels, has been discretionary, often assuming hegemonic designs while vetoing dialogue and democratization. Thus, the Muslim anger is rooted in indigenous and external factors—mostly of an extra-religious nature—though certainly it is exhibited through an increased emphasis on religiosity or a self-assumed introversion.

Western politicians largely share a common ideology and strategy on terror, and while attributing it to Muslim groups, are confident of their eventual invincibility. It is a different matter whether their high-sounding ideals for the developing world including the Muslim regions, would ever reach fruition given the powerful forces of multiple control at their disposal. Exaggeration as well as underestimation of a *Muslim* threat, which largely occurs due to a pervasive anguish and anger, characterizes their disproportionate responses, often unilateral and massive in terms of their impact and scale of destruction. Western apprehensions and ambitions are widely shared and supported by a whole strata of ideologues and pundits representing professions such as politics, law, education, media, defence, religion and business, who have been regimenting a consciousness based on the partisan memory of the Muslim–Western relationship. To a significant extent, they share a derogatory view of Islam as a religion and Muslims as a trans-regional community embodying clandestine demographic, cultural and geo-political challenges. These ideologues are certainly the true descendants of the Orientalists of the colonial era, who, like the Crusaders, fiery priests and Inquisitioners before them, always perceived Islam as an eternal foe. Led by known intellectuals these powerful elites have revived a sordid and antagonistic discourse on Islam while retaining closer alliances within the Bush Administration. George W. Bush himself is supported by an entire breed of politicians such as Tony Blair, Silvio Berlusconi, Jose Maria Aznar, Ariel Sharon and John Howard, from amongst many, who see eye to eye with Washington's grand design of a modernist world anchored on market fundamentalism and supported by unchallenged military unilateralism, over and above the UN and such other multilateral prerogatives. Most of these leaders are motivated by an evangelical mission, seeing it as their moral duty to pursue aggressive policies vis-à-vis Muslim regions and Diaspora. It is not surprising at all that, once again, several Christian missionary organisations and rhetoricians such as Frank Graham, Pat Robertson, George Carey and Jerry Falwell have chosen to join the bandwagon both to denigrate Islam and also to convert impoverished Muslims and numerous war orphans in West Asia.

It is a widely shared Muslim belief—not usually aired on the Western media—that the proponents of Pax-Americana, Greater Israel, Hindu Rashtra, an unassailable Mother Russia or such other forms of unitary nationalism all unite in their hatred as well as fear of Muslims. Muslims, in general, apprehend that 9/11 was just a symptom of a larger malaise rooted in Western official double standards, though most of them do not support terror, yet are all significantly affected by retaliatory policies. More and more of them see several sinister lobbies working behind the US-led campaign on terror. Seeing multitudes of Palestinians, Afghans, Chechens, Kashmiris, Gujaratis, Iraqis, Thai Malays and Moros losing their lives with official Muslim leadership staying sidelined, they worry that not only in Diaspora but also in the traditional lands of their abode, their cultures, history and religion are once again under a serious spotlight. Like the Orientalists and evangelists of the near past, Islam is being imperviously and holistically essentialized as an innate culture of violence, irrationality, sexism and authoritarianism. Excepting some extreme elements, Muslims are not preoccupied with the idea of conquering the entire world for Allah, since to most of them the mundane problems of day to day life are more than enough to keep them occupied. Of course, like other evangelical religions Muslims idealize a global Islam and a united *ummah*, but they are aware of their own serious limitations, especially in a world where plain spirituality, otherworldliness and devotion are overshadowed by a hegemonic modernity, itself rooted in competition and individual gains. Commentators like David Selbourne or 'Will' (Harry) Cummins may chide the world for loosing the battle eventually to a victorious and global Islam and can admonish the Left for not being able to foresee the rising tide of radical Islam, yet the fact remains that all such predictions are premature and simply alarmist.[56] As a matter of fact, pervasive poverty, high rates of illiteracy, authoritarian regimes kowtowing to specific interests and a constant external interventionism continue to exacerbate Muslim anguish, with the age-old dictum of divide-and-rule determining the fate of millions of have-nots. The Neoconservatives and their other ultra right counterparts may have vast military and economic resources at their disposal, whereas radical Muslims may have a strong concept of holy war and martyrdom to enthuse scores of young men, yet they all have their limitations and the world cannot be left to their simplistic and insidious designs.

Within this contentious and immensely dangerous mode of thinking and politicking, histories of religions and peoples have been rewritten to substantiate a clash of cultures, with an attendant media and other racist xenophobes justifying this polarization. In the name of patriotism, these closely allied establishments within otherwise fully-fledged democratic polities demanded an ideological and racial uniformity. Critics, peace marchers and moral refuseniks were all seen as subversive liberals, Muslim-lovers or traitors in league with the enemy from *within*. Religion, nationalism and patriotism—often uneasy bedfellows in the past—came to be allied together in this multi-faceted campaign whose moral, class-based and racial undertones have been unswervingly hegemonic. Even five years after 9/11, there are exhortations for further intense campaigns targeting Muslim regions and communities. For instance, a former CIA official—possibly Mike Scheuer—felt that the West was losing the war on terror and had to assume more militarist strategies. To this 'Anonymous' strategist with expertise on South Asia, most of the 1.3 billion Muslims did not hate the West for what it is but what it had done to their lands, faith and resources. To him, the only way to defeat the Muslims was by undertaking total campaigns without any sympathy for civilians, population centres or water and food resources: 'With killing must come a Sherman-like razing of infrastructure. Roads and irrigation systems; bridges, power plants, and crops in the fields, fertilizer plants and grain mills—all these and more will need to be destroyed to deny the enemy its support base.'[57]

This study looks at the root cause of Western views on Islam spread over the last fifteen centuries mainly to establish whether it is the lack of knowledge, or instead the partisan and gullible nature of information on both sides that quickly transmutes political problems into religious and cultural conflicts. This research is fully alert to the dangers of monolithicizing Islam and the West, yet applies them plainly as the familiar paradigms without rejecting the Islam-in-the-West and West-in-Islam equation. In the host of writings on Islam simply focusing on well-rehearsed themes such as terror, Al-Qaeda, Jihad, modernity and other related subjects, this volume attempts a comparative and a rather overdue Muslim perspective. It also brings in an integrated discussion of some prominent issues such as Afghanistan, Iraq and Palestine, besides dilating on the Indo–Pakistani conflict, Muslim secularism and politics of gender.

Chapter 1 ascertains the mutual acrimonies, especially in the post-9/11 perspective, and identifies the areas of tension all the way from the early Prophetic era through Spain, Sicily, the Crusades, the Ottoman Empire, and colonialism to Orientalism. It offers a valid overview of Western scholarship—secular as well as sacred—until recent times by throwing a searchlight on the academe. Writers such as Dante, Shakespeare, Goethe, Pococke, Gibbon, Renan, Margoliouth, Massignon, T.E. Lawrence, Marshall Hodgson and several others have been briefly revisited within the context of institutionalisation of Islamic studies at premier Western universities.

Chapter 2 links up the Orientalist and neoconservative traditions in the contemporary era with a specific focus on Professor Bernard Lewis, the doyen of scholars on Muslim history. His various books, especially the recent best-sellers, have been reviewed, offering a critique and an 'alternative' view. Chapter 3 is a further in-depth study of some of the leading writers, publicists and journalists such as Daniel Pipes, Paul Berman, Gilles Kepel and Bernard-Henri Levy whose abrasive and inimical opinions on Islam, Jihad, Muslim history, Diaspora and related subjects are widely read and have even been influencing important policy matters. Chapter 4 is devoted to the study of V.S. Naipaul, Patrick Buchannan, Ann Coulter and some known figures from the media and evangelical enterprise to establish their stances on Islam and the Muslim world. Chapter 5 surveys diverse and recent Muslim opinions on classical Islam, modernity and Western civilisation. Here, the focus is on Fazlur Rahman, Abul Ala Mawdudi and Abul Hasan Ali Nadwi, and towards the end, and following a brief encounter with some progressive Muslims, it locates their position on [Muslim] feminism and secularism.

The next two chapters attempt a detailed analysis of West Asian regions under Western and Israeli attack. Chapter 6 focuses on Afghanistan and Iraq, which were targeted by George Bush and Tony Blair for military invasions in pursuit of the war on terror. The rise of regional warlords, escalating ethno-sectarian schisms and strains on gender issues are a few glaring commonalities in both these countries where the coalition has had ample opportunity to help construct fresher, all-encompassing and judicious orders, away from partisan interests and security imperatives. The chapter on Afghanistan and Iraq is meant to seek out conflicting policies on issues of democracy and nation-building as contested by all sides under the Anglo–American occupation.

Chapter 7 tries to understand the often-ambivalent relationship between Judaism and Zionism within the context of a growing criticism of Israeli policies. Many of Israel's protagonists have tried to juxtapose this criticism with anti-Semitism in their effort to make Tel Aviv sacrosanct despite its continued high-handed policies. Recent pro-Israeli Jewish views and their critique are the mainstay of this chapter. Israel's often controversial policies in the Middle East and their support from the North Atlantic region vocally reverberate within the Muslim discourse at all levels, increasing anguish over their own weaknesses besides underpinning a worldwide anti-Americanism. While some European Jews such as in Britain, may be apprehensive of Neo-anti-Semitism, the violent Middle Eastern politics keep infecting the Muslim–Western discourse in several ways. The unquestioned official Western support for Israel only exacerbates Muslim anger along with not too often unjustified accusations of neo-colonialism and double standards. This chapter also focuses on the intertwining of Judaism with Zionism seeking an essentialised and unquestioned support for Israel, which remains contentious among several Western and Israeli Jews. The section on Israel and Palestine not only seeks the root cause of this major bleeding wound but also responds to some aspects of neo-anti-Semitism, where Diaspora Muslims, for example in France, are being projected as the new perpetrators, though splashing swastika and other racist graffiti on Jewish buildings has been the work of the Neo-Nazis.

The Epilogue acknowledges forces sensitive to the Muslim predicament and also offers a short resume on the Indo–Pakistan conflictive relationship, underlining the imperatives for a fresher paradigm on this costly and taxing bilateralism.

NOTES

1. The US commission led by Congressman Thomas H. Kean presented its 567 page report of findings and recommendations to President George W. Bush in July 2004. Created by the Congress and the President in November 2003, this bipartisan commission mostly focused on recent and technical aspects such as the lack of co-ordination among US intelligence agencies and avoided analysing global contentious issues where US foreign policies have received serious criticism and rebuke. Most of the narrative is about Islamist groups such as Al-Qaeda and their hostility towards the United States. Its recommendations included an efficient pre-emptive regime and a centralised system in the country, and thus avoided recommending overdue substantive changes within the realms of foreign and defense policies. But, as an authoritative document, it certainly offers detailed information on the events immediately preceding 9/11. See, The National Commission on Terrorist Attacks Upon the United States, *The 9/11 Commission Report*, Washington D.C., & London, 2004. It can be read in conjunction with works by other analysts, who offer a wider arena of theorization and empirical research. They can be found further below and in the Bibliography.

2. Oliver Miles, 'Lewis gun', a review of Bernard Lewis's *From Babel to Dragomans*, *Guardian*, 17 July 2004.

3. James Mann, *The Rise of the Vulcans. The History of Bush's War Cabinet*, London, 2004. The book focuses on biographical, ideological and political orientations of Dick Cheney, Colin Powell, Donald Rumsfeld, Paul Wolfowitz, Richard Armitage and Condoleezza Rice.

   A British journalist looks at the United States as one of the oldest nations where the problematic of temporal and religious unleashes diverse reactions including the Midwestern paranoid of globalisation, which is otherwise celebrated by big business. Thus, the negative ramifications of a heightened nationalism engender a greater sense of insecurity and chauvinism—a phenomenon that, according to this analyst—is missing from post-national Europe. See, Anatol Lieven, *America Right or Wrong: An Anatomy of American Nationalism*, London, 2004. For a well informed review of this book see, Timothy Snyder, 'The old country', *Times Literary Supplement*, 25 March 2005, p. 32.

4. The authors warn against such daredevil views and feel that a closer and uncritiqued collaboration with Israel while debunking of Muslim views and interest in a blind self-confidence will only add to further chaos. See, Stefan Halper and Jonathan Clarke, *America Alone: The Neo-Conservatives and Global Order*, Cambridge, 2004, pp. 3-11. Francis Fukuyama is not a member of this group though on occasions he has supported some of their views. Similar is the case with Samuel Huntington.

5. For first-hand information on Neoconservative views and agenda, see Douglas Feith, Robert Kagan and William Kristol (eds.) *Present Dangers: Crisis and Opportunity in American Foreign and Defense Policy*, San Francisco, 2000; also, Aftab Ahmad Khan, (ed.) *The Empire and the Crescent: Global Implications for the New Century*, Bristol, 2003.

6. For a first-hand perspective, see Irving Kristol, *Neoconservatism: The Autobiography of an Idea*, New York, 1995; also, Gilles Kepel, *The War for Muslim Minds: Islam and the West*, London, 2004. A chapter in this study by the French specialist on Islam is devoted to the Neoconservatives. Perle and Wolfowitz have been the major pillars of the Bush presidency during the first term, while Alan Keyes is a former Assistant Secretary of State. Fukuyama, known for his thesis, 'end of history', has been on the President's Council on Bioethics, whereas Gary Schmitt headed the Project for the New American Century as an Executive Director. For further details, see Earl Shorris, 'Ignoble Liars: Leo Strauss, George Bush and Philosophy of Deception,' *Harper's Magazine*, June 2004. (http://wwww.findarticles.com), accessed on 14 May 2005).

7. Irving Kristol, a founder of the Neoconservative movement, acknowledged the influence enjoyed by Leo Strauss both on political philosophy and US foreign policies. Irving Kristol, 'The Neoconservative Persuasion: What it Was and What it Is,' in http://www.weeklystandard.com/content/Public?articles/000/000/003/000zmlw.asp, accessed on 14 May 2005.

8. Leo Strauss, *Natural Right and History*, Chicago, 1965, pp. 2-3.

9. Gregory Bruce Smith, 'Leo Strauss and the Straussians: An Anti-democratic Cult?' *PS: Political Science and Politics*, XXX, 2, (1977).

10. Lynne V. Cheney, *Telling the Truth: Why Our Culture and Our Country Have Stopped Making Sense*, New York, 1996, pp. 29-30. Gertrude Himmelfarb, the historian wife of Irving Kristol and a specialist on late Victorian society, has been quite critical of relativist and post-modernist discourse found in 'history from below' which, to her, can only be countered by a moralist reading of history. Her views on working mothers, divorces, out-of-wedlock births, and divorces are all too familiar and might have underpinned the compassionate conservatism of President Bush. Gertrude Hammelfarb, 'Postmodernist history and the flight of fact,' in John Tosh (ed.) *Historians on History*, Harlow, 2000.

11. Tristan Hunt, 'Historians in Cahoots', *Guardian*, 16 February 2005.

12. Leo Strauss, *Natural Right and History*, p. 29.

13. See, Lawrence F. Kaplan and William Kristol, *The War Over Iraq: Saddam's Tyranny and America's Mission*, San Francisco, 2003.

14. Ibid., p. 125.

15. A well-informed book on this subject reveals the American and global interface in this venture. See, George Crile, *My Enemy's Enemy. The Story of the largest Covert Operation in History: The Arming of the Mujahideen by the CIA*, London, 2003. For a first-hand Pakistani account of the ISI-CIA collaboration in fighting a proxy war, see Mohammad Yusuf and Mark Adkin, *The Bear Trap*, London, 1992. Certainly, such celebratory works only focus on achievements and avoid the human and related cost to Afghans and Pakistanis.

16. For all the details, see Craig Unger, *House of Bush, House of Saud: The Hidden Relationship Between the World's two Most Powerful Dynasties*, London, 2004. Michael Moore's documentary, Fahrenheit 9/11, used similar facts and figures to show an unexplained relationship between the Bushes and Sauds.

17. It was during the closing months of the Clinton presidency that the New American Century Project came up with a plan of Pax-Americana stipulating an invincible American politico-economic control across the globe, further underpinned by the Christian Zionists waiting in the wings for the return of Jesus Christ.

18. For details, see Robert Fisk, *The Great War for Civilisation: The Conquest of the Middle East*, London, 2005.

19. There is no doubt that there have been some reshuffles following the re-election of President Bush. In 2005, Bolton was nominated as the US Representative to the United Nations, despite his strong opposition to the concept of this world body. Concurrently, President Bush appointed Paul Wolfowitz to the presidency of the World Bank.

20. Israel not only enjoys a steady and multiple American support, it has also benefited from highly secret information on US policies and strategies in the region. Once in a while, to placate some critical opinion groups, Washington would leak news on investigating some officials for relaying vital information

to Tel Aviv. See, Paul Harris, 'FBI probes 'suspect deep inside' the Pentagon,' *Observer*, 29 August 2004.

21. His European spouse, while researching for the Rand Corporation, advised further isolating orthodox Muslims while patronizing the secularists and moderates.

22. David Frum and Richard Perle, *An End to Evil: How to Win the War on Terror?* New York, 2003; and, Lawrence F. Kaplan and William Kristol, op. cit.

23. Jean J. Kirkpatrick, 'American Power—For What?' *Commentary*, January 2000.

24. For a comprehensive study of this intermingling of religion and politics in the post-9/11 phase, see David Domke, *God Willing? Political Fundamentalism in the White House, the 'War on Terror' and the Echoing Press*, London, 2004

25. Jonathan Steele, 'US claims over Iran's nuclear programme sound eerily familiar,' *Guardian*, 27 August 2004.

26. Michael Ignatieff, *Empire Lite: Nation-building in Bosnia, Kosovo and Afghanistan*, London, 2003.

27. Fareed Zakaria, *The Future of Freedom*, London, 2003.

28. Christopher Hitchens, *Regime Change*, London, 2003. This volume consists of his columns from 2002–3 in support of the invasion. The columns, penned after the fall of the Saddam regime, reflect euphoric and rather premature optimism. Like Guardian's David Aaronovitch, Hitchens—the columnist and essayist—has been an ardent supporter of the invasion. Aaronovitch, following a persistent criticism of his support for the war, eventually left the prestigious British liberal newspaper after writing a defensive peace on 11 May 2005.

29. For instance, see Arundhati Roy, *The Ordinary Person's Guide to Empire*, London, 2004, and, Patwant Singh, *The World According to Washington: An Asian View*, Cheltenham, 2004.

30. The statements by George Carey, the former Archbishop of Canterbury, and those of the Cardinal Cormack O'Conner, head of the Catholic Church in England and Wales, have consistently downgraded Islam's contribution to global civilization. To them, Islam simply adores and promotes violence while ignoring science and reason. Bishop Michael Nazir-Ali, one of the senior-most Anglican Bishops and of Pakistani origin, fully supported the Anglo-American invasion of Iraq irrespective of several legal and moral questions. Even with the absence of weapons of mass destruction and no proof of Baghdad's links to Al-Qaeda, the British senior clergy, in most cases, refused to acknowledge the travesties of this unilateral decision. Even when the British and American media as well as Amnesty International and the International Red Cross exposed the serious moral, sexual and psychological abuse of Afghan and Iraqi internees at Bagram, Guantanamo Bay and the Abu Ghraib Jail, the senior clergy kept quiet. Of course, Bishop Tutu has

been a persistent critic of Western policies in the Muslim world, yet American evangelists like Pat Robertson, Frank Graham, Jerry Falwell and several other notables from the Moral Majority, like the missionaries of the colonial era, vocally supported Anglo–American and Israeli policies. Important broadcasters such as Robert Kilroy-Silk, Oriana Fallaci, Robert Kaplan and politicians like Denis MacShane and the Prime Ministers Silvio Berlusconi of Italy, John Howard of Australia and Jose Maria Aznar of Spain took it upon themselves to popularise the myth of Western cultural and moral superiority over Muslims. Their frequent outbursts along with full diplomatic and military support to Washington and London, gave impetus to an existing anti-Muslim sentiment. In several cases, the embedded media refused to offer any alternative view while politicians frowned at Arab television channels such as Al-Jazeera for telecasting the Iraqi and Palestinian versions of the traumatic events. The Russian campaigns in Chechnya causing serious human rights violations were almost ignored by the media whereas countries in Eastern Europe joined the anti-terror bandwagon to appease the Americans. For instance, senior officials in Macedonia during February 2002 arrested seven transit passengers on their way to Western Europe and brutally murdered them in a staged encounter as if they were Muslim terrorists. As was revealed in 2004 in a Skopje police inquiry report, these seven unfortunate victims were illegal immigrants simply passing through the Balkan country, and merely to appease Washington, the ministers ordered their cold-blooded murders. After shooting them down, the Macedonian police dressed them in military fatigues and put some weapons and explosives next to them as if to show they were planning terrorist activities. Thus, a vast combination of powerful sections of the Euro–Atlantic societies, with a similar support from Israel, Thailand, Australia and several obliging Muslim leaders, zeroed in on Muslim groups, even if the latter had nothing to do with terror or just happened to be refugees, or were simply working for charities. Even the regimes confronted with the demands for self-determination quickly maligned such movements as terrorist ventures.

31. John Gray challenges the commonly held view that gradually we are all becoming modern and thus our intents and actions may also become more reasonable. To him, even Al-Qaeda and such other groups are products of modernity and globalisation, and many more such forces may still emerge to cause further dislocations. John Gray, *Al Qaeda and What it Means to be Modern*, London, 2003. His views are certainly contested by Francis Wheen, Nick Cohen and several other analysts, to whom Enlightenment-based modernity remains sacrosanct.

32. Several serious commentaries, other than popular critique of the US policies, suggest alternative policies and perceptions. For instance, see George Soros, *The Bubble of American Supremacy*, New York, 2004; Emmanuel Todd, *After the Empire*, London, 2004; Chalmers Johnson, *The Sorrows of Empire*, New York, 2004; and, William Pfaff, 'A new American dream', *Observer*, 16 May 2004.

33. 'The claims of western values are mocked by Iraq and the rise of Asia'. Martin Jacques, ' Our moral Waterloo', *Guardian*, 15 May 2004.

34. This 'orientalisation' of Islam is not merely an intellectual construct, rather it entails a wider and multi-faceted agenda. It is the feminisation and infantisation of the Muslim peoples, rendering them as 'pliant, sensuous, passive, awaiting penetration by the rational masculine west'. It provided an easy canopy to justify military campaigns and other discretionary attitudes and policies. Jonathan Raban, 'Emasculating Arabia,' ibid., 13 May 2004.

35. As is borne out by recent studies, Israeli intelligence agencies had already orchestrated a smear campaign against Yasser Arafat even before Barak-Arafat parleys at Camp David in 2000. While President Clinton blamed Arafat for not rising to statesmanship, several new works have revealed a pervasive animus against Palestinian leadership. For Clinton's views, see Bill Clinton, *My Life*, London, 2004, pp. 943-5. The role of Israeli intelligence agencies led by Amos Gilad in drumming up hatred against Arafat, as confirmed by Amos Malka and Robert Malley, has been fully documented. See, David Hirst, 'Don't blame Arafat', *Guardian*, 17 July 2004. Israeli agencies and lobbies in America played a vital role in urging the Bush Administration to mount the invasion of Iraq. For details, see James Bamford, *A Pretext for War. 9/11, Iraq and the Abuse of American Intelligence Agencies*, New York, 2004. Seymour Hersch published a long piece outlining the Israeli infiltration in Iraq and Iran to incite and train Kurds against Iraqi Arabs, Iran and Syria. Some Israeli agents were even involved in interrogating Iraqi prisoners in the notorious Abu Gharaib Jail. See, Seymour Hersch, 'Plan B', *New Yorker*, 28 June 2004. .

36. Terry Waite, 'Were my captors worse than the Guantanamo jailers?' *Guardian*, 23 November 2005.

37. 'US guards "filmed beatings" at terror camp,' *Observer*, 16 May 2004. The Red Cross and the Amnesty International had highlighted these issues to London and Washington but a wall of secrecy prevailed until Samuel Hersch's pieces in the *New Yorker*, similar photographs in the *Washington Post*, a special programme on the CBS's '60 Minutes' and illustrated reports on the NBC and ABC carried the shocking pictures and details on brutalisation of the internees. According to Hersch, the Bush Administration fully knew of ongoing serious abuses but chose to do nothing. See, Seymour Hersch, *Chain of Command*, New York, 2004. The former detainees, in their interviews, also offered first-hand information on their routine maltreatment, in contravention of the Geneva Conventions of 1949. Following admission by President Bush and regrets by Donald Rumsfeld, Sir Jeremy Greenstock also apologized for overlooking the reports from the Red Cross and Amnesty International on the serious violations of the Geneva conventions. Jeremy Greenstock was the British envoy to the UN during the build-up to invasion of Iraq and was working with the Paul Bremer-led Provisional Coalition Authority (PCA) in Baghdad. The confession and apology from the former British diplomat were made in an interview with Jon Snow on Channel Four on 19 May 2004.

38. Ahdaf Soueif, 'This torture started at the very top,' *Guardian*, 5 May 2004.

39. Haifa Zangana, 'I, too, was tortured in Abu Ghraib,' ibid., 11 May 2004.

40. *Guardian*, 12 May 2005.

41. 'To insist that the ends now justify the means is morally disgraceful,' Geoffrey Wheatcroft, 'Blair still took us to war on a lie,' Ibid., 5 March 2005.

42. He even refused to appear in a television debate together with Michael Howard and Charles Kennedy, the opposition leaders of the Conservatives and Liberal Democrats. Nearly all the questions from the audience in this special programme, 'Panorama', were about his decision to lead the country into an otherwise unnecessary war. 'Panorama', BBC TV1, monitored in Oxford, 28 April 2005. The next day all the British and several European papers commented on war proving a major electoral setback for the incumbent prime minister.

43. Sami Ramadani, Dr Kamil Mahdi, Haifa Zangana, Professor Kamal Majid, Tahrir Numan and Sabah Jawad signed the letter. See 'Iraq war still a factor at the ballot box,' *Guardian*, 4 May 2005.

44. Christopher Meyer, *DC Confidential*, London, 2005.

45. 'Bush plot to bomb his ally', headlined the pro-Labour *Daily Mirror* on 22 November 2005, followed by reports of possible official curbs on such publications. 'Legal gag on Bush–Blair row', Guardian, 23 November 2005. In an interview with the British television channel, the director-general of Al-Jazeera expressed deep concern over the memo and doubts about the 'incidental' bombing of their bureaus in Kabul and Baghdad in 2002 and 2003. Sky News, monitored in Oxford on 27 November 2005.

46. Christina Lamb, 'The return of the Taliban,' *New Statesman*, 22 March 2004, p. 30.

47. An obviously shaken Hamid Karzai, on his return from Europe, asked for calm, though offering a slight criticism of the policies of the US military in his country. It was noted that even the Chief Justice, Fazl Hadi Shinwari, demanded an apology from the US, as he said: 'If the Americans have done this, then they should admit it and punish those who did it and apologise to Muslims.' 'Karzai slams anti-US protesters', BBC World Service, 15 May 2005, http://news.bbc.co.uk/1/hi/world/south_asia/4547413.stm

48. 'Guantanamo: A Scandal Spreads,' *Newsweek*, 9 May 2005. In the same week, *Washington Times* carried a cartoon of an American soldier patting a dog for helping to catch a Libyan member of Al-Qaeda. The problem with the cartoon was that the dog had 'PAKISTAN' written on its back, which deeply shocked and hurt millions of Pakistanis.

49. *Daily Telegraph*, 16 May 2005.

50. This was borne out by several academic studies undertaken at Cardiff and Glasgow. See, Justin Lewis, 'Biased Broadcasting Corporation,' *Guardian*, 4 July 2004; Greg Philo and Mike Barry, *Bad News from Israel*, London, 2004; and John Lloyd, *What the Media are Doing to Our Politics*, London, 2004.

51. The Amnesty International's official statement was carried in the evening news on Channel Four on 18 May 2004 and was reported next day in the global media.

52. This was highlighted in an editorial in a liberal weekly soon after the killings of Palestinian leaders by Israel. It was noted: 'A return to its original boundaries would not only guarantee Israel's security, it would also ensure the future integrity of the Jewish state.' See 'The only solution for Palestine' (leader), *New Statesman*, 29 March 2004, pp. 6-7.

53. Baruch Kimmerling, *Politicide: Ariel Sharon's War Against the Palestinians*, London, 2003, pp. 3-4; also, Israel Shahak and Norton Mezvinsky, *Jewish Fundamentalism in Israel*, London, 2004; and, John Rose, *The Myths of Zionism*, London, 2004.

54. Other than billions of dollors spent in maintaining the Occupation and hundreds of settlements, each week at least two Israeli soldiers were being inflicted with moral and psychological trauma owing to the unjust policies of their government. For instance, just from October 2000 to June 2003, 360 soldiers underwent investigation on various charges including 153 cases of homicide. Many more cases have remained unreported. For details, see Martin van Crefeld, Defending Israel, as reviewed in Max Hastings, 'Their best defence,' *Guardian*, 29 March 2005.

55. While defining and identifying the evolution, nature and kind of Muslim countries, or for that matter several other states, one needs to be quite careful in applying Eurocentric theoretical models. The typologies such as weak/strong, developed/developing/post-colonial or unitary/plural may be useful in delineating some shared characteristics among the nations, but they may not be totally helpful in comprehending a more complex and varied phenomenon. Robert Cooper's categories of post-modern, modern and pre-modern states and nations again are fraught with problems. While countries in the North Atlantic regions or Japan may account for post-modern states, even Spain, Belgium or the United Kingdom could still be confronted with volatile ethno-regional issues that some of the so-called pre-modern nations may have. Even modern states such as Russia, Italy, China and India could not totally fit in within the same theoretical jacket of nationhood. In 2004, India's electorates, by a clear majority, were willing to offer prime ministership to a foreign-born Christian widow with a Muslim already heading the country as the president, while a Cooperian post-modern state such as the United States may take several decades before electing even a white woman to head the country, not to talk of an African-American or a Hispanic. In the same vein, the possibility of a non-White, non-Anglican monarch to head Britain is as distant as of a Muslim becoming the Chancellor of Germany or president of France or even an Indian becoming the prime minister of Italy. States and nations may evolve as well as break for a variety of reasons and modernity could certainly prove a twin-edged sword in such processes. One could list a host of writings on statehood vis-à-vis nationhood but for an

interesting perspective from Tony Blair's former advisor on foreign relations, see Robert Cooper, *The Breaking of the Nations: Order and Chaos in the Twenty-First Century*, London, 2003. It is interesting to note that in the post-Cold War global politics, analysts keep differing over the ideological and geo-political contours of the world. On the one hand, Islamophobia remains a major worry whereas some scholars may still see the world already interconnected through similar interest groups of technocrats and trans-regional institutions. Anne-Marie Slaughter in her *A New World Order*, New York, 2004 has aired this view. Ian Buruma thinks that antiwesternism across Asia and Africa was nurtured in the West itself whereas Muslims generally have disallowed themselves the benefits of post-Enlightenment modernity. See, Ian Buruma and Avishai Margalit, *Occidentalism: A Short History of Anti-Westernism*, London, 2004. On the contrary, Noam Chomsky, Arundhati Roy, Norman Mailer, Samantha Powers and George Soros see the emergence as well as a certain decline of American power where 9/11 has provided a quick justification for militarism and economic expansion. Such volumes offer an ever-increasing historiography on perceptions about US military power versus its soft power and various domestic and external challenges. The works focusing on anti-Americanism across the continents, as authored by Naomi Klein, Zia Sardar and Michael Moore, account for another area of critical analysis. However, the revitalised interest on the past empires and the American imperium have also led to an interesting debate involving analysts such as George Monbiot, Joseph Nye Jr., Michael Ignatieff and several others. Niall Ferguson's works reveal nostalgia for the British Empire and recommend its relearning by the US. His first book on the subject was written for a television audience and thus expectedly lacks the full scholarly vigour. His second book, *Colossus*, not only lacks substantive theorisation and comparative analysis but also reveals lacks of immersion into US history and government including crucial developments like the Vietnam War. See, *Colossus: The Rise and Fall of the American Power*, London, 2004. For its review by Leonard Gordon, see *Times Higher Education Supplement*, 30 July 2004. A better-documented book falling in the realm of diplomatic history is by an American historian who traces an unbroken continuity in American foreign policy amongst all the post-Second World War administrations. Accordingly, Washington has been attempting 'openness' since the 1950s, and the end of the Cold War, opposed to common perceptions, did not herald any crisis in policy directions and formulations. See, Andrew J. Bacevich, *American Empire: The Realities and Consequences of the U.S. Diplomacy*, Cambridge, Mass., 2003.

56. David Selbourne's *The Losing Battle with Islam* was widely quoted on the Internet and in broadsheets. See, *Sunday Telegraph*, 25 July 2004; and *Guardian*, 31 July 2004. The manuscript had been rejected by six publishers though the media projected as if these publishers were apprehensive of a Muslim backlash over his observations. In fact, his views on Muslims posing

a constant and destabilising threat since the Second World War and an allegedly Diaspora support for terrorists are neither new nor in any way offer persuasive arguments.

'Will' Cummins, in his four serialised articles expressed his Islamophobic views such as that of an enemy from within, and Muslims, like dogs, share common characteristics, and that Islam with a black heart and a black face, is based on false prophethood. His racist tirades appeared on 4, 11, 18 and 25 July (2004) and the newspaper even highlighted some letters reflecting similar hostile opinions. When probed by Marina Hyde, the *Guardian* Diarist, the *Sunday Telegraph* refused to divulge the real identity of 'Will' Cummins. Further investigations by her identified 'Will' Cummins to be Harry Cummins, the press officer at the British Council in London. Initially, like the newspaper, the Council was also reluctant to admit his existence but due to several entries in the *Guardian* and protests by Muslims, it finally dismissed his services. See, *Guardian*, 30 July and 3 and 4 August and 3 September 2004. For serialized pieces, see 'Dr Williams, beware of false prophets,' 'We must be allowed to denigrate Islam,' 'It is the black heart of Islam, not its black face, to which millions object' and, 'Muslims are a threat to our way of life,' *Sunday Telegraph*, 4, 11, 18 and 25 July 2004. It is amusing to note that as a senior executive at the British Council, Harry Cummins had earlier sent a circular to the press in his official capacity to initiate cross-cultural debate with younger elements. The Council, itself meant to foster a better cultural understanding and purported to attract foreign students including Muslims to Britain, was deeply embarrassed as the case substantiated the claims of institutional racism and Islamophobia in the academic and such other organisations, otherwise funded with tax money. Borrowing heavily from Bernard Lewis, Ian Buruma—a Japan specialist—felt that given their history and religion Muslims were being propelled by forces of contempt and violence. The British columnist used to write for the *Guardian* before moving on to *The Times*. See, Ian Buruma, 'Driven by history and hate: Islam's holy warriors,' *The Times*, 3 August 2004.

57. Anonymous, *Imperial Hubris: Why the West is Losing the War on Terror?* Washington, 2004, p. 241.

1

ISLAM AND THE WEST: OLD RIVALS OR AMBIVALENT PARTNERS

'There had been no systematic campaign of forcible Islamization in Spain after the Muslim conquest. Yet within two centuries the Christians of Al-Andulas had for the most part adopted Islam. The vigorous methods pioneered by Jimenez de Cisneros (leading Inquisitioner in Granada) were dictated by political motives and they seemed to succeed in the short term. By law, and on paper, Islam was ended and the whole nation made officially Christian'.
– Andrew Wheatcroft, *Infidels: The Conflict between Christendom and Islam 638-2002*, London, 2003, pp. 140-1

'Britain and the US did everything to avoid a peaceful solution in Iraq and Afghanistan,' George Monbiot, 'Dreamers and idiots'.
– *Guardian*, 11 November 2003

'I'd rather be a Paki than a Turk'.
– English football fans in Hastings, 2003

'Were my captors worse than the Guantanamo jailers?'
– Terry Waite, *Guardian*, 23 November 2005

Without subscribing to a clash of cultures or feeling apologetic about the relationship between Muslims and the West, the unevenness in their mutual interface is certainly an ironic reality. Whether it is owing to an age-old theological contestation or more recent geo-political tensions the fact, however, remains that powerful sections from amongst the Western politicians, media and academia—not just the ordinary masses—perceive Islam as a most unnerving threat. In a rather abrasive way, they find the fault lying entirely with the Muslims. The events of 9/11, though largely condemned by Muslims but not without protestations over Western double standards in Western Asia and elsewhere, not only caused massive attacks on countries like Afghanistan and Iraq, they have equally intensified the Muslim predicament in Palestine, Chechnya, India and several other places. The unprecedented rolling back of civil liberties, internment of several hundred undefined Muslim internees in Guantanamo Bay and at several other CIA-operated secret facilities, strict visa restrictions for Muslim applicants, profiling of millions of Muslim Americans, the daily reports of harassment of Muslims in the Diaspora and a pronounced negative spotlight on Islam are some of the sad components of this so-called war on terror. Of course, there are millions of people in the West and elsewhere who, through a rainbow peace movement or by demanding equal rights for everyone, have been vocally critical of such multi-faceted campaigns, but their demonstrations even in the world's oldest and proudest democracies failed to restrain official jingoism. The cohabitation between an exclusive nationalism and evangelical Christianity, anchored upon permeating undercurrents of Orientalism, has never been so intense in the North Atlantic region. President Bush, Prime Ministers Tony Blair, Antonio Berlusconi, John Howard and Jose Maria Aznar were driven by a strong religious (Christian) righteousness and so were Ariel Sharon, L.K. Advani and several other leaders across the globe, to whom undertaking a campaign against Muslim activists has been more than a political expediency.[1]

The popularisation of the Republican Party in the American South eventually leading to President Bush's re-election and a vigorous Christian Right zealously trying to convert Muslims in Iraq and Afghanistan through direct evangelical activities or by distributing aid and charity goods, are some of the features of this Neoconservatism. Frank Graham, the son of Billy Graham, led Operation Christmas Child aimed at sending shoes to Iraqi children, attuning them for conversion. The outbursts by Italy's

Berlusconi on the superiority of the Christian civilisation over the rest and especially Islam, and the unrestrained outbursts of US General William Boykin against Muslims with the reverberations of similar policy postures in France, Germany and Australia revealed a wider convergence among official and private prejudices. Islam, certainly, after 9/11 emerged as the 'new enemy' with Muslim life and culture deserving no substantial respect but rather being referred to as the greatest and oldest threat to superior Western cultural norms and values. Undoubtedly, some Christian elements within the North Atlantic region felt unease over this opportunistic and unnecessary campaign at a time when Muslims across the world accounted for a huge underclass caught between indigenous suffocation and external derision. It was feared that the evangelical activities hidden behind the mask of charity both in the United States and Britain on the heels of massive destruction in Western Asia would only accentuate anti-Western resentment in the Muslim world.[2] This is not to deny the fact that there are Muslim rejectionists as well, to whom the West symbolises only hostility and arrogance and the best way to deal with it is either through confrontation or sheer indifference. Though both Islam and the West are trans-territorial and allocating them an essentially regional or cultural specificity is ahistorical, yet for the sake of convenience, one has to depend upon such denominators.

Other than the military onslaught, it is the academic and media vilification of Islam and the resultant Muslim marginalisation that retain the most damaging and inimical portents. The translation of military and political campaigns or even of racist typologies into religious idioms is certainly spawning cultural conflicts, though often not unwittingly. The events of 9/11, military campaigns and a pervasive Islamophobia following the London blasts of July 2005 have certainly resuscitated the harbingers of the 'clash of civilizations' though in reality this is already a one-sided and ominous ploy. The ragtag Taliban, secular yet authoritarian Ba'athists or a few solitary vocal groups high on slogans yet unable to obtain a basic iota from rote knowledge dispensed in traditional *madrassas* are no comparison to the massive killing machines at the disposal of the Western regimes. The powerful monopolies over media, diplomacy, economy and the presence of loyal intermediaries all across the Muslim regions make it quite difficult for any Muslim factor to make its presence felt across the board. Even a minor semblance of ideological or logistical unity amongst the disparate activist groups has not been possible though their disgust with Western hegemony and duplicitous policies in the Muslim regions converges with the rising tide of anti-Americanism and a serious critique of an unblemished modernity. These turbaned and bearded activists, with all their emotive rhetoric, are certainly no match for the organized forces of some of the most powerful states in the world. On the contrary, their outbursts, even to resist hegemonic presence, claim more blood from their co-religionists.

Characterized by its clear-cut class-based features, the war on terror, despite its altruist rhetoric, has resulted in further devastation of some of the poorest regions in the world and a denial of civil liberties to millions. It might be a clash of similar fundamentalisms with some clerics hijacking the Muslim ideology of *jihad* and the Neoconservatives and ultra-right elements hoodwinking the Western voters. The Zionist–Christian alliance, like the Likudists, Russian nationalists and Hindutva ideologues, posit Islam as the main obstacle to overcome before the Second Coming of Christ, yet the fact remains that since 9/11 the world has become more dichotomous. While the dissolution of the Cold War could have augured a better, self-respecting, peaceful and less polarized world—short of the end of history—it did not need to be led into still another catastrophe. The issues of environment and poverty or epidemics such as AIDS have been sidelined by unilateral militarization amidst the strictest immigration controls and a serious rollback of civil rights even in the most vocal democracies. The intolerance of one type has spawned several others of immense proportions on all sides. The Western governments, to evade their own poor performances in social sectors, find in Al-Qaeda a useful alibi whereas the racist elements seek their pound of flesh by scapegoating mostly non-white and predominantly Muslim communities amongst them. The war on terror, soaked in its

Judaic–Christian syllogisms and by assuming the garb of a moral crusade against illiberals, terrorists, savages and non-democratic forces of evil arrayed against higher Western moral virtues, underwrites a reinvigorated Orientalist discourse. The moralist postulation uttered by Bush, Blair or Berlusconi are not to be simply brushed aside as mere political asides or slips of the tongue as they have represented the tip of an iceberg by virtue of being rooted in the legacy of an extended and often acrimonious past. Such a discourse goes back to the core of a Europeanised modernity, which assumed the responsibility of redesigning a colonized world in its own image.

While modernity offered enlightening precepts such as secularism, democracy, human rights and greater respect for diversity, it equally resulted in physical and cultural control of vast sections of the human population in consonance with a continued denigration of their heritage. Racism, slavery, economic restructuring to suit the 'core' countries and a persistent legacy of hegemonic polices towards impoverished regions are all part of the project of modernity that bequeathed scores of wars, the Holocaust and ethnic cleansing. The scientific revolution added to the human life span but also turned human groups into the most violent and annihilative species on earth causing millions of deaths in the name of empire, nationalism, and patriotism, and now, the war on terror. Naturally, such a significant project had to be deified with some 'koshering' that came through moral righteousness, the erstwhile 'White Man's Burden' and is presently being justified through terms such as democratisation, restructuring and development. In a sense, it appears that even after centuries of efforts to transform the Western Hemisphere, the Pacific Rim, Africa and Asia, if these masses have not yet absorbed the West European and the American constructs of development and advancement then there must be something irreparably wrong with them. Modernity is a mixed blessing and many of these tensions and dissensions are rooted in its transgressions. The West has been using European modernity to suit its needs and whims, and Muslims, like several others in the former colonies, wrestle with it in their own way. It is both

seductive and destructive as all kinds of groups, including
fundamentalists of various shades, harness it for their own specific
needs.[3]

The main hypothesis in this section is to show that the current
mis-images of Muslims and stereotypical if not totally derisive views
of Islam have been rooted in more recent times where colonisation,
the slave trade, slavery, racism and Orientalism ran the roost. It is
not the lack of knowledge among the Western elite that has
unleashed a multi-dimensional assault on Islam; it is instead the
restatement of hegemony and power politics and the lack of
willingness to allocate due space to Islam that continue to
underwrite such attitudes and inanities. These slanted views, in
fact, emerged a long time back in history with the priests, popes,
politicians and poets all sharing an exaggerated and concurrently
undervalued view of Islam as a multiple threat while constantly
refusing to accept it as a fellow Abrahamic tradition. Scepticism of
the Prophethood and of the authenticity of the Quran and viewing
Muslim politics as an eternal *jihad* purported to eliminate
Christianity and Judaism have been ever-present. Given the unique
and often contested nature of mutual contacts and encounters such
discretionary discourse generated partisan attitudes and biased
policies towards Muslims. Periodically and more often, such misimages and suspicions were rekindled to substantiate partisan
policies both in the past and especially since the end of the Cold
War, making Islamophobia a pervasive cliché. The political
prerogatives and even personal refrains, as at the present, have
always been couched in religious connotations and that is why
powerful groups in the North Atlantic region and elsewhere tend
to see in Islam the greatest-ever threat to their cultural norms and
political stability. Accordingly, not only humanity at large but
Muslims as well have to be emancipated from an insidious threat
so as to reincarnate a peaceful world shorn of the Islamic threat.
Renaissance and Reformation have to be endowed to the Muslims
to create proto-Western communities instead of hooded, chest
beating, bearded, sabre rattling and untiring hordes of Muslim
fanatics. Islam, fanaticism, terror, irrationality and violence have all

become interchangeable terms to define Muslim history and religion. The events of 9/11 as well as bomb blasts in Madrid, Bali and London have dramatically reignited this zeal, bringing politicians, evangelists, hate mongers and Neo-Orientalists together to legitimise the ongoing campaign.

Whereas Osama bin Laden and Saddam Hussein or even Muslim monarchs or military dictators do not represent and reflect a diverse and humane civilization like Islam, the agony of the Muslim populace certainly gets aggravated both by this authoritarianism combined with an enduring injudicious foreign intervention. Such an ideology of self-professed Judaic–Christian superiority over others, as symbolised by the present North Atlantic and several other proto-Western states, received manifold resuscitation under the political hegemony dating from a recent past, though the origins of this unevenness date back from the early era of the Crusades and the Inquisition. The resurgence of this multi-fanged ideology since 9/11 is not incidental and in a way, has seriously replenished the negative views of Islam and Muslims.[4] It is important to revisit some of those opinion-makers and transmitters whose analyses of Islam and Muslims, in most cases, have provided the historical backdrop to specific views on Islam. They also offer a unique overview of Western/European legacies in Islamic studies, though it will be incorrect to say that the entire Western scholarship on Islam has been antagonistic. Other than laudable exceptions, outpourings from many of these immensely powerful individuals fully influenced people in powerful positions unleashing a plethora of policies reverberating in the new century, making it more violent and costly in terms of human life in our history.

Before one deals with a few representative specialists on Islam and their more recent views, it may be useful to seek an overview of the European intellectual and religious encounter with Islam as an important backdrop for contemporary discourse. However, it is imperative to state at this stage that Western opinions about Islam are largely divided into the two main categories of protagonists and antagonists. Both these groups, over the centuries, have manifested a wide variety of professional multi-disciplinary and are not confined to mere ecclesiastic sections or politicians, as artistes, travellers, academics, courtiers, converts, spies, poets, novelists, journalists, filmmakers,.aid workers, travellers, businessmen, NGOs and even ordinary people have reflected this ideological duality, which in more recent years, especially following the Salman Rushdie affair and the First Gulf War of 1991 has grown sharper. The Bosnian crisis in the mid-1990s allowed some sensitivity to a better understanding of Muslims—not as perpetrators rather as victims—yet the events of 9/11 have unleashed a new energy for proponents of the clash of civilisations and erstwhile efforts such as the Runneymede Trust's *Islamophobia*, seem to have been already overtaken by a pervasive anti-Islam animus. Invasions, war mongering, brutalisation of Muslim population groups, especially in politically contentious areas such as Palestine, Kashmir, Chechnya, Kosovo, Gujarat and elsewhere all have been taking place in an arena of wider anti-Muslim malaise. The incarcerations of thousands of Muslims in the Diaspora on minor suspicions, bans on charities, and the worst of all, the ignored agony of internees at the Delta Camp in Guantanamo Bay are some of the sordid realties of this new war on terror. In the same vein, Israel, India and Russia and several other states, by applying a wider clamp down on their dissenting population groups have established their own special detention centres. Israel maintains its own secret 'Guantanamo Bay' in the form of Facility 1391 and has been persistently violating Palestinian human rights over the last six decades. Ariel Sharon's disregard for Palestinian life and property as perpetrated through an intense campaign of dispossession, wide-spread killings, destruction of the infrastructure and erection of the twenty-foot high wall further partitioning and ghettoising Palestinian communities has gone on unhindered by any moral, legal or international restraints. To the shock of many Israelis, not only have some of their pilots and soldiers, driven by guilt, refused to kill Palestinians by turning 'refuseniks', their own country has been globally viewed as the greatest threat to world peace. In a survey across the European Union in late 2003, 59 per cent Europeans viewed Israel as the most serious threat to world peace—even greater than Iran and North Korea. Such opinions coming from an otherwise supportive Europe gravely shocked Israeli leadership and their American supporters who tried to portray it as the age-old manifestation of anti-Semitism.[5]

Western opinion, divided into the above mentioned two respective broad groups of critics and supporters, is anchored upon a set of complex, historical, religious, political and intellectual reasons. The antagonists—the mainstream opinion group for our purpose here—have always found fault with Islam by seeing in it an eternal foe, whereas the supporters perceive it to be a part of the human heritage instead of an enemy. To the diehard antagonists, Islam, especially after the dissolution of the Cold War, is a significant and multi-dimensional threat to Western societies and interests. To such elements—assuming a higher moral and powerful pedestal—Islam represents a Janus-faced fundamentalism and terrorism and has to be contained through stringent military-centred policies. However, some of them believe that the Muslim world needs some external *putsch* towards democracy and liberty and the West holds a historical and moral responsibility to bestow these virtues on the otherwise 'backward' Muslims.[6] This group differs widely over strategies to refashion the Muslim world, with one section suggesting military means, and has included Paul Wolfowitz, Daniel Pipes, Ann Coulter, Bill Kristol, Elliot Abrams, Richard Perle, Douglas Feith, and such other proponents of the New American Century, who sought religio-political justification for their 'moral crusade'. Inclusive of Jewish and Christian elements with a sprinkling of some immensely ambitious Muslim-Americans such as Fareed Zakaria and Zalmay Khalilzad, and camp followers from amongst the political exiles, this group has been led by Dick Cheney, the Republican US Vice-President. The evangelical rationalisation for this group is provided by Franklin Graham, Pat Robertson and the other leaders of the Jewish-Christian Right, who, in league with the Likud Zionists, desire a new Middle East under the aegis of American military and economic power. Sceptical of the United Nations or even the European Union, they are least concerned about the Muslim factor or the underlying conflicts within the contested domain of modernity, and are irritated by the lack of wider Muslim reciprocity for their project. They are at best patronising if not outright dismissive altruists, though intentionally insensitive towards Muslim concerns. Any indigenous dissent, to them, is merely linked with Al-Qaeda, or some Muslim irrational penchant for *jihad*. To such a powerful group, the Bush administration has been a timely blessing to implement their plans wherein Israel, pro-Western and dictatorial Muslim regimes, and most of all, the Pentagon provide instruments for implementing a new order in West Asia.[7] It will not be out of place to suggest that many of these people may harbour colonial and racist views without a forthright admission, and are puzzled by research such as by the Pew Center, on global public opinions towards the United States. To them, Washington under a diehard Republican Administration, militarily unassailable and fully reflective of the ideas of the Neoconservatives, can afford to be irreverent to global criticism including that of liberal Europeans. To them, America is inherently a moral force created for the wider good, but only in their unique way, as Democrats, Liberals and Islamists are not only irresponsible, they are the main hurdles to the American enterprise. It is interesting to note that, despite being abhorrent of a predominant European critique of American policies, they reflect a long-held Christian legacy of European views and scholarship on Islam. Despite the support from certain conservative European sections for the US-led campaigns in the Muslim world, including 'the lite' imperial control, American views of Islam and the Muslims reveal to a significant extent a continued tradition of Orientalism and derision, though the emphasis and style may be uniquely *American*.[8]

Westernism and Christianity: Crusaders against a Common Foe

It will be simplistic to suggest that the Muslim–Western relationship is all about religion where Islam and Christianity (and now Judaism and others) have always behaved as perennial enemies. Simultaneously, it is also ahistorical to remove religion as a core factor in the often-acrimonious relationship, nor will it be helpful to suggest that relations between Muslims and Christians have been characterised by eternal conflict, though these do tend to receive more focus. In the same vein, a careful observer cannot afford to overlook the tribal, imperial, national and international rivalries that spawned conflicts as well as occasional unison on all sides. Moreover, instead of seeking a single-factor explanation, the relationship has to be seen within the context of centricity of power and multiplicity of factors such as language, class, culture and colour.

Muslims, over the recent centuries, present a huge underclass of predominantly non-White clusters where hegemonies such as colonialism and 'Orientalist attitudes' have only added to their stigmatisation, though their predicament has been largely due to the underlying forces of the politico–economic variety. Poverty and disempowerment, combined with internal authoritarianism and external hegemonies, have exacerbated the pervasive Muslim plight and also the anger. Muslims of various orientations and nationalities find themselves in a typical 'catch-22' situation and the ameliorative efforts have to come from multiple directions.

Whereas the politico–economic malaise may have occurred due to several forces and accompanying causes, the ideological trajectories accompanying the colonial hegemonies frequently used higher religious ground both to legitimise and to underwrite such control and conquest. The various decisive epochs in their past until 9/11 and especially ever since have coincided with a flurry of writings, sketches and policies where Islam, the Prophethood, Muslim cultures and histories have mostly received negative spotlight. One may say that all the religions and ideologies of the world may have had their due share of derision but certainly 'Islam was both misunderstood and attacked most intensely'.[9] The periodic tensions have always tended to be contemporaneous with derisory outpourings. Bordering on sheer hostility and racism, such typologies and caricatures have often reverberated with partisan, patronising and occasionally violent postulations. Western politicians, priests and scholars have often collaborated in positing Muslims as enemies, barbarians, anti-Christ, uncultured mobs and sheer terrorists. They have never shied away in using age-old lexicons dating from the Crusades, the Inquisition, Expulsions and colonialism to relegate the Muslim heritage into some perennial time warp. Undoubtedly, the recent evolution of the peace movement and greater trans-disciplinary sensitivity for the Muslim predicament is nascent though quite a significant development otherwise, the Christian West, as per tradition, has been intolerant if not totally annihilative towards Muslims. Certainly, Muslims have their share of injustice and demonisation directed against non-Muslims though their counterparts frequently give out as if Muslims may have the lion's share in violating and brutalising human rights. Historically, such a discretionary view does not hold ground when one looks at the diversity and massive scale of violence committed against non-Whites and non-Christians, usually under the pretext of Christianisation and modernisation. The Crusades and the accompanying massive violence, the Inquisition and the total extermination of Muslims and Jews from the Iberian Peninsula and Sicily, ethnic cleansing in the Balkans since the Turco-Greek tensions all the way until the recent times and the millions of deaths and internment of Muslims from Mauritania to the Philippines during the colonial phase inclusive of centuries of pogroms in Russia are cases of holistic and large-scale violence. Added with the slave trade, slavery, elimination of Natives across the three continents, the Holocaust and the intermittent imperial and global wars the total tally of human losses may well exceed several hundreds of millions owing to Europeanization and Westernisation of the world. Thus, in a powerful way, violence against Muslims, Jews and other non-Western communities in the last few centuries—with the West (inclusive of Russia) at the prime of its power—does not make pleasant reading in human history.

It is curious to note that the traditional Muslim communities in the Western heartlands totally disappeared whereas, on the contrary, non-Muslim minorities and majorities not only survived, in some case, such as Jews, Bulgarians, Greeks and Hindu Brahmins, they duly benefited from the Muslim sultanates and caliphates. Europe, during its internationalisation not only turned intolerant to ethno-religious minorities amidst its own populace, its modernising project radically depopulated several other continents. Such dramatic demographic changes can be countenanced only if scapegoating the Natives, indigenous and other such non-Western communities including Muslims receives a more critical and balanced perspective. For instance, the growth in violence in the Balkans since the nineteenth century is a rather complex and modernist phenomenon and was sadly perpetrated by all sides though the Ottomans were always apportioned the major blame. The focus on Turks fitted in with the preceding traditional misimage of Muslims—'the terrible Turks'—and thus Turkey got all the blame, while the Greeks, Bulgars, Serbs and others were presented either as victims or fellow Christians fighting against the barbarian 'other'. Likewise, the characterisation of the Middle East or Central Asia as eternally conflict-prone Muslim regions is rooted in the recent external interventions dating from the colonial era. There is no doubt that Kosovo, Palestine, Bosnia, Iraq, Afghanistan, Kashmir, Moroland, Lebanon, Chechnya and Sinkiang making most of the contemporary news on violence are predominately Muslim regions, but violence therein is largely owed to foreign invasions and not due to some specific Muslim penchant for terror. Muslims have used Islamic symbols of community-building to resist foreign encroachments and have been quite vocal about it. Of course, some groups, as expected in such situations, undertook extreme measures but they still cannot override the root cause of these ongoing conflicts.

To a great extent, the emergence of the Western Neoconservatives using religion, culture and history from the powerful political pulpits in Washington, London and Tel Aviv is rooted in the preceding centuries when Islam was viewed as the major enemy. The interplay of religio–political hostility towards Muslims, contemporaneous with various crucial political developments, began soon after the death of the Prophet in AD 632. In 638, when an austere Caliph Omar reached Jerusalem to guarantee a peaceful coexistence to this plural city under Muslim rule, Sophronius, the Orthodox Patriarch of the city, observed in Greek: 'Surely this is the abomination of desolation spoken of by Daniel the Prophet standing at the holy place'.[10] Muslims were not merely a religious threat they were also considered a political menace and resistance to them had to be justified through scriptural rationale. Soon, St. John of Damascus (675–749), despite his erstwhile appointment at the caliph's court until 716, came out with a scathing attack on Islam by declaring the Prophet Muhammad (PBUH) as the Antichrist. This characterisation led to the subsequent unfair treatment of the Messenger in the host of secular and sacred writings varying from the Venerable Bede to Dante and others. In fact, Bede had popularised the myth of Islam as Hagarism by seeking the birth of Ishmael—the son of Abraham—from Hagar, who in the Christian view, was not a wife rather a concubine. St. John's followers, especially the priests in Constantinople and Rome, feared a Muslim conquest of these Christian–Byzantine citadels and kept up a persistent attack on Islam, and like St. John, considered Muslims as infidels. It was the Muslim conquest of Spain, Portugal and Sicily and forays into Central Europe and France that further infuriated the various Christian elite. The papal call for the Crusades coincided with vital political changes in an increasingly fragmenting Europe, though northern Spain helped by the Christian knights and volunteers undertook a leading role in counterposing a multi-dimensional campaign against Muslims. As articulated by Montgomery Watt, Christian Europe at that time suffered from a serious inferiority complex and Islam as the most serious religious and political threat led to a keen sense of unity and escapism.[11] The Muslim conquest of Spain[12] is well documented with an ever-increasing focus on a successive pluralism and splendid aspects of the Islamo–Spanish culture, but the conquest of Southern Italy and similar cultural and social synthesis largely remain unexplored. Muslims had attacked Sicily since 652 AD—long before their incursions into Spain—but were only able to make major

inroads in the early ninth century when they captured Palermo in
831. Led by the Aghlabids of North Africa (Tunisia), the Muslims
conquered Naples in 837, Messina in 843 and Syracuse in 878.
After capturing Bari on the North Adriatic, they threatened Rome
in the 840s. Pope John III (872–82) paid tribute to Muslims for
two years to ward off any direct conquest. Following the Aghlabid
expulsion from Tunisia by the Fatimids in 909, Southern Italy
became a Fatimid province. But the eastward shift of the Fatimid
interest with a major focus on Egypt since 948 weakened their hold
on Italy, though the province, being ruled by the Kalbite family,
offered good governance. It was during their rule that the Islamic
culture established its roots in Sicily, and like Muslim Spain, a
successful pluralism and an active commerce flourished. But
Muslim rulers soon lost their control to the invading Normans who
captured Messina in 1060 and took charge of the entire southern
peninsula by 1091. Unlike Catholic Spain, the Normans did not
expel the Muslims and co-opted them fully in their set-up. Norman
Kings like Roger II (1130–54) and his grandson, Frederick II
(1215–50), despite contemporary tensions, protected their
prosperous Muslim subjects and came to be known as 'the two
baptised sultans of Sicily'.[13] The conquest of Sicily by the Normans
initially tolerated the Muslim presence by co-opting them in
agriculture, industry and other urban professions. The Arabo–
Norman culture, as reflected in the arts, architecture, language and
cuisine, showed the possibility of a plural co-existence but papal
bulls were soon to mount an annihilative campaign against these
early Italian Muslims. A Spanish Muslim, Ibn Jubair, visiting Sicily
in 1184—a century following the Norman conquest—could still
witness plural culture and felt exuberant not only in Palermo but
also in the countryside. He named Palermo *al-Madinah al-Kabir*,
the great city, resplendent with diverse cultural activities. 'It has
Muslim citizens who possess mosques, and their own markets, in
the many suburbs. The rest of the Muslims live in the farms of the
island and in all its villages and towns.' He further noted that
William II, the Norman King, was 'admirable for his just conduct,
and the use he makes of the industry of the Muslims' and goes

about 'in a manner that resembles the Muslim Kings'.[14] But owing to xenophobic calls, this pluralism was soon to end with the re-Christianisation of Southern Italy and elimination of the Muslim community from the island, not so far from papal Rome, itself spearheading the Crusades. Soon, the mosques and other religious buildings were turned into churches and cathedrals and forcible conversions became the order of the day. This drama was again to be enacted in Portugal and Spain and eventually Southern Italy would become the launching pad for a decisive naval encounter with the Turks in 1571 at Lepanto.

The Crusades destroyed pluralism not only in Italy and other Mediterranean islands but also played havoc with Christian, Jewish and Muslim groups across the Levant and the Holy Land. They also implanted two powerful enduring legacies for Muslim–Christian relations. Firstly, they solidified a distorted image of Islam in the West, which continues to reverberate even today from political polemics to serious studies. Secondly, Islam became an obsession for West Europeans—collectively called Franks by their Muslim contemporaries—though their lack of knowledge of the objective realties in the Levant is equally shocking.[15]

Transporting so many armies for such a long period of time for demolition purposes became an enduring Western tradition, which has been repeated quite often ever since. The resistance by the locals was as much undervalued as it is today with the Anglo–American troops in West Asia and Israelis trying to dispossess an entire local population from Palestine. After the Fall of Granada in 1492, the massive scale of ethnic cleansing in Castilian Spain went on for a century and by the early seventeenth century Muslims, Moors or Moriscos had totally disappeared from their native land.[16] The descendants of Ferdinand and Isabella such as Charles V and Philip I and II ensured the elimination of the Muslim presence from Spain, lent substantial help against the Ottomans, captured territories in North Africa, exiled many remaining Muslims to the new colonies and played a major role in Mediterranean warfare until the Armada was destroyed in 1588. Seventeen years earlier, the Castilian/Hapsburg princes had led the naval war against the

Turks and defeated the hated Muslim enemies near Greece. Sicily was the headquarters for the Battle of Lepanto, while the leadership was provided by Spain and Christian volunteers filtering in from all over Europe. The Pope led the prayers and efforts to defeat the hated infidels and sent his closest bishops to Messina to bless the departing warriors. The Spanish colonists, showing a similar level of contempt and zeal, tried to subjugate Muslims in Southern Philippines. They were even named as Moros by the Spanish colonials who tried to convert them to Christianity. History was to repeat itself in the Balkans during the nineteenth and twentieth centuries though not before the extermination of the Natives across the Western Hemisphere where Christianity and colonisation joined hands besides initiating the 'peculiar' institution on an unprecedented scale. But as in Sicily, Spain eliminated the Muslims physically yet it could not obliterate their cultural and architectural heritage which remains so powerful through its Moorish and Mudejar representations across the converted mosques and numerous other edifices.

In the era of the Crusades and Christian conquests in the Mediterranean regions, European Muslims were declared outsiders, barbarians, brutish and the deadliest enemy whose religion, culture and heritage were to be decimated. The Crusades encouraged the Spanish and Italian Christian elite to mount military campaigns against these 'infidels', and the creation of the myth of St. James and of the Holy Pilgrimage in Galicia (Santiago of Compostela) duly helped foster the crusading fervour amongst the Asturian kings.[17] While Muslims—called Moors, for understandable reasons of differentiation and denigration—had mostly guaranteed respect for pluralism, the conquering Christian monarchs pursued a dual-edged policy of conversion and expulsions. The end of Muslim rule in Granada in 1492 and the subsequent elimination of Muslims from Andalusia was the decisive phase in *Reconquista*. The Muslim conquests in the early era, in the Near East, Sicily, Iberia and Eastern Europe, have been presented for centuries as an unmitigated desire by the adherents of Islam to subjugate Christians. Instead of looking at the historical events within their political and related multi-dimensional causation, they were always posited as the rise of the Crescent over the Cross. Of course, like the West European conquests since the rise of the Catholic kings, Columbus and Napoleon were also perceived by many Muslims as a transcendent Cross annihilating a weakened Crescent. However, European writers and ecclesiasts, following the critique of St. John of Damascus and the priests in Spain and Rome, never allowed Islam its own space by simply denigrating it as a mere heresy. Medieval European misimages of Islam focused on denying prophethood to Muhammad (PBUH), who, for instance in Scotland, was called Mahound. The Ottoman retreat from Vienna in 1683 and the subsequent wars in the Balkans vehemently regimented the Christian–Muslim divide. By this time, Western Europe had already established its hegemony over vast tracts across the Muslim world and previous misperceptions and misimages were reincarnated through the willing generations of Orientalists.

Western Discourse(s) on Islam

The study of the relationship between Muslims and Europeans and post-Columbian North Americans is a fascinating subject of mutualities as well as of acrimonies. Long before the traditions of Colonialism, both Orientalism and Neo-racism—inclusive of the massive slave trade and slavery—manifested ambiguity, rivalry, hostility and curiosity on all sides. This encounter was characterised by images and misimages and permeated through religious, political, intellectual, military and economic channels. Even in the twenty-first century the same five channels seem to be carrying the historical burden though the media and the Diaspora, and greater trans-regional factors have added to the complexity of this encounter. The continuing images and misperception of Islam and Muslims, despite the hyped-up globalisation and greater inter-cultural encounters, have refused to go away and instead, in several cases, have been reinforced.

How were these images established and who instrumented them even in a pre-Orientalist phase, is itself a fascinating area. While the non-Muslim Orient (East and South-East Asia) lacked proximity with Europe until recent times, it is the predominantly Christian Europe and overwhelmingly Muslim West Asia and North Africa which shared proximity as well as rivalries. Jews and Christian in the Muslim heartland and Muslims in the Christian heartland proved to be trans-cultural agents long before the media and other technology-based channels set in. While to some observers, the lack of massive channels may be the root cause of mutual discord, to others, the very multiplicity and longevity of the mutual encounter itself might have spawned disharmony.

The following section, before an assessment of the views of some of the representatives of the above-mentioned groups in the contemporary era, seeks to summarise the historical background to this often acrimonious and occasionally cherished relationship.

More than anywhere else, Islam 'was a problem for Christian Europe'.[18] The personality of the Prophet Muhammad (PBUH), his claim to have received divine revelations as accumulated in the Quran, and the Muslim views of Jesus Christ and other biblical prophets as prophets of Islam were the focal points of this early Christian ire.[19] Islam was often called Mohammedanism despite the Prophet's exhortations on being a messenger of God and not the founder of any personality-centred theology. However, Muhammad's marriages, his role as a commander of the faithful, his critique of early Judaic and Christian scriptures for having been tampered with by the priests, and Islam's expansion across the regions all intensified this rebuke. Islam, rather than waiting for a polity to adopt it, had created its own state following the Prophet's migration to Medinah. The expansion of this highly politicised religion to the lands of urban civilisations of Sassanid Persia and Byzantine Rome was unnerving, especially given its roots in the backwaters of the Arabian desert. The Crusades were as much an effort to wrest control of the erstwhile Christian heartland from the Muslims, as they were a part of the efforts by Christians to gain supremacy over fellow Christian lords and nobility. The papal desire to seek a *de jure* authority over princes and the aristocracy posited a common target whereas the motives and strategies ran parallel to the stated goal of conquering the Holy Land. The wrath against fellow Christians, Jews and Muslims knew no bounds for almost two hundred years until Saladin decisively terminated the European onslaught in 1091.

Medieval Europe benefited from, as well as envied Muslim Spain until its western regions, in the wake of political, religious and commercial redefinition, embarked on the road to modernity. It was during the medieval age that one finds the first Quranic translation into Latin by Robertus Ketenesis in 1143 though the contemporary European knowledge of Arabic outside Muslim Spain was quite limited. The same translation was formally printed in Basel four centuries later owing to Martin Luther's personal interest, and in 1616, a German rendition was accomplished by Salomon Schweigger. A Dutch version followed soon afterwards. Islam's Middle Eastern origins, similarities as well as differences with the other two main Abrahamic traditions, and most significantly, its political role as a conquering ideology germinated interest in understanding its classical heritage like the Quran.

The redefinition of Christian Europe on sectarian, national and absolutist lines happened within the backdrop of Renaissance and Reformation. The Europeanization of the world—a development of immense historical and cultural significance—had begun at a time when Jews and Muslims were being expelled from the Iberian Peninsula; new routes were being discovered to the East and the West and the three Turkish/Timirud dynasties had established themselves in the Near East, Persia and the Indian subcontinent, respectively.[20] Soon, the emerging West European intellectuals, writing in Latin and emerging 'vernacular' languages found Islam to be both exotic as well as the 'other', which was to be feared and envied for its vitality, simplicity and devotional appeal. The rise of the Ottoman dynasty increased European religious and intellectual interest in Islam and Arabic, though mostly reflecting hatred instead of any objective or serious scholarship. Like the contemporary arts, the emerging 'national' literatures in Europe reflected embodied ambivalent and curious if not totally hostile views on Muslims, who by now, had graduated from being referred to as Arabs or Barbarys into Turks. Dante's relegation of the Prophet in the Inferno remained the pervasive view in contemporary Europe and the converts to Islam—commonly known as renegades—were always unacceptable like the marauding North African pirates, whose escapades resulted in loss of ships and kidnappings for ransom. The 'new' encounter with the Sub-Saharan Africans and their subsequent enslavement was fully justified through moral and religious scriptures adding to ambivalent if not totally indifferent attitudes towards Muslims. This was the beginning of the European politics of enslavement and encroachment though the Ottoman Caliph was still considered a possible ally at least by the Tudor monarch, Queen Elizabeth-I, against rival European powers such as Spain and France. The distant Mughals and Safawids were also viewed as potential allies whose riches and cultural vitality amazed the explorers, travellers, traders and special ambassadors. Even the Turkish coffee became controversial as it was thought that it might spread the word of the 'Saracens' among gullible elements.[21] However, some minor ecclesiastic interest in Islam as a rival phenomenon remained present among specific sections of West European societies, especially in France and Britain. William Shakespeare and Christopher Marlowe often dilated on Islam-related themes in their plays and poems, seeking both exotica and a historical parallel based on a perceived 'otherness'.[22]

It was in 1587 at the College de France in Paris that regular Arabic classes began, soon to be followed by similar efforts in Holland and England. The chair at Leiden was established in 1613, to be followed by one at Cambridge in 1632. Two years later, Oxford created a similar chair with Edward Pococke (1604–1691) as the pioneer scholar. He had spent some time in Syria as a chaplain to English merchants and had translated some of the works of Imam Ghazali, a medieval Islamic theologian. However, it was George Sale (1697–1736) who offered the first proper, full-length translation into English of the Quran, though erstwhile several individuals in the preceding decades had undertaken some fragmentary efforts. Sale's translation was from the Latin text, originally rendered by Lodovico Marracci. Sale duly recognised the Prophet Muhammad's apostolic credentials and infinite wisdom. *History of the Saracens,* the first-ever work on Muslim-Arabs in English, was authored by Simon Ockley (1678–1720), which like Sale's prefatory remarks accredited Muhammad (PBUH) with distinct capabilities. Another contemporary, Robert Boyle (1627– 1691), a founder of the Royal Society, developed a lasting though not so positive interest in Islam and Judaism, mainly purported to authenticate Christianity.

The post-Columbian curiosity in the 'Orient', typified both by powerful Timirud empires and the emergence of a new West European overseas empire, coincided with the commercial expansion of a divided but deeply energised Western Europe. The joint stock companies, under the tutelage of private directors or owned by the crowns initiated European globalism that reverberated in the contemporary literary works highlighting exotica as well as extravaganza. The European emissaries visiting Agra, Fez, Isfahan and Constantinople came back not only with magnificent presents but also with stories of self-sufficient and even prosperous Muslim empires over vast lands and diverse peoples. Unlike coastal Africa, the Eurasian and Mediterranean Muslim regions were centres of political power and cultural development, and any Western relationship had to be based on mutual respect and strictly for political–economic motives. It is only in the subsequent centuries that these very factors eventually led to the creation of full-fledged empires but not until the central authorities had begun to stagnate. The Eighteenth century turned out to be the threshold of Muslim decline and the concurrent rise of the European maritime empires. A vibrant, unchallenged and expansive Western Europe led to the depopulation of several continents and the establishment of colonial hegemony, often erected with the participation of the indigenous elite, occasionally called intermediaries or the predecessors of present-day surrogates. While trading companies from France, the Netherlands and England had already begun establishing 'factories' and trading posts in the Muslim coastal towns, their Iberian predecessors exhibited greater zeal in physically transporting and converting indigenous populations to Catholicism. This newly energised and highly ambitious Western Europe pursued colonisation and the slave trade without any remorse or challenge. Consequently, millions of Africans were transported to the Western Hemisphere, of whom a sizeable portion were African Muslims, generally known as Moors. Within a generation or two these Africans became *proto* Americans taking on the religion and culture of their masters, though nonchalantly, and the early Islamic factor in the Western Hemisphere submerged until it was rediscovered in the twentieth century.[23]

The Inquisition fell hard on Muslims, Jews, Africans and Native communities in the Western Hemisphere and even in the Far East. However, it was Napoleon, fresh from his exploits during the French Revolution, who undertook a massive campaign to encounter and conquer the Muslim heartland. In 1798, he landed in Egypt in the company of soldiers and more than two hundred scholars to formally build closer amity with the Muslims. Earlier, he had been in correspondence with Tipu Sultan of Mysore, who was engaged in fighting the British in India. Tipu Sultan had, in fact, invited Napoleon to attack India, and had employed some French military commanders to train his Muslim and Hindu troops to fight the British East India Company. In a crucial battle at Seringapatam in 1799, Tipu was killed and his prized belongings were taken to Britain with the credit of victory going to the Wellesley brothers in India.[24] Napoleon, on his arrival in North Africa, tried to soothe Egyptian fears by proclaiming that the French 'worship God far more than the Mamluks do, and respect the Prophet and the glorious Quran...the French are true Muslims'.[25] During this period of Enlightenment, amidst a widely subscribed idea of progress, Europe had assumed the flagship role to civilize the world in its own image. The secularising impact of modernity was reflected in contemporary writings on Islam where admiration as well as dismissal characterized writings by known authors like Voltaire. Edward Gibbon devoted a chapter of his monumental work to the Prophet Muhammad (PBUH) and the ascension of Islam. His verdict, after an initial applause for the prophetic career in Makkah, soon turned into a critique of the polity that the Prophet had created in Medinah. Gibbon had problems in relating with the Prophet as a politician. However, some exceptional intellectuals of this Enlightenment era such as Henri de Boulainvilliers (1658–1722) saw Muhammad (PBUH) as preaching a rational religion. Herman Reimarus (1694–1768) felt that people were unduly criticising 'the Turkish religion' without having 'read the Alcoran...'.[26] Even George Sale, after having published his English translation of the Quran in 1734, was not apologetic. David Frederick Megerliu followed Sale in 1772 by publishing a German translation of the Quran directly from the original Arabic text. Johann Jacob Reiske (1715–1774) can be accredited for pioneering German works on Muslim history. However, Goethe is often referred to as one of the most prominent names in this generation of Enlightenment intellectuals, especially in Germany, to have recognized Muslim contributions towards the classical heritage. He adopted several Arabo–Persian words dating from the era of the Crusades.

In the world of literature, it was Joseph von Hammer-Pugstall (1774–1856), who translated several leading Arabic, Persian and Turkish classics into German and introduced his readers to appreciate great Muslims writers of the early medieval era such as Hafiz, the Persian poet of Shiraz. He also completed a monumental ten-volume *History of the Ottoman Empire*. The German tradition of Oriental scholarship was carried on by his student, Friedrich Ruchert (1788–1866). But, as observed earlier, European Enlightenment traditions, followed by the Romanticists, more often showed a kind of 'literary hatred' towards the Turks in particular and Muslims in general.[27] After the establishment of Fort William College in Calcutta by the British East Company in the 1770s, there emerged a greater curiosity for the 'Orient' owing to direct dialogue between West European and South Asian literary traditions. However, by that time it had already become almost a unilateral discourse reflective of European globalism and the outpourings by widely quoted authors such as Gustav Weil, William Muir, Aloys Sprenger and D.E. Margoliouth tended to draw visibly negative portraits of Islam and the Prophet. Concurrently, the missionaries had also become well established in the Muslim regions such as in South Asia and pursued their evangelical activities displaying an unassailable vigour. However, from amongst certain traditional Muslim elite—*ulama*—several took it upon themselves to engage these Western missionaries in debate on the Prophethood, similarities and differences between Islam and Christianity and how Islam was a revealed message despite all the sceptical views held by the latter. Karl Pfander, a German enthusiast from the Church Missionary Society, soon engaged in a debate at Agra with a Muslim scholar, Shaikh Rahmatullah al-Kairanawi, though he withdrew only after the second session.[28]

India had by then emerged as the focal point of this Islam–Christianity encounter and several British officials such as William Muir (1819–1905) extended the domain and works of early Orientalists like Sir William Jones (1746–1794), who had devoted most of his attention to philological issues.[29] Muir, who had been a participant at the Agra debate, returned to Scotland to head Edinburgh University and published his *Life of Muhammad*, which received wide attention in British literary circles. The book presented a mixed portrait of the Prophet and showed Islam merely as a branch of Christianity. Thomas Carlyle, the famous Victorian essayist, saw in Muhammad (PBUH) a not-too-unfamiliar hero and accepted him as a full-fledged prophet. Another of his contemporaries, Charles Forster—the grandfather of the novelist E.M. Foster—in his volume, *Mahometanism Unveiled*, offered rather unbecoming opinions on the Prophet of Islam. It is interesting to note that his own grandson considered his works totally pedestrian. Charles Forster's views on Islam were typical of his generation, which was imbued with a self-professed sense of racial superiority and exhibited a moral uprighteousness while interacting with non-Christian non-Whites.

The early encounters with such people (as in India) based on equality and curiosity had given way to sheer regimented imperialist attitudes underwritten by neo-racism. This was the high water mark of Orientalism when missionaries, writers, intellectuals, colonial administrators, artists, women visitors and even home-based scholars produced tomes of writings and sketches, creating non-European societies in their own images. There was a massive outburst of writings, paintings and commentaries of both a secular and a sacred nature, which, in the wake of 'reorganization' and 'redefinition' of the colonized societies and the imports of the curious and exotic, left permeating imprints on contemporary consciousness. The museums, imperial exhibitions, military parades, civilian shows, biographical literature and official gazetteers on the colonized societies added to a masculine view of the nationalist-imperialist discourse in West Europe. The colonized were shown to be in a state of cultural and intellectual inferiority and in need of modernist European initiatives inclusive of colonial edifices to put them on the road to self-discovery and better living. Social Darwinism was not only the legitimising principle of the powerful class of entrepreneurs at places like the United States it was the main ideology underwriting Victorian norms and mores. Curiously enough the stereotypical and derogatory images of non-Christian Asians, Africans and other Natives were not merely confined to people in the 'home' countries, most of the colonial administrators themselves were fully imbued with them. They operated as the redeemers out on a civilising mission and posed as the *mai bap* (li: parents) of the indigenous peoples. In several cases, the former had popularised such misimages in the first place portraying a strong religious (Christian) component. Accordingly, while Hindus and Buddhists may have been perceived as too ascetic and less challenging, the Muslims were always viewed as formidable opponents whose acculturation required urgent initiatives. Here, Islam was not seen as an identity marker but rather as a bane of problems for its believers, as it commanded complete subordination and utmost sacrifice. Muslim resistance to colonial rule, often justified in the name of religion and *jihad*, was used to substitute a widely subscribed Muslim otherworldliness, which had to be harnessed by sheer force.

It is fascinating to see how the Crusade-based misperceptions were revived during the height of European colonialism, though in the latter case they were more varied and supported by complex economic and military factors, with intellectual justification also fully in attendance. The French, while confronted with the revolt in Algeria led by the Salafis, felt that their secularism in a Christian garb could wrestle with the Islamist forces and thus citizenry was discreetly allowed to only those North African Muslims who were willing to renounce Islam. Such Western policies were the components of a multifaceted project of imperialism, which refused to be contented only with political or economic matters. The Dutch avoided the extreme civilizing measures though in British India, a hierarchal view of Indian societies—the latter being essentially communal and premodern—received full publicity and efforts were fully devoted towards Westernisation. W.W. Hunter, an Indian civil servant (ICS) and latterly an academic in Oxford, saw Muslims 'eagerly drinking in the poisoned teaching of the Apostles of Insurrections'. Alfred Lyall, Syed Ameer Ali and Syed Ahmed Khan contested Hunter's view the way the Muslim founder of the Aligarh movement challenged William Muir on his views of the Prophet.[30] Other than his detailed biography of the Prophet of Islam, Muir, quite unabashedly believed that 'the sword of Muhammad (PBUH) and the Quran are [were] the most stubborn enemies of civilization, liberty and truth which the world had ever known'. William Monier-Williams, another head of the Oxford-based Indian Institute, viewed Islam as 'an illegitimate child of Judaism'.

The Revd Malcolm MacColl found Islam unacceptable because of its tolerance for polygamy though some colonial administrators of this Victorian era including Alfred Lyall, Theodore Beck and William Becker duly recognized Islam's tolerance towards non-Muslims.[31] But the Orientalists, in most cases, dominated contemporary discourse and known authors such as Jane Austen, Rider Haggard, Joseph Conrad, Richard Burton, Lord Byron and their contemporary literati vocally upheld specific, uneven and strong views on non-Western peoples. Their generation was to be followed by another generation reflective of the Victorian imperial idioms and included writers such as Rudyard Kipling, E.M. Forster, Katherine Mayo and Albert Camus. By that time, it was not merely South Asia or North Africa which were the focal points of this modernist intellectual altruism; a steady growth of writings on the Ottomans also revived the age-old scare of 'the terrible Turks'.

The Greek war of independence had invoked the British romanticists like Lord Byron, and the Eastern Question elicited unrestrained support for Christian communities in the Balkans whereas the massacres of Muslims and their expulsions were glossed over by both the West European politicians and intellectuals.[32] Only the massacres of the Christians—Bulgarians, Armenians, Greek Orthodox and others—received prominent coverage in the diplomatic and press reports and the near elimination of Islam from Eastern Europe remained almost under-reported.[33] Likewise, Russian expansionism in the wake of intermittent pogroms of the Muslims in the Caucuses and Central Asia went on unchecked. By the 1860s, Ming rulers in China had already captured the vast Turkic lands in Central Asia following some of the worst ethnic cleansing of Muslims in the kingdom itself.

As researched by Rana Kabbani, benefiting from the Saidian paradigm, Orientalists such as Goland, Chardin, Chateaubriand and Lady Montagu along with the romanticists of the nineteenth century including Shelley, Keats, Byron, Coleridge, Moore and others fully exoticised the East. Their romanticist outpourings on non-Western societies such as Muslims further objectified the colonized peoples. They were considered infantile, childlike or even childish, exotic, vulnerable, well meaning but equally dubious, lost in the torpor of primitive traditions with the Anglo-Saxons and Gaels heralding their deliverance. The East, to such writers, was essentially the land of *The Arabian Nights* where women, in particular, were not only tormented but were equally prone to spellbinding manoeuvres. Metaphorically, empire, to the French, British and even Dutch writers, was an alluring woman, whose nearness was guaranteed through sheer control and subordination. The contrasting images of the imperialised women varied from vulnerable victims to scheming witches.[34] Travellers and fortune seekers like Richard Burton, Charles Doughty and subsequently T.E. Lawrence and Louis Massignon found this East mysterious, alluring and complex and needing Western patronage and guidance to modernise itself. Westernisation was the major component of this multi-dimensional scheme of modernity, though some writers such as Wilfred S. Blunt tried to offer an opposite but strictly a minority view of respect for these traditional societies. It is not surprising that Bernard Lewis, Wilfred Thesiger, Elias Canetti, Linda Blandford, Emma Duncan, Richard Reeves, Christina Lamb, Daniel Pipes, Ann Coulter, Richard Perle, Oriana Fallaci, V.S. Naipaul, Thomas Friedman, Charles Krauthammer and an ever-growing circle of experts on Islam are the latter-day purveyors of the same imperial tradition, though in some cases, more sophisticated but essentially paternal, detached yet self-righteous.[35]

The contemporary Orientalist discourse is not merely confined to professional writers, it also includes a vocal section of roving journalists, travellers and some individual writers sharing nostalgia for the bygone days of empire. A growing number of expatriates or Diaspora writers such as Salman Rushdie, who feel uncomfortable with being called Commonwealth writers, also reflect a growing yet complex genre emanating from within the Orientalist tradition. Certainly, a critical discourse as articulated by intellectuals including Frantz Fanon, Leopold Senghor, Aime Cesaire, Albert Hourani, Edward Said, Eqbal Ahmad, Gyatri Spivak, Immanuel Wallerstein, Stuart Hall, Ziauddin Sardar, in league with the liberal and critical groups within the former 'core' countries, has also made its mark in the contemporary debate.

Despite the lack of any colonial connection between the German states and the Muslim world, several German scholars, over the past several centuries, showed some religious and philosophical interest in Islam and often compared it with Christianity and Judaism. For instance, to J.G. Herder (1744–1803), Islam was basically a primacy of the Arab spirit, a view that reverberates in the works of G.W.F. Hegel (1770–1831). The philological research by William Jones, the pioneering Indianist, deeply benefited German Orientalists including Franz Bopp (1791–1876) and Wilhelm von Humboldt (1767–1837), and was reflected in the works by F. Max Muller (1823-1900). Like anthropology—a major ingredient of colonial-plus-orientalist reconstruction of non-Western societies—the development of philology as a significant academic pursuit remains the hallmark of the Victorian era.

In France, Ernest Renan (1823–1892), while deeply immersed in neo-racism, played a crucial role in fashioning European views of Islam. His writings covered a wider terrain and led towards the categorization of human societies on the basis of their languages. According to his hierarchical dictum, human societies consisted of three groups: firstly those who, to him, lacked collective memory and thus lacked a defined culture. Over and above them were the second category of civilized races such as the Chinese and others who had obtained a certain level of civilization but were incapable of going beyond that status. The third and the most competent category mainly consisted of the two great peoples of the Semitic and Aryan races. The Semites had pioneered religions such as Judaism and Islam whereas the Aryans excelled in sciences, philosophy, arts and literature. Compared to the Semites, the Aryans were multi-disciplinary and forward-looking who carried the burden of refashioning the entire humanity by demolishing both the Semites and other counterparts. In pursuance of the true traditions of neo-racism, Aryans epitomized human perfection, and the rest, as laid out by Ernest Renan, were mere appendages.

Such continental views reverberated across the width and breadth in the West where gypsies, Jews, Catholics, Muslims and other Afro-Asian peoples were defined as inferior races. Within the heart of Europe, Jews became the 'enemy within' and Catholics were perceived as emotional, half-cultured and essentially superstitious people, vulnerable to authoritarianism. Even the Weberian explanation of capitalism vocally hinged on Protestant ethics just like present-day hierarchical views where Muslims are presumably locked in some pre-Reformation and pre-Enlightenment time warp. But Renan's views did not go unchallenged by contemporary Muslim modernists like Jamal-ud-Din al-Afghani (1839–97), who engaged the former in some discussion in Paris on the subject. Afghani brought out his magazine, *Urwathul Wusqa* and sought a reinterpretation of Islam without feeling apologetic towards its classical traditions. Living in colonial Paris after travelling across Muslim lands including the Ottoman Empire, Afghani influenced a generation of Indian and Arab modernist Muslims. His espousal of Pan-Islamism, away from the political overlordship of any particular dynasty, also won him a major following among Muslim intellectuals, especially in British India and Egypt.

The other major intellectual to challenge Renan's views was a Hungarian Jew who was to emerge as the leading scholar of Islam in the modern era and whose treatises were to establish an independent and more judicious tradition of Western scholarship on Islam. Ignaz Goldzihr (1850–1921) refuted Renan's views on Judaism and then immersed himself in Islamic studies by focusing on the Prophetic traditions. His first-hand initiation into Islamic literature and Arabic by virtue of living in the Middle East led to his recognition of Islam both as a fully-fledged religion and a distinct culture. In Cairo, he met Muslim scholars including Afghani and became the first-ever Western scholar to study Islam from its primary sources by immersing himself in the contemporary centres of Muslim learning such as Al-Azhar.[36] He applied critical methods in his study of Islam, especially the Prophetic traditions, and resisted the temptations of working for any university or such other establishment. He was vocally uncomfortable with some Jewish and Christian groups displaying patronizing attitudes and thus preferred to stay independent of any peer pressure.

In the last quarter of the nineteenth century, when Oxford was more occupied with Indic studies under the tutelage of Indologists like William Monier-Williams and Max Muller, the discipline of Islamic studies remained peripheral allowing a lead to Cambridge with W. Wright (1830–1889) being appointed to the Arabic chair.

He had, in fact, studied at Leiden and was soon joined by several other distinguished colleagues such as R.A. Nicholson (1868–1945), W. Robertson Smith (1846–1894) and E.G. Browne (1862–1926). Subsequently, Oxford exhibited some interest as well by appointing D.S. Margoliouth (1858–1940) to undertake teaching and research on Islam, followed by his successor, H.A.R. Gibb (1895–1971).[37] In London, owing to its increased interaction with the vital Middle Eastern regions, especially after the First World War, and due to a growing need for area specialists for all types of reasons, the School of Oriental and African Studies (SOAS) was founded. Still, most of the teachers and researchers at the British universities lacked first-hand exposure to Muslim societies and regions. Other than administrator–scholars attached with the Royal Asiatic Society and the Asiatic Society of Bengal, a few individuals left their imprint on the contemporary views of Islam. E.W. Lane (1801–1876) had lived in Cairo for a number of years and other than his *Manners and Customs of Egyptians,* produced a distinguished Arabic–English dictionary.[38] However, the most influential traveller–writers of the Muslim Middle East during the twentieth century were Louis Massignon (1883–1962) and T.E. Lawrence (1882–1935), who spent years in the region; learnt Arabic, interacted with the colonial administrators and tried to assume vanguard roles for their individual countries in building up links with the Muslim Arabs. They both were the last of the 'romantics'—though one may also include several more like Wilfred Thesiger, Eric Newby and William Dalrymple, whose works have also shown a fascination for and an often-complex relationship with their non-Western associates.

Louis Massignon, with a strong Christian background in France and education in metropolitan Paris, travelled across North Africa and stayed for a while in Cairo and Iraq. At one stage in Basra, he was arrested and during the tense period of internment underwent some spiritual transformation featuring a deeper immersion in Arabic.[39] Massignon's postgraduate research had been on the great Muslim Sufi, al-Hallaj (d.922), who had been hanged by the Abbasids in Baghdad for his radical ideas. Subsequently, Massignon sympathized with the anti-colonialists in Madagascar and Algeria fighting French colonial rule. However, he remained deeply rooted in his personal Catholic traditions yet greatly respected Islam for its unequivocal views on monotheism. He was greatly influenced by Islamic mysticism and hoped for a greater Christian–Muslim interface. As is seen by subsequent research on his work, Massignon remains a permeating influence on the French scholarship on Islamic mysticism, and is accepted as a mentor in this field.

Like Massignon, T.E. Lawrence also combined the roles of an empire builder, a scholar and a romantic figure whose own life, later disillusionment with the regime and rather an early death in 1935 have left an indelible impact on British attitudes towards the Middle East, Arab nationalism and Orientalism.[40] He had met his contemporary, Massignon, during his youth and led the Arab revolt in the Hejaz against the Ottomans. He certainly had a complex relationship with the Arab rebels led by Sharif Hussein and must have felt deeply betrayed not only by the system of Mandates but also with the British turn-about on their former allies. Lawrence's book *Seven Pillars of Wisdom* reveals not only his personal immersion into the Arabo–Islamic world but also his effort to be seriously taken as a specialist on Islam. David Lean's film, *Lawrence of Arabia,* has further popularised his romantic mystique and dashing personality but, like Robert Byron, Baden Powell and Wilfred Thesiger, he remained a puzzling figure until his early death in a traffic accident in 1935. At times, Arabia and Lawrence seemed to be intertwined with all their myths and heroism. Both Massignon and Lawrence, like other fellow colonists, were stupendously complicated personalities representing contemporary contradictions inherent within the colonizing societies. Lawrence, for instance, suffered from acute paranoia, which turned severe after the British betrayal of his Arab associates Sharif and Feisal.[41]

As can be seen from the above brief resumé, the non-Western world and the former colonies including the entire width and breadth of the Islamic world, have been the focus of a diversity of scholars, missionaries and colonial administrators, all imbued with curiosity for their own reasons but still believing in some inherent inferiority of these cultures. Christianity, despite its origins in the 'East', was appropriated as a *European* heritage whereas Islam was characterized as an Asiatic religion and Judaism was seen located somewhere in-between depending upon the variable contemporary attitudes towards Jews. The rising trajectories of exclusivist nationalism and racism in the near past underwrote an overpowering ideology of imperialism especially in Western Europe, which was subsequently adopted in the United States. By the late-nineteenth century, Holland, owing to its colonial enterprise in South-East Asia, had also begun some scholarly efforts on Islam, mainly at Leiden University. Interestingly, Britain, France, Germany and Holland all remained interested in researching Islam yet it did not elicit any major following from amongst the students.[42] H.A.R. Gibb, expecting a more receptive American scholarship for his works on Islam, moved to the United States after teaching at SOAS and Oxford. Gibb's influence was felt among many of his students and contemporaries including Marshal Hodgson and Clifford Geertz. Hodgson (d. 1968), known for inventing terms such as 'Islamicate', 'Irano-Semitic, 'Timurids' (for Mughals), or 'Jama'i' (for Sunnis), sought the explanation of human civilizations including Islam in reference to three factors: ecology, group interests and creative individuals. Influenced by Arnold Toynbee and Oswald Spengler, he focused on 'Oikumene'—the Afro-Eurasian region in its centrality to the evolution of cultures—and produced his well-known *The Venture of Islam*. Geertz is known for pioneering anthropological studies on Muslim regions.

During the post-Second World War decades, a new generation of specialists in Britain such as Kenneth Craig, W. Montgomery Watt and Norman Daniel undertook diverse studies on Islam. Contemporary United States, due to its pronounced global role in the Cold War and owing to geo-political interests in the Muslim world, also began a significant phase of historiography on Islam. The emergence of a Muslim Diaspora and the evolution of groups such as the Nation of Islam have further added to this interest in Islam though geo-political considerations, specific lobbies and a common lack of comparative analysis have characterized American views of Muslims. Numerous American scholars have been dealing with the various academic realms of Islamic studies, yet it is in the areas of geo-politics and journalism that most of the energies have been concentrated. The national interests as well as dramatic portrayals of Muslim societies have allowed both these two areas to steal a march over more serious academic disciplines. While the Western politicians have been making all the vital policy decisions, it is the media coverage that, to a large extent, still betrays images of Muslims varying from sworn enemies to 'different' clusters. Like their former colonial counterparts in Europe, the American, Australian and Canadian perceptions of the Muslim peoples are deeply impacted by specific discretionary views and are underpinned by a pervasive civilizing sentiment. The traditional support for Israel, especially due to a Holocaust-related guilt, has made it still more difficult for them to assume a fully balanced view of Muslim sensitivities.

Scholars of Islam in the United States have come from diverse backgrounds reflecting various preferences and have included known names such as Bernard Lewis, John Esposito, Daniel Pipes, Carl Ernest and several Diasporic Muslims such as the late Professors Ismael Faruki, Aziz Ahmad and Fazlur Rahman at Temple, Toronto and Chicago, respectively. American Muslim academics include men and women as well as some local converts, besides a growing number of Muslim women academes.[43] They are joined by an astounding number of media specialists, though often reflective of cursory and Orientalist views, whereas some novelists have taken on Muslim themes and certainly Hollywood has its due share as well. In the United Kingdom, it is only in the past two decades that a growing interest in Middle Eastern studies has begun to increase, though Islamic Studies as a discipline remains divided into several regions. Often these disciplinary and regional divisions create wider gaps. For instance, teaching and research on South Asia, accounting for the world's largest concentration of Muslim population, remain mainly focused on Indic studies with Islam either non-existent or just an incidental part of it. Somehow, Western scholarship still keeps on treating the Arab regions as the core areas of Islam, whereas Central, Southern and Southeast Asian Muslim communities and likewise the Sub-Saharan areas remain largely peripheral. There are some exceptions to this reductionist view, yet Islam continues to be perceived as an Arabian particularism.[44]

The lack of immersion in Persian, Arabic, Turkish, Bengali, Hausa, Malay and Urdu also hinders academics from promoting studies on Muslim communities and in addition, absence of familiarity with Islam as a religion also presents a major impediment for many of these academics who are either Westerners, Russians or even Indians holding important chairs of international history with very few Muslim academics occupying key academic positions.[45] Places such as Durham University are already experiencing an institutional decline in Middle Eastern studies though a growing number of younger Muslims along with a few British Muslims like Martin Lings and Gai Eaton—mostly on their personal basis and in the footsteps of Muhammad Asad— have pursued their studies on Islam. The Muslim media—both print and visual—and some emerging think tanks are the new post-Rushdie developments. However, research by British academics such as Ernest Gellner and Fred Halliday is widely quoted whereas some British academics such as Michael Gilsenan and Roger Owen have already moved to the United States. In France a growing professionalisation is gradually allowing Muslim scholars to make their presence felt and academics like Muhammad Arkoun have made their due impact. Maxime Rodinson, Olivier Roy and Gilles Kepel, who, other than the first, are mostly interested in the contemporary issues of political Islam, follow noted names such as Louis Massignon. However, a steadily growing number of European Muslim scholars seems to be gradually building up a tradition of progressive Islam though it is still early to estimate their influence on the long-held Western views of Islam. Despite a major Turkish presence, studies on Islam in Germany are either being pioneered by the German scholars or by a few Sufi converts.

In a nutshell, Islam still remains a peripheral discipline in academia, and for politicians and journalists it is contemporary politics which remains alluring. Holland, especially Leiden, carries on with its age-old tradition of scholarly works on Islam including the *Enclypoedia of Islam* and other periodical literature. The periodic seminars and special publications, as reported in the *ISIM Newsletter* offer a growing Europe-wide curiosity if not full-fledged disciplinary interest in the Muslim peoples, arts, history and politics. The European Union has been sponsoring such research institutes and diverse think tanks across Europe to provide sufficient expertise on Muslim polities though the effort remains divided into regional studies.

However, one has to be careful before overestimating a scholarly interest in Islam in the West, especially after 9/11 when official and private misimages of Muslims have become quite familiar. Many Muslims, including from academia, feel further marginalized. Following the terrorist attacks in the US, Spain and Britain and the official retaliatory policies, the research centres and especially Muslim think tanks in the West have assumed a diminished profile, which is not helpful to a no-holds-barred debate. Apologia, introversion, along with some cases of aggressive reaction, reflect subterranean tensions within the Muslim communities. The profiling of Muslim individuals, internment and expulsion of thousands of Muslims across the regions, ban on headgear like in France and Germany, routine negative media portrayals, partisan focus on Islamic fundamentalism and harassment of several second-generation young men on mere suspicion have relegated Muslim minorities to an immensely low status.[46] Certainly, efforts for a better, plural and multi-cultural world have been nefariously pushed back by decades.

As is obvious, the political and economic interests in the West, often justified through moral and cultural excuses, have usually vetoed other cultural or social prerogatives. While European domination of the rest of the world introduced Christianity—both by intent and as an accompanying reality—the intellectual and literary interface with non-Western societies such as Muslims has reflected a self-righteous imperial baggage. Modernity came in with its mixed imprint in the wake of Europeanisation of the world and that is where slavery, racism, Orientalism and uneven inter-regional and inter-communal realties took precedence. Even though the slave trade and subsequently the institution of slavery were banned in the early nineteenth century, and in the United States in 1863, the hierarchical realties of an uneven world still remain evident, more than half a century after the de-colonization itself. No wonder, Western moral postulations and exhortations for the developing world evoke mixed feelings and more often engender mistrust. Though it will be only half true to suggest that only the Crusades, the Christian conquest of Muslim Spain followed by the Inquisition and ethnic cleansing, or the recent colonization have been responsible for this unevenness in perceptions and relationship, yet it is nevertheless important to remember that even today, geo-political and economic objectives, often at the behest of specific interest groups, neutralise individual efforts for a positive and reconstructive human discourse. The hegemonic policies of the colonial era anchored on racist typologies and derision continue to persist, often characterized by a direct intervention or through obliging intermediaries. The interest in natural resources and other geo-political assets across the Muslim regions, combined with security concerns for regional allies such as Israel in the post-colonial era, have only intensified a massive public disillusionment both with the local regimes and their Western backers. Amidst a rising tide of Islamophobia and the deep economic and political dichotomy between the rulers backed by the West, and the ruled has angered radical Muslim elements desirous of creating Islamic utopias by expelling their ruling elite and their Western backers. Humiliation, anger, grudge and betrayal have spawned anti-American sentiments among some Muslim radicals including Al-Qaeda who decided to take on the United States as a symbol of Western power and invincibility. Never before did the acts of a few cost so much anguish to so many. The common Muslim inability to forestall the destruction of the Muslim populace in several regions and a multiplied anger over continued Anglo–American unilateralism, amidst a multi-prong campaign—often defined as the new Crusades by several Muslim opinion-makers—regimented the premise of a clash of civilisations on all sides. Once again, it has become obvious that the anomalous political relationship between the Muslims and the North Atlantic regions is far from improving, and instead, seems to have deteriorated significantly.

NOTES

1. For details, see Stephen Mansfield, *The Faith of George W. Bush* (New York, 2003). Both Bush and Blair are reported to have prayed together though the latter would often deny that. 'Bush says God chose him to lead his nation', *Observer*, 2 November 2003. In his interview with David Frost, President Bush unequivocally confirmed that both he and Blair were firm believers and practicing Christians. 'Breakfast with Frost', BBC1TV, 16 November 2003. According to the US President, they both believed in speaking the truth though, on several occasions in the recent past, Blair would not admit to having prayed with the American President or would simply divert the question. In response to another BBC journalist, Blair did not know the extent of power held by the Neoconservatives in Washington and was equally naive about the intricacies of Middle Eastern politics and was thus doubtlessly and 'accidentally' roped in by the Americans in the war on Iraq. See, James Naughtie, *The Accidental American: Tony Blair and the Presidency* (London, 2004). In October 2005, it was widely revealed in the press that President Bush personally believed in having been led by divine forces to invade Afghanistan and Iraq.

2. The Revd. Giles Fraser, 'The evangelicals who like to giftwrap Islamophobia', *Guardian*, 10 November 2003. A few letters appearing next day further expressed anger and surprise over the way missionary activities were being taken up in Iraq with unstated support from officials. In the following few weeks it was further revealed that certain American charities working in the Middle East had even prohibited their British counterparts from referring to the British–America invasion and 'occupation of Iraq. The terms, 'invasion' and 'occupation' were to be dropped in conversation or correspondence forcefully—a kind of subjectivity to the superior American geo-political imperatives. Many of these charities such as Action Aid, Christian Aid or Oxfam are supported by Washington and London and thus are careful not to condemn military campaigns.

3. A recent study seeks this experience in a universal context. See, John Gray, *Al-Qaeda and What It Means to be Modern* (London, 2003).

4. Gilles Kepel and a few other European writers may trace the evolution of anti-Muslim feelings in events such as the Arab–Israeli War of 1973, the Oil Embargo, the Iranian Revolution (1979) and the furore over Salman

Rushdie's *The Satanic Verses* or the scarf issue in France in 1991 and 2004. Such a view may be partially true but it puts the blame on global Muslim events and ignores the racist and discretionary legacies before and after these events. See, Gilles Kepel, 'Islamic Groups in Europe: Between Community Affirmation and Special Crisis', in Steven Vertovec and Ceri Peach (eds.) *Islam in Europe: The Politics of Religion and Community* (London, 1997).

5. For details on the public opinion survey, see *Guardian,* 29 October 2003. On the defiance by the Israeli conscripts, see Linda Grant, 'What the War Does to US?' *Guardian Magazine,* 29 November 2003.

6. Ann Coulter, Daniel Pipes and Fareed Zakaria are some of the main proponents of this school of thought. To them, the United States, in particular, holds an unprecedented upper moral ground due to its democratic norms and attendant global responsibilities and thus must refashion the Muslim world or especially the Middle East in that context. For a recent version of this view, see Fareed Zakaria, 'Iraq is not ready for democracy', ibid., 12 November 2003.

7. Some of them have already lost patience for kowtowing regimes such as Saudi Arabia and feel confident enough for the United States to undertake this 'reconstructionist' enterprise.

8. While British historian, Niall Ferguson, now teaching in New York, in his television series, *Empire,* (2002) may advise present-day Americans to learn from the British in empire building, Michael Ignatieff, another Russian–Canadian–British writer, has been advocating cultural imperialism to establish democracy in the Muslim world. See his *Lite Imperialism: Nation-building in Bosnia, Kosovo and Afghanistan* (London, 2003). Fareed Zakaria finds in the American concept of liberty a well-needed redemption for Muslim nations. See, *The Future of Freedom* (New York, 2003).

9. Annemarie Schimmel, *Islam: An Introduction* (Albany, 1992), p. 1.

10. Quoted in Andrew Wheatcroft, *Infidels: The Conflict between Christendom and Islam 638-2002* (London, 2003), p. 47. Some of his followers thought that the Muslim conquest of the Holy Land was in fact a predicted curse.

11. W. Montgomery Watt, *The Influence of Islam on Medieval Europe,* (Edinburgh, 1982), p. 82.

12. It was in 1832 that the publication of *Tales of the Alhambra* by Washington Irving, the American writer living in Granada, introduced Spain and the rest of the world to the splendors of a lost era. Spain's own rise and fall and its colonial and Christian rivals also criticised it for destroying a glorious heritage. For instance, the Victorian interest in Muslim Spain was a retort to post-1492 policies. Stanley Lane-Poole's book, *The Moors in Spain* (London, 1888), not only romanticized the Spanish Muslim past, it equally criticised post-Inquisition Spain. To the famous British author, Spain's rise was solely due to the Muslims and its decadence occurred when it eliminated and expelled them. Professor Reinhardt Dozy's study of Muslim Spain, originally published from Leiden in 1861, and its English translation in 1913, proved

to be a groundbreaking work in the reconstruction of the tenure of Muslim Spain. The second major scholarly work on Muslim Spain was undertaken by Levi-Provencal whose three volumes on the subject besides his revision of Dozy's research covered Muslim history in Spain until 1031, as his death did not allow the completion of his monumental project. In more recent times, Watt and Hitti have tried to provide single-volume studies of the entire Muslim experience in Spain. See Watt and Cachia, *A History of Islamic Spain* (Edinburgh, 1965); and Philip K. Hitti, *History of the Arabs* (London, 1961). Hitti's book, by that time had already undergone several editions. Anwar Chejne, Bernard Lewis and Albert Hourani, besides a host of writers on Arab history, have sections on Muslim Spain, though in the Islamic world, there are works of history and fiction focusing on Muslim Spain, generally known as Al-Andulas or Hispaniya. Muhammad Iqbal, Abdul Haleem Sharrar, Nizar Kabbani and Nasim Hejazi have immortalized Muslim Spain in their literary works.

13. Watt, p. 5.

14. Quoted in Ihsan Aslam, '...in Sicily', *Daily Times* (Lahore), 10 December 2003; also, www.pakistanhistory.com. When the South Asian poet-philosopher, Muhammad Iqbal (1875–1938) visited Sicily in the early twentieth century, he was deeply moved by its by-gone past and wrote a moving poem about Muslim Sicily comparing it with the devastation of Delhi after 1857 and that of Muslim Spain. He had, in fact, visited Andalusia and gone through a similar moving experience there.

15. Watt, p. 54.

16. Wheatcroft in the second section of his book has capably discussed details on Muslim elimination following the fall of Granada. See, pp. 63-161.

17. Watt, p .47.

18. Albert Hourani, *Islam in European Thought* (Cambridge, 1993), p. 7. For a detailed study, see Norman Daniel, *Islam and the West* (Oxford, 2000).

19. Posited both as barbarian and wasteful ventures as well as the struggle for the internationalization of Europe—at the expense of Jews, Muslims and some fellow Christians—the Crusades displayed an unusual velocity. It was, in a way, a painful, arduous yet not totally wasteful enterprise, if one looks at extra-religious aspects. Steven Runciman, *Crusades*, 3 volumes, London, 2002 (reprint).

20. See, Montgomery Watt, *The Influence of Islam on Medieval Europe* (Edinburgh, 1994); Bernard Lewis, *Islam and the West* (Oxford 1994), and, *The Muslim Discovery of Europe* (London, 1982). I have discussed the attendant developments in my other volume. See, *Islam and Modernity: Muslims in Europe and the United States* (London, 2004), especially the first two chapters on Spain and the third chapter on Britain. Also, Jason Webster, *Andalus: Unlocking the Secrets of Moorish Spain*, London, 2004.

21. For details see, Nabil Matar, *Islam in Britain, 1558–1685* (Cambridge, 1998).

22. Malik, pp. 71-78. Dr Johnson wrote: 'There are two objects of curiosity—the Christian world, and the Mahometan world. All the rest may be considered barbarians'. Quoted in Hourani, p. 10.

23. It is only in the recent past that with books such as *Roots* and *The Autobiography of Malcolm X* that the Muslim factor began to elicit some serious attention. The most comprehensive work on this subject is owed to Allen D. Austin, whose research has unearthed biographical information on several known African slaves who were Muslims and who tried to maintain their contacts with Islam through various means (see, Allen D. Austin, *African Muslims in Antebellum America* [London, 1997]). The film, *Amistad*, based on the true events of 1839, also shows several African Muslims being smuggled into the United States. Such discourse has led to a renewed interest among several African–American groups on Islam.

24. Richard Wellesley, later Marquess Wellesley (1760–1842) was the Governor-General of India who ensured a steady expansion of the Company's rule whereas Arthur Wellesley, later the Duke of Wellington (1769–1842)—the younger brother—was eventually to gain victory over Napoleon at Waterloo. Plays on Tipu were popular in contemporary Ireland since he was considered o be a distant friend fighting the common enemy. His sword, turban and most of all, a wooden harmonium embodying his anti-British sentiments, are kept in the Victoria and Albert Museum. His musical instrument shows a Company's Red Coat being strangled in the jaws of a tiger and crying helplessly for help. The tiger in this prized item at the Museum symbolised Tipu who wanted to expel the Company from India with help from revolutionary France. For more on Tipu Sultan, the Wellesleys and the Company, see William Dalrymple, *White Mughals* (London, 2003), pp. 58, 140-8, 177-8 and 192-7. Dalrymple, however, through this popular book and other writings has been advocating 'chutnification' of the various cultures in regions such as South Asia. By focusing on intermarriages between the British and Indians—especially Muslim women—the travel writer–historian has been trying to refute the 'clash of cultures'.

25. Quoted in Hourani, p. 15.

26. Quoted in Schimmel, p. 5.

27. Ibid., p. 2.

28. For further details on this inter-faith debate and dissension, see Avril Powell, *Muslims and Missionaries in Pre-Mutiny India* (London, 1993).

29. Basically a judge, Sir Jones worked closely with the Indian Muslim elite and established historical links between Sanskrit, some European languages and Old Persian. Jones's interaction with the Muslim elite established a curious but still equal relationship between the Islamic East and Christian West. His own interaction with Mirza Abu Talib Khan, Ghulam Husain Khan and several other early 'Occidentalists' offered him a rare opportunity to seek out the intellectual and theological moorings of the 'old' East. Some of these Persian-speaking Muslim elite had been to Europe and could offer first-hand

a comparative perspective on inter-faith and inter-cultural issues. For details, see Gulfishan Khan, *Indian Muslim Perceptions of the West During the Eighteenth Century* (Karachi, 1998). By that time, some Indian citizens like Dean Mahomed or the wives of British Indian officials had settled in Britain and Ireland and left favourable impressions in their newly adopted lands. See, Michael H. Fisher, *The First Indian Author in English: Dean Mahomed (1759–1851) in India, Ireland, and England* (Delhi, 1996); also, (ed.) *The Travels of Dean Mahomed: An Eighteenth-Century Journey through India* (Berkeley, 1997). For a comparative overview, see C.L. Innes, 'Black Writers in Eighteenth-Century Ireland', *Bullan: An Irish Studies Journal,* V, 2, 2000.

30. Syed Ameer Ali was an eminent Indian Muslim jurist from Bengal, who wrote two comprehensive studies of the Muslim past so as to counteract Western assaults on Islam. *The Spirit of Islam* and *A Short History of the Saracens* remain two well-argued and authentic studies even after a century of their earliest editions. Ali subsequently migrated to London and established the London Branch of the All-India Muslim League in 1908. He died a few years later in London. His work was carried on by his contemporary, Allama Yusuf Ali, a former Indian civil servant and academician whose English translation of the Quran is widely read and whose contribution towards Muslim renaissance in Lahore remains crucial. He had returned to India on the invitation of Muhammad Iqbal and made Lahore his base. Yusuf Ali died in London in 1952.

31. For a valuable study on the subject, see K.K. Aziz, *Britain and Muslim India: a Study of British Public Opinion vis-à-vis the Development of Muslim Nationalism in India, 1857–1947* (London, 1962).

32. Of course, one may find exceptions such as the reportage of the Russian atrocities in Chechnya during the nineteenth century, as reported by W.H. Russell of *The Times,* who also earned his name because of his extensive coverage of the Crimean War.

33. For a pertinent work on this less-known subject, see Philip Mansel, *Constantinople: City of the World's Desire* (London, 1997). I have discussed this fully in reference to the late-nineteenth century ethno-national movements in the Ottoman Balkans. *Islam, Modernity and Globalisation: The Tragedy of Bosnia* (Lahore, 2004).

34. Rana Kabbani, *Imperial Fiction: Europe's Myths of Orient* (London, 1994), p. 26.

35. This is not to underestimate the general value of their works, or the significance of especially those whose recent encounters with the former colonies are based on genuine human concerns and also rooted in rigorous and honest research.

36. Hourani, pp. 37-8.

37. He was the teacher of a number of Islamists and Islamicists including Fazlur Rahman. However, in his private views, he did not acknowledge any Muslim

contribution towards the reawakening of Europe. (This information was personally confirmed by a retired academic, who happened to have a discussion with Professor Gibb in the early 1960s following the former's lecture at Oxford's Majlis—the South Asian student body. Based on an interview with Professor Tapan Raychaudhuri in Oxford in January 2004).

38. His correspondence, some personal belongings including his Egyptian clothes and early editions of his works were put on display in early 2003 at Ashmolean Museum in Oxford.

39. Hourani, pp. 43-4.

40. T.E. Lawrence once again became quite popular following the UK–US invasion of Iraq and due to local resistance in 2003–5. His book underwent several editions and broadsheets carried special comments on his association with the Arabs.

41. He frequently changed his name, shifted jobs and brought out several different versions of his book. For thirteen years, he employed John Bruce, a Scot, to physically beat him up on a regular basis for some physical gratification. For details, see Michael Asher, *Lawrence: The Uncrowned King of Arabia*, London, 1998, pp. 17-20. Earlier, in his years at Oxford, Lawrence would exhibit strange behaviour by diving into the Cherwell, periodically going on strange diets or cycling endlessly and aimlessly. Since his return from the Middle East after having staged the Bedouin revolt against the Ottomans during the First World War, he was confronted by the realities of the mandate system solidified through the Paris Peace Settlement. The Sykes–Picot Pact, the secret Anglo–French covenant on the distribution of the Middle East, and the Balfour Declaration certainly added to his psychological torment and guilt.

42. It is only since the 1960s and onwards that one finds a gradual increase in studying Islam-related subjects including Middle Eastern or African studies. By this time, the displacement of the traditional colonial powers had been superseded by the induction of the United States as a dominant force in the post-colonial world though in strong competition with the Soviet Union, and Muslim regions began to gain some following in the major American universities.

43. Some prominent names are Amina Wadud, Barbara Aswad, Leila Ahmed, Asma Barlas, Riffat Hasan and Ayesha Jalal.

44. No wonder V.S. Naipaul, in the tradition of the Victorian Orientalists, keeps viewing Islam as the Arab Imperialism. His works such as *Among the Believers* or *Beyond Belief* refuse to see the acculturative influences within Islam and its numerous cultural expressions. For an interesting alternative, see Richard Bulliet, *View from the Periphery* (Albany, 1994).

45. At places like Oxford, London and Cambridge, South Asian history has either become an appendage of Indic studies or only focuses on the British phase. As a consequence, the Muslim era or studies on South Asian Islam remain almost non-existent. One or two academics claiming to lead studies

on Muslim topics ironically lack lingual as well as disciplinary training in these areas. Islamic Studies forms a rather subdued part of Middle Eastern studies, where geo-political subjects of contemporary or recent significance dominate the debate and curricula.

46. In the two years following 9/11, the British authorities arrested nearly six hundred Muslim individuals amidst a dramatic media focus whereas only five had to confront some charges and those too not related to terror. But compared to the very low and rather trivial and miniscule level of indictment or conviction, the damage to the entire community has been manifold. *Guardian*, 6 December 2003. Following 7/7, more Muslims are being rounded up while several others are under surveillance by security agencies.

2

NEO-ORIENTALISM AND MUSLIM BASHING: BERNARD LEWIS ON ISLAM

When one keeps hold of all the facets of the medieval confrontation of Christianity and Islam, it is clear that the influence of Islam on western Christendom is greater than is usually realized...Because Europe was reacting against Islam it belittled the influence of the Saracens and exaggerated its dependence on its Greek and Roman heritage.

– W. Montgomery Watt, *The Influence of Islam and Medieval Europe,*
1994, 84

An Arab-American waiter who reported for work at a presidential fundraiser last Friday was sent home because the US secret service believed he posed a security risk....He was escorted from the Hyatt Regency hotel in Baltimore, where he has worked for seven years, after just one question from the manager: 'Is your name Mohamad?'

– *Guardian,* 12 December 2003

The relationship between the Muslim East and a predominantly Christian West, especially in its recent phases, has been usually conflict-prone though there have been areas of mutualities varying from culture, literature, cuisine, arts, technology, politics, economy, trade and Diaspora. The dichotomous interface has been both due to a lack of proper information on both sides, simultaneously, it owes to pervasive misperceptions and mismages. While there is no single-factor explanation, yet religious and politico–economic factors—often hand in glove—have played a pronounced role in widening the chasm. The role of opinion makers, varying from missionaries to academics, politicians and media pundits has been equally problematic, further exacerbated in recent times by hegemonic policies and discretionary interventions in the Muslim regions. While the Islamic conquests of the Christian heartland had been a debilitating development, the Crusades, Inquisition and colonialism only added to serious imbalances. The post-colonial geo-political imperatives in the developing world obtained through surrogacy, protection of specific interests by imposing new territorial and ideological entities and policies often characterized by invasions and denigration have certainly underwritten Muslim anguish.

The discretionary typologies as reflected in the Orientalist discourse and institutionalised racism meted out to an overwhelmingly non-White Muslim Diaspora since the dissolution of the Cold War and more so after 9/11 and 7/7 have re-ignited the acrimonious tradition of Islamophobia. Books on Islam, *jihad*, Muslim militancy, Islamic terror and on groups such as Al-Qaeda or the Taliban have mushroomed in the last few years. Saddam Hussein and Osama bin Laden, in most of these dramatic studies, have come to typify ordinary Muslims by fitting them in with the age-old images of Islam as a dangerous heresy. Mullah Omar and Imam Khomeini remind all of *Mahound,* as the army of experts and Islam specialists take turns in the print and visual media to pontificate on *jihad.* Chest beating, wife beating, turbaned and bearded crowds are seen as the latter-day Moors whose Diaspora counterparts in the West may pose a threat from within. While the Islamic world has to be presumably retrieved from its pre-Renaissance time warp, the superior Western values must be protected not only through military-led invasions but also through a rollback of civil liberties of these Muslim immigrants and their descendants. Thus, the war on terror, in the tradition of the Crusades and colonialism, is a new moral, socio-political, economic and cultural enterprise targeting the present-day barbarians by applying multiple channels and instruments. While Presidents George W. Bush and Vladimir Putin and Prime Ministers Tony Blair, Jose Maria Aznar, John Howard, Ariel Sharon and Silvio

Berlusconi hyped up this civilizing mission, its reverberations were felt in the Caucasus and in South-East Asia where an entire generation of cold warriors underwent resuscitation. A tier of ideologues whose own unabashed views of Muslim religion, history and the present day problematics converged with the geo-political dictates of these rulers, and were coopted by the Neoconservative politicians. The discussion, in this and the following chapter, is devoted to a few of those whose works not only reflect their own serious and often hostile biases but also represent a recurring and often myopic tradition in Western scholarship. These individuals do not simply belong to a wide variety of disciplines; they are also the flag carriers of a persistent, nebulous and immensely pernicious attack on Islam and Muslims. In their often reductionist and patronising manners, they share a common hostility to Islam, its relationship with the West and the rest, and in some of their post-9/11 outpourings they have focused on seeking faults only with the Muslims.[1] These academics, writers, journalists, clerics and politicians are the front-runners in this recent phase of insidious attacks on Islamic cultures by manifesting a pervasive Western antagonism.

Instead of recapping the critique of Samuel Huntington's clash of civilisations, this selection largely concentrates on Bernard Lewis, Daniel Pipes, Ann Coulter, V.S. Naipaul, and Pat Buchannan with a few references to some others to show the spread of a cross-disciplinary yet monologous Neo-Orientalism displaying its vicious portents. Combined with the ignoble institutionalisation of extra-Geneva convention institutions such as Camp X-Ray on Guantanamo Bay, the notorious Abu Ghraib Prison, Israel's Facility 1381 or Britain's Belmarsh Jail and hundreds of their counterparts elsewhere, the forces of a pervasive Islamophobia amidst a triumphal moralism surely make a painful subject in human history. This chapter focuses on Professor Bernard Lewis while the rest will be reviewed in the subsequent sections.

Bernard Lewis, 'the principal guru of the neocons, the proponent of the Iraq war', is one of the most influential academics on Islamic history.[2] Born in 1917 into a British Jewish family, Lewis studied at London University's School of Oriental and African Studies (SOAS) before moving to the United States. For the past several decades, Professor Lewis has been teaching at Princeton and has authored several valuable studies on Muslim history and has, in general, concentrated on modern Turkey and the Arab Middle East. However, since the 1990s, Lewis has been focusing on more contemporary issues by positing an unbridgeable gap between the West and Islam and has been the vanguard proponent of the clash of civilisations even before Samuel Huntington's well-publicized piece appeared in *Foreign Affairs* in 1993. Lewis's historical studies including *The Emergence of Modern Turkey, The Arabs in History* and *The Middle East: 2000 Years of History from the Rise of Christianity to the Present Day* have long been used as text books at several universities. His familiarity with the original source material and a focus on relationship between Muslims and non-Muslims reveal recurring legacies of tensions and conflicts.

Islam is puzzling to Lewis and to him it is the bane of diverse problems for the Muslim peoples—both Arabs and Turks—until the encounter with the West ushers in a new era of hopes and uncertainties. Islam in the Middle East and Spain is shown as a civilisational force that uses *jihad* to obtain power and thus the Quran and the sword become intertwined. However, it is the traditional Christian and Jewish communities within the Muslim world, which, according to Lewis, suffered as *dhimmies* yet, maintained a loyal relationship with the Muslim masters. In Lewis's works, Muslims usually come about as power-crazed warriors whose penchant for violence against non-Muslims or even fellow Muslim sects remains undiminished. Lewis apportions most of the Muslim agony to something intrinsically violent in Islam and its encounters with the West—Crusades, colonialism and modernity—despite their pangs holding a retrieving impact for an otherwise lost and fragmented Muslim world. His focus on Islamic community building, relationship between Islam and politics, idealism for Pan-Islamism and a sustained suspicion of Judaic–Christian precepts are some of the most decisive causes of decline and disillusionment within the community.

To Lewis, Western Europe and its models of governance, politicking and prioritisation of modernity offer the only hope for Muslims. To him, even the glorious past is interspersed with interpersonal and doctrinal rivalries with Muslim culture and polities lost in a perennial torpor. His unabashed Eurocentric views find an Islamic deliverance only in a Western modernity. Lewis, occasionally, and quite intentionally, focuses on controversial areas of the Islamic past and in a perfectly Orientalist tradition, subtly turns into a demolition man. His discourse is steeped in an exoticisation of Islam with emphasis on its internal differences, violence and vulnerability to irrational tendencies with the total focus on a supposed Islamic exceptionalism, but that too in a negative sense. He dwells mostly on the conflictive aspects of the Muslim–Christian relationship though Jews appear in his narrative but as non-contentious individuals who, in several cases, by accepting Islam played a vanguard role in preserving the best of both the East and West. Lewis cannot hide his anger over Islam's emphasis on self-sufficiency and its low-profile interest in the West, which to him, remains the ultimate model of human excellence. In addition, Israel, instead of being seen as a creation and instrumentation of a policy of dispossession, or its continued brutalisation of the Palestinians quite irreverent to global opinion, either disappears from his discourse on discord in the Middle East, or innocuously stays on the sidelines. Lewis's major preoccupation with the intra-Muslim and Muslim–Christian dichotomies also absolves Israel as a major cause as well as the instrument of this uneven relationship. His apologia for Israel and post-9/11 defence of Israel as a wronged state unequivocally reflect his unquestioned sympathy for Zionism. After, 9/11 Israel is the victim of Muslim terror while earlier on it was an exceptional project aimed at civility and to induct order in an otherwise world of eternal chaos and totalitarianism.

Other than routinely seeking Muslim problems within the context of Islam and an intermingling of religion and politics, Lewis devotes a single-minded attention to violence largely as the Islamic legacy *per se*. His book on the Assassins quite cleverly reinforces the element of intra-Muslim violence and is thus a reiteration of Orientalist preoccupation with Eastern peoples as irrational, childish and unruly, who have to be controlled and forcibly guided towards a cherished culture. Despite its academic ingredients, the volume essentializes the Western view of an unforgiving force of vendetta within Islam. *The Assassins* reads like a story from *A Thousand and One Nights* and seems to suggest as if 'the Old Man of the Mountain' was the Prophet Muhammad (PBUH) himself or maybe a Khomeini or Osama bin Laden of the medieval past. To Lewis, they were history's first terrorists who did not spare even their fellow believers. Due to paucity of good literature on the subject and also in the perspective of the Iranian Revolution, such a study fulfils both academic needs as well as Orientalist imperatives. Since its first publication in 1967, the entire practice of terror by this fanatical Muslim Shia group during the Crusades, has assumed 'contemporary relevance', especially after 9/11 and more so after the second Intifadah in Palestine. The suicide attacks on the United States and against Israelis, according to Lewis, have rekindled interest in the Assassins, despite their rationale for suicide being quite averse to pristine Islamic teachings. In his recent preface to the volume, he observes rather clearly: 'Certainly, the resemblance between the medieval Assassins and their modern counterparts are [sic.] striking: the Syrian–Iranian connection, the calculated use of terror, the total dedication of the assassin emissary, to the point of self-immolation, in the service of his cause and in the expectations of heavenly recompense. Some have seen a further resemblance, in that both directed their attack against an external enemy, the crusaders in the one case, the Americans and Israelis in the other'. In the study of their methodology, he considers them the role models and 'the forerunners' of the present-day suicide bombers. He invokes classical Islamic abhorrence of committing suicide and condemns the twentieth century Muslim clerics for 'blurring of this previously vital distinction'. He repeats himself to underline their Middle Eastern origins so as to posit them as the forerunners of today's militants fighting the US and Israel: 'The story of the medieval Assassins, who appeared in Iran and spread to the Syrian and the

Lebanese mountains, can be instructive. And of all the lessons to be learnt from the Assassins, perhaps the most important is their final and total failure'.[3]

Allegorically, Lewis has been referring to Al-Qaeda, Hamas, Hizbollah and such other groups though it is rather too simplistic to group together so many parallels whereas most of the these groups, except for Hizbollah, happen to be Sunni and their war is against the Israelis and Americans and not against fellow Muslims—though they certainly decry Muslim ruling elite as surrogates.[4] But, these outfits, despite their intermittent attacks in Saudi Arabia or Iraq, are not eliminating some rival Muslim clergy in a systematic way, which was certainly the hallmark of the Assassins. The resistance in Iraq is altogether different and is aimed at collaborators though the US remains the ultimate target not merely as a representative of some monstrous West but simply because of its exploitative and hegemonic policies in the region. The unquestioned US support for Israeli dispossession of Palestinians and its opportunistic relationship with authoritarian regimes while simultaneously sermonising on justice and human rights, cause a massive backlash. Anti-Americanism may have many manifestations outside the United States but it is not merely confined to the Muslim regions and likewise the critique of Israel is quite pervasive and widespread even in the European heartland, where in several public opinion polls Israel has been overwhelmingly viewed as the most dangerous threat to world peace. Thus, using selective events from the Muslim past to essentialise some unique Muslim obsession for violence is not only incorrect but is equally far-fetched. For instance, sectarian conflict in Pakistan has a different character unto itself where several local and regional forces are at play but to read these activities as the ditto copies of the Assassins is certainly a dubious argument. Surely, the Ismailies themselves would understandably like to avoid more critical studies of Hasan bin Sabbah—the old Man of the Mountain—and would instead focus on Nasir Khusrow, the eleventh century intellectual and theologian, yet the Assassin experience cannot be enlarged or explained as a totemic legacy for all the subsequent activisms.

It appears that Lewis is more interested in locating unsavoury details from the Muslim past to substantiate a partisan and insidious view of Islam. Such a slant, found in almost all of his writings, seriously compromises his otherwise prolific scholarship. For instance, his *Race and Slavery in the Middle East* is mainly set to prove that Muslims were slave owners and suffered from racist attitudes as reflected in their socio-political life.[5] Of course, Islam tried to humanise contemporary society, and the Prophet, in his exhortations and through personal example, tried to eradicate age-old colour and culture-based typologies. The concept of *ummah,* the daily five-time congregational prayers and the annual Hajj were not merely aimed at community building but were also purported to override racist and clannish proclivities. However, it is equally true that Islam did not ban slavery once and for all and many Muslim feudatory and monarchical families thrived on slave labour. Muslim slaves, inspired by Islam's egalitarianism, often resorted to rebellions against such dynasts. Muslims, especially in the Arabian Peninsula, inherited a long-held tradition of slave owning though subsequently the West Europeans enslaved African, Barbary and even Arab Muslims themselves. The class-based regimentation and feudalisation only prolonged enslaving traditions but there were noble exceptions across North Africa and South-West Asia where former slaves were able to establish ruling dynasties. Lewis, time and again, tries to show that the West ended the slave trade in the Muslim world during the colonial period while many Muslims including the Peninsula Arabs had been justifying it on a religious basis until the late nineteenth century.

Slave owning was not as regimented and institutionalised among Muslims as it was in the American South nor was it such a massive and lucrative enterprise as was seen during the early modern era with the 'peculiar' institution dominating the Middle Passage and a major portion of the Atlantic economies. Arabs and Africans enslaved fellow Africans but the Europeans and Americans cannot use such a reality to justify their own massive enslavement of Africans nor can one see total similarity in both case studies. If Israel, the former colonial powers and the United States were so transparent on issues of racism and slavery then how come at the UN-led first-ever conference in Dublin in 2001, they tried to block all efforts to confront these legacies? These countries were even unwilling to tender a formal apology to the Africans.

Professor Lewis's short study on identity politics in the Middle East focuses on the forces of change and continuity though he only detects a contestation between Pan-Islamism and territorial patriotism, which may overrule trans-regional loyalties as witnessed in the Iran–Iraq war. However, as a true Eurocentric, he feels that Muslim societies will take longer to accept change and stabilize themselves as modern communities.[6] In his rather comprehensive study of Muslim–European interaction, *The Muslim Discovery of Europe*, one encounters Lewis at his most as an Orientalist. Not only does the title itself suggest a Eurocentrism in his approach, it vividly situates the West as the core region in all kinds of human activity with Muslims not only as its periphery but also the *other*. The book is based on some selective Arabic, Persian and Turkish sources to show that either the Muslims did not care about discovering the creativity and ongoing changes within Europe, or they were simply handicapped by their unquestioned belief in their own religious and cultural self-sufficiency. His source material and the parameters of discourse are quite selective though no less significant and the interpretations as well as the consequences predictably fall in line. One may simply ask: why Europe has to be the barometer of the knowledge or extent of any other civilisation? The Chinese, Japanese, Hindus, Mongols, Africans, Native Americans or the indigenous people of Australasia never visited or interacted with Europe until recent times: does that make them less human since they did not learn from this citadel of science, democracy and modernity that Lewis is so preoccupied with? Muslims, compared to anybody else, have had a rather lasting interaction with Christians, Jews, Zoroastrians, Hindus, Buddhists and several African religious groups—though not always peaceful and nor so conflictive either—and maybe, it is the enormity of contacts and interaction that may explain these numerous contestations. To Lewis, Muslims have been bad learners largely because they did not become pseudo European, presumably out of something innately wrong with Islam, though he would not say so openly yet that is what he implies every few pages of this massive study. However, in complete fairness to Lewis and the objective realities on the ground, Muslim agony in recent centuries owes itself to a reversal from scientific inquiry and logic while opting for imitation and conformity.

Consisting of twelve chapters, *The Muslim Discovery of Europe* begins with a survey of the contacts and acculturative impact on all sides. Based on Muslim sources, it explores the extent and quality of the knowledge that the Muslims had of Europe over the centuries in areas such as languages, translations, media, religion, economy, politics, law, science, culture and socio-personal lives. He finds Muslim contact very meagre, temporary and partisan, only seeking transient gains rather than absorbing the European advances in vital areas. In other words, Muslims were bad pupils and remained in the dark about all the significant changes in a predominantly Christian and subsequently secular Europe. And, this could be the bane of their predicament. For instance, the Arab historian Ibn Hakam (803–871), while writing about the Muslim conquest of North Africa and Spain only gives a passing reference and that too in regard to booty. Tabari (d. 923) and Ibn al-Quttiya (d. 977), the early reputed Muslim historians, did not even mention the Battles of Tours and Poitiers in the 730s, which had steeply reversed the Muslim attack on France, though they devoted several pages to the intermittent invasions of Constantinople.[7] To Lewis, Muslims, exhausted with the internal schism especially under the Abbasids, had resigned themselves to more eastward ventures and settled for a limiting extroversion. They preferred to ignore vast Christian territories across Europe though the fact is that the Muslims both in Spain and Sicily were culturally and politically quite active and never ashamed of interacting with the non-Muslims. In the same vein, the Ottomans and Mughals patronised non-Muslim elite for both civil and military purposes and it is a different matter that our knowledge of related written traditions remains only confined to the retrieved manuscripts.

Lewis censures Muslims for ignoring the Crusades, both politically and intellectually, and even the contemporary familiar terms, to him, are owed to the Christian Arabs. Certainly, the discussion of the Crusades has remained a Euro-Christian monopoly but their deeper and permeating impact upon the Muslim consciousness must be based on some oral and written traditions. While, on the one hand, he accuses Muslims of ignoring the Crusades *per se*, simultaneously he considers the conflict to have left two serious legacies. Firstly, the status of Christians in the Muslim world became quite precarious, and secondly, the relationship between Muslims and Europe took a nose dive. Certainly, under the Crusades everyone suffered in the Levant and the Holy Land but Christians and Jews survived in this otherwise Muslim heartland whereas following the Inquisition and ethnic cleansing, Muslims from the Iberian Peninsula, Sicily, Greece and the Balkans almost disappeared within a few decades. Muslim metropolitan cities like Delhi, Lahore, Hyderabad, Salonika and Constantinople were Muslim-minority centres until the recent demographic changes transformed their contours.

Lewis is justified in finding the Mongol invasions immensely debilitating for Muslims which further turned their attention to the eastern regions while Europe—the West—looked further west and eventually triumphantly found new routes and new continents. However, to Lewis, the Ottomans, while claiming to be the descendants of the Byzantines, never rose above seeking land and booty, as recorded by some contemporary Turkish historians. To him, by not conquering Italy after their conquest of Constantinople, the Turks committed a blunder, as this region soon became the hotbed of Renaissance and Counter Reformation ushering in a modern Europe. Their defeats in 1571 at Lepanto and then in 1683 at Vienna further distanced them from the crucial regions destined to redefine Europe. Their preoccupation with the eastern regions and wars with fellow Persian Muslims further blinded them to the vital scientific discoveries in the West. Though they were shocked by the calibre of the English ships sent by Queen Elizabeth I and by the tenacity of the Venetian rivals yet never tried to gain knowledge and technology from these 'infidels'.[8]

Lewis finds early Muslim sultans and scholars lost in the abyss of ignorance and a self-created sense of unassailability. Thus, by seeking out selective examples, he finds even conquering rulers like Selim I (1512–1520) refusing to listen to some solitary sane voices like that of the vizier, Lutfi Pasha, who had advised him to invest in a more competent navy before he could dream of conquering the Franks. Even after Ibrahim Muteferrika, a Hungarian convert to Islam, had been able to establish the first modern printing press in Constantinople in 1731, its output remained miniscule. The Muslim envoys to Paris, London and Vienna, while privy to Western progress, merely critiqued the moral characters of their hosts instead of exploring their scientific and artistic achievements. As a consequence, when Napoleon attacked Egypt in 1798, the age-old myth about Ottoman self-sufficiency lay shattered and the entire Muslim world was soon to be subjugated by the emerging Western powers. Lewis makes it read like a long-time Muslim tardiness accompanied with self-delusion and aggravated by a violence-prone and anti-intellectual baggage. One wonders, how a scholar of this era could still reverberate the once-familiar legacy of the imperial armies of pundits issuing derogatory judgements on non-Western peoples in the spirit of invincibility, often joined by a missionary zeal!

Lewis tends to forget that Europe for centuries suffered from its own ethnic and religious schisms which caused anguish to many others across the continents, but decrying Europeans for their past and holding present generations responsible for the sins and crimes of their ancestors is as foolhardy as being judgemental about non-Europeans. The Muslim global perspective, according to Lewis, was always limited as they never tried to build up pacts and cultural linkages with non-Muslims. They were more interested in capturing and converting them: 'The Muslim conviction of their own predestined final victory did not blind them to the significance and the uncertainty of this wide-ranging and long drawn-out conflict between two faiths and two societies. In Muslim writings, the

Christian world becomes the House of War par excellence, and the war against Christendom is the very model and prototype of the jihad'.[9] It is ironical to seek the mainstay of long-enduring Muslim empires only on the basis of coercion and conversion, as Lewis would like us to believe. Islam's acceptance of several norms and mores from other cultures and a tolerance for syncretic values besides protection of non-Muslims within a contemporary context are totally ignored by Lewis. Muslims certainly evicted Jews and Christians from the Arabian Peninsula, yet in general their record of tolerance towards non-Muslims has been certainly higher than many of their contemporaries and adversaries.[10] Islam's own acculturative potentials as is seen in the case of the Mongols is totally forgotten by this historian, who is perceived to be a doyen in his field.

Bernard Lewis painstakingly and presumptuously focuses on unabashed Muslim reluctance in translating European classics into their own languages besides their aversion to learning Western languages. In the areas of philosophy and medicine he acknowledges the vital Muslim link between the ancient Greco-Roman heritage and more modern era, yet in all other areas of inquiry and research he finds Muslims seriously lacking interest and wherewithal. The few books translated from the European languages into Arabic or vice-versa mainly owed to the Europeans themselves, who in several cases, happened to be converts. When Europe was establishing efficient means of communications including the print media, Muslims still depended upon traditional modes, and despite exhortations by some rare eminent intellectual-diplomats, the Muslim world refused to show any interest in the industries of contemporary Europe. After Ibn Jubair, the Spanish Muslim who undertook visits to Sicily and the Levant during the Crusades, he does not find Muslims operating as effective intermediaries well until the late eighteenth century. These recent Muslim observers also appear to be more preoccupied with contemporary moral and religious dimensions rather than undertaking serious scholarly efforts to transmit vital information on modern Europe. However, he offers some qualified credit to two Indian Muslim visitors to

Europe: Itisam ud Din and Mirza Abu Talib Khan who came from Bengal and visited Western Europe in the late eighteenth century. He, however, forgot to say anything about Dean Mahomed, the first Indian writer on multi-cultural issues. Rather abrasively, Lewis blames Muslims and especially the Turks for not making any effort to learn from powerful Westerners instead of continuously belittling the latter: 'In the face of this growing threat, all that the Islamic histories offered about these people was manifest lies and grotesque fables'.[11] Most of the information about the West in the past had come to Muslims from the Greeks though in between Ibn Jubair and such other occasional writers added to the existing knowledge, yet most of the emissaries, according to Lewis, still happened to be non-Muslim citizens.

Lewis feels that being sent abroad as an official ambassador was often not a cherished assignment and was more often allocated to 'undesirables'. Such a view is not charitable, as how would any proud ruler send a suspect abroad when the purpose was mainly to impress the hosts! The record of Moroccan, Turkish and Persian ambassadors reveals their positive impact on the elite and laity of the Western nations. Even if they were not permanently based in the Western countries much to the detriment of their patrons, at least they did not engage in subversive activities against their host countries as one saw intermittently in the case of the Venetian, Russian, French and British envoys in Constantinople, who routinely engaged in intrigues against their hosts. The Venetians were so hostile to the Ottomans that just in the case of Suleiman the Magnificent, they organised fourteen attempts on his life by trying to poison him.[12] Count Nikolai Ignatiev, the Russian envoy to the Ottoman court during the nineteenth century and the great-grandfather of Michael Igantieff, used his embassy premises and funds to recruit and train Bulgars and other Balkan insurrectionists to destabilise the Ottomans.[13] The record of his other European colleagues was not pleasant either, who saw to it that the Ottomans would never be able to stand on their feet. Of course, the First World War was the last straw when the Balfour Declaration officially koshered Zionism, and the secret Sykes-Picot Pact between

Britain and France on dividing the Middle East following the War caused a grave sense of betrayal among Muslims. Lawrence of Arabia's escapades with the Arabs in Mesopotamia, Syria and the Arabian Peninsula were blatant mechanics not only to defeat the Ottomans but also to further humble and divide the Arab communities. Senior to Thesiger by a few years and romanticised through films such as *Lawrence of Arabia*, T.E. Lawrence was an emotionally broken, psychologically torn apart and immensely confused person suffering from schizophrenia. His mythification often overlooks his own split personality that eventually led to his own death, and in a way, symbolises many of those imperial and imperious administrators whose partisan and racist attitudes have been the bane of enduring schisms and turmoil in the Middle East. The entire generation of Muslim surrogates from Sharif Hussein to contemporary authoritarian and corrupt Western surrogates certainly do not inspire a great eulogy for some of these modernist norms that Lewis admonishes the past generations of Muslims for ignoring at their own peril.[14]

Reading any of Bernard Lewis's books, even without a slightest Muslim background, leaves one agitated and equally confused. Initially, one feels angry with Muslims for being so casual about the West and since one reads the same accusation time and again in all his books, one grows tired of his litany. While he is more adept in seeking Muslim inefficiencies, the reader gets confused for not finding an answer to a continuing Muslim factor in the world. Their rise from a humble background in the backwaters of Arabia and a steadfast loyalty to their faith for fifteen hundred years is no remarkable achievement if one uses the strict cultural yardstick that Lewis only allocates to his West. However, in their case, as Lewis puts it, the West had to literally come to them: 'In other Arab countries [other than Muhammad Ali Pasha's Egypt], and in Iran, the awakening of Muslim interest in the West came much later, and was the result of an overwhelming Western presence'.[15] One wonders how much more altruist one could hope to be! Lewis is aggrieved over Muslim visitors to Europe and their compatriots back home for not being able to identify the Europeans nationally instead of insisting on their Christendom. Is Lewis not falling into the same trap when he, like his several other predecessors and contemporaries, uses a similar straitjacket for all Muslims? He praises 'solitary' exceptions such as Persian Rashid al-Din who, in his authoritative book written during the fourteenth century, offered some details on Western Europe. But, to Lewis, his credit basically owed to his Jewishness though he had converted to Islam during the Mongol rule over Persia. In the same manner, Ibrahim b. Yaqub, the Catalonian envoy of the Ottomans to several European countries, was also a Jewish convert to Islam. Lewis accredits the Jewish communities for keeping the Muslims aware of the outside world besides manning their trade, diplomacy and other scientific departments, which is in itself a tribute to the Muslim patronage of Jewish professionals who had suffered for so long under the Christians. As he himself earlier posited in *The Jews of Islam*, Lewis reiterates this vanguard role by Jewish professionals, especially of physicians within the Muslim empires:

> Several of these Jewish doctors played a political role of some importance. Their access to the persons of sultans and viziers on the one hand, and their knowledge of European languages and conditions on the other, made them useful to both Turkish rulers and foreign envoys, and enabled some of them to achieve positions of power and influence. Some were even sent on diplomatic mission abroad.[16]

Such a patronage and utilisation of Jewish skills should be taken as a compliment to Muslim sultans, though Lewis would not imply that, but that could be one major reason for the lack of anti-Semitism across the Muslim regions for so long unlike Europe. Lewis is angry over Muslim irreverence for watches and even time keeping that he himself experiences when many Muslims, to him, do not seem too self-disciplined. It may cause inconvenience yet is too small and rather an awkward argument to denigrate an entire civilisation. Lewis is not generous enough to acknowledge Muslim contributions in architecture, and instead suggests that they heavily borrowed from others including the Italian baroque ornamentation. One wonders about his views on the Central Asian architecture or even the Mughal monuments in South Asia. He censures Muslims for not leaving any archives or sketches on even as traumatising a development as the Crusades since, to him, only one portrait survives from the entire two centuries of Euro–Muslim altercations. How could one reconcile such a brash assertion with the recent research on the subject, which, in some cases, is totally based on Muslim sources, earlier unknown to scholars including Lewis? One may simply refer here to Carole Hillenbrand's *The Crusades: Islamic Perspectives* and her almost total dependence on the contemporary sources and some recent books on the subject. Even Steven Runciman's three-volume *A History of the Crusades*, despite being written in the 'Western mode', does not shy away from some translated Arab sources.[17]

Lewis, however, finds Muslims perpetually lacking interest in learning European languages until very recent times, underpinned by their traditional nonchalance towards Western sciences, industry, socio-cultural heritage and the astounding discovery of 'new' continents. In conclusion to his exhaustive volume highlighting a series of Muslim 'failures' in encountering a changing and growingly powerful West, Lewis finds three unprecedented developments of far-reaching significance that changed this cultural contest finally and decisively in favour of the latter. Firstly, the discovery of a whole new world energized Europe; secondly, Renaissance ushered the rediscovery of classical heritage and promoted the spirit of inquiry; and finally, Reformation weakened the ecclesiastic authority over thought and expression. All these crucial developments put Europe ahead of all including Muslims, and to him, that is the only way forward so as to break an enduring legacy of Muslim indifference. Lewis's celebration of these three powerful movements not only reflect his Eurocentricity but also an uncritiqued celebration of modernity, which caused so much anguish to so many millions including the successive generations of Europeans themselves. Lewis lacks interest in reflecting upon the failings and disasters of modernity that some of his contemporaries have been highlighting in recent years. He is naturally at ease in objectifying Muslims by passing judgements on their entire tenure extending over fifteen centuries while ignoring the various epochs of plural coexistence, not seen so often even in Lewis's own celebrated West.

To seek out Bernard Lewis's early research on Islam and his acumen in reproducing the same arguments over the last five decades one may briefly assess one of his earliest works. After military service, Lewis published *The Arabs in History* (1947) written during the war when several West European countries, while propounding to fight fascism, were stubbornly reluctant in allowing independence to their own colonies. Lewis, an official in imperial Britain, could foresee decolonisation and the emergence of a new Jewish state achieved through colonial machination and forced dispossession of the Palestinians, already promised in the Balfour Declaration. His volume does not allow Islam its own autonomous space and rather attributes several of its traditions to Judaic and Christian influences, so as to deny its originality. In his view, the Arab civilisation, a microcosm of the medieval Muslim world, at the most, consists of 'atomistic' communities lacking a coherent and pervasive body politic.[18] In an age of nation-states, justified through a 'liberationist' creed of nationalism, Lewis does not see Muslims ever being capable of congregating together like their European counterparts. Such an argument was quite popular during the imperial era but reiterating it in the 1990s was both ironic and even simplistic. Nationalism—the modern-day tribalism and Lewis's cherished European partake—is no more a venerated reference. As a Jew, despite his relentless support for the Zionist state, he should have been the first to highlight its xenophobic ills, as reflected through pogroms, expulsions, exclusion and the Holocaust. He feels as if Muslims had been least moved by such a massive onslaught on their heartland and instead woke up with a 'delayed response' and that too in the form of *jihad*, which certainly to him is a violent bloodshed. Despite *jihad* being a defensive strategy during the colonial hegemony, Lewis is not willing to allow it any space and defines the Muslim response merely as a war against war.[19]

Lewis explains the Muslim predicament in reference to two factors: the intrinsic problem, which he ascribes to Islamic particularism, and secondly, the steady rise of a technologically (and even culturally and intellectually!) superior West that Muslims had been negligent of for so long. Well, this is not for the first or last time that the British-American historian has asserted as such. Ignoring the intra-Muslim diversities and lack of his immersion into debate among the Muslims strata, he locates Muslim 'backwardness' in some sheer reluctance to absorb modernity. To him, the ideological conflict among Muslims in the recent decades owes itself to polarisation between the traditionalists and modernists. Without allowing any space to their several convergences and even a slow and rather unnoticed development of Muslim civil societies, he feels as if this strife is purported to take Muslims back to the early roots precluding any progress. Muslims, in his opinion, have to seek their future in modernisation as otherwise this polarity may claim a higher toll. Muslims, to Lewis, will have to choose between Islamic theocracy and liberal democracy: 'The future place of the Arabs in history will depend, in no small measure, on the outcome of struggle between them.'[20]

One of Bernard Lewis's recent best selling books, *What Went Wrong? Western Impact and Middle Eastern Response,* again posits the Muslim–Western relationship only within a dialectical paradigm. It essentialises conflict and certainly bestows an unassailable triumphalism to the West whereas within the Muslim world and history there is nothing comparable except for indolence, drift and drudgeries. The book has nothing new to offer and is a summarisation of Lewis's known positions since 1947 but its publication soon after 9/11, amidst a flurry of writings on Islam, and his own personal life-time career as a known teacher of Middle Eastern history at a premier American university, guaranteed a major success. Other than critical and well-familiar voices, most of the reviews of this book have been laudatory and within the pervasive context of unbridled Islamophobia both at the official and private levels, which is not surprising at all. He, innumerable times, repeats his well-known position of Muslims being caught unawares by the Western institutional might. He apportions the blame to the Muslims for residing in a self-adulatory atmosphere of self-sufficiency considering Islam to be the greatest and best civilisation. Based on his lectures during 1999, the slim volume consists of seven chapters and offers a handy chronology of Muslim failures. It is amazing that, on the one hand, Lewis perceives only conflict as a recurring pattern in the Muslim–Western relationship but, somehow, keeps highlighting only the Muslim drawbacks. If the Muslims were such a disaster then why waste so many decades and pages on them repeating oneself umpteenth times! Either he is not sure of his own views or is lost between simultaneously overestimating and underestimating Muslims. For instance, in the beginning of this book, he laments the absence of scientific learning from amongst the Muslims as he finds only one European book on medicine to have been translated in almost two centuries (1655 to the late eighteenth century).[21] Even their successive military defeats, to Lewis, could not compel Muslims to confront the technologically and economically more powerful West. Their monarchs, unlike their European counterparts, did not care to appoint full-time envoys to keep them abreast of the latest on this side of the Mediterranean. They never scrutinised their relationship vis-à-vis the West, especially after the Columbian discovery when a resourceful Western Europe controlled the seas and trade. The Muslim kings and sultans had become dependent upon the European channels and ships for importing their favourite goods, but still showed no curiosity to learn about the West. Muslim elite at their own peril neglected such a sea change in the global political economy. Their subsequent and half-done reforms in the nineteenth century, as was the case under the Ottomans, came too late and only through piecemeal arrangements.

Bernard Lewis focuses on three areas where Muslims, until recent times, have been reluctant in inducting overdue reforms and finds himself in the company of some liberal and conservative clusters of opinion, whose only mutuality is in finding fault with Muslim values. Slaves, women and non-Muslim minorities, to them, have remained oppressed and equally ignored sections in the Muslim world whereas the contemporary West had already made strides in all three areas. There is something old and new in this material. Lewis has been critical of Muslim attitudes towards the underprivileged, and as seen above, has tried to prove that Islam was equally and rather more forcefully colour-conscious as anyone else. In a way, he found Islam supportive of slavery despite its egalitarian ideals and instead used slaves for various domestic and defence purposes. In the past, he produced a monograph on the subject, but given his penchant for repetition and lack of any fresh input, he uses such material to substantiate his current tirades against Islam.

In the same vein, his views on the status of non-Muslim minorities have been all too familiar though it is a different thing that he attributes academic accomplishments such as translations and historiography to non-Muslim intellectuals within the Muslim empires, besides allocating such non-Muslim individuals a vanguard role as diplomats to Western metropolises. Lewis shies away from comparing such case studies with his cherished and equally monolithicised modern West, which transformed the slave trade, slavery and racism into highly organized, massive and enduring pursuits. However, on women, this is the first time that one finds Lewis brandishing his whip, though certainly he is not the first one to do so. From veil to polygamy and from harem to public arenas, Muslim women are depicted as the perennial victims in scores of writings and visual portrayals. Irrespective of the fact that women may be the victims of male chauvinism and sexism; the Western Muslim women donning scarves and asserting their Muslim identity are mostly doing it out of their own choice and not always under peer pressure.

It is interesting to note that an academic of Lewis's stature is totally unaware of the valuable debate on post-coloniality, gender, identity, multi-culturalism and racism, which has characterized a number of Western academic disciplines. The powerful critique of Western adulation of modernity and Westernism, characterized by Frantz Fanon as pathology at the heart of Western culture, seems to be unknown to Lewis. Lewis's obsession with modernity ironically leads him to the denial of difference and overlooks the colonial mutilation of the oppressed that has, in several cases, unleashed contradictory pathologies.[22] Lewis is totally negligent of a liberal tradition of this counter critique in the Western thought dating from the 1960s, which has found serious gaping holes and contradictions in the Western canon.[23] As a growing number of critical researches in the realms of imperial and cultural studies reveal, variables such as gender, class, culture and colour cannot be seen as categories in total isolation. They have to be analysed within the complex contours of an uneven relationship among cultures and communities, especially during the imperial and post-colonial phases.

Power was both the epitaph and the anchor-stone for imperialism which itself created a poetics of ambivalence as well as of violence. The theoretical and empirical research focusing on post-coloniality, Orientalism, subalterns and Feminism have offered powerful and equally alternative interpretations on modernity and identity formation especially amongst the underprivileged communities. Thus, the issues of racial and gender discrimination cannot be simplistically attributed to any particular culture such as Muslim, and must be seen in a larger historical context and power politics.[24] One can easily understand his context due to a pervasive critique of the Taliban soon after the euphoric Anglo–American invasion of Afghanistan and also the Saudi dualism over the past several decades. However, 9/11 has offered greater and greener opportunities for the breed of Neo-Orientalists to further their agendas while simultaneously appearing to be politically correct when it comes to gender. Sympathizing with Muslim women and minorities would insidiously silence many liberals, to whom issues of Muslim human rights in Palestine, Chechnya, Iraq and Afghanistan may be deserving of more assertive sympathy. This is not to suggest that the Muslim women have an ideal status within the Muslim countries, but they are an integral part of a universally disempowered mass where elites—Westernised and orthodox—nefariously unite to veto wider democratisation.[25] Ironically, all these regimes and even the clerical elites including the Saudis and Taliban have often been protected and supported by the Western powers. While the West may justify the pursuit of unbound material gains as the ultimate purpose in life, and could eliminate major sections of non-Western societies for such a goal, the wider Muslim disempowerment owes itself to a combination of indigenous and external factors.[26]

While seeing Islam as an eternal *other*, Lewis keeps on identifying the modern West as the Christian heartland or even a Judaic–Christian construct, which is self-contradictory, since he rebukes Muslims for the same. He is not happy with the Muslim characterization of the West as a Christian monolith and snubs them for not valuing the West's transcendent march since the early times when Muslims formulated their unchanging views of an inherently Christian Europe and beyond. In his best seller, *What Went Wrong?* he cannot restrain himself from these religion-based differentials when he posits development of secularism in the West totally owing to the separate ways that the Christian and Muslim histories traversed.[27] This divergence between these two religions, to him, explains why Western democracies have nothing in common with Islam since Muslim status is akin to that of the pre-Christian West and resembles not at all its post-Christian phase. Here, for the West the march from Christianity to secularity emerges as an essentialised discourse that the Muslims have failed to assimilate. One wonders about non-Western and non-Christian democracies such as India, Malaysia, Japan and several others who may have established their own democracies without essentially following this Christian/Secularist route. Moreover, secularism is not the end of Christianity, it still seeks its reference and legitimacy from the former, either as a reaction, as in France or as a fully-fledged partner like in several other Western polities. Lewis's touchstone of Christianity and modernity all within the epicentre of the West seems to have bypassed the Islamic world where 'things had indeed gone badly wrong' and compared to Christendom, Muslims 'had become poor, weak and ignorant'.[28]

Lewis finds the West moving far ahead of Muslims in the three inter-related areas of politics, economy and military power, which are the main attributes of progress as witnessed by the former. To him, these vital developments affirm a successful modernization and characterize today's powerful West whereas, on the contrary, Muslims suffer both under the domestic tyrannies and are deeply anguished over a continuum of humiliations. Even South Koreans have performed better than Muslims, who, especially in the Arab world, keep making scapegoats of others. In the past, according to Lewis, Arabs blamed the Turks for their malaise but since 1948 it is Israel that offers a convenient alibi. However, to him, still this cynicism does not explain how many times more numerous and equally proud Arabs were so easily cowed down by half a million Jews, imbued with a political vigour.[29] His reference imputes the creation of the state of Israel over and above the teeth of Arab/ Muslim opposition and the former's stratagem of victories against a determined foe. Here Lewis, like a naughty child, locates Arab defeat owing to some intrinsic and enduring legacy without, of course, acknowledging the Western props for Israel. His arrogant and seemingly gleeful simplification, premised on a clash of civilisations, refuses to see the geo-political complexities, though one has to admit that it is certainly a failure of the Arab leaders in countering Israeli expansion and policy of dispossession.

Any scholar of Lewis's stature, even with such Zionist biases, would refrain from expressing such glee over the Middle Eastern tragedy. To most of the Muslims, it is neither the invincibility of Israel nor a vulnerability of Islam that might have cast these events in such an embarrassing manner; it is the failure of corrupt and inept political leadership that the region has been bedevilled with. Nor does a victorious Israel herald the total decimation of Islam though such an argument, if turned around on its heels would be quickly perceived as anti-Semitism. In the same vein, Lewis opines that the historic Judeo–Islamic tradition has been totally replaced by the Judeo–Christian tradition, which not only brings back religion into the core of his arguments but also implies that Jews and Christians, after centuries of hatred and pogroms have finally found some common interface. This may be true in the case of Jewish–Christian Neoconservatives but it cannot gloss over the powerful tragedies brought about by their polarity until recently. Given the unrestrained Israeli violations of human rights in Palestine and the age-old anti-Semitism in a predominantly Christian West, Lewis's optimism could prove immensely misplaced. If this tradition of newfound mutuality was already mature then it would be wise for Zionists to bury the age-old scare of anti-Semitism and simply focus on Muslims. Several of his Jewish detractors would not feel comfortable with his optimism, as many of the staunchest critics of Israeli and Likudist policies have been Christians including the Pope and Christian Palestinians in the Holy Land, representing the Orthodox, Armenian and Coptic Churches.

Lewis traces the phenomenon of suicide bombers to the humiliation of the Arabs at the hands of Israel and within the larger context of political, economic and military backwardness of the Muslims. His solution is to brush aside the pervasive sense of victim-hood by undertaking 'a common creative endeavour'.[30] Muslims are certainly angry over their political and military defeats yet to premise that they *en mass* suffer either from vengeance or from a perpetual victim-hood is a misreading of Muslim consciousness. It is, in plain words, a sheer trivialisation of such a large civilisational community. Muslims would rather leave this eternal victim-hood for some other communities who have already made quite a case out of it and Lewis will be well placed to advise his compatriots to renounce it since it might have already outlived its utility. Societies and countries cannot survive merely by reminding others of their sheer guilt and misbehaviour in the past nor can they gain strength by simultaneously operating as perpetrators. Posing victim and a perpetrator concurrently has its own serious paradoxes and moral contradictions.

Bernard Lewis's other recent best seller, *The Crisis of Islam: Holy War and Unholy Terror,* is a further detailed charge sheet against Muslims, where the collective problems of Islam, aversion to modernity, recourse to terror and violence justified in the name of

Jihad, are probed. The title is totally judgemental as it perceives Islam lost somewhere in a serious crisis within the only two trajectories of terror and *jihad*—both justified in the name of Islam. To any reader, the title itself comes about as a powerful verdict on an entire civilization. Lewis finds the last three centuries very significant in the history of Muslims and their relationship with the West, interspersed with nonchalance towards modernity, defeats by the Europeans and disregard for democracy. He finds a pervasive Muslim anger having shifted to the United States, seeing in it an extension of a hated Europe. Poverty and tyranny rule the roost in the Muslim world, largely due to their own contempt for change, especially when the West flags it. Accordingly, in the recent decades, the Second World War, the centrality of the Saudi regime in distributing puritanical literature, defeats at the hands of Israel, the Soviet invasion of Afghanistan, the Iranian Revolution and the growing hatred of the West reflect a pervasive Muslim agony.

Following an introduction situating the entire Muslim history in the context of 9/11, the nine chapters of medium length form this book, which in its analysis and contents is not totally different from his previous works. It is a powerful and widely read yet totally critical—often-negative—statement on Muslim history, religion, politics and present situation. His dialectical view of history—based on a clash of civilizations—is obvious from each page where maps, selective quotes and references to historical occurrences in the past reveal a presumed irreconcilability between Islam and a Judeo–Christian West. His monolithicisation of these two eternal antagonists refuses to accept their internal pluralism or presence of the Judeo–Christian West within Islam and vice versa. He feels that despite Western pronouncements on the war on terror not being a war on Islam, Muslims stubbornly refuse to believe in it. Muslims may be naïve but the invasion of Iraq in 2003 under the three pretexts of finding weapons of mass destruction, links between Baghdad and Al-Qaeda and Iraq being a threat to the West, as reiterated by Bush and Blair, all make one of the major lies in human history.

President Bush, as recorded by Paul O'Neill, the former treasury secretary, had already made up his mind to attack Iraq long before 9/11. The dictums of pre-emption and of regime change over and above legal and moral justification were applied to unleash the invasion of yet another Muslim country. If millions and rather absolute majorities in the West persistently refused to accept this rationale for war, how could one blame Muslims for not reposing trust in London and Washington. Lewis finds Osama bin Laden as a prototype Muslim whose predecessors in the past several centuries had been similarly sceptical of the Christians and people have often believed in them. Lewis, like in his other books, blames Muslims for seeing the West and especially the US, as they 'tend to see not a nation subdivided into religious groups but a religion subdivided into nations.'[31] When Bush and Blair themselves used Christian symbols and offered an intermingling of religion and politics, how could Muslims deny them and their powerful establishments their Christian credentials. It may be as ahistoric as to divest Israel seemingly of its Jewish, racial and ideological particularism because without that Israel will not be Israel even to its detractors.

To Lewis, Muslim historical consciousness dwells on selective memory and celebrates an ideal of a trans-regional *ummah*, underpinned by a shared religion. It only encompasses certain chosen episodic details of conquest and victory from the Pharaohs to the Qureshites and from the Crusades to colonialism and thus is at a loss to assimilate any other relationship nor is fully reconciled to the idea of a nation-state. Lewis must be one of the few remaining scholars who still use nationalism as a reference point and rather a prized development, whereas to several of his colleagues this so-called cornerstone of modernity and the bedrock of Westphalian order might have already outlived its utility.

In fact, that a scholar of avowed Jewish and Zionist persuasion may have some nostalgia for nationalism even after the Holocaust, is certainly ironical. Nationalism is a new tribalism though earlier it was posited as a post-tribal aggregation of political communities offering liberationist and professional alliances over and above family, kinship and tribal loyalties. Nationalism, to its proponents such as Gellner, Kohn, Kedourie and Anderson, is a modernist construct, further solidified by state systems and common lingual and historical traditions all shared through print capital. Globalisation, regionalisation and even a vehement form of ethnification are threatening this kind of nationalism while the representatives of present-day nationalist ethos are none other than the British National Party, Neo-Nazis, KKK, Le Pen's National Front and such other outfits across the West and Australasian regions. The BJP's Hindutva spearheading a mixture of religion and politics is also augmented by selective and equally insidious historical accounts. The Likudniks in Israel offer a similar exclusive form of nationalism with serious ramifications even for Palestine's own native populations. Lewis considers Osama bin Laden as a proto-Muslim type, very much in the tradition of the early Muslims, or, even Imam Khomeini whose use of historical symbols from the past only sees a long-time enemy in the West, which many Muslims may be willing to accept. Ordinary Muslims may be as gullible as the ordinary Americans when their chief executive invokes historical Christian symbols and underlines a new crusade to protect civilizational values against the barbarians.

Time and again, Lewis comes back to his favourite game of seeing Christianity and Islam as two divergent forces where the latter, unlike the former has no separation of sacred and the secular. God and Caesar are the same since the times when Prophet Muhammad (PBUH) combined the roles of a prophet and head of state. This duality, to Lewis, explains the main difference between the two and also the secret of Western supremacy. To the American scholar, 'the difference between Islam and the rest of the world, though less striking, is still substantial.'[32] This is because the Muslim world is still not post-*Muslim* as has been the case with Christian Europe. But this is a feeble argument, as in the case of Japan the emperor until 1947 held both temporal and spiritual powers whereas the Vatican and Israel stay professedly Christian and Jewish states. India, likewise under the BJP, had been heading towards a similar dispensation. Thus, Muslim utopianism may not be that exceptional, which certainly defeats the argument of characterizing Muslims as unique and ahistorical in their approach to politics and religion. At least, unlike Israel and Hindutva, Islam is colour blind and does not specify a peculiar racial type to qualify for membership of the political community.

The erstwhile Orientalist demarcation between the House of Belief and House of Nonbelief has already become redundant with the Muslim Diaspora all across the globe and a sizeable Muslim population living under non-Muslim rule. Lewis's ascription to Muslims, of the highest level of religious faith and practice is not totally sound as it lacks any empirical evidence. Reverberating the current American exaggerated fear of the *madrassa*-based Islamic instruction, he fails to see the class dimension in this category of a huge underclass and only imputes nefarious portents to this age-old tradition. To Lewis, these seminaries are the hotbeds of Islamic fundamentalism and anti-Westernism, well beyond the access of the most powerful regimes. One can see his study of the Assassins reflective in such statements. To him, fundamentalists have taken upon themselves the articulation of a societal anger against pro-Western leaders besides exploiting the Muslim memories of a glorious past interspersed with victories and political power. This may be partly true but Muslim disempowerment and dismay are not due to religious reasons and are rooted in political and economic malaise, though being on the receiving end for so long would also spawn a similar response from any other community caught in a similar situation. Muslim humiliation is due to the elite surrogacy and impotence in the post-colonial phase and the fundamentalist response is not the sole and unitary reaction to it. Given the absence of other civic institutions including democratic processes, the fundamentalists appear to be noisier than others. While a vast majority of Muslims, despite serious criticism of Western double standards, will not support terrorism specifically against civilians, a few disgruntled elements, especially those with some past alliance with the West, may be tempted to do so. Most of the alleged perpetrators of 9/11 and other leading members of Al-Qaeda have been associates if not favourites of powerful Western institutions including the CIA. Lewis is not being fair in his assertion that Islam, in the past, 'inspired in some of its followers a mood of hatred and violence. It is our misfortune that we have to confront part of the Muslim world while it is going through such a period, and when most—though by no means all—of that hatred is directed against us.'[33]

Islam's pristine teachings and traditions celebrate tolerance and forgiveness for all. The acts of defiance, political dissent and activism for self-determination are certainly different from sheer terror and the desperate acts of self-immolation, by no means, symbolize a holistic hostility towards other communities. The criticism of American foreign policies or Israel's policies of oppression and dispossession do not represent a consensual Muslim hatred for Americans or Jews. Muslim anger needs to be taken aboard rather than defining it as a routine part of Islamic traditions, since the problems are political and of a mundane nature, and by giving them a religious identity, Lewis is being both incorrect and extremely partisan. Muslims are not questioning Jewish or Christian teachings as their position has been clear on such theological issues for a long time; it is their elite-based negation and aggression on Muslim issues as such that understandably invited criticism. The painful politics and imprints of the Inquisition, colonial evangelical enterprise, slavery and even the Holocaust still do not justify a complete negation of Christian ethics by attributing such tragedies to some inherently Christian ethos.

Bernard Lewis, while assessing common Western views on the contemporary Muslim situation, finds two broad categories of opinion: firstly, that Islam is a genuine and major post-Cold War threat to Western lifestyles and societies, while to the second group, Muslims including the radicals are inherently good people who have been wronged by a dreadful West and are now reacting in an equally damaging way. To him, both these opinions are ill considered despite retaining some basic truth. To him, except for Muslims, 'both here and there' who desire friendly relations with the West 'a significant number...are hostile and dangerous, not because we need an enemy but because they do'. Such Muslims see in the United States a reincarnation of 'the ancient and irreconcilable enemy' who has to be fought with. Still, there are people who, despite being sensitive to flaws in Western culture, are appreciative of 'its inquiring spirit, which produced modern science and technology; its concern for freedom, which created modern democratic government.' Yet, still another opinion group, aware of the West's unlimited power but not relenting in their hostility to it, is prepared to seek a 'temporary accommodation'. The last two are not so similar and it 'would not be wise to confuse the second and the third'.[34] The essentialisation of this dialectical nature of the Muslim–West relationship and universalisation of some elements such as anger, jealousy and reactionary fervour to a vast majority of Muslims do not make a convincing argument, especially when one is not purporting to be a polemicist. It is true that the West-led modernity has registered varying responses from all—not the Muslims alone—but to perceive them rooted in an eternal hostility or even religion-based *priori* is absolutely wrong and dangerous.

While meandering through his favourite subject of *jihad* as the militarist venture of Islamic internationalism, Lewis focuses on the Muslim–Western relationship since the Crusades. Interestingly, he finds the Crusades imprinted deeply in the Muslim consciousness but, in his typical manner, he is quick enough to trivialize their causes. This is quite different from what he had been writing before 9/11 when, according to him, contemporary West Asian Muslims, in general, did not care much about the Crusades. He posits them as an aberration manifested through attacks on Muslim trade caravans that prompted Saladin to undertake some decisive action, where otherwise ordinary Muslims were being fatalistic or sheer negligent. Osama bin Laden's references to the present-day Crusaders remind Lewis of fundamentalist reconstruction of anti-Western discourse anchored in the bitter memories of the past. He is not willing to give Muslims any credit for offering any new discourse on such a momentous encounter with the West as it was all due to Christians —Franks— that the terminology was inducted into history. This is not for the first time that Professor Lewis has honoured his Christian heroes with his usual aplomb. How amazing that it is only in the nineteenth century that, once again under the European influences, the Muslims rediscovered the Crusades and presently, it is Osama bin Laden and Al-Qaeda who have been trying to hammer this into an otherwise indolent Muslim consciousness. While characterizing Muslims as immensely history-conscious and Islam being such a well-documented tradition, Lewis is certainly contradicting himself. One wonders whether to accept Muslims as primitive, pre-literate and emotional masses with no sense of history since the Prophetic era, or peoples with a strong historical memory. Lewis may help his readers by offering a clearer view.

As a committed Zionist and Neo-Orientalist, Lewis does not lose any chance of disputing Muslim spiritual and historical claims on Jerusalem. To him, the construction of the Dome of the Rock by the Umayyad caliph in 691–2 was a clear signal to both Christians and Jews that from now onwards Muslims had due claims on Al-Quds.[35] Lewis tends to forget that even before the Dome and long before even the elevation of the Kaaba as the Muslim *Qibla*, Jerusalem held that status. Over successive centuries, until 1967, Muslims never denied civic and religious rights to Jews and Christians in Jerusalem. In the same vein, post-Napoleonic European expansion in the Muslim world, characterized as imperialism, is widely viewed by Muslims as the salience of *takfir*.[36] However, Muslims, like many other Western observers and scholars from a wider Afro–Asian world, are aware of the powerful, multidimensional and far-reaching imprints left by imperialism in its wake. To any sensible Muslim, imperialism has been more than a religious onslaught and is, in fact, a profound and enduring form of Westernism. Lewis does not have the patience to see the contradictions and ramifications of imperial legacies in the Muslim world or the various forms of neo-imperialism. However, he is quick to defend his favourite state of Israel seeking out the Mufti of Palestine during the inter-War decades when he approached Hitler's Germany for a possible alliance against the British. Such a move on the part of the Mufti should have not surprised anyone as imperialism itself had been implemented through an unabashed dictum of divide-and-rule and withdrew as well through a similar stratagem of divide-and-quit. If the colonials had the remit to refashion the world according to their own dream or to suit their needs, why would not one allow the same to the colonised, at least to preserve their lands and basic rights? Britain, through the Balfour Declaration, the Mandate system, encouragement of Jewish influx into Palestine and discretionary policies under Lloyd George, Churchill and Samuel Hoare had already alienated the Arabs by siding so openly with the Zionists.

Chapter 7 of *The Crisis of Islam* is a twin-track attack on Muslim attitudes towards the United States. The 'discovery' of the Americas is cited both to remind readers of the Muslim indifference to a modernized and expansive Europe simultaneous with the enduring power of the West which, in recent decades, has only earned Muslim wrath. In an ironic manner, Lewis reminds his readers that the earliest and the only surviving copy of Columbus's map— though in a Turkish translation—survives in the Topkapi Museum in Istanbul, yet other than that, Muslims did not share any concern with this historic development. Except for a few solitary passing references in some Arabic or Turkish books, the Western Hemisphere remained unknown to Muslims whose interaction, both at the elite levels or through immigration, began somewhere in the last fifty years or so. Lewis would have been in better place as an historian, if he could have consulted some of his Princeton colleagues on many early Muslim slaves shipped into the two continents. The emergence of the Nation of Islam in the 1930s and a half-century of growing interest in African American studies have already established ample proof of a historic Muslim factor in the 'discovery' and 'making' of the Americas.

From the unfolding events in Andalusia, the Catholic kings used Moorish human and monetary resources until slavery was solidified as a lasting trans-continental institution. African Muslims, other than the Moriscos, made a major share of the human cargo transplanted across the Atlantic until Lincoln's Emancipation Proclamation in 1863 stopped the slave trade as well as the peculiar institution. Even after the Civil War and for more than a century, Africans as well as Asians were officially barred from immigration into the United States as the melting pot was only confined to largely white and predominantly Anglo-Saxon groups. Non-Whites, including Africans, Indians, Arabs and Chinese were all declared ineligible for American migration and citizenship.[37] Amidst the pervasive Jim Crow laws and other racist typologies such as the Yellow Peril, non-Whites had no chance to enter the land of 'rags to riches', so powerfully articulated by Horatio Alger or by a similar welcoming dictum on the Statue of Liberty. It was Henry Ford, the inventor and automobile magnate, who allowed some Arab workers to work at his factories in Dearborn, Michigan, though the numbers remained significantly small.

Lewis, apparently, does not have any explanation for the Muslim criticism of the United States, though he finds both the laity and the elite in the Muslim world imbued with a vocal anti-Americanism. One could refute his Muslim criticism of America as an immoral place by narrating the plain historic fact that until recent decades, the United States as a society did not invoke any collective derogatory Muslim reaction. Though the Muslim factor within the United States or the establishment of a pronounced American factor in the Muslim world is a post-Second World development, even during the very tense years of the Cold War, or despite the US unassailable support for Israel, Muslims did not holistically denigrate the US. Most Muslim professional settlers in the country admired its plural and accommodative ethos, and the religious amongst them, even found America more receptive to Islamic egalitarianism. Of course, like elsewhere, many Muslim societies did not appreciate the commercial and popular cultural imports besides the growing role of American political and economic establishments, solely at the expense of the local cultures and economies. This kind of criticism, despite the strains of the Cold War was quite in league with similar contemporary reservations about America in Europe or Japan. Migration to the United States or higher education in the American universities have been the hallmark of Muslim adulation for some of the noted American institutions, but like other non-Protestant immigrants, the Muslim Diaspora and the religious elite outside North America have remained wary of an unhindered acceptance of individualism, materialism and market-based fundamentalism. The double standards in foreign policy, the support for Israel at the expense of the Arabs and similarly the defence of corrupt and coercive Muslim regimes have been the traditional root cause of Muslim anger.

Successive United States administrations lost credibility amongst the developing societies including Muslims largely due to partisan policies and prioritisation of particularist interests. Thus, to highlight Muslim criticism of the United States simply as an anti-Christian sentiment, is incorrect; it is all due to political, economic and official factors, often justified by a traditionally anti-Muslim media generating a pervasive angst. The US vocal support for the Shah of Iran and other similar regimes, as documented by Lewis himself in the same chapter, only revealed time and again that Washington was totally committed to its own interests and not interested in the welfare of the people in West Asia and elsewhere. Most of the Muslims were shocked and saddened by 9/11 but the overwhelming and disproportionate American retaliation including the invasions of Muslim countries like Afghanistan and Iraq, followed by arm-twisting of several others, have only transformed this anguish and criticism into a fully-fledged anger. And, certainly, it is not confined to mere Muslim regions. The Guantanamo Bay internees, forced deportations of thousands of Muslims, fingerprinting, spread-eagling and other violations of human rights in such gigantic proportions would anger anyone with a semblance of respect for basic human rights. Thus, one wonders, how come a seasoned academic like Bernard Lewis is unable to seek out the causes of Muslim criticism of the United States and only keeps searching for answers in some essentialized Muslim demonization of the Christian world. He finds Muslim anger on the increase, which is true and understandable if one looks at the global peace movement, that has confirmed the view that anti-Americanism is not just a Muslim pursuit. He fails to see Osama bin Laden and his ilk being atypical of Muslims and likewise does not comprehend that the acts of desperation in Palestine or the resistance against foreign occupation across several disputed regions are rooted in enduring sore points. His verdict on the permanence of this Muslim anger is worth noticing: 'What we confront now is not a complaint about one or another American policy but rather a rejection and condemnation, at once angry and contemptuous, of all that America is seen to represent in the modern world.'[38] One wonders how a scholar of Lewis's stature can blind himself to the Muslim desire to settle and live in America as opposed to what he misinterprets as a pervasive desire to eliminate America.

Lewis, instead of looking at serious geo-political issues and the contradictory nature of American political and economic policies, only seeks the roots of Muslim anger and grievances within the teachings of Sayyid Qutb, an Egyptian Muslim scholar. Qutb had studied in the US soon after the War and turned critical of American culture on moral grounds. US support for the establishment of a Jewish state in the Arab land deeply disheartened him. Qutb, to Lewis, is both the architect as well as the instrument of some widespread Muslim hatred of America. Born in upper Egypt in 1906, Qutb, an official in the Egyptian administration, came to the United States in 1948 and stayed on for two years. He decided to go back and engage himself in some revivalist activities. Egypt had undergone a military coup in 1952 led by military officers such as Naguib and Nasser. Their nationalist fervour, due to the overthrow of the monarchy and rejection of extra-territorial rights enjoyed by the British, had earned them great support amongst the general Egyptian population. But Qutb wanted Egypt to return to its Islamic roots and thus developed ideological differences with the revolutionary officers in 1955. After a hasty trial, he was convicted to a 15-year prison term and was released in 1964 due to intercession by the then Iraqi president. His release coincided with the publication of his Arabic work, *Signposts on the Way (Ma'alim fil Tariq)* that became a popular reference work for Islamists in the Middle East. The nationalist regime soon rearrested Qutb in 1965 on charges of inciting treason against President Nasser and sentenced him to death on 21 August 1966. Eight days later, he was executed, but his influence on Muslim revivalists has proven quite formidable.

Qutb feared that the Jews and several Christian groups, in their hostility to Islam, would influence US policies and thus his critique of the American establishment. During his stay in the United States, he had witnessed powerful support for the establishment of Israel and gained a first-hand exposure to specific influences on US foreign policies. Lewis notes: 'Sayyid Qutb was shocked by the level of support in America for what he saw as a Jewish onslaught on Islam, with Christian complicity.'[39] This further proves that more than culture, it was political unilateralism that underwrote his critique, and like any other revivalist, he not only advised going back to Islamic roots but also tried to inculcate a common sense of 'Muslimness' across the divided communities. Certainly, Qutb felt that the Muslims had to steer themselves out of a pervasive laxity that he called *jahliyya* (ignorance) yet his memories of post-War American societies reverberated with a gnawing consumerism and sexism. Being a Muslim scholar, he may sound quite judgemental on dances in the church halls and emphasis on 'fun' and 'a good time', yet the baby boom era was not without its own problems either.

Qutb was in America when the country assumed leadership in several areas around the globe, and instead of offering a fresher perspective, it strictly followed the former colonial powers. It had involved itself in the Cold War both to gain and perpetuate its multiple influence worldwide. The Middle East had the strategic and economic potentials, urgently needed by the United States and its allies, but Washington's primacy often lacked the farsightedness, equanimity and fairness that should have come about with the assumption of the role of a super power. While Japan, Germany, China, Canada or the Scandinavian countries can redefine their relationship with the developing world without surrendering their own interests, the US could have also exhibited a similar magnanimity instead of abrasiveness. Even now if the US undertakes overdue ameliorative and helpful initiatives across the troubled regions, instead of demonisation and militarization, which have added to global insecurity, most of the criticism of its foreign policies will certainly subside. But this is for the Americans and their government to decide.

Lewis' reference to Qutb as the pioneer doyen of Muslim anti-Americanism is similar to the suggestion that Muslim criticism of Britain may be solely because of anger over *The Satanic Verses,* or that Muslim critique of France owes itself to French policies in Algeria, or is solely due to some exhortations by Algerian clerics. Millions of protesters across the world voicing their concern and criticism of Washingtonian militarist unilateralism and a dangerous dictum of pre-emption, as confirmed by the Spanish elections of 2004, were least motivated by Qutb, as most of them are not Muslim by persuasion. Lewis may be aggrieved over Muslim double standards, since they may gloss over Soviet and Russian atrocities against their coreligionists but would instead single out the United States for its policies. To him, their criticism of pro-Israeli policies conveniently overlooks the American pro-Muslim role in Bosnia or Kosovo. Such an argument ignores the fact that the Muslims for generations have suffered due to the religio-political equation under the Czars and then were further brutalized under the long Communist and nationalist decades. In addition, the Soviet role in Afghanistan and the Caucasus has been persistently rebuked costing millions of lives, something that should have been known to Lewis. Thus, seeking Muslim anger only as a unidirectional trajectory is simply ignoring the recent and equally sad realities of aggression and resistance. In fact, Israeli policies are both a reminder of the incompetence of the Muslim elite as well as of the partisan policies with their roots in the North Atlantic regions.

Lewis is closer to the truth when he highlights the pathetic situation of human development indicators, as documented by the Arab Human Development Report of 2002. Not only do the areas of health, education and other basic needs fall miserably low compared to several other regions, official policies simply show a self-immolative preference for expenditure in non-development sectors. Since the time of the Caliph Mamoun in Baghdad during the ninth century, the Arabs, as Lewis painstakingly quotes the figures, have translated about 100,000 volumes altogether compared to that number per year in present-day Spain. Contemporary Arab output in translations is 330 per annum, which is quite below that of any West European nation. He also quotes the total GDP of all the Arab countries totalling at $531.2 billion, compared to $595.5 billion for just Spain. Lewis, while celebrating Israel's performance without any reference to the US largesse, finds its per capita GDP three and a half times higher than that of Syria and Lebanon and twelve times that of Jordan and thirteen times that of Egypt.

The truth is that we are dealing with politico-economic disempowerment and serious issues of poverty, which are the results of a dangerous liaison between domestic and external discretionary factors. Certainly, it is not a failure of modernization itself, it is a reflection on the way modernization has been carried out in these regions. Muslim criticism of the Western world, in that sense, becomes more real when one looks at the forces of political economy, rendered so incongruous by a combination of domestic and external aberrations. However, Lewis is not ready to seek such a complexity of factors which has made modernization and development so disputatious everywhere but he is insistent on making it into a Muslim–West problem: 'Broadly speaking, Muslim fundamentalists are those who feel that the troubles of the Muslim world at the present time are the result not of insufficient modernization but of excessive modernization, which they see as a betrayal of authentic Islamic values.'[40] Given his above-quoted statistics one may not be so sure about his claims as Muslims everywhere are eager to modernize but certainly many of them do not desire to westernize.

Lewis is quite unsparing whenever he finds a chance to find fault with the Muslims. To him, despite the Islamic emphasis on peace, there have been Al-Qaeda-type terrorist groups who 'arise from within Muslim civilization, just as Hitler and the Nazis arose from within Christendom,' and one simply cannot find any rationality to see them akin.[41] Such an observation is not only fallacious, it is equally callous and incorrect. Muslims, like any other human societies, may have their phases and periods of violence against non-Muslims or even against one another yet one does not find several cases of collective and massive massacres or ethnic cleansings ever carried out by Muslims. On the contrary, Muslims have more often protected pluralism and despite occasional violence or social stratification, non-Muslim minorities survived among their midst. Furthermore, violence against Muslims has been more often massive and large-scale as seen in the case of the Crusades, Inquisition, ethnic cleansing campaigns in Eastern Europe, India and Russia until the 1990s and post-9/11 that have been visibly characterized by genocides. In our times, Palestine, Chechnya, Caucasus, Bosnia, Kosovo, Afghanistan, Kashmir, Gujarat, Moroland, Southern Thailand, and Iraq are recurrent cases of massive violations of human rights, dispossession and aggregate elimination, mostly at the hands of 'external' and majoritarian forces.

Hitler's case was of a modern state in the heart of Lewis's ideal and favourite Europe where a systemic elimination of the Jews took place under the Nazis, with Christian elements either staying indifferent or supporting the genocide. The Muslims never had a regime like the Nazis where millions of citizens would be en masse gassed or totally decimated; that credit goes only to modernity. All across Europe, Lewis's co-religionists faced cleansing and periodic pogroms while they prospered under the Muslims. Using the Assassins as an enlarged and universalised model of Muslim violence is too far-fetched and makes a rather feeble argument. They were selective and only targeted fellow Muslims whereas Nazis and other European expansionists, both in recent times and in the past, organized long-term campaigns against Jews, Muslims, Gypsies and even fellow Christians, not to forget millions in Africa, the Western Hemisphere and Australasia.

Professor Lewis's likening of the Assassins to Al-Qaeda is equally strange as these are two different trajectories altogether. However, he is quite right in being an optimist since, like in the past, the present-day terrorists will also be defeated. Still, it is a travesty that while claiming to be the student and rather leading specialist of Muslim civilization, Lewis could find only one solitary example and that too one that does not fully fall behind his argument. Given his essentialization of the polarity between Islam and the West with the latter representing development, learning and progress and all the best for all times, and the former being embodied by Al-Qaeda and the Assassins, Lewis's persistently pernicious thesis of a clash of cultures may not surprise anyone. His recently published collection of articles and a vanguard role in pushing the case for the invasion of Iraq and Iran, besides offering rather antagonistic caricatures on Islam and the Arab Middle East, only compromise an otherwise lifetime work as an academic specialist on the Middle East. His lack of immersion into the Arab lands and unfettered sympathy for Israel over and above intellectual objectivity reverberate in *From Babel to Dragomans*. To him, the Arab/Muslim criticism of US policies had nothing to do with Israel, and stemmed from some inherent anti-Americanism. As an apologist for Israel, to him even the terms such as 'Palestine' and 'Palestinian' were invented during the war of 1967, without realising that Theodore Herzl had, in 1896, suggested 'Palestine' as the Zionist homeland in his preface to *Der Judenstaat*.

Lewis constantly egged on the Neoconservatives and Washington for the invasion of Iraq (and of Iran) by changing his role as apologist for Israel to sheer propagandist. That is why the *Wall Street Journal* in February 2004, while commenting on Lewis's role within the cabal of strategists in Washington, noted: 'The Lewis doctrine, in effect, had become the US policy.' It certainly validated Edward Said's observation of Lewis being 'an academic whose work purports to be liberal objective scholarship but is in reality very close to being propaganda against his own subject material.' Oliver Miles, while concluding his review of *From Babel to Dragomans*, reflected: 'It is tragic that such an admired scholar may be remembered for a policy which history is likely to categorise as ill conceived, illegal and a costly failure.'[42] His simplistic, selective and judgemental views on Muslim history and on a diverse civilization like Islam, displaying an enduring tradition of hostility, only betray a partisan and equally dangerous view, which thanks to a post-9/11 eagerness to know more about Islam, does not shy away from its often repetitive, reproductive and negative features. Like his nineteenth century predecessors, Lewis's propagandistic tirade will certainly surprise as well as sadden his readers a few decades from now. But by that time, given the enormity of the damage, it may be too late!

NOTES

1. It is both ironic and tragic that many important opinion and decision makers cannot even differentiate between Islam as a religion and Muslims as its adherents. For instance, in an interview regarding the undefined internees—the terrorists-suspects—, David Blunkett, the British Home Secretary used both these terms interchangeably. To him, these 'Islams', apparently lacking a defined British citizenship, could leave this country on their own choice. In fact, by these *Islams* he supposedly meant *Muslim internees* in British jails such as Belmarsh. The BBC24, monitored in Oxford on 21 December 2003. It may be relevant and equally ironical to remember that the Home Secretary Blunkett had previously been the Education Secretary in the Tony Blair Government. His interview appeared a day after one leading British newspaper, on its front page, published a letter—the first-ever—from an undefined internee in Belmarsh Jail. This Palestinian internee had been in an undefined solitary and immensely painful confinement since December 2001 and had begun to experience mental and physical illnesses. Like several hundred such other suspects, not only does his own status remain undefined, even the authorities had failed to bring about any charges against him despite criticism from Amnesty international and such other organisations. See *Guardian,* 20 December 2003.

2. Oliver Miles, 'Lewis gun', review of Bernard Lewis's *From Babel to Dragomans, Guardian,* 17 July 2004.

3. Bernard Lewis, *The Assassins: A Radical Sect in Islam* (London, 2003), pp. viii-x. His earliest work was on the Ismailis, based on his doctoral research. See, Bernard Lewis, *Origin of the Ismailis* (Cambridge, 1940).

4. The assassins, or *Hashisheen,* built their fortresses in the mountains between Persia, Syria and the Caspian including the present-day Kurdish areas of Iraq. Their largest fort was at Al-Mut, where the Old Man of the Mountain was based. The Mongols, led by Hulagu Khan in 1256, finally attacked it and the violent finalé to the Assassins came within a few months. Soon, Baghdad was destroyed by the Mongols and until their conversion to Islam, the descendants of Chingiz Khan and his grandson, Hulagu Khan, remained a scourge for Western, Central and Southern Asia.

5. Bernard Lewis, *Race and Slavery in the Middle East: An Historical Inquiry* (London, 1974); also, *Islam and the West* (New York, 1993), and, *The Political Language of Islam* (Chicago, 1988).

6. Bernard Lewis, *The Multiple Identities of the Middle East* (London, 1999).

7. Bernard Lewis, *The Muslim Discovery of Europe* (London, 2003; reprint), p. 19.
8. Ibid., pp. 40-8
9. Ibid., p. 66.
10. Mark Mazower's recent study focuses on Salonika, the second most famous city in the Ottoman Empire that prided itself on pluralism all the way until 1911, when Greece captured it from the Turks and Muslims were cleansed from the city. Like in Spain earlier on, all the mosques were converted into churches and the city's fabulous skyline was totally transformed. Interestingly, Salonika under the Ottomans was a Jewish majority city until they left for other places in the twentieth century. See, Mark Mazower, *Salonika, City of Ghosts: Christians, Muslims and Jews, 1430–1950* (London, 2004).
11. Lewis, p. 135
12. Philip Mansel, *Constantinople: City of the World's Desire* (London, 1995), p. 26.
13. Ibid., p. 300.
14. Churchill offered him a temporary job, lower than his exalted expectations, and his tenure with the RAF remained equally perplexing. He would change his name quite often and would withdraw his books from the market soon to follow them up with newer versions. Such a tormented personality is both romanticised as well as archetypal of an era of British supremacy over one-fourth of the world. He felt bitter towards his government for ditching the Arabs and died a broken man. For details see, Michael Asher, *Lawrence: The Uncrowned King of Arabia* (London, 1999), pp. 26-7, 42-3, 76, 111-12, 233-4 and 309. For his own views see, T.E. Lawrence, *Seven Pillars of Wisdom* (London, 1997; reprint). Earlier, Cecil Rhodes represented a similar generation of empire builders whose ego, avarice and greed knew no bounds.
15. Lewis, 2003, p. 170.
16. Ibid., p. 228.
17. In fact, Hillenbrand, in the preface to her illustrated volume, has used this term for Runciman's volumes published more than half a century ago. Carole Hillenbrand, *The Crusades: Islamic Perspectives* (Edinburgh, 1999).
18. Bernard Lewis, *The Arabs in History* (Oxford, 1993; reprint), p. 133.
19. Ibid., p. 164.
20. Ibid., p. 208.
21. Bernard Lewis, *What Went Wrong? Western Impact and Middle Eastern Response* (London, 2003), p. 7.
22. For a detailed discussion on the complexity of enduring colonial cum racist typologies unleashed on the Afro-Asian peoples, see Frantz Fanon, *Black Skins, White Masks* (London, 1986; reprint).
23. Jacques Derrida, Stuart Hall, Gyatari Spivak, Edwad Said and several others have pinpointed these issues where even an otherwise *neutral* discourse, thanks to the power of the medium, itself becomes a 'revealed' truth

imposing a so-called consensus. For a quick overview see, Stuart Hall and Sarat Maharaj, *Modernity and Difference* (London, 2001).

24. Anne McClintock, *Imperial Leather* (London, 1995).

25. As was feared, despite all the promises for Afghan women, Bush and Blair, soon after the invasion of Afghanistan, lost interest in the socio-economic issues of that country. It appeared that they were more interested in eliminating Al-Qaeda and the Taliban than in ameliorating the situation. After displacing the Taliban, the country was given back to regional warlords whose stories of rape, kidnap and violence were all too familiar for Afghan women since the 1990s. The Northern Alliance, Mullah Ismael Khan and Rashid Dostum re-established their hegemony under Western tutelage and the country fell into another precipice where drugs, guns and feuds ruled the roost. For an Afghan woman's view see, Mariam Rawi, 'Rule of the rapists', *Guardian,* 12 February 2004.

26. Within this context, in France, the issue of *hijab*—not veil as erroneously identified—assumes a rather complex dispensation. It is neither Muslim men compelling women to wear *hijab* nor is it a rebuke to France's secularist educational system. In some cases, it may accrue from peer pressure but in several cases, women consider it to be a matter of self-empowerment and thus it becomes a voluntary act. On the contrary, superimposing secular uniformity in the name of liberalism, itself turns fallacious as it does not allow any choice or space to both individuals and communities. In addition, superimposition of *laciete* only shows panic and eagerness to defend secularism, which should have sufficient credentials to make itself acceptable. If the state is to impose this unilateral Frenchness based on secularist assimilation then what is the difference between colonial and post-colonial French models of enforced integration. Moreover, in a dangerous way, it may further alienate a largely underrepresented Muslim minority in the country. See, Madeleine Bunting, ' Secularism gone mad', *Guardian,* 18 December 2003. Also, Yasmin Alibhai-Brown, 'The West must get humble and honest—fast', *Independent,* 5 January 2004. German official impatience to follow the French suit, without the former's espousal of a secular system, also raises serious issues of identity, racism and empowerment.

27. Lewis, 2003, p. 115.

28. Ibid., p. 168.

29. Ibid., p. 172.

30. Ibid., p. 178.

31. Bernard Lewis, *The Crisis of Islam: Holy War and Unholy Terror* (London, 2003), p. xviii.

32. Ibid., p. 12.

33. Ibid., p. 19.

34. Ibid., pp. 20-1.

35. Ibid., p. 33.

36. Literally, the term would mean rejection or disbelief. Always used for non-believers, the term is not applicable to the People of the Book. Thus, Lewis's use of the term is rather complex. (Ibid., 43)

37. For instance, it was in 1884, a year after the installation of the Statue of Liberty and the inscription of Emma Lazarus's historic words of the US inviting the wretched and hapless of the earth that the Chinese Exclusion Act was promulgated to stop the Chinese and East Asian immigrants from entering the country. Already the Chinese immigrants had played a leading role in the construction of railway lines when the entire continental USA was mapped and in 1867 at Promontory the main lines met to herald a new era in American industrialization. In the 1890s, many Chinese single women in the United States ended up in brothels on the West Coast largely because they were non-English speaking and there were no Chinese men to marry them. Largely exploited by criminals within the wake of 'a Yellow Peril' hundreds of these Chinese Americans ended up in the urban red light areas.

38. Lewis, pp. 57-8.
39. Ibid., p. 59.
40. Ibid., p. 103.
41. Ibid., p. 107.
42. Oliver Miles, op. cit.

3

WESTERN NEO-CRUSADERS AND ISLAM: PIPES, BERMAN, KEPAL AND LEVY ON MUSLIMS

'What are the chances of suspending other prominent Americans in a glass cage from Tower Bridge?'
— A letter in *Guardian*, 15 September 2003

'It sounds like a bit of red herring to me.'
— Paul Bremer's reaction to Tony Blair's claim of finding WMDs in Iraq, quoted on Sky TV, 28 December 2003

'Islamism is perhaps the most vibrant and coherent ideological movement in the world today; it threatens us all.'
— Daniel Pipes, *Militant Islam Reaches America*, p. xiii

Daniel Pipes is 'a perfervid anti-Muslim, whose main characteristic is that as an Orientalist he 'knows' Islam for the appallingly dreadful thing that it is.'
— Edward Said, *Covering Islam*, p. xviii

'But I know this country (Pakistan) is crazy and lives under the watch of the secret services, which really *are* paranoid.'
— Bernard-Henri Levy, *Who Killed Daniel Pearl?* p. 360

The United States offers an interesting case study in the Islam–West interface by virtue of being a recent entrant and also the speed with which it has become the flag carrier in redefining this bilateralism. Its emergence as the super power, especially after the dissolution of the Cold War, gigantic interests and stakes in the Muslim regions, the salience of Neoconservatives, the retaliatory campaign since 9/11 featuring invasions of Afghanistan and Iraq amidst rolling back civil liberties of Muslim visitors and residents have allocated it an unchallenged profile. Its multiple, active and often contentious involvement across the globe usually perceived as hegemonic, is confronted with the dissent from a wide-range arena of critics. The global peace movement, characterized by the liberal and conservative critics of US policies—often derided as the usual anti-Americanism— has prompted several ambitious and often abrasive American writers, policy planners and opinion makers to offer their own extreme views on all subjects, including Islam. Benefiting from the legacy of the Orientalists but using more powerful and far reaching channels for diffusion of their ideas, these Christian–Jewish elements across the United States and elsewhere are not detached academics but run several think tanks, and through their official and public positions, proffer policies affecting billions across the world. They belong to a variety of professions and use politics, religion, media, economy, military prowess, lobbying and public diplomacy to implement their dreams of Pax-Americana, anchored on a strong Judeo–Christian worldview. They are professedly religious, and perhaps, offer a rare time in history when two hostile religious traditions known for millennia of hatred and pogroms are collaborating against what they perceive as a common enemy. Their views, in most cases, are motivated by religious zealotry like the Second Coming of Christ and certainly they all converge on the US as the divine republic ordained for a universal good. To them, the US is not an ordinary republic but one designed in God's image with a mission to spread the gospels of capitalism and Christianity. The dissolution of the Soviet Union has put America in an unprecedented position to spearhead their message and if this is not to take place through evangelical or peaceful means then military strategy has to be employed. Once again, religion and politics are together in the duty of a larger-than-life ideal where like the erstwhile *godless* Soviets, the misdirected Muslims— prototypes of a barbarian-terrorist such as Osama bin Laden— urgently require redemption.

These Neoconservative proponents and activists of the Ultra Right see in the dissolution of the Cold War a divine will, which has to be furthered at all costs. They are not mere nationalists, but xenophobes to whom American writ must reign supreme as the reluctant irritants from 'the Old Europe' can be ignored at their own peril. Muslims and all the other flag carriers of any alternative ideology or morality are to be confronted with full force, without any respect for multilateral alliances and covenants including the United Nations Charter or the Koyto Agreement on environment. Their belief in the sanctity of their mission and their confidence in the self-assured invincibility of the American military and economic might is unwavering, and with a vulnerable Bush Administration they found a willing establishment to implement their crusades. 9/11, in a way, came about as a blessing from the blue to set their agendas into action with the American juggernaut on the move across West Asia—the land of Biblical Prophets. These Neoconservatives awoke to their strength under Ronald Reagan when the Iranian Revolution directed their energies against political Islam. Alliances with the Mujahideen in Afghanistan or with Saddam Hussein against Iran costing millions of deaths were two major projects undertaken by Reagan's Republican Administration. Clinton's comparatively soft-peddling on defence and his sex scandal provided them with unlimited oil to fuel an anti-liberal campaign as they saw in the 'end of history' a chance to establish their utopias. Samuel Huntington's clash of civilisations, originally articulated by Bernard Lewis, redirected their focus and that of others at the Pentagon, Langley, Capitol Hill, Rand and numerous other think tanks to focus on Islam as 'the old-new enemy'. The Soviets were ideological enemies who had been brought down but generations had grown up seeking an enemy and now somebody else was needed as their replacement. Muslims were not only different-looking due to colour, class and creed but had been historical rivals if not the enemies who certainly did not like Israel, and could be resurrected as a major *enemy*. The sought-after opportunity came about with 9/11 when some of the former surrogates and collaborators like Osama bin Laden and Al-Qaeda turned against the former benefactor.

The Neoconservatives, both in the US and elsewhere, seek sustenance from a staunchly uniform nationalism, neo-racism, biblical teachings, imperial pride, hegemonic agenda, unbound moralism, and subscribe to an unbound market fundamentalism. They are the defenders of the US-led globalisation and oppose any form of multilateralism by virtue of sharing an unflinching belief in American military inviolability. The American Neoconservatives and their counterparts elsewhere all unite in banning immigration or shelters for asylum seekers, and are usually white supremacists backed up by full-fledged parties propounding unitary nationalism in almost every Euro-Atlantic country and Australia. These leaders may not vocally pronounce their racist typologies but often apply anti-immigration and racist rhetoric to gain wider support and thus are not enamoured of pluralism. They are multi-disciplinary in their professional backgrounds but like George Bush, Donald Rumsfeld, Richard Perle, John Ashcroft, Paul Wolfowitz, Condoleezza Rice, John Bolton, William Kristol, Robert Kagan, Douglas Feith and several others they hold very important positions. The powerful Bible belt and conservative Midwest are their strong power base while the Pentagon is the instrument along with the ever-willing media such as Fox News and several others, mostly owned by a few conglomerates. Religious evangelists including Pat Robertson, Frank Graham, Jerry Falwell, Christopher Catherwood and others provide the moral concrete whereas money and material come in from collaborative corporations and pro-Israel groups. The intellectual justification is offered by academics and writers such as Bernard Lewis, Daniel Pipes, Paul Berman, Robert Kaplan, and V.S. Naipaul; the populist tirades are delivered by Neoconservative publicists like Ann Coulter, Patrick Buchanan and by media celebrities like Oriana Fallaci, Charles Krauthammer, Simon Jenkins, William Safire, Judith Miller, 'Will' Cummins and Jim Hoagland.[1] Ambitious individuals such as Fuad Ajami and Fareed Zakaria, seeking their own pound of flesh, follow these frontline pundits closely. They represent a new generation of ambitious globetrotters who have taken upon themselves the role of powerful intermediaries for American political and economic interests.[2]

Globally, these Neoconservatives have been supported by leaders including Tony Blair, John Howard, Silvio Berlusconi and Jose-Maria Aznar, without forgetting the East European states vying to prove their loyalty to Washington by sending in troops and imposing similar anti-Muslim policies through their police and immigration officials.[3] The Neoconservatives, spewing racist and millenarian ideologies, have not been merely confined to the United States; they are everywhere including Europe and Australia. The European Ultra Right, fuming with rage at growing non-Christian pluralism, and nostalgic for an imperial past, includes a multitude of writers and publicists such as Bernard-Henri Levy, Gilles Kepel, Robert Kilroy-Silk and Denis McShane whose tirades have been adroitly memorized by racist outfits. This section deals with some notable opinion makers whose partisan views have been feeding into this pervasive Islamophobia.

Even before President George W. Bush appointed Daniel Pipes to head the Institute of Peace Studies in 2003, concerned quarters and educated Muslims were aware of periodic asides from this American specialist on Muslim history. He had earned enough notoriety through his persistent and self-righteous critique of Islam, Muslim pursuit of warfare, slaves in the past Muslim societies and a growing profile of Muslim Diaspora in the West presumably with its own exaggerated ramifications for societies such as the United States. Pipes, through his books, papers and media interviews came across as a person of strong, unitary and partisan opinions who would not miss any opportunity to slander Muslims.[4] His academic research on Islamic history only strengthened his serious prejudices and reservations about Muslims. Middle Eastern politics, the Arab-Israeli conflict, Syrian defiance of American and Israeli policies in the region, furore over *The Satanic Verses* and the volatile Balkan politics had already supplied him with sufficient material to portray Muslims as violent and perpetually emotion-ridden masses. To him, Muslims were presumably suffering because of their uncritiqued pursuit of Islamic teachings and also due to their reservations on an enlightened and progressive West.

Pipes, in the tradition of Bernard Lewis, had already assumed the role of a populist Orientalist to whom 9/11 came as a blessing in disguise as he could justify his claims on the Muslim penchant for violence. Pipes had been a student of Muslim history at Harvard where he researched Islamic attitudes towards slavery, especially in reference to statecraft and military systems. More than two decades before the publication of his recent best seller, *Militant Islam Reaches America*, Pipes had launched himself with a doctorate from Harvard in 1978 through a dissertation on slave soldiers in the Muslim empires. Three years later, the research was reissued in the form of a book: *Slave Soldiers and Islam: The Genesis of a Military System*, published by the Yale University Press.

Pipes, in his research volume,[5] uses *Muslim* and *Islam* interchangeably without realizing that they may not mean the same. For instance, defining Muslim history as Islamic history itself is an unresolved debate. For some, Islamic history might have ended with the early Pious Caliphate to be followed by more mundane monarchies, whereas to others, some periods of Muslim political history could still be qualified as phases of Islamic history. In the same vein, seeking all the socio-political acts including slavery and its legitimacy through Islam may not hold ground especially if one is confronted with a single-factor explanation. One cannot ignore the worldly nature of these monarchies, their warfare for both defensive and offensive imperatives and the role of several other inter-disciplinary factors in fashioning Muslim attitudes on race and colour. This is not to say that Muslims have never been colour blind or resolutely abhorred or abolished slavery but seeing in comparative and qualitative terms, one definitely finds Muslim legacies totally different from those of the pre-Islamic empires and starkly different from the North Atlantic traditions of racism and slavery in the early modern period. The Prophet Muhammad's (PBUH) own personal background, prioritisation of human rights over everything else and the examples of friendship with his freed slaves formed radical pioneer traditions, which many Muslims carried on, though there were exceptions as well.

Not all Muslim kingdoms were kind to Africans though one finds several former slaves making it to the top and then ushering in their own ruling dynasties such as the Mamluks in Egypt and the Slave Sultans in Delhi. One reason for Islam's continuing growth was its practical emphasis on equality frequently seen in congregational activities on a daily and periodic basis besides clear injunctions on properly treating the slaves. Islam certainly stopped short of abolishing slavery, which still does not mean that a gradualist approach to abolition and a mutual egalitarian reciprocity were absent from Muslim ethos. Muhammad (PBUH) formally adopted Zayd bin Harith as a son and Bilal was not only his favourite *Muezzin* (a caller for prayers) but also a highly respected companion. His farewell address after his final pilgrimage to Mecca focused on his exhortation for basic human equality and rejection of racism and all other related hierarchies. Even now, in the wake of the UN and Geneva conventions, Muhammad's address delivered to the world at large reads as a radical document vetoing colour, region and class-based differences.

Pipes leaves the impression as if Muslims, unlike the common *image* of being egalitarian, have been exploitative of slaves who they depended on to defend them during aggression. It must be an interesting claim since conquering huge and otherwise mostly inhospitable regions across the three continents and then sustaining a permeating influence upon them for so long could not be simply owing to a slave-based defence mechanism. Pipes singles out Islam to be the only religion to have used slaves for military purposes. He attributes this to Islamic law (*Sharia)* and the Prophetic traditions where conscious attempts were undertaken to train and arm slaves to fight for Muslim communities. During the caliphal era, slaves were effectively used to spearhead Muslim conquests. Thus, the earliest tradition, as formulated by the Prophet and the Pious Caliphs, was further sophisticated by 'Islamic', 'Islamicate' and 'Islamism', as represented through subsequent dynasties. The Abbasids used Turks as slaves who, in their time, sought slaves from the Balkans and Africa. In a rather selective manner, Pipes picks up his data to prove that Islam, instead of abolishing slavery, institutionalised it to suit defence imperatives. He quotes Ibn Khaldun, the well-known North African intellectual, for delineating a specialized training programmes for slaves. Quoting from other Muslim administrators and jurists including Nizamul Mulk, the Seljuk Prime Minister, he detects well-patterned programmes of inducting slaves into Muslim defence hierarchies. To Pipes, a 30-year period was usually required to lapse before a slave could qualify to rule. To him, the main reason for the promotion of slaves as warriors by Muslims was simply because of the latter's reluctance to carry on fighting.[6] There is no denying the fact that certain Muslim groups of Arab or Berber origins and even some Sub-Saharan Muslims pursued slavery but that was without any religious justification. The enslavement, with all its serious human rights violations, reflected political and military exploits and did not carry any 'green' badge as religious teachings simply abhorred mistreatment or bondage of fellow human beings.

The feudalisation of Muslim dynasties and tribal raids across Africa underwrote enslavement, though the use of slaves for military purposes gradually declined. The import of African slaves into India was an episodic reality spread over centuries and predated the Muslim factor. The Turks in India, like in neighbouring Persia or Turkey, were mostly rulers and came in as invaders to graduate into empire builders. In pre-Mughal India, the Turks were again rulers though the Slave Dynasty was an intra-Turkish affair. The Turks, following their conversion to Islam—especially subsequent upon the Mongol onslaught—benefited as well as consolidated Muslim rule over vast tracts of three continents. Presumptions that the Turks had been simply slaves or mere convenient instruments for acquiring power fall flat since it is a universal case and secondly, if the former slaves became the founders of the three most powerful empires—the Timurids in India, Persia and the Near East—then that is itself a unique case in Muslim egalitarianism. Former slaves becoming powerful kings in the early modern period, definitely may itself be a challenge still waiting to be surpassed. Pipes equally forgets the fact that the European enslavement of Africans accounted for a major Muslim section where Moors, Berbers,

Spanish Muslims, West Africans and Arabs along with several Bantu tribes were shipped across the Mediterranean and Atlantic. It is only in the recent past that historians, especially in the United States, have begun to unearth this unknown chapter in international history.[7] The Ottoman system of *diversheme* of adopting and training Balkan adolescents for civil and imperial purposes is a rather complex subject and cannot be simply categorized as a case of outright enslavement. It evolved out of several indigenous and external push factors and was a novel tradition of creating a new yet loyal and efficient hierarchy to support an expansive and equally complex Ottoman system. The sultans having *harems* and appointing African men to guard their sanctity offered an alternative system of control though it was not void of oppression when it stipulated castration of young African boys. One other related area worth exploring could be the ultimate or contemporary fate of the descendants of the former slaves. Some of the most modern and sermonizing societies, including that of Professor Pipes himself, are still seriously and dangerously segregated whereas so-called traditional societies such as Muslims, despite some class-based or ethnocentric preoccupations, do not suffer from any such serious and large-scale colour bars spawning fully-fledged apartheid.

Other than these historical and sociological issues and his outpourings on Syria and Salman Rushdie, Pipes's ascension to fame and notoriety owes itself to 9/11 when he was rediscovered as a media expert on Political Islam, terrorism, fundamentalism and the concept of *jihad*. More like Bernard Lewis, but strictly in a populist and jingoistic mode, Pipes has portrayed Islam as the most dangerous threat to the West by offering partisan and often offensive views on Muslim history. Like Lewis and several other Neo-Orientalists and populist rhetoricians, 9/11 came at a time when their views could have otherwise been discarded into the bin of history. Edward Said's critique of Orientalism and an emerging sensitivity to Islamic history had begun to de-dramatise Muslim politics but the terrorist attacks reinvigorated Islamopobia, which over the last few years has obtained centre stage in media and academia as the second line of offence against Islam. The current form of Isamophobia is not merely a racist typology, it is a more holistic and comprehensive amalgam of several components, including a subtle yet more dangerous form of Orientalism. Thus, the views of people like Lewis, Fallaci, Pipes, Pat Robertson or Frank Graham are not mere hearsay or temporary outbursts but instead reveal a more pervasive form of anti-Islam discourse.

In his best selling volume, Pipes ascertains the travesty and scale of 9/11 as an unprecedented act of terror against American lives, costlier than what Khomeini might have caused. Most of all, the attacks only led to a 'focused attention on this foe', by affirming a continuous connection between Islam and violence. Pipes, while claiming to write for 'fellow non-Muslims', promises to take a neutral approach in his book, which turns out to be a one-sided assault on Muslims, their religion, history, politics and Diaspora ensuring a negative view of Islam. To him, Islam is 'the most vibrant and coherent ideological movement in the world today; it threatens us all.'[8] Given such powerful and highly judgemental views one wonders about his claims to neutrality. A few pages down in the preface, he lashes out at immigration policies, which, to him, had become the most contentious issue in post-Cold War years. Here, he not only reiterates the typical Neoconservative xenophobia but also subtly suggests that the new immigrants may be linked to terror, as they may be Muslims and certainly non-Whites. Playing on such American vulnerabilities is an age-old game usually popular among the racist elements that concurrently never tire of celebrating America as the abode of the wretched and dispossessed of the earth.

While carrying on with his unmitigated attack on Muslims, especially in the opening pages of his volume, Professor Pipes occasionally turns defensive by positing that it is not Islam but its militant version which poses the real threat. Muslim militants, as Pipes claims, account for 10 to 15 per cent of the total Muslim population. One wonders how one differentiates a *normative* Islam from the *militant* Islam and on what scientific evidence it is possible to determine the percentage of militants in an international and highly diverse religion like Islam! To Pipes, these militant

Muslims aim at capturing governments to impose their agendas, which he fails to analyse at desirable length, and only centres on their aspirations for political ascendancy. However, his patronizing attitude towards the Muslim past becomes quite apparent when he quotes Martin Kramer, the historian, who had noted in a similar vein: 'Had there been Nobel Prizes in 1000, they would have gone almost exclusively to Moslems.'[9] To Pipes, more like Lewis, Muslims ignored the emergence of a powerful West at their own peril, and even an astute Ibn Khaldun in 1400 just made a passing reference to the changing times in 'the land of Rum' without alerting his co-religionists to the harder times ahead. However, it was in 1798 that, with Napoleon's invasion of Egypt, Muslims, to their chagrin, encountered a powerful Western outreach, which caused some consternation, yet did not fully awaken them to the new formidable challenges. Since then, Muslims have been constantly clustering towards the bottom of all the denominators of progress and development while presenting a vast spectacle of impoverished millions. Their politico-economic marginalization and psychological setback within the context of a difficult interface with a powerful West, according to Pipes, have collectively led to three types of responses: secularism, reformism and fundamentalism. The fundamentalist response, to him, is inherently a militant version of Islam and reflects three features. Firstly, it reaffirms devotion to the sacred law; secondly, it vehemently rejects Western influences and precepts, and thirdly, it has been turning faith into a fully-fledged ideology. To Pipes, fundamentalist and militant versions of Islam, in all cases except for the Taliban, are strictly modern and urban. It is a different case that while looking at the ingredients of Muslim fundamentalism, one does not find anything distinct from their Jewish, Christian or even Hindu counterparts. One would have expected a scholar of his calibre to look at the sociological, political and economic factors underlying such articulation instead of merely focusing on age-old Orientalist discourse centring on religion. He is, however, sharp enough to differentiate it from the traditional Islam, though one wonders whether he is being nostalgic for Sufism. Traditional Islam, as Pipes perceives it, is living by the Divine precepts whereas militant Islam is geared to capture power so as to create a new order. Unlike a confident traditional view, fundamentalist Islam is highly defensive. Though, it is not a 'new' enemy yet fundamentalism among Muslims, to Pipes, made its major entry during the 1970s. Apparently, he is referring to the Iranian Revolution, and maybe, to the Oil embargo of 1973 following the third Arab–Israeli war. He censures Western regimes for not realising the level of threat posed by militant Islam though writers like Leon Uris, the author of the novel, *The Haj*, had been forewarning them.

Juxtaposing Islam both as an 'external' enemy and an 'internal' threat in the form of Muslim immigrants is the usual Neoconservative ploy to express their racist biases besides spewing a xenophobic populism. While the Western regimes may have been lax on immigration, Muslims themselves, as Pipes believes, refuse to integrate. Pipes opines that the Muslim immigrants, instead of assimilation are more interested in converting local communities and are exploiting the forces of demography which are otherwise not favourably inclined to the West due to diminishing and quickly greying populations. Such a position, other than its clear racist undertones, is totally incorrect. Firstly, immigration to the West is still immensely restricted and the Western regimes including Australia and New Zealand since the 1970s have been erecting barriers and unassailable structures to debar new immigrants or even asylum seekers from coming into these regions. Fortress Europe has been pursuing the American-style exclusionary policies dating from the early 1920s when most of the non-European immigrants were officially disqualified for migration to North America. The colonial regimes like Britain and France also sided with Canada and the United Sates in seriously disallowing aspiring Asian and African immigrants. The selective immigration since the 1960s is only meant to acquire skilled professionals or the dependents of the immigrants.

The second premise of the Muslim immigrants being reluctant to integrate is too simplistic given the sociological discourse on acculturation, multi-culturalism, integration and assimilation.

Similar views were held about the Irish, Catholic, Jewish and East European immigrants a century back; thus Pipes is simply reverberating the age-old Neoracism by scapegoating Muslims. As an alarmist, his verdict is that there is a hope only if Muslims were willing to modernize and enable themselves to integrate, which is itself no less disputatious. In his third chapter titled 'Battling for the Soul of Islam', he posits Iran and Turkey as two antagonistic models for Muslims, where the latter should be helped to export its secularist model to the rest. While Iran since the Revolution of 1979 has nothing pleasant to offer, Turkey, according to Pipes, deserves being inducted into the European Union, and accordingly, the US must emphatically persuade its European partners.

His next chapter, 'Do Moderate Islamists Exist?' is more polemical and less academic, and plainly finds no moderates among Muslims. His stated dilemma is that the ordinary Christians do not understand the extent of the Islamist threat and many of them end up idealising democratic politics for Muslims without realizing that even with elections Muslims will stubbornly remain anti-Western. Such a view, besides being extremely pessimistic, is totally negative as it posits a holistic value judgement on a huge community by showing a complete lack of faith in its humanity. It equally overlooks their predicament, which may not be solely of their own making. Electoral politics and democracy are certainly the best possible human achievements for a common and greater good, several times better and efficient than even the most benevolent dictatorships yet there is no guarantee that as seen in India, the US, Israel or South Africa under Apartheid, specific groups may not hijack it. Not only are the Islamists, to Pipes, inherently non-democratic, they are radical utopians who vocally subscribe to extremism and are immensely non-moderate.

For understandable reasons and more like Bernard Lewis and diehard Zionist groups, he finds Islamists to be anti-Semite, though one wonders how he would otherwise define the Arab ethnicity, if the Semites themselves were deemed to be anti-Semites![10] In his partisan style, Pipes, while enumerating all the negative features of the Islamists, finds them instinctively anti-Western, unwilling to coexist with non-Muslims and thus extremely dangerous. Daniel Pipes urges the US to accept militant Islam as an ideology and not merely a faith and fully confront it. While substantiating this clash of cultures and of ideologies, Pipes is so carried away that he ends up erroneously identifying his own country as a secular state. However, he recommends a strategic plan to deal with the Islamists and accordingly recommends a few policy measures. He advises the shunning of any form of debate and appeasement by warning against assisting them in any form and instead advocates an open support for anti-Islamist forces. He, however, sensibly urges Western governments to prevail upon the Muslim regimes for gradual democratisation and to reduce their repressive policies.[11] Other then the last two points, his other measures could be termed as alarmist unless he could really identify and quantify the enemy, because merely declaring Muslim critics as militants and then coming down hard on them would only stipulate the clash of societies and stifling pluralism and dissent.

True to his Orientalist credentials, Pipes finds Islam inherently anti-West and refuses to accept socio-economic causes underlying fundamentalist fury. On the contrary, to a liberal argument seeking politico-economic explanations of Political Islam, Pipes, more like Jessica Stern,[12] feels that economic growth has instead helped the Islamists in assuming a higher profile. Such a view is not only unsubstantiated, it is equally an effort to forestall the possibility of any class-based analysis. However, to Pipes, militant Islam simply aims at acquiring absolute political power, which may be partly true but it does not explain the underlying congregative force of have-nots and their desire for alternative policies. Of course, Islamists are not uneducated in all the cases as some of them are even familiar with the Western classics and have been graduates of Western universities. Leading exponents of Political Islam such as Hasan al-Turabi of Sudan, Khurshid Ahmad of Pakistan, Mehdi Bazargan of Iran, Sayyid Qutb of Egypt, Necettin Erbakan of Turkey, Abbas Madani of Algeria and Rashid al-Ghannoushi from Tunisia have studied in the West, and in several cases, have observed Western societies from close quarters. Pipes portrays them as inherently anti-Western but equally finds them assimilating some of the modernist achievements in the areas of science, feminism and governance, which, in fact, weakens his argument of situating them all in one essentially anti-Western camp. He acknowledges hybridity in the Islamist discourse, which must make it difficult to categorize them all as inherently rejectionists. However, reiterating his faith in the Neoconservatives, he criticises the liberals for seeing in them the architects of a new anti-Capitalist ethos, especially following the dissolution of the Cold War. He lambasts the liberal sections for failing to see the extent of this threat and their naive acceptance of a greater evil simply to justify their own anti-Americanism. He has an acute problem—though often undefined—with both the Islamists and the Western liberal groups. Forgetting Guantanamo Bay detainees or the Anglo–American invasions of Western Asia, he, on the contrary, deems Washington appeasing and pandering to the militants. Certainly, he is not happy with the level and extent of Islamophobia, when he observes: 'Without anyone quite realizing it, the resources of the federal government have been deployed to help Muslims spread their message, and, in effect, their faith. If the 'war on terror' is to have any larger purposes, it must be to free people from the yoke of politicized Islam. There can be no better place to begin that than right at home.'[13] Pipes is either not aware of thousands of Muslims having been deported and interned across the continents over the past few years, nor does he seem to realise or care for the extent of devastations of Muslim regions. His ironical observations do not reflect even an iota of responsible scholarship. If we follow his logic than the Western regimes like the US have to demolish Political Islam for some larger interest; can we use the same logic to mete out the same to Political Hinduism, Likudist-Zionism and Neoconservatism?

In his tenth chapter, 'A Monument of Apologetics', Pipes turns into a diehard polemicist and does not hesitate from delivering a harangue against fellow Western scholars on Islam. Quoting works such as *Oxford Encyclopaedia of the Modern Muslim World*, Pipes seriously and rather unnecessarily questions the academic standing

of John Esposito, which is certainly in bad taste. He accuses the
four volumes of subjectivity especially in reference to Zionism and
Israel. This is one of his favourite McCarthyist themes as he
apportions blame to Western scholars of Islam for allegedly being
in cahoots with the militants—as if writing about Islam was itself
a major crime. He soon comes back to his favourite subject of
singling out Muslim Americans as a threat from within who
harbour 'worrisome aspirations for the United States. Although not
responsible for the atrocities in September, these people share
important goals with the suicide hijackers: both despise the United
States and ultimately wish to transform it into a Muslim country.'[14]
Such aspersions coming from a known academic would even put
the Ku Klux Klan to shame.

Quoting the example of Siraj Wahhaj, an African American
Muslim, Pipes finds American Muslims pursuing double standards.
When talking to the general Americans they are soft but leave no
stone unturned in radicalising these co-religionists. Tracing the
history of Islam in America, he focuses on the 1920s when the early
Muslim immigrants came to North America, though he
conveniently ignores the long phase of slavery. It was with the
efforts of Muslim scholars such as Ismail al-Faruqi, a Palestinian
academic at Temple University, that various Muslim think tanks
including the International Institute of Islamic Thought (IIIT) and
Muslim Students Association (MSA) were founded during the
1960s, further growing in the subsequent decades. Within a few
years, to Pipes, Muslim academics such as Faruqi, Masudul Alam
Chodhary and Shamim A. Siddiqui were spearheading *dawah* or
Islamic propagation in the United States by reposing some
optimism in its ultimate Islamisation. Pipes devotes several pages
to some Muslim ideal of converting America, both through
unrelenting evolutionary and revolutionary processes. Juxtaposing
the Muslim publicists with the Nation of Islam (NOI), he sees a
great destabilizing force brewing up within the country, as Muslim
revolutionists undertake initiatives with the Muslim evolutionists
supporting them in their own ways.

While repeating his early categorization of Muslims, Pipes differentiates between traditional and militant versions of Islam. To him, 15 per cent of Muslims are militants who pose a serious security threat, and diehards such as Omar Abdar Rahman and Osama bin Laden would exhort them for revolutionary tactics. One million American converts including the followers of Louis Farrakhan are to be watched through vigilante action before they cause some major trouble. In the long run, he suggests strict control regimes including surveillance and profiling of Muslim activists and especially of 'sleepers'. Other than keeping a watchful eye on the think tanks, he advises a vigilant scrutiny of the Council on American-Islamic Relations (CAIR), as such organizations may also harbour sleepers. Not only should there be strong checks on Muslim immigrants, Muslim students need to be thoroughly vetted with a discreet scrutiny of their areas of academic specialisation.

Building on this Muslim threat, Pipes finds an average Muslim immigrant enjoying a higher income than an average American. To substantiate his racist typology he picks up selective individual cases to prove that Muslims *en masse* are geared towards dangerous plots, which is a sheer travesty and an irresponsible use of data. On several occasions, he becomes the mouthpiece for Israel when he offers case studies of Arab Americans sympathizing with the Palestinians and hastily brands them supporters of Hamas and Al-Jihad. If Jewish Americans are entitled to enjoy the rights and privileges of dual citizenship and are not censured for harbouring and even implementing Zionist plots in the Occupied Territories, then merely sympathizing with the Palestinians or sending funds for refugees should not be caricatured as a support for terror. And the vast majority of the world's population realises it is the Palestinians who are themselves the victims of terror.

Pipes, in his unremitting rancour, does not keep his discussion confined to contemporary issues and instead goes back to the early period in the Muslim past. He cannot hide his jubilation over the works of some Western historians like Patricia Crone and Michael Cook who have tried to deconstruct some consensual areas in Muslim history. Their nebulous tirades as presented in their work,

Hagarism (1977), question the prophecy and attribute several myths to the early era. Pipes's own antagonism, combined with his Orientalist views, is quite apparent when he quotes from William Muir and such other Muslim-hating colonials in trying to demolish myths about the Prophet Muhammad's statesmanship. As a committed supporter of Zionism, he finds an excuse to tarnish Yasser Arafat while simultaneously critiquing the Prophet on his peace treaty with the Meccans. The way he draws parallels between the two different personalities and two eras, simply to suggest the untrustworthiness of the Muslims, is, in fact, a reflection of his unswerving animus towards everything Islamic.

Pipes is unforgiving to Muslim members of the African American community and criticises them severely though he allocates some space to evaluating various views about African slaves in the Western Hemisphere and the eventual marginalization of Islam from both the continents until the early twentieth century. He is, however, not so sure about Sylviane Diouf's claim that the ancestors of Frederick Douglass and Harriet Tubman, the well-known African American abolitionists of the nineteenth century, were also Muslim.[15] While giving a history of the Nation of Islam (NOI), he devotes ample space to dissension between Farrakhan and Warith Deen Muhammad, the son of the late Elijah Muhammad. While Warith has merged his section into mainstream Islam, Farrakhan's intermingling of racial militancy and bourgeoisie mores makes an 'odd combination'. Pipes sees the NOI as a leading anti-Semite group though he does not delve deeper into the complex context of relations between American Jews and African Americans. To make it into an Islam-versus-Judaism issue or positing Neo-antisemitism as an Islam-specific matter is not only simplistic, it is equally incorrect. It nefariously absolves the predominant and many times more powerful White population groups of any responsibility in sharing racist legacies; besides, such a view is aimed at tapering down a growing critique of the Israeli policies of occupation and dispossession in Palestine.[16] However, African Americans, especially members of the NOI, according to Pipes, 'are two hundred times more likely to convert to Islam than whites'.

But he still appreciates their overall good-naturedness, especially after full conversion to Islam, though he relishes in offering details on Jamil al-Amin, the formerly H. Rap Brown, who was implicated in a publicized murder case in Atlanta. Such cases, to Pipes, are 'the mirror-images' of radicals who may end up flagging several extremist causes. But he lashes out at Muslim organizations for not disowning Al-Amin and instead defending his case as a victim of racism. To Pipes, 9/11 gave a chance to moderate Muslims to disown such extremists but 'they missed this opportunity and militant Islam's hegemony remains in place, as strong as ever.'[17] Pipes is eager to press his government to be proactively vigilant on an undeniable threat—'the Enemy'—and it should also persuade the other Muslim nations to curb radical clusters amongst them.

Pipes is certainly unforgiving to those American and Muslim academics who offer a 'sanitized' view of Islam and especially of *jihad*. To him, the militant version of Islam is on the ascendance and the American 'multi-culturalist' academics cannot ignore a long tradition of military offensives carried out in the name of *jihad*. Unlike scholars such as Bruce Lawrence, John Esposito and several others, he forcefully perceives in *jihad* a strategy mainly to propagate Islam and create an Islamic empire by force.[18] He uses his last chapter to show that Islam is being misrepresented by scholars who view *jihad* as a toothless ideology whereas it aims at a total physical conquest and transformation of both the Muslim and non-Muslim worlds. To him, unlike modernists, Muslim revivalists such as Mawdudi, Qutb, Al-Banna, Khomeini and activists like Osama bin Laden and several other jihadist outfits are all vociferous practitioners and propounders of an armed struggle, without ever forgiving their fellow Muslim rulers. To Pipes, the armed struggles in Palestine, Chechnya or elsewhere are merely to wrest political power through terror and are not genuine efforts for self-determination.[19] In that sense it is not surprising, since the war on terror itself does not differentiate a genuine struggle for rights from sheer violence.

Pipes and his Neo-Orientalist and Neoconservative colleagues have used 9/11 as an opportune event to vent and expand their own narrow-mindedness and xenophobia. Their denigration of Muslim religion, history and societies including Diaspora underwrites a holistic and equally pernicious discourse. They have insidiously presented a selective perspective while pushing an agenda for confrontation. Instead of looking at the issues rather dispassionately these Islamophobes are in fact hate mongers, while concurrently proclaiming to be unbiased academics whose only preoccupation is to find fault with Islam and Muslims. Unlike the Cold Warriors, these elements share an immensely dangerous outlook and by controlling media sections and political echelons they have been using their influence diligently, no matter at what cost. They tend to forget that the Muslim world, having been ruled and redesigned by the colonial masters, is yet not able to augur a new politico-economic beginning. Problems of poverty and disempowerment abound while their surrogate rulers and corrupt elite remain totally dependent upon Western largesse. The Western control on their policies, thanks to the Pentagon, IMF, CIA, DFID, or the World Bank and through a powerful public diplomacy emanating from Washington, London and Paris have turned freedom into a mere charade for billions across the South. Like Michael Ignatieff, the Canadian author, Pipes suggests a proactive role for the United States in weakening militant Islam through a more aggressive interventionism at different levels, and in his enthusiasm for such a policy anchored on an unflinching belief in American might and self-righteousness, he conveniently forgets the sad legacies of colonialism.

Pipes, through his army of followers and researches and his web site (Campuswatch), leads the witch-hunt against any scholar who may have balanced views on Islam and, through his web site and peculiar way of petitioning, is helped by several like-minded groups arrayed against Muslims. Even reputable Muslim scholars based in the West are not spared. For instance, Tariq Ramadan, the European Muslim intellectual and the author of several well-received books, was offered a professorial position at Indiana University. After having issued him the visa, the US authorities led by the Department of Homeland Security rescinded it on the eve of his joining the university in the summer of 2004. The main objection was on his being a grandson of Hasan al-Banna, the founder of Muslim Brotherhood, while the officials totally ignored his 'intellectual pedigree.'[20] Noam Chomsky and many other distinguished American scholars are already protesting against such an ebullience for empire-building, as was warned by Michael Mann: 'The American empire will turn out to be a military giant, a back-seat economic driver, a political schizophrenic and an ideological phantom… a disturbed, misshapen monster stumbling clumsily across the world'.[21]

Intermingling of religion and politics, backed by sheer militarization, are not just Muslim-specific but happen to be a global phenomenon. Muslims have certainly had their share of violence in history but compared to it the modern slave trade, American slavery, European colonialism and especially the depopulation of the four continents, an overpowering racism, a continued degradation of the environment and massive violence perpetrated through global wars, the Holocaust, or ethnic cleansing are all legacies of that great Western heritage that modernity bequeathed and to which Lewis, Pipes and their camp followers belong.[22] If Muslims have not fared well on this rather painful barometer of modernity, they may be the lucky exception like the Native Americans or Australasian Aborigines. As the post-colonial studies and critical theories amply reveal, Orientalism has been itself both an instrument and an architect of violence and brought legacies of serious psycho-political and economic disruptions in its wake.

For a long time in the modern era, Orientalists and their successors kept Muslims objectified in their writings through occasional caveats surreptitiously stating that the Muslims were not yet able to write objectively about themselves. Nationalism, modernism and even revivalism were all explained by most of the colonial administrator and missionary scholars as positive attributes and results of the Western encounters with the East. In other words, a powerful, superior yet benevolent West had rediscovered and redefined the East for the latter's benefit and thus the colonial discourse turned into the grand narrative overshadowing everyone else. This Orientalist construct was unabashedly uneven, hierarchical and racist, and looked down upon Eastern cultures and traditions. Modernity, Westernism and progress were posited as the ultimate Western assets, which were to empower otherwise subordinate, devious, often childish and irresponsible mobs from the colonies. This civilizing project was not only hegemonic it was equally pompous and derogatory. And when some scholars or dissenters started to redefine the equation either by going back to the roots or by emphasizing synthesis, Western pundits usually mistrusted them. Both the revivalist and reformist responses were deeply distrusted though the former was apportioned a larger share of responsibility for dissuading people from a total submission to imperial control. Thus, when Muslim jurists and scholars such as Sayyid Qutb, Mawdudi, or other Salafis raised the flag of resistance they were branded as obscurantists. The reconstruction of Islamic responses was seen as amateurish, irresponsible and anti-West. Some of these Islamists were deeply suspicious and critical of Westernism which they considered both immoral and hegemonic, and persuaded their Muslim communities to resist modernisation if it meant Westernisation. Their intellectual articulation may have had its own limitations but they certainly symbolized the contemporary ideological polarity among the Muslim elite. After 9/11, once again, there is a renewed interest in understanding these Islamists who seem to have offered an ideological legitimacy to the armed resistance against alien influences and control. Concurrently, the entire ideology of *jihad* has come under a major searchlight.

Paul Berman, an American commentator, has tried to focus on Sayyid Qutb to seek out an ideological foreground to Muslim activism and militancy as espoused by Osama bin Laden and such other extreme radicals. Highly opinionated, though claiming to be an intellectual purveyor of liberal traditions, Berman seems to have joined the bandwagon of Islamophobes by picking on selective events from the recent European and Muslim past. A supporter of President Bush's war on terror with his unflinching belief in its liberating ramifications for all, especially the Europeans and

Muslims, he flags the stars and stripes as a benevolent force geared for a larger humanitarian good. Quoting from Lewis, though he does not take the trouble of offering any references for his citations, Berman has been introduced as one of the pre-eminent commentators on European and Islamic totalitarianism, though his knowledge of Islamic activism, which he often defines as Islamism, derives merely from the three translated volumes of Sayyid Qutb's *magnum opus*. Wherever he finds a chance he inserts a positive caveat for Israel and certainly views it as a citadel of liberalism confronting Islamic fascism. Beginning with Kafka's *The Rebel*, he takes the reader through Lincoln's Gettysburg Address; selectively focuses on Sayyid Qutb's *In the Shade of the Koran*, whose twenty-seven volumes he admits not to have read, and then towards the end of his book, offers a survey of developments since 1989. Here he focuses on the Middle East, Afghanistan and the gradual growth of Islamism that finally takes on the United States largely owing to some Muslim totalitarianism and partly because the USA, in the 1990s, refused to tackle this major threat on the horizons. In a veiled manner, he thus critiques the Democrats and vocally supports Bush on his apparently clear-mindedness in confronting Osama bin Laden and Saddam Hussein, though, in the latter case, he fails to elaborate the rationale for invasion. Instead, he glorifies it as a humanitarian interventionism, which may establish democracies in the region as had happened in Europe since the Second World War, and in Eastern Europe after 1989.

Berman's problems are his simplistic generalizations due to his lack of immersion into world history, especially those of Muslims; his opinionated self-righteousness, his unflinching belief in the American dream and policies, and his delinking of Western hegemony in the Muslim world that have, to a large extent, created serious anomalies. Without saying it clearly, despite a personalised and often racy style, his analysis not only defends Huntington's clash of civilisations, but also goes a step further and makes it a battle between good and evil, where evil is certain to lose. In reaching such conclusions, he reaffirms his faith in Lewis to whom Muslims are a long lost case and even democratisation may end up bringing the terrorists into power through the ballot.

To Berman, European totalitarianism began earnestly after the First World War in the form of Stalinism and Fascism, and developed a close relationship with terror. In the same vein, he goes on to describe Muslim totalitarianism, which is nihilistic, anti-Western and feeds itself on a cult of murder and suicide. He traces its root in the twentieth century to the teachings of Sayyid Qutb whose unease with the moral aspects of Western life styles such as prevailed in the United States during his student days had left a lasting imprint. Qutb had been a student in Colorado and turned into a life-long critic of materialism and individualism, as symbolized in a highly industrial society. He felt uneasy with American sexual mores and opted to return to his native Egypt where he strove for an Islamic revolution, more in line with classical Islamic teachings. From the pulpit of Hassan al-Banna's Muslim Brotherhood, he developed a close relationship with Gamal Nasser and other young military officers. After the coup in 1952, the military officers turned hostile to the Muslim Brotherhood and eventually imprisoned its top leadership. It was in prison that Qutb wrote his thirty-volume *In the Shade of the Koran,* which continues to influence generations of Islamists including Osama bin Laden and Ayman al-Zawahiri. Qutb was hanged in 1966 whereas his other academic brother went into exile in Saudi Arabia.

Mawdudi, the Taliban, Al-Qaeda, Hamas, Indonesian and African Islamists have all been deeply influenced by Qutb's critique of Western 'hideous schizophrenia' and a strong reaffirmation of Islam's self-sufficiency.[23] To Qutb, dying for Islam while pursuing *jihad* offered a continuous renewal of the only perfect Message, which makes Berman focus on him as the architect of contemporary Muslim totalitarianism and the cult of suicide bombers. Berman's problem is that he does not differentiate between state-led terrorism and individual or group-based acts of terror, and rather packages them together as totalitarianism. Like the Islamists, Pan-Arabists all the way from the Egyptian nationalists to the Baathists in Syria and Iraq are presumably also fascists, as they subscribe to a similar idealisation of the past and venerate the cult of suicide and violence. Berman is at pains to justify the invasions of Afghanistan and Iraq by espousing a form of moral idealism. He suggests at great length that the United States has never been anti-Muslim: 'In all of recent history, no country on earth has fought so hard and consistently as the United States on behalf of Muslim populations—a strange thing to say, given what passes for conventional wisdom'.[24] This author conveniently tends to forget the deaths of thousands of innocent civilians in Iraq since 1991 and again since April 2003, and also in Afghanistan. The unflinching support for Israel through an idealization of Ariel Sharon and post-9/11 internment of Muslims in numerous jails including Guantanamo Bay certainly are some of the constant reminders of a complex American interface.

American scholars such as Lewis, Pipes and Berman, the media pundits, religious networks and numerous powerful think tanks are discreetly and vocally anti-Muslim and any solitary voice sympathetic to Muslims promptly elicits the title of Muslim lover, which is like being decreed a fascist. Berman is right in positing Political Islam with the forces of modernity though he blames Islam for lacking a tradition of defiance and critique from within. Quoting Tariq Ramadan, a Muslim scholar based in Switzerland and the grandson of Hassan al-Banna, he tries to prove that Islam only demands an unquestioning subordination, which again only reveals his own sketchy knowledge of Islam. Muslim history is replete with questioning and dissent by religious scholars and Sufis arrayed against clerical and political authorities. The Shia tradition, despite it own hierarchy of clergy, has been an enduring proponent of dissent for almost fourteen centuries. Berman characterizes Islamists, especially those trained in Western institutions, as 'hyphenated personalities', who are modernists during the day— especially in Diaspora—but by night go back to their particularist Islamic identities. Berman ignores the fact that this is not unique to Muslims, as people in general have multiple identities and countries like the United States and Britain have in recent years taken great pride in identifying themselves as plural and multicultural societies. Moreover, people are not sure that even after a total assimilation they will still be considered equal.

Berman, while celebrating the idea of progress in the West, finds it absent from the Islamic ethos where all is already perfect—though he does not realise that even the Western concept of progress is so contentious that using it to judge non-Western societies may itself be self-defeating. Berman's serious unease with Qutb and other Islamists, as is evident from his narrative, is due to their critique of Israel and its substantial support from the West, especially the United States and thus his discourse frequently turns into a defence of the Israeli and American policies. While he traces the history of liberalism from within a conflict-ridden England of the seventeenth century, he finds it prospering in the United States since the nineteenth century. It was replenished by Wilsonian idealism and more so since the Second World War, when America undertook the reconstruction of Europe and Japan. After 1989, the end of totalitarianism came about partly because of liberal traditions in Eastern Europe and partly due to the American leadership, an act that needs to be repeated in the Muslim world. To him, Jews and Christians may have their own reasons to subdue Islam and vice versa but eventually it is liberal democracy and feminism, which hold the key for a new Muslim dawn.

To Berman, Muslim totalitarianism assumes more dangerous proportions as these Islamists are inherently anti-women. This is an old whip in the hands of Islamophobes that they use so often, but singling out Muslims as the only post-1989 totalitarians is too simplistic and would certainly spread glee among many supremacists. The Likudniks (Gush Emunim), Hindutva (RSS and Shiv Sena, amongst many others), Neoconservatives (all the way from xenophobes/evangelists to Timothy McVeigh, Pat Robertson and others), Orthodox Christians (exponents of Greater Serbia or Loyalists-exclusivists in Northern Ireland, or Uganda's Lord's Army), Buddhists (Aum Shinrikyo) and several other supremacists elsewhere do not figure at all in Berman's discussion of totalitarianism and liberalism.

As suggested by Mary Kaldor, an academic at the London School of Economics (LSE), such groups 'all share the Armageddon myth. They are obsessed with the potential of extreme violence to shock, with ideas of sacrifice and martyrdom, and with fear of hated enemies. These new terrorists are often linked to parts of the state apparatus, as in Afghanistan or Saudi Arabia, but, more often, they flourish best in failing states rather than in powerful, self-sufficient administrative frameworks.'[25] Kaldor takes Berman to task for his idealisation of Israeli policies and apportioning of blame to Palestinians. She observes: 'I share Berman's horror of suicide bombing, but it is worth considering how its victims perceive war. Many more Palestinians, including civilians and children, have been killed by Israeli military during the second intifada, than suicide bombers have killed Israeli civilians. Why should we think that Israeli behaviour is justified because soldiers carry it out whereas suicide bombers are terrorists? The same argument can be made about the recent wars in Afghanistan and Iraq.' She is definitely questioning the means and their horrendous cost in human lives in those poor nations. She prioritises international law over military pre-emption when it is surreptitiously carried out in the name of liberating people or ending terrorist networks.[26] Berman, like the American power elite, is sceptical of international law as, to him, annihilating terrorists should remain a consensual point and certainly an American prerogative. The mythification of this war on terror has created its own cycle of violence, which could be self-defeating by incurring more in human lives and miseries. Berman's rash optimism hastily overlooks the long-term human costs globally and even in terms of civil rights within the Western nations and may even offer encouragement for further suicide attacks, as more and more communities are seriously affected by the revengeful American war on terror. One wonders how a liberal analyst can justify war and still idealise it when those unfortunate lands are becoming awash with can innocent blood!

Berman finds Muslim totalitarianism aiming at capturing political power by adopting a three-tier strategy as suggested by Qutb: fighting *jahliya* (ignorance among Muslim elite), *jihad*, and the creation of a utopian Islamic state. Using this as a criterion he meanders through the Muslim world seeking out several movements including the Khomeinites, Hizbollah, Islamic Jihad, Taliban or such other groups spearheading their idealism. The Iranian Revolution carried out in the name of 'purest Islam', like other such radical movements was in fact not 'a war between love and piety ...[but] a war between cruelty and suicide.'[27] This only reveals his sheer ignorance about Iran under the Shah. After a recap of several other Islamist movements, Berman delivers his verdict: '...the Muslim totalitarianism of the 1980s and '90s turned out to have been fully as horrible as the fascism and Stalinism of Europe—fully as murderous, as destructive of societies and moralities, as devastating of civilizations.'[28] Such an edict from an established analyst only deserves to make a banner head line on the racist web sites run by the British National Party (BNP) or KKK! The problem with this approach is that it is premised on the *othering* of Islam and presumes any party expressing Islamic orientation to be a totalitarian outfit. It essentialises Islam as a sinister and inherently anti-Western ideology. That is why media and academia end up asking routine questions such as: does Islam allow democracy, as if they are simply antithetic. Or, in the same vein, does Islam grant women any rights, as if Islam is merely sexism!

Berman's viewpoint—not so unique—equally presumes that Muslims without democracy and feminism are simply barbarians and for them to qualify as modern they have to shun Islam and be something else altogether.[29] Needless to say, such views are both myopic and illiberal. Islamic history largely affirms recurring traditions of synthesis and diffusion, though in several recent cases, emphasis has also been on a literalist application of religious ethos. The question of democracy or women's rights does not have to presuppose the annulment of Islam from these societies; instead, there is a need for universal empowerment, judicious egalitarianism and economic redistribution. Berman, Pipes and Lewis, and other writers such as Nick Cohen, Christopher Hitchens and John Keegan—despite having written thousands of pages critiquing non-Westerners such as Muslims—usually avoid talking of regimented stratification, colonial legacies, external hegemonies, Western interventionism and an imbalanced global economy collectively operating at the expense of developing countries and beleaguered communities. Good governance, unfettered democratisation, guaranteed peace and civic rights are not merely theocratic or ideological issues, they are rooted in wider political and economic anomalies and without taking them into account, plain Islam-bashing is a mere waste of time and energies. Defending Enlightenment may be an act of devotion yet overlooking the contemporary salience of racism, slavery and imperialism and their enduring imprints may only weaken the defence of a mixed bag such as modernity. Celebration of Enlightenment-based liberalism by these Western scholars should ideally not lead them to offer a *carte blanche* validation of Europeanization of the world. It only feeds into the Huntingtonian clash of cultures, concurrently stressing the redundant Fukuyamian ebullience. Lewis, Pipes and several other analysts seem to be relishing the idea in their commentaries by positing Islam as not a mere anti-liberal totalitarianism but a significant threat to Enlightenment itself.[30] Posting Islam as the bane of the problem—anti-Enlightenment and the sponsor of terrorism— is neither a new argument nor a convincing explanation of complex issues involved; it is merely a convenient escapism and name-calling, so favoured by Orientalists and evangelists.

Berman moves on to wrestle with liberals such as Noam Chomsky, Breyten Breytenbach (the South African–French critic of Israeli genocide of Palestinians) and Jose Saramago (the Portuguese Nobel-Laureate) for criticising, the American and Israeli penchant for violence. His counterattack is not patterned as a response to their respective arguments but is directed more against their disciplinary and personal acumen, which is like hitting below the belt. These liberals, to him, are not fully aware of the apocalyptic and death-obsessed mass movements among Muslims and instead are barking up the wrong tree. The Left, to Berman, is naïve in its support for peace, Palestinian rights, and also in its critique of American interventionism. Berman, while posing to be a defender and propounder of liberalism, is placed in closer proximity with the Neoconservatives. Interestingly, Berman's 'study window' in his Brooklyn apartment allows him 'to conclude that Islamism in its radical version of present poses every imaginable danger.' The richest Saudis, brainiest Egyptians and bravest Afghans, duly helped by intelligence agencies such as those in Pakistan or similar other clusters, will keep on promoting the death culture by causing more terror.[31] Curiously, his vantage Brooklyn point allows Berman to ruminate on Europe's policy of 'do nothing' while faced with a global threat such as Muslim fascism and terror. He singles out Sweden and Switzerland in particular for their opportunistic wait-and-watch policies during the wars and crisis while others have fought and suffered for them. As Western Europe bled to rid the world of the global menace of fascism, these two countries bided their time to reap their posthumous benefits though they knew that a victorious Hitler would not have left them 'neutral'. Berman is unforgiving to German philosophers like Fichte for allowing Muslim thinkers to be imbued with their idealisation of romanticised fascism. He uses the Bosnian crisis to censure French socialists under Francois Mitterrand for hyping up anti-Serb sentiment, though it was only the United States that, through its humanitarian interventionism, came to Europe's rescue.

Bush might have been naïve and ignorant of international law but his clarity on the issues of terror, though defined in uncouth Western terms, has been, to Berman, the best safeguard for global liberal values. The US invasion of Afghanistan amidst the premise to rid Afghan women of oppression, according to Berman, makes it the 'first war in which women's rights were proclaimed at the start to be a major war aim. No one seemed to notice, though.'[32] In hindsight, one could say that while in his enthusiasm for the US-led interventionism, both Afghanistan and Iraq in particular and West Asia on the whole, still seemed ages away from the promises of a new tomorrow. Even Afghan women's groups including the Revolutionary Association of Women of Afghanistan (RAWA), have felt betrayed and forgotten by the Bushes, Blairs and other high-sounding moralists of 2001.[33]

France has always tried to assume intellectual and ideological leadership of the rest of the West by highlighting its achievements such as secularism, which is part and parcel of an unchallenged republicanism. The French revolutionary ideals certainly continued through the generations of revolutionaries across the world but the country itself remained a diehard imperialist. Its empire was second to that of Britain and was characterized by a strong policy of centralization and forced assimilation that the French colonial administrators tried to impose on the colonies. France was also quite reluctant in withdrawing from its former colonies in Africa and Asia as was seen in Algeria and Indo-China where a long trail of bloodshed followed their exit. The French liberals, in several cases, supported decolonisation but also remained focused on the essentialisation of secularism. The reluctance to accept minorities—an enduring legacy—has deeply divided and disheartened not only its plural communities but has divided its liberal intellectuals. In their zeal to liberate women and other underprivileged communities, many of them, while espousing a forced integration, sound more like dogmatists to whom French identity remains sacrosanct. Muslims, who always played a crucial role in the economic and military affairs of France, have often been treated abysmally.

While France has been in the vanguard of the study of Islam, its governments and pressure groups have been specifically intolerant to Muslim communities in the country. As seen in the debate on headgear/scarf in the early 1990s and again in 2004, the French centrist regime of Jacques Chirac seemed to be in competition with Le Pen's National Front in scapegoating Muslims to seek more votes. The ban on headgear, especially after 9/11 was used in the name of integration of Muslims (and others) but in effect it was a sordid reflection of the French discretionary attitude rooted in the Algerian war of independence. The Iranian Revolution, the Salman Rushdie affair and the crisis in Algeria following France's resistance in accepting the electoral verdict that would have brought the FIS—the religio-political party—into power, and then 9/11, all fed into anti-Muslim sentiments. Curiously, the French Government and several intellectuals perceive secularism as an effective medium to empower plural communities, especially women; simultaneously its leaders do not hesitate in showing Christian solidarity with the rest. For instance, the experts who were led by Valery Giscard d'Estang, the former French president, in fact, drafted the EU constitution draft defining Europe as a Christian community. Moreover, when Pope Paul John II died in 2005, the French flag flew at half-mast all across the nation while President Chirac himself participated in the papal funeral at the Vatican.

There are two groups in France holding divergent opinions about French politics of race and culture. The first group is of those to whom secularism and assimilation are indisputable and have to be imposed by banning headscarves and other religious symbols from schools. To them secularism is the cornerstone of republicanism and any concession, in the name of multiculturalism, is self-defeating and a reversal of France's long political journey. The liberals are not prepared to listen to sociological and economic arguments where a strict imposition may further marginalize already underprivileged Muslim women or even young Sikhs. The second group, though a minority, wants to redefine secularism in the context of changed demographic and economic issues and is prepared to modify some old precepts governing the *laicite* school system, where education remains totally nonreligious.[34] These groups have their supporters and opponents across Europe though anti-Muslim feelings have remained dangerously high across North Atlantic regions.

Gilles Kepel is the leader of the first group to whom Muslims, if given a choice, will only debilitate the republic. As a Jacobin republican, his studies focus on a minority of Muslim activists to whom he allocates stupendous powers of destabilising the rest. His book, *Allah in the West*, mainly focuses on radical elements and does not show any interest in the heterogeneous composition of Muslim communities. As a 'classical Orientalist', he believes that Islam is simply not for democracy, and radical groups all across the North Atlantic regions harbour greater and dangerous designs. He is always preoccupied with 'communalism' with all its negative connotations and believes that multiculturalism will simply lead to further fragmentation. He is unwilling to recognise that assimilation is power-centric, and refuses to allocate any space to minorities as the paradigmatic decisions and mechanics are already in place, ordained by peers disallowing them any choice or even pedagogical participation.[35] Kepel was opposed to the idea of opening a special institute at Strasbourg University to help European Muslims learn more about the modernist exigencies and interpretations of their religion. Kepel, in his short monograph, based on visits to the Middle East and the United States, has tried to gather his impressions of the Muslim world following 9/11. His impressionistic travelogue reads more like Naipaul's narrative and similar other rather superficial works by travelling specialists. To him, Muslims are torn between the distrust and adoration of the West, though largely remaining distrustful of Western regimes while being supportive of Osama bin Laden.[36]

There is no doubt that Kepel has been studying Muslim politics since the 1980s when he mainly focused on Egypt, and since then all his other books continue to dilate on groups like the Muslim Brotherhood and Islamic Jihad. In the process he repeats himself quite often.[37] He is right though in suggesting that Al-Qaeda is not a well-knit group with a specific hierarchy; instead it is a hotchpotch of several disgruntled, educated and urbanized Muslim groups, who are using religion and politics to replace or even displace the ruling hierarchies across the Muslim world. To Kepel, these activists remain abysmally distrustful of Western policies and the Muslim elite's surrogacy to the former, and use information technology for networking with similar other disgruntled groups. Like Huntington, he notices widening chasms but reposes all his trust in the Muslim Diaspora for salvaging the malady, without assigning any major responsibility to the North Atlantic ruling elite and discretionary lobbies. Like other neo-Orientalists, he simplistically suggests Eurocentric remedies without realising that the latter might have itself aggravated the malaise in the first instance. To Kepel, Muslims are confronted with a new Andalusia where Western intellectual and political power reigns supreme, unlike the era when it was the other way around, and the only way forward is through learning from the West.[38]

Analysts like Bernard-Henri Levy, a French populist writer of very strong and rather myopic views, support Kepel. A philosopher of Jewish descent, Levy was born in Algeria (1948) and enjoys the media limelight. His books usually embody autobiographical information owing to his narcissistic tendencies and he does not shirk mixing fact with fiction.[39] When he lacks facts, he quickly builds up fabulous images, owing to his photogenic personality and associations with the world of fashion and media. An egocentric, Levy relishes exaggerated narratives about himself, especially those which depict him as the most influential contemporary French philosopher. Many of his critics, in fact, hold him responsible for lowering the philosophical debate to the extent of facilitating its appropriation by ultra right groups in France.[40] In his twenty-ninth book, *Who Killed Daniel Pearl?* Levy blames Pakistanis in general and the government in particular for several types of devious acts. This book is about Daniel Pearl, an American journalist for the *Wall Street Journal* (WSJ), who was murdered mysteriously in Karachi in 2002, and a shocking video of his execution was shown around the world. The Pakistanis arrested and convicted Omar Sheikh—a British Pakistani—for masterminding the murder. Levy, in his own fictional and flamboyant style, blames educated and cosmopolitan Muslims like Sheikh who use radical Islam to promote their own careers in countries such as Pakistan. He asserts that Pearl knew too much about the trafficking of nuclear secrets from Pakistan to Afghanistan's Taliban and that is why he was heinously executed in January 2002. To Levy—the former French diplomat and a flamboyant journalist—mad scientists and Islamic fundamentalists had joined hands to create the first 'Islamic' bomb. In his own name-dropping style, he makes his book into a thriller, especially when writing about Pearl's execution. The book not only mixes history and fiction, it is a 450-page long harangue against 'Pakistan that I saw turning into the devil's home'.[41] He simultaneously tries to empathise in an unrestrained Orientalist mode, as he observes: 'But I know this country is crazy and lives under the watch of the secret services, which really *are* paranoid.' However, his tirade against the country is not new since he has been writing about South Asia for more than four decades and admits in *Indes Rouges* (Red India*)*—an earlier book—to being 'scarcely sympathetic to Pakistani policy'.[42]

In the patronizing style of such other *liberals*, who conveniently assume a higher moral ground by championing the cause of women in Muslim societies, Levy's touristy reportage does not allow him to fully investigate the complexities of this society. It is both amusing and rather silly to assume 'that Rawalpindi is the only place that I see women's faces.' It is as if one determines the nature of society—its inter-gender relationship only—by using the criterion of seeing women out on the streets! The same city, however, depresses him as he finds it 'bizarre' and 'cruel' as he encounters a dwarf usherer at a hotel.[43] One wonders about his reaction if the same dwarf had been begging in the bazaar! Even his references to 300 Indian virgins arriving in Dubai and the charity being used for terrorist purposes are plainly ludicrous. Several visits to 'the black hole of Karachi' and other cities across the country were meant to interview people on the circumstances leading to the murder of the American journalist.[44] He does not find anything positive about Karachi where, according to our author, one could buy a little adolescent Bengali girl for 70,000 rupees, out of which 10 per cent would be meant for the police. Brimming with confidence, he informs his readers of 3,000 virgins arriving in the port city just the previous night via India to be sold.[45] His fantastic claims do not end here, since posing as an authority on Islam and terrorism, he offers an interesting Freudian explanation: 'Islamism and women, this depth of pain and terror, this fear and, sometimes, this dizziness in front of the feminine sex I've always thought was the real foundation of the fundamentalist rage.'[46] This can be certainly considered as a unique interpretation of Political Islam by the leading French thinker. Surely, he juxtaposes Islam and terrorism by allocating them modernist portents as 'terrorism (is) a bastard child of the demonic couple: Islam and Europe.'[47]

Amongst others, he wanted to meet some elusive Pir Mubarak Shah Gilani, the leader of Al-Fuqrah and presumably the mentor of the 'Shoe Bomber'. In the process, he pieces together the story of Pearl's kidnapping and brutal murder as owing to some nexus between the *jihadists* and the Pakistani intelligence agencies. Other than his opinionated statements on Pakistan, its people and Pakistanis in Britain, Levy's forays into the case do not spring any surprise as his final summation hinges on three possibilities. Firstly, to him, Pearl was murdered as he knew too much about the linkages between the Pakistani *jihadis* and the Taliban and a possible exchange of information on nuclear weapons between Al-Qaeda and a few Pakistani scientists. Secondly, he blames a pervasive Anti-Americanism for the journalist's cold-blooded murder. His third interpretation is that Pearl's contacts such as Omar Sheikh and affiliates of the Binori Town seminary in Karachi had come to know of his Jewish identity and the concurrent American and Israeli citizenships. It would have been more relevant if, in place of devoting so many pages to unnecessary details, he could have simply focused on the CIA, WSJ and Al-Qaeda, but that would have required rigorous research resulting in a slimmer yet analytical volume.

On the contrary, the book by Mariane Pearl, the widow of the slain journalist and herself a reporter, uncovers several hidden aspects of her husband's murder. Based in India, Daniel Pearl came to Karachi to write reports on radical groups for the *Wall Street Journal*. He received local hospitality from a large number of people, including some Islamists. When his computer broke down, he was loaned a laptop, which had been owned in the past by some Al-Qaeda leaders in Kabul. The American journalist discovered some secret files about Al-Qaeda and its command on the computer's hard disk and sent it off to New York. The WSJ handed over the computer to the CIA, which used the secret information to bomb safe houses in Kabul and elsewhere. 'The hard drive contained documents which the WSJ took the unusual step of handing over to the US intelligence then bragging about it in print, perhaps endangering Pearl's life.'[48] In one of these attacks, Muhammad Atef, the head of the military wing of Al-Qaeda, was targeted, which caused consternation among its sympathizers and followers in Pakistan. This is where Pearl's collaborators turned into his tormenters and kidnapped him and took him to some secret location. His pregnant wife, Mariane, sought help from his employers but presumably it was not forthcoming. Without any financial and legal support, she acted on her own and eventually hired a Pakistani attorney. According to Mariane Pearl, the perpetrators were not sophisticated Muslims, but instead came from a semi-literate and uncouth background though they happened to be computer-literate.[49] While Pearl's employers may be nonchalant towards the cruel murder of Daniel Pearl, Levy has certainly used it in his own preposterous way, mixing facts with fiction to present an egoist thriller about educated Muslims waging a multi-dimensional war on the West. The disclosure of an illicit nuclear technology transfer between Pakistani scientists and countries such as Libya and Iran in early 2004 further emboldened Levy in his denunciation of Muslims. Curiously, he presents himself as a great champion of moderate Muslims without mincing words in an exaggerated discomfort with Islam.[50] Levy has been known for his close association with Bosnia's late president, Alija Izetbegovic and Ahmad Shah Mahsud, the murdered leader of the Northern Alliance in Afghanistan. He never forgave the Pushtun Taliban and their Arab supporters for killing Mahsud, just two days before 9/11.[51] According to Levy, Omar Sheikh, Osama bin Laden, Masood Azhar, Pir Gilani and such militant-activists while contrasted with Izetbegovic and Mahsud, in fact, represent the two faces of Islam. However, amongst his several cherished possessions, Levy owns a gigantic mansion in Morocco and has dozens of North Africans waiting on him. His espousal of the rights of North African Muslims in France appears akin to his claims of being active in pro-Algerian protests during the 1960s, which have been found wanting in truth.

Though the ban on religious symbols including headgear and forcible integration of Muslims are not just confined to France, as Germany and some other countries have been pursuing a similar policy, still it is gratifying to note that the local-born Muslims are getting more politicised. In the process and at a very difficult juncture in their history they are also receiving support from several other think tanks and civic groups. The studies by scholars such as Jocelyn Cesari and Farhad Khosrokhavan are focusing on economic and social issues, as confronted by the smaller Muslim communities in local estates, and are not enamoured of grand narratives by Kepel or Levy. Neil MacMaster sums up his succinct assessment on a note of caution: 'What we may be seeing in France is a strange gap between current Islamophobia, whipped up by the racist FN or by secularist Socialists and specialists like Kepel, and a deeper level of change toward integration and adaptation'. Though a population of five to six million makes Muslims a visible minority in France, several other communities such as Sikhs, Jews and Catholics are equally perturbed over a uniformist secularist juggernaut.[52] However, the same Muslims, despite their annoyance with the French official unilateralism, were holding processions and rallies in September 2004 in support of the release of the two French journalists, who had been taken hostage by Iraqi militants.[53] Perhaps it is time for Berman, Kepel and other proponents of modernity to open their vintage windows towards the horizons nearer their neighbourhoods!

NOTES

1. The hypocrisy of some well known journalists and other writers came into full view in early 2004. While a decade earlier, in the wake of the Rushdie affair, they had criticised Muslims for being barbarians, when Robert Kilroy-Silk published his racist pieces in the *Sunday Express* targeting Arabs, these proponents of human rights including Fay Weldon, Simon Jenkins and Connor O' Cruise, all opted for a mysterious silence. For a pertinent reminder, see Yasmin Alibhai-Brown, 'The West must get humble and honest—fast', *Independent*, 5 January 2004.

2. Individuals like Zalmay Khalilzad, Hamid Karzai, Ahmed Chalabi, Iyad Allawi and such other political, ideological and even intellectual 'exiles' have often worked in close league with oil companies and several public and private agencies in Washington. With their powerful backers in the US government and multinational corporations and aided by some 'native' authenticity, these individuals are apparently success stories in acquiring coveted jobs. Like their American colleagues, specialising on foreign countries, these individuals, in some cases, assume professorships at well known American universities occupying well-endowed chairs.

3. The cases of Germany and France certainly baffle many observers. On the one hand, both Chancellor Schroeder and President Chirac resisted the Anglo American efforts to launch the invasion of Iraq without a UN mandate, while simultaneously they supported legislation to ban headscarves, which affected millions of Muslims in both the countries. Some people thought that Chirac was pandering to the racist lobbies so as to seek more votes for his party by making scapegoats of Muslims whereas, to others, it was the typical hegemonic form of secularism vetoing tolerance. However, even the critics of scarves or other headdresses felt that secularism without tolerance and freedom of expression and lifestyles is in itself a new tyranny. The majority of analysts felt that the Franco–German Muslim communities, already beleaguered in socio-economic areas, would be further disadvantaged by this legislation which apparently seemed to have a majority support from non-Muslims in those countries. However, women's demonstrations in France and elsewhere on 18 January 2004 elicited various responses though Muslim women claimed not to have been under peer pressure at all. See, 'Anti-Muslim feeling in France takes on a murderous angle' (leader) *Independent*, 19 January 2004; and Natasha Walter, 'When the veil means freedom', *Guardian*, 20 January 2004. (Quoting from Leila Ahmad and Salma Yakub, she finds the veil affording space to Muslim women instead of repressing them)

4. For instance, see Daniel Pipes, 'There are no Moderates: Dealing with Fundamentalist Islam', *The National Interest*, Fall 1995.

5. Daniel Pipes, *Slave Soldiers and Islam: The Genesis of a Military System* (New Haven, 1981).

6. Pipes' explanation makes Muslim rulers appear like Ante-Bellum Southern plantation owners who used African-Americans for plantation economies, though he does not refer to it.

7. Following *Roots* and powerful epochs such as *The Autobiography of Malcolm X* or through the literature and oral traditions of the Nation of Islam, contemporary knowledge of Muslim victims of European slavery is gradually expanding. It is here that Pipes's perpetrators themselves turn into victims.

8. Daniel Pipes, *Militant Islam Reaches America* (New York, 2002), pp. xi-xiii.

9. Quoted from *Jerusalem Post* (31 December 1999) in ibid., p. 4.

10. Interestingly, he is not the only one who would divest the Arabs of any contribution to the world heritage. A former Labour MP and well-known BBC presenter, Robert Kilroy-Silk, in his weekly column in a newspaper used similar pejorative terms in demonising the Arabs. To him, the world did not owe them anything and even the oil was discovered, used and paid for by the Westerners. The Arabs, to Kilroy-Silk, were basically 'suicide bombers, limb amputators and women repressors'. See, *Sunday Express*, 4 and 11 January 2004. On protests from Muslims and the Commission for Racial Equality, the BBC suspended his programme though the newspaper and the columnist both refused to apologise for such an explicit and uncalled for denigration. *Independent on Sunday*, 11 January 2004. Instead, he was

supported by many viewers of Sky-Fox Network, an overwhelming majority (92 per cent) of whom felt that the BBC should have not suspended his programme. Sky TV News Poll, 11 January 2004.

11. Pipes, pp. 38-51.

12. Jessica Stern, 'Pakistan's Jihad Culture', *Foreign Affairs*, November–December 2000.

13. Pipes, p. 103.

14. Ibid., p. 112.

15. Ibid., p. 218.

16. Pipes is not the first or the only Western scholar to have focused on the NOI's tensions with the Jewry, several others have offered similar views and have more often apportioned the blame to the former. One wonders whether it is out of a newfound love for Jews, or, merely racism, or simply Islamophobia that has made such writers offer such slanted views. See, Gilles Kepel, *Allah in the West*, London, 1997, chapters 1-3. The French scholar on Islam, like Pipes, offers a detailed narrative of the Nation's critique of American Jews. It singles out Minister Louis Farrakhan for his outspoken comments and soft corner for some Muslim leaders.

17. Pipes, pp. 227-41.

18. Like Karen Armstrong, Fred Halliday and several other British scholars with balanced views on Muslim history and politics, there are several American writers whose integrity is beyond dispute. Works by Roxanne L. Euben, Joel Benin, Joe Storks, O.J. Stewart and Robert Van De Veyer are certainly noteworthy.

19. This penultimate chapter, 'Jihad and the Professors' was published in a leading British academic magazine, to be followed by several letters in the subsequent weeks mostly challenging Pipes's way of naming and 'shaming' his American colleagues besides censuring him for his myopic views on Islam. See *Times Higher Education Supplement (THES)*, 3, 10 and 17 October 2003.

20. For details, see Tariq Ramadan, 'An oft-repeated 'truth'', *Guardian*, 31 August 2004.

21. Michael Mann, *Incoherent Empire* (London, 2003), quoted in Laurie Taylor, 'Mann vs. military giant', *THES*, 9 January 2004.

22. Michael Moore is rather too vocal in suggesting that white men have caused most of these acts of collective violence and even the spread of gun culture, certain diseases, or ethnic cleansing. Michael Moore, *Stupid White Men* (New York, 2002; especially the chapter, 'Whitey').

23. Paul Berman, *Terror and Liberalism* (New York, 2003), pp. 76-8. Berman was preceded by a British author in focusing on Qutb as the precursor of contemporary Political Islam. Malise Ruthven, a former BBC correspondent, had zeroed in on Qutb and Mawdudi for their articulation of Islamic activism. As admitted by him, his volume was rushed in the wake of 9/11. See, Malise Ruthven, *A Fury for God: The Islamist Attack on America* (London, 2002).

24. Ibid., p. 17.

25. Mary Kaldor, 'Armageddon myths', review of ibid., in *New Statesman*, 26 May 2003.

26. Ibid.

27. Berman, p. 108.

28. Ibid., 112. The travesty is that Berman, further down in the same chapter, aggregates all the Islamist movements into one category being monolithically run by Al-Qaeda as the vanguard group. Such a view is totally incorrect as there are several political and intellectual movements across the Muslim world and many of them have serious differences over interpretations and strategies. It is like overlooking the diversity within the West and identifying it simply as one Christian or Ultra Right monolith.

29. Other than writers reviewed in this study, several other analysts including Christopher Hitchens, John Keegan, Nick Cohen and Francis Wheen feel that Islam is somehow averse to modernity. To them, modernity may have its problems yet Enlightenment remains sacrosanct to any criticism. See, Francis Wheen, *How Mumbo Jumbo Conquered the World*, London, 2003. See the review of this volume by Johann Hari in *Independent on Sunday*, 15 February 2004. While most of the writers have been against the war on Iraq, some such as John Keegan have supported it due to their views of Islam as an anti-Enlightenment ideology. For a selection of such views, see *Guardian* (Saturday Review), 14 February 2004.

30. Thus, it is not surprising that all these *liberal* writers and analysts fully supported the invasion of Iraq. Like New Labour they are Neo-Liberals whose ideological outlook is closer to Neoconservatives

31. Berman, p. 118. One wonders about this special window that opens not just on Manhattan's skyline but also across the Muslim regions!

32. Ibid., p. 195.

33. See, Mariam Rawi, 'Rule of the rapists', *Guardian*, 12 February 2004.

34. A very good expose of the headscarf issue and a rather paranoid French official viewpoint, see Natasha Walter, op. cit.

35. For a useful discussion, see Neil MacMaster, 'Islamophobia in France and the 'Algerian Problem'', in Emran Qureshi and Michael A. Sells, (eds.) *The New Crusades: Constructing the Muslim Enemy* (New York, 2003), pp. 307-10.

36. Gilles Kepel, *Bad Moon Rising: A Chronicle of the Middle East Today* (London, 2003).

37. The focus, like in the case of Paul Berman, remains on Sayyid Qutb. See, his *The Roots of Radical Islam* trans. by J. Rothschild (London, 2005; reprint).

38. Gilles Kepel, *The War for Muslim Minds: Islam and the West* (London, 2004). At places, the book appears impressionistic and less orientated towards interpretive research. Beginning with the failure of the Oslo Accords, the volume reviews Neo-Conservatism in the United States, the situation in Iraq and Saudi Arabia whereas the last section deals with the Muslims in the West.

In a way, this work combines his earlier works on North Africa and the Muslim Diaspora,

39. Gaby Wood, 'Je suis un superstar', *Observer*, 15 June 2003.

40. See various reviews on his work in: www. Periscope.blogs.com

41. Bernard-Henri Levy, *Who Killed Daniel Pearl?* transl. by James X. Mitchell (London, 2004), p. xix.

42. Ibid., p. 360.

43. Ibid., p. 266.

44. Ibid., p. xix. He finds himself once again 'in chaotic, feverish Karachi, with its wet, smoky autumn sky…Karachi is the only city in the world where mafia are so much a part of the mainstream of life in the city that their clashes, their incessant split-ups, their compromises, have the same importance as episodes of political life back home in the West'. P. 179.

45. Ibid., pp. 179-80.

46. Ibid., p. 150.

47. Ibid., p. 101.

48. Chris Petit, 'Searching for the truth', *Guardian* (Review), 21 February 2004.

49. Marianne Pearl, with Sarah Crichton, *A Mighty Heart* (London, 2003), pp. 150-2. She is critical of Levy for claiming to know Daniel Pearl's feelings before his murder and finds a Pakistani police captain to be the real hero, 'who risked his own life trying to recover her husband'. Emma Brockes, 'Living bitter is living dead', *Guardian*, 20 April 2004. In fact, in her book it is this 'Captain', who comes out as a hero while she does not dwell on any nuclear-related details that the French philosopher dramatises in his work.

50. See, Johann Hari, 'A Very Political pin-up', *Independent*, 8 March 2004.

51. He often comes back to the slain Afghan leader by eulogising Mahsud for championing 'moderate' Islam. Levy had met him during the 1980s when the Tajik commander was fighting the Russians and then visited him again in Badakhshan during the 1990s while he was aligned with the Russians to fight the Taliban. Like the West Pakistanis in the former East Pakistan, the Taliban, according to the impassioned French writer, were totalitarian tormentors. His forays into other trouble spots, presented heroically and prosaically, appear to build him into the champion of the oppressed all over the world. One of his recent works focuses on the bloodshed in the Sudan, Sri Lanka, Colombia, Burundi and Angola, as he narrates his dramatic adventures amongst the oppressors and the oppressed, though misses out the culpability of external forces in spawning and arming such conflicts. See, Bernard-Henri Levy, *War, Evil and the End of History*, transl. by Charlotte Mandell (London, 2004).

52. It was reported that five thousand Sikhs in and around Paris were deeply upset over the headgear issue and many of them threatened to emigrate. See *Guardian*, 23 January 2004. The BBC, in its report, highlighted the dilemma

of about 3,000 Sikh students in Paris to whom turban and beard were too important to be shunned. www.bbc.c.uk/southasia

53. Based on extensive media reports and personal visit to France, 1-6 September 2004.

4

OLD ENEMY, NEW WARRIORS: WESTERN POLEMICISTS, POLITICIANS AND PUBLICISTS ON ISLAM

'We should invade their countries, kill their leaders and convert them to Christianity'.
    – Ann Coulter in her column on Muslims, 13 September 2001

'What is perhaps most disturbing about the Kilroy-Silk episode…,is that he plainly knew he could rely on the support of many Britons in expressing his anti-Arab and anti-Muslims views…Such (racist) incidents testify to a culture of active racism in Britain that is the product of levels of ignorance inadequately addressed by education authorities and fostered by the sneering, casual racism of much of the tabloid press'.
    – William Roff, a letter, *New Statesman*, 26 January 2004, p. 34

'We are not hated for who we are. We are hated for what we do. It is not our principles that have spawned pandemic hatred of America in the Islamic world. It is our policies'.
    – Patrick Buchanan, *When the Right Went Wrong*,
    New York, 2004, p. 80

'It is absurd to argue that the decision of a Muslim woman to cover her hair is inherently evidence that she is oppressed, any more than a Sikh man's turban—also among the religious symbols to be banned in French schools—is evidence that he is being oppressed'.
    – Natasha Walter, 'When the veil means freedom',
    Guardian, 20 January 2004

'And as the public response to Robert Kilroy-Silk's recent gratuitous anti-Arab rant in the *Daily Express* has shown, most agree that Muslims are universally dangerous people hell-bent on destroying the West'.
      – *Cherwell*, Oxford Student magazine, 16 January 2004, p. 10

It is not just the known professors and analysts such as Bernard Lewis, Daniel Pipes, Paul Berman, Gilles Kepel, John Keegan and Bernard-Henri Levy who have provided ample material to the politicians and several racist outfits to mount their campaign against Islam, a whole generation of literary and media personalities have joined the bandwagon of Islamophobia. While Arundhati Roy, Noam Chomsky and several other writers may focus on hegemonic Western polices, several renowned writers such as V.S. Naipaul and pre-eminent Church personalities continue to spew their hatred and anger towards Muslims. Such a multi-layered discourse of contempt and dismissal exaggerates a presumptuous Muslim threat to the Western civilisation while concurrently casting Muslims as barbarians. Both the extreme forms of exaggeration and trivialization of Muslims not only provide fodder to the culpable forces they equally offer a wider convergence among a vast array of groups and powers banking on racism, exclusion, derision and violence.

Viewing Islam both as a victor and as a victim is nothing new yet the proponents come from a wide variety of backgrounds and disciplines with powerful instruments and trajectories at their disposal. They are backed by strong establishments and publicize their inimical views through global print and visual media, which is again anchored upon powerful cultural expressions such as English, French, Italian, or German. Thus, Islamophobes cannot be dismissed merely as partisan or deranged individuals; these are articulate, widely read and immensely dangerous clusters of ambitious and energised interest groups enjoying institutional support and global outreach. They peculiarise Islam; view it as a repressive dogma and focus on the status of Muslim women by making veil and related issues the touchstones of their own moral and civilisational superiority. They overlook the role of modernity and colonisation in engendering the unprecedented cases of collective violence on an international scale in the last few centuries and rather focus on the positive attributes of Enlightenment, with Islam as its nemesis. To them, Islam-bashing is more than a leisure past-time; instead it is a full-time pursuit and a moral espousal with a strong intellectual justification. It is safe to suggest that, in most if not all the cases, strong elements of ignorance and arrogance underlie such suppositions and stratagem. In a continuation of the last three chapters, we turn to individuals like V.S. Naipaul, Patrick Buchanan and Ann Coulter as we unearth a whole generation of missionaries and journalists, who have already transformed Neo-Orientalism into a flourishing multi-disciplinary enterprise. To them, Muslim men are all bearded, turbaned, chest beating and Kalashnikov toting terrorists whose women are veiled multitudes entirely draped in black and also a living agony. In between just these two familiar caricatures, most of the Western literati, academia, media and other polemicists would not recognise any diversity or vicissitudes characterising 1.5 billion Muslims, nor would they be eager to explore the seamy role of foreign (mostly Western!) interventions, always at the expense of local communities.

Naipaul, A Leading Polemicist

V.S. Naipaul is certainly one of the most influential and articulate image-makers when it comes to post-colonial societies such as India, Trinidad and the non-Arab Muslim world. Even before his Nobel Prize and knighthood, Naipaul, of Trinidadian-Indian descent, was a well-known fiction writer and opinion maker. Born in 1936 and having studied at Oxford before embarking on a full-time career as a writer during the 1950s, Naipaul has never been far from controversy whether it is his relationship with his father, his colleagues and disciples like Paul Theroux, or secular India and the post-1979 Muslim world. Along with works of fiction like *Miguel Street, A House for Mr. Biswas* and *A Bend in the River,* Naipaul wrote, among others, two narratives on India: *India: A Wounded Civilisation* and *India: A Million Mutinies*, which turned out to be quite controversial for many Indians.

Soon after Khomeini's Revolution in 1979, Naipaul, amidst a growing accent on Political Islam in the non-Arab world, decided to visit Indonesia, Iran, Pakistan and Malaysia resulting in his book *Among the Believers: An Islamic Journey* (1981). The volume earned him notoriety in the Muslim world and was seen as an impressionistic reportage, often lacking in substantial evidence anchored in rigorous research. In 1995, he returned to these countries for five months and the result was a rejoinder, *Beyond Belief*, which is not only tinged with satire but is equally imbued with sweeping generalisations about these predominantly non-Arab Muslim societies accounting for the two-thirds of the global Muslim population. Written during the Bosnian tragedy and accompanying ethnic cleansing and thousands of rape cases of mostly Muslim women, the book was widely hailed by liberals, conservatives and Islamophobes, who saw in it a serious and rather debilitating critique of the non-Arab Muslims. The book fed into ever-increasing anti-Muslim feelings, especially when the former cold war warriors needed a new enemy and Huntington had already given his verdict of a cultural clash with Islam as a civilisational threat characterized by bloody borders.

Of course, like his other works especially on India, Naipaul's own identity crisis was a significant reason for his life-long pursuit of revolting diatribes about non-White communities. He is quite unsparing of Islam and communism, as, to him, they both console the harassed without ameliorating their lot. His tirades against the Arabs—like those of Robert Kilroy-Silk and several others—refuse to recognise them as cultured peoples by positing them as imperialists who have erased the histories and identities of billions of others.[1] He does not realise that Islam did not mean a reassertion of Arabism, it had rather denoted the pre-Muhammad Arab past itself as *jahliya* (age of ignorance). In the same vein, Arab Muslims did not simply displace the Iranian past and identity, they helped them usher in a new synthesis. It may not be out of place to suggest that even Shiaism, popularised by the Turkish Safavid dynasty in Iran, was partly a rebuke to the Arabs, though millions of Shias in Southern Iraq and Bahrain also happen to be Arab.

While his *Among the Believers*, at a few places, ascribed some aesthetics to Islam, this new volume finds Muslims devious, aggressive, thoughtless and irredeemable, who pursue a religion embodying foolish, taxing and inflexible dogmas. According to him, this patriarchal religion is practised without any critique or introspection as the followers idealise a romantic past and demand the formation of an Islamic state unaware of its serious cost or even sheer impossibility. Naipaul does not realise that the Muslim demand for an Islamic state means rejection of injustice, corruption and humiliation that millions of them go through daily. Certainly, both activists and Muslim governments use Islam to justify their stances and interests yet none denies the fact that Islam inherently manifests social justice and compassion. Like the Orientalists and their successors, Naipaul finds Islam totally oppressive and especially for women it is too coercive as it demands exclusion, domesticity and veiling. Naipaul does not take into account that as researched by a whole generation of Muslim feminists such as Fatima Mernissi, Leila Ahmed, Asma Barlas, Riffat Hasan and several others, Islam offers a secure space to women and other underprivileged communities. It is the feudal structures and the clergy who are primarily responsible for women losing out besides the lack of democratic institutions that women, like other underprivilged groups, tend to remain disempowered. A veil or even a scarf could be oppressive to some while to others it may be a means of empowerment, though this is not to suggest that the Muslim women live in an ideal situation. They are, in fact, a major section of a vastly disempowered Muslim world where economic and political marginalisation, owing to internal and external factors, keeps on claiming a major cost.

Interestingly, Naipaul's new book is dedicated to his Pakistani wife, who is perhaps responsible for giving him some of the details on the life of Nawab Abbasi of Bahawalpur. Nadira Alvi, a journalist herself, comes from this town in South-western Pakistan.[2] Naipaul is unforgiving to Arabs for imposing their Arabised religion on non-Arabs who, for centuries, have tended to deny their own histories to reclaim Arab history as theirs. At the start of his

'Preface', on the very first page, Naipaul is anxious to convey his personal judgement on Islam, which he persistently equates with the Arab imperial culture:

Islam is in its origins an Arab religion. Everyone not an Arab who is a Muslim is a convert. Islam is not simply a matter of conscience or private belief. It makes imperial demands. A convert's world view alters. His holy places are in Arab lands; his sacred language is Arabic. His idea of history alters. He rejects his own; he becomes, whether he likes it or not, a part of the Arab story. The convert has to turn away from everything that is his...the turning away has to be done again and again.

Naipaul fails to recognise that most Europeans, Americans and Australasians are converts to Christianity (and to other *Eastern* religions) in the same sense; the East Asians and South-East Asian Buddhists are converts as well, since Christianity came from the Middle East and Buddhism originated in India. Thus, the contemporary problems in these societies cannot be attributed solely to conversion that took place centuries ago. In the same manner, if presumably Hinduism is not native to India that does not mean that Hindus cannot be good Indians until or unless they return to their pre-Hindu (Dravidian) past. Conversions to Islam happened mostly without coercion and the local sufis played a crucial role in its propagation amongst usually underprivileged people in otherwise highly stratified societies. In fact, Muslim cultural and political centres such as Delhi, Agra, Lahore, Constantinople and Salonika until very recently were Muslim minority cities.

Islam's classical texts are in Arabic and like the European classics in Greek and Latin, the scholars prefer immersion in these languages but there is no compulsion in Arabising oneself merely to prove one's Islamicity. Islam's coexistence with numerous other plural societies has been unique and more enduring than that of its counterparts and though there is quite a bit of violence in the name of Islam including against Muslims, still it will be ahistoric to suggest that Islam only permeates conflicts. It is like assuming that since Muslims in Britain are comparatively less advantaged than some other communities, it may be because of Islam. In the same Afro-Asian world or in Diaspora, Ismaili Muslims happen to be usually well placed and prosperous and their Islamicity does not stop them from being rich. Also, how would one justify the poverty, violence and stratification in non-Muslim regions including the American Hemisphere and Africa?[3] Going for pilgrimage or wearing Arab dresses by some people still would not mean Arabisation of these societies which are inhabited by native and indigenous communities and where the folk and liberal cultural traditions seek pride in locating their pre-Islamic past. Educated Pakistanis have never denied their Indus Valley culture nor have Turks, Iranians, Iraqis or South-East Asians ever underrated their pre-Islamic histories. Even becoming a Muslim is not a painstaking experience, though the religious practices may require more time and energy.

Between Naipaul's hateful and presumably taxing Muslim Arabia and a romanticised Greater India, nothing genuine, original and positive exists. His Greater India includes present-day Pakistan and the countries of Indonesia and Malaysia. He does not know their history well and as a 'New Hindu' imagines a trans-regional Hindu civilisation which might have been left asunder by Muslims. It is only the Europeans in recent times who helped the Hindus resuscitate their identity. Tracing the history of Islam in Indonesia, he strongly feels nostalgic for its supposedly Hindu and Buddhist past, which is again contentious as there is no consensus on these islands ever having been abodes of these two Indian religions. The existence of a Greater Mother India is still mythical and not proven by history—though lingual and architectural similarities exist even today yet dating from more recent times. His verdict is thus quite controversial and also betrays his own prejudices about the 'new' enemy that he has found since he developed closer affinities with Hindutva: 'Islam and Europe had arrived here at the same time as competing imperialisms, and between them they had destroyed the long Buddhist–Hindu past. Islam had moved on here, to this part of Greater India, after its devastation of India proper, turning the religious-cultural light of the subcontinent, so far as this region was concerned, into the light of a dead star.'[4] This is not only incorrect it is equally polemical especially when Naipaul, in his prefatory remarks, had promised to offer the honest accounts of his interviewees. Instead, he proffers a dangerous, partisan and even vicious verdict on two vast regions without being aware of their histories.

One of the greatest contributions of Islam in India was the formation of a synthesised Indo-Muslim culture, also called the Perso-Indian culture which permeates every walk of life in South Asia, from languages, literature, architecture, arts, cuisine, music, clothes, folk traditions to the globalisation of India until the British conquest. For instance, the Mughals (1526–1858) not only patronised Hindu artists and aristocracy they preserved their holy books, temples and even allowed their Hindu wives to pursue their own religious practices inside the palaces. Except for a few solitary cases, Muslim rulers preserved and protected Hindu, Buddhist and Jain scriptures, while allowing Jews and Christians to fully contribute towards a plural culture. Indian pluralism flourished under the Muslims as it became the heartland of various cultural and intellectual traditions, and despite their Central Asian origins, all the Muslim dynasties settled in India and preferred it over their ancestral lands. One wonders, how Naipaul could view them as the destroyers of Greater India. While recording his meetings with several Indonesian Muslims, such as Abdul Wahid and others, he makes several glaring mistakes. For instance, while commenting on Madden, a US-educated Indonesian, he blames a well-known Pakistani modernist at the University of Chicago for misdirecting him. Naipaul, without checking his facts, describes Fazlur Rahman as 'the Pakistani fundamentalist fanatic...himself enjoying, bizzarely, academic freedom at the University of Chicago, and sleeping safe and sound every night, protected by laws, and far away from the mischief he was wishing on his countrymen at home'.[5] Professor Fazlur Rahman was a reputed Muslim modernist—perhaps one of the vanguard—and had to leave his native Pakistan in the late 1960s as the clerics turned against his emphasis on the reinterpretation of Islam. Thus, he was far from Naipaul's fanatic, who is a different person altogether and has been a recent supporter of the Taliban.

Islam is the main enemy for Naipaul and it has to be dealt a blow every now and then, as he notes:

> The cruelty of Islamic fundamentalism is that it allows only to one people—the Arabs, the original people of the Prophet—a past, and sacred places, pilgrimages and earth reverences. These sacred Arab places have to be the sacred places of all the converted peoples. Converted peoples have to strip themselves of their past; of converted peoples nothing is required but the purest faith (if such a thing can be arrived at), Islam, submission. It is the most uncompromising kind of imperialism.[6]

Only a polemicist, imbued with a superficial view of history, could hold such views as they do not reflect any historical truth or objectivity. An intellectual of Naipaul's stature here volunteers to lead the neoconservatives and Islamophobes. Excluding 200 millions Arab Muslims—not to talk of Christian Arabs, who do not have any problem about their being non-Muslim—Naipaul finds more than one billion Muslims of various hues and kinds to have lost their histories and identities. This monolithicisation of Islam is a redundant and rather obscure position since it plainly ignores a vast mosaic that Islamic civilisation itself embodies, varying from creed to class.

Islam, despite some essential unity in belief, celebrated pluralism as was seen for the first time in Spain, Italy and the Balkans. Naipaul may need to know that Muslim minorities vanished from the Christian heartlands—the various *Andalusias*—while non-Muslims survived and even prospered in the predominantly Muslim regions. In Iran, he only finds disillusioned Shia intellectuals whereas the ayatollahs are all hangmen. His sojourn in Isfahan makes him nostalgic for the Zoroastrian past and he brings in his favourite, India, to show that the Parsees survived and flourished only in their Indian Diaspora where tolerance reigns. It is rather strange that while writing so soon after the Ayodhya incident of the demolition of the Babri Mosque and slaughter of thousands of Muslims at places like Mumbai, Naipaul only finds the example of Indian Parsees to score some quick points vis-à-vis Muslim regions.

He is an abrasive supporter of imperialism as he applauds Western colonialism for Hindu India's retrieval from its lost past, of which Iran and other Muslim regions appear to be resentful of. It is obvious that either Naipaul is unaware of the discourse on imperialism, colonialism and modernity or is totally disinterested in immersing himself in their critique. He does not shy away from mimicking the imperialists when it comes to offering his opinions and rather asserts that many communities had originally welcomed colonialism. He had harboured an early fear of a Muslim in his Trinidadian neighbourhood but never seems to outgrow his views on Islam.[7] Islam, like communism, remains a ghost, which not only requires exorcising but also a total displacement. He does not care to read about the countries and their religious histories before undertaking his tours, as he admitted in an interview to *Newsweek*.[8] A man of strong views and a supporter of the demolition of Ayodhya Mosque in 1992 by Hindu Kar Sevaks, Naipaul has been an avid admirer of the BJP, and accompanied by his Pakistani Muslim wife, he has never shied away from offering his personal appreciation. He enthusiastically welcomed the BJP's victory in the Indian elections in 1995 and its cultural onslaught ever since to Hinduise India. As an ardent supporter of Hindutva, he never minced his laudatory words by declaring it 'a mightily creative process.'[9] It is rather axiomic that the Nobel Prize Committee in their recommendations in 2001, had applauded him for his critical analysis of fundamentalism.[10]

However, it is in Pakistan that Naipaul is at his crudest in his attack on Islam, the Muslim state and its architects and inhabitants. Nothing pleases him more than lashing out on Islam for everything wrong in this young polity. Women, peasants and servants fair abysmally low in this 'criminal enterprise' which was idealised by Muhammad Iqbal—the poet-philosopher—in his address to the Indian Muslims in 1930 at Allahabad. Naipaul, of course, cannot forgive the creation of Pakistan, which, to a supporter of Hindutva and of a Great Hindu India, was a sin committed through a heinous act of separation. His respondents and contacts in Pakistan might have delved into their own nostalgia, yet he sees in them the pathetic cases of lost souls. Some of them, like a certain Shahbaz, became revolutionaries *a la* Che Guevara while attending private schools and Oxbridge in Britain. A few others, after their higher degrees abroad, turned even more oppressive to their serfs and servants whom they kept dirty and humiliated like their feudal, uncouth ancestors. Pakistani advocates, journalists and students, to Naipaul's consternation, repeat the mantra of Islam while tracing their origins from non-Indian lands. Naipaul does not shy away from betraying the trust of his companions and hosts, as was notably explained by Eqbal Ahmad:

> There is another aspect to this, which is rather typical of this type of Orientalist, racist scholarship. That is, Naipaul cannibalizes his friends. The Shahbaz of his book is a man who is my friend, Ahmed Rashid. He took Naipaul as a personal guest during his six-week visit to Pakistan, showed him around, and introduced him to a myriad of people, including me. Ahmed was generous to a fault. He dropped a lot of other things he was doing to help Naipaul in his work. Naipaul has repaid him by writing a caricature. He changed his name but only in such a way that every educated Pakistani would recognize Ahmed Rashid in that book and will pity him for having befriended this cannibal of a man. Naipaul is...a very sick man. The book is actually beyond belief, perhaps because it's a book driven by ghosts. Islam is one of his ghosts.[11]

It is Islam, which, to Naipaul, continues to rob and deny non-Arab Muslims of their roots, and is the bane of their problems. To him, this is the typical 'Muslim convert's attitude to the land where he lives. To the convert his land is of no religious or historical importance; its relics are of no account; only the sands of Arabia are sacred'.[12] One wonders what would Naipaul say to Zionism and Israel, and in case of holding similar views on them would he be able to air them so vocally and get away with it! Pakistanis are uprooted, repressive and immature, that is what he finds time and again, though he prefers a visit to Lahore's red light area to substantiate his claims. He finds Pakistanis continuously berating one another 'because of their uncertainty in the wider world'.[13] Of course, he cannot forget and forgive that Pakistanis are overwhelmingly Muslim, and had opted to separate from his 'Greater India'. Islam is the reason for their turning away from their Indianness: 'It is a dreadful mangling of history. It is a convert's view; that is all that can be said for it. History has become a kind of neurosis. Too much has to be ignored or angled; there is too much fantasy. This fantasy isn't in the books alone; it affects people's lives.'[14]

The inhabitants of the Indus Valley converted to Islam more than a thousand years ago and one wonders if for them, according to Naipaul, history stopped then and there. He is ignorant of the fact that it was not the Arabs who ruled India; instead, all the ruling Muslim dynasties happened to be Turkish, with one or two exceptions, and they too happened to be Afghans. Muslims did come into India over the successive centuries but most of them were natives who opted for this religion to escape caste and class-based oppression. Islam, especially as preached by sufis, offered equality and human respect along with establishing trans-territorial linkages, though it will be incorrect to assume that given the Muslim rule, the entire Muslim community in South Asia had some inherent advantage over non-Muslims.

Naipaul, in his prefatory observations, promised to be just a listener to others so as to offer their accounts as honestly and as unadulterated as he could. But, ironically, every page is resplendent with his opinions, verdicts, and even blasé generalisations. However, in Pakistan, he is at his best in his quest for exotic details to tinge his narratives, and that is why he visits the prostitutes in Lahore, though one may never know whether his aim was to ridicule their poverty or merely to show a seamy side of Pakistani culture. Maybe, Pakistan is no different from several other nations where, despite a greater accent on religion, life, in general reflects its own mundane and often bitter realities—though focusing on shadowy areas around London's King's Cross would not be a sufficient source to locate the multiplicity of a metropolitan culture. Naipaul's narratives of the last Abbasi ruler of the princely state of Bahawalpur is certainly a bird's eye view of a decadent princely India of irresponsible, corrupt and sexist rulers who enjoyed full protection and respect from the British government. There is no doubt the Nawab used his British and Arab connections to perpetuate his lax and often decadent rule over a population which was simply helpless. It is true that he, like his other counterparts across India, exploited religious symbols but his advice and security came from the British residents including Penderel Moon. The Nawab of Bahawalpur, like the Nizam of Hyderabad or 565 princes and rajas across South Asia, represented an intentional waywardness of the Raj, though Naipaul apportions the blame only to Islam while being irreverent to a history of the entire millennium in lower Punjab:

> The Arab faith, the Arab language, Arab names, the fez: twelve hundred years after the conquest of Sindh, this affirmation of separateness, of imperial and racial and religious authority: there probably has been no imperialism like that of Islam and the Arabs. The Gauls, after five hundred years of Roman rule, could cover their old gods and reverences; those beliefs hadn't died; they lay just below the Roman surface. But Islam seeks as an article of the faith to erase the past; the believers in the end honour Arabia alone; they have nothing to return to.[15]

Ashoka promulgated Buddhism in his Indian empire whereas the Romans adopted Christianity, and the same has been the case with different conquering rulers and ideologies. Even long after their cherished Revolution and secularism, the French were converting people to Frenchness—a process that did not aver any hesitation. As late as 2004, in the name of a majoritarian ideology, they disallowed religious minorities from donning their headdresses. In the 1960s—during a period of upheavals and human rights— France was responsible for murdering more than a million Algerians whose only fault was their demand for independence. France had done the same in Indo-China and other colonies, where citizenship of France was not a right but a privilege available to those who renounced their own religion such as Islam. The former Tunisian president, Habib Bourgiba, long after independence, chose to appease the French by suppressing the Islamo-Arab identity of his people. He appeared on television drinking juice during the month of fasting and openly encouraged Tunisians not to fast during Ramadan. He displaced Arabic in favour of French the way France, even thirty years after independence, was disallowing Algerian Islamists any role in running their country. France vetoed the election results in 1990s, which could have brought the Islamists into power, and since then Algeria has become once more a cauldron of bloodshed and agony.

A small country like Belgium chose to eliminate hundreds of thousands of the Congolese in the late nineteenth century to appease King Leopold's insatiable avarice for collecting diamonds. Soon, the British, egged on by an imperialist, Cecil Rhodes, were engaged in the Zulu wars[16] while the Germans during 1903–4, eliminated more than one hundred thousand South-West African tribesmen (Namibians) who demanded civic rights while refusing to vacate their ancestral lands for German planters. Earlier, Portugal and Spain had unleashed their forces of colonialism, conversion, and conquests that totally changed the demography of so many continents, and the victims continue to suffer even today. La Casas would chastise fellow Iberians for their mistreatment of the Natives but would countenance enslavement of millions of Africans and Muslims. The Russians under the Csars like Ivan the Terrible, frequently promulgated pogroms of Muslims, Jews and other minorities in the East—something which has not ended even today with Yeltsin and Putin applying unchecked force on Chechnya and other defiant communities in the Caucuses. The only super power, after its Korea and Vietnam, did not hesitate to decimate two Muslim countries, though as admitted by several American writers, both the Afghans and Iraqis had no direct connection with 9/11.[17] Just to single out Islam as the only permeating tradition of a taxing imperialism is rather too selective and highly irresponsible. Naipaul's own ancestors accounted for an Indian Diaspora that the

British had created to meet their imperial needs in the three continents, and which a British historian has named as 'a new kind of slavery', since the slave trade had been formally outlawed in the previous decades.[18]

Naipaul mixes history with religion and the past with the present, the way he avoids a deeper analysis by hiding behind sweeping generalisations. A corrupt, Britain-returned and Britain-supported Nawab—despite his use of Arab symbols, is definitely a modern moron and a jewel of another empire which zealously protected its own hegemonic interests by perpetuating such inept intermediaries. Naipaul, while commenting on Nawab Abbasi, remembers Ibn Batuta, a Moroccan traveller to India, Europe, Africa and China in the fourteenth century and selectively uses his multiple marriages to show that the Nawab was living the age-old Arab tradition of polygamy. Naipaul's journey ends in Karachi as he focuses on the Muhajir Qaumi Movement, a lower middle class urban political party established for decentralisation that often fell victim to rhetorical leadership. However, Naipaul, like elsewhere, did not see anything positive in Pakistan and nor did he respect the dignity and privacy of his hosts from amongst the 'converted peoples'. His verdict is: these people, whether traditional Muslims or Westernised individuals, are all corrupt, repressive and lost in their own ways. He does not see any future for them as long as they do not retrieve that pre-Islamic past, but, hypothetically speaking, is there any guarantee that an uncritiqued Westernisation may hold all the truths and solutions to their predicament? One of his reviewers asks a pertinent question:

> Naipaul repeats vigorously that the Muslims are fools for turning their backs on necessary historical process. Fair enough. It is a fallow time for the community of Muhammad. They lack the energy to invent. So they fall back on the glories of a dead past. It is a shame. But if Islam is expected, rightly, to evolve, why should the certainties of liberalism remain forever fixed?[19]

Buchanan, Coulter and Muslim Bashing

The Neoconservatives castigate the Clinton interlude as a wayward and morally inept era, and since the Clinton–Lewinsky affair have pursued their push to the right. They consider the end of the Cold War as an American triumph and want to move further in demolishing other threats including the Muslim terrorists, who may be working in league with some liberals. They believe in strict immigration controls, support profiling non-White immigrants and visitors, and are deeply suspicious of the enemy from within. They are against pluralism, decry women's rights, see the disempowerment of the underprivileged in America due to their own intrinsic failure and are vehemently opposed to abortion and gay rights. They, like staunch Zionists, idealise a new Middle East, eventually made safe for Christianity. To them, America is for a moral good and cannot go wrong. Thus, by virtue of their significance in the most powerful country in the world and with the Republican Administration in Washington, these Neoconservatives have represented some of the most racist and exclusionary ideologies. Patrick Buchanan, a conservative in the style of Barry Goldwater and Ronald Reagan, has been very close to the White House as an advisor to the Republican Presidents, and following his expertise as a speechwriter, has carried on with his periodic columns, interviews and books on contemporary American politics, foreign policy, immigration and the need for an ideological shift to a Conservative Right. Buchanan, like Ann Coulter, is an articulate conservative and a former presidential hopeful, whose views reflect a considerable section of American society. Until the invasion of Iraq in 2003, he shared ideological unison with most of the Neoconservatives, yet, in recent time, has developed unease with some of their extreme views and an immense influence over Bush policies. He lashes out at the culture of the 1960s when liberalism took root in the West, and among its several ramifications, a decrease in the White population turned out to be a development of significant proportions. In his book, beckoning with a clear yet dramatic title, *The Death of the West,* he uses the race card to its hilt by giving out figures on the decrease of the White population amidst an influx of Asian and African immigrants. He writes as a master propagandist and plays on the insecurities of supremacist lobbies. To him, the steady arrival of the Islamic-Arab and African immigrants since the 1960s has created a nation within a nation that seems to benefit from growing demographic imbalances. America, to him, has already become a two-nation country. For instance, when President Nixon took his oath, there were nine million foreign-born citizens but at the time of George W. Bush's inaugural ceremony there were thirty million Americans who had been born abroad, in addition to another nine million illegal residents in the country. Reflective of the insecurities of the ultra right and trumpeting the racist mantra, according to Buchanan, the United States was annually receiving one million legal and another one-half million illegal immigrants. This demographic revolution with all its ethnic, economic and ideological connotations, to Buchanan, remains the most significant threat to a *traditional* America. It may, to him, balkanise the culture and would definitely fragment its single nationhood.[20]

Before the publication of Samuel Huntington's *Who We Are,*[21] Buchanan flagged the changing demographic contours of the United States by focusing on a steady increase in non-Anglo-Saxon groups. Like his own country, to Buchanan, Europe, was also a loser due to a zero population growth. Such a view is not only the cornerstone of neoracism it also proffers an argument routinely offered by racist outfits and tabloids across the North Atlantic regions and in Australia, despite the fact that a growing service sector and manufacturing annually need more working hands from abroad to replace an aging population. But Buchanan is not going to balance his extreme views by bringing in such facts; his is a unilateral verdict. While seeking an *other* among non-Whites, Buchanan is deeply worried about the future of the Euro-American world, which to him is essentially White and certainly superior of all:

In Africa, there will be 1.5 billion people. From Morocco to the Persian Gulf will be an Arab-Turkish-Islamic sea of 500 million. In South Asia will live 700 million Iranians, Afghans, Pakistanis, and Bangladeshis, and 1.5 billion Indians. There will be 300 million Indonesians, and China, with 1.5 billion people, will brood over Asia.[22]

He sounds more like an Antebellum Southern planter, or an Afrikaner supporter of Apartheid, and the KKK, BNP, or Le Pen must be proud of his predictions to scare more people into their fold. The United States and the rest of Western Europe have deeply benefited from immigration, and unlike the erstwhile racist typology of immigrants being a burden, they are a proven asset. On the contrary, mass immigration and refugee movements have been occurring within developing countries with Pakistan and Sudan heading the list, whereas the West strictly accepts only qualified professionals, trained by the poor taxpayers in the developing world. Owing to severe inequities in their own countries, however, many younger hopefuls keep on trying to reach Western shores, though a vast majority of them cannot make it.

Buchanan, as an astute politician and rhetorician, knows that by presenting monstrous figures and a scary future, he will be hyping up exclusivist nationalist feelings among his readers. His columns reverberate with shock-therapy, and by using non-White immigrants as a bait, he has been nefariously adding to the worries of Western people besides playing on their ignorance of the facts about immigration and its economic benefits. He blames the low turnover in the Western population on abortion, neo-feminism and the attitudinal changes brought in by leftist writings that have, to him, already replaced the classics. From amongst the Left, he selectively focuses on the Frankfurt School of Social Research which, in his opinion, has been responsible for the diminution of family, capitalism and Western culture. Following in the footsteps of Karl Marx, scholars like Adorno, Gramsci and Marcuse, through their development of critical theory, have been recruiting women and students as neo-proletariat. He sees a similar decline in Russia with its main threat of destabilisation coming from the Islamic South while the Turks may swamp Germany, making the entire European continent a 'dead man walking'.[23] He moves on to another predominantly Western country, Israel, where a low fertility among the Jews is supposedly faced with a greater population threat from the Palestinians. Jews have 4.5 children per woman while her Arab counterpart in the West Bank has 5.5 and in Gaza, 6.6. Though it is not a big difference, especially in view of the continuous policy of expulsions, killings and refugees not having a right to return, but still he notes: 'In twenty-five years, there will be two million Palestinians in Israel, seven million Palestinians living cheek-by-jowl with six million Jewish Israelis.' His support for Zionism does not allow him to pause and reflect on the Palestinian exodus thanks to the European legacies of colonialism and the Holocaust. Instead, he reaffirms his concern for Israel while ignoring the natives and soon reverts to his favourite theme of Islam 'rising again' though Muslims stay far behind in science and technology. Here, like other Neoconservatives, he minimises as well as maximises Islam as a civilisational threat and notes: 'But the Islamic world retains something the West has lost: a desire to have children and the will to carry on their civilization, cultures, families, and faith.'[24]

Buchanan is deeply concerned about violence, martyrdom and militancy, which he faithfully attributes to Muslims. It is the future of his own country that he sees within the context of external threats and refuses to see the role of immigrants in its *making*. Immigrants are pollutants who prefer separatism to integration besides imposing pagan norms over Christian virtues. Such a paranoia is quite typical of Neoconservatives whose state of siege refuses to see anything positive in other cultures.

In his subsequent book, Buchanan is wary of the overzealous Neoconservatives and censures them for leading the United States into a quagmire by pushing for the invasion of Iraq. *When the Right Went Wrong* is less emphatic about demography and more concerned about US foreign policies and relations with the Muslim world. Buchanan's tirade against Islam is slightly tempered down here though he still views it to be a major threat yet advises for withdrawal from the Muslim regions in pursuance of more even-handed policies towards the Israeli–Arab conflict. In this volume, he is nostalgic for Barry Goldwater and Ronald Reagan as he attempts to redefine conservatism by seeking its origins from

George Washington's farewell address of 1793. However, he begins his work by emphatically highlighting the American might, an unprecedented and rather exceptional reality never seen before in history:

> Not even the British Empire at its zenith dominated the world in the way the United States does today. US forces are deployed in lands that the soldiers of Victoria never saw. Our warships make port calls on all continents. Our military technology is generations ahead of any other nation's. Our GDP is 30 per cent of the global economy.[25]

However, all this, according to Buchanan, has been put at grave risk due to the daredevil policies of the Bush Administration as dictated by the Neoconservatives, who have wrecked the Reagan Revolution steeped in his favourite conservatism. He fears an 'imperial overstretch' due to the attack on Iraq 'that did not threaten us, did not attack us, and did not want a war with us'.[26] In a chapter devoted to the Neoconservatives, he offers a critique of ideologues and policy-makers such as Paul Wolfowitz, Richard Perle, and Douglas Feith and decries them as the 'War Party'. To him, the dream of bringing democracy into the Muslim world through military interventions would prove counterproductive on many counts. Firstly, interventionism offers no solution and would instead only increase anti-Americanism besides leading to the accusations of 'democratic imperialism'. Secondly, he is not at all optimistic in the future of democracy in the Islamic world, as Muslims 'have never been democratic'. Thirdly, he finds the US military presence on Arab soil itself being responsible for 9/11, as he notes: 'The terrorists were over here because we were over there'.[27]

Buchanan traces the history of Islam all the way from the earliest times, and quoting from Bernard Lewis, finds Muslims eager to recover their lost glory whereas the American policies have only exacerbated the anger among them: 'We are not hated for who we are. We are hated for what we do. It is not our principles that have spawned pandemic hatred of America within the Islamic world. It is our policies.'[28] Thus, to this influential conservative ideologue

Islam might he a heresy and an enemy yet the Muslims themselves are braced for internal schisms: 'Today's struggle for the hearts and minds of Muslims and Arabs is between Ataturk and the Ayatollah.'[29] One may disagree with Buchanan but he deserves credit for his forthright analysis as he takes his own country to task for pursuing unilateral and partisan policies in the Muslim regions. While citing Avraham Burg, the former speaker of the Israeli Knesset, he urges the American and Israeli leaders to follow judicious and balanced policies towards the Arabs. Vocally highlighting his discomfort with Israeli policies and their unquestioned support by the US, his advice for his own country is to be even-handed: 'Israel is free to choose. But America needs a Middle East policy made in the USA, not in Tel Aviv, or at AIPAC or AEI.'[30] Certainly, he has the temerity to be critical of Israel and Washington at a time when even a minor hint of disagreement could be misconstrued as sheer anti-Semitism. His suggestions, offered towards the end of the volume, include withdrawal of American troops from the Middle East and other such regions in the spirit of non-intervention and fairness to all.

Ann Coulter, unlike Buchanan and other overbearing Neoconservatives is a youthful, glamorous woman who appeared on the political scene during the closing days of the Clinton era when the ideologues aggregated their efforts to mount a multi-dimensional offensive. In her columns,[31] television interviews and two books, she has left no stone unturned to attack American liberals, blaming them for all the ills. In her best seller, *Slander: Liberal Lies,* Coulter finds political debate in America 'insufferable' due to the Clinton decade, which led to the liberal ascension.[32] Coulter accuses liberals of hating Christians, Jews and profit motives, and even after 9/11 when the country got united, they continued grumbling. To her chagrin, they even defended John Lindh Walker, an American *Talib*, without sharing a pervasive wave of patriotism: 'Indeed, an attack on America by fanatical Muslims had finally provided liberals with a religion they could respect'. They even insisted on praying rights for the internees of Guantanamo Bay.[33] In other words, her McCarthyism would not allow any dissent or concern for human rights especially when it comes to patriotism and conformity, and likewise her paranoia does not allow her to see the complex ideological issues. While Buchannan has been more concerned about White Americans by dramatising demography and immigration, Coulter is deeply anguished over intra-American dissensions and would not allow any space to critics. As her first book, *High Crimes and Misdemeanours: The Case Against Bill Clinton,* reveals, she considers liberals in league with the American enemies. She does not realise that Clinton, despite his liberal rhetoric, was responsible for decade-long sanctions against Iraq, which were nefariously and less brightly defended in 1996 by Madeleine Albright, his Secretary of State. When Leslie Stahl of the CBS's '60 Minutes', queried her about the death of one-half million Iraqi children due to sanctions—a larger number than the Japanese deaths in Hiroshima and Nagasaki—Albright had nonchalantly observed: 'I think that is a very hard choice, but the price, we think, is worth it.' She has herself affirmed this in her autobiography.[34] The Clinton Administration was responsible for the largest number of sanctions ever imposed on several developing nations, and always ignored countries like Pakistan while befriending India.

Coulter is a staunch defender of Fox TV, notorious for its jingoism, yet is hyper sensitive to even mild criticism, rarely aired in some solitary columns of the *New York Times.* Her yardstick for authenticity is an unquestioned loyalty to her kind of exclusionary patriotism. Her heroines are women like Linda Tripp, Paula Jones and Katherine Harris, who made news in the 1990s for all kinds of reasons whereas feminists seeking equality and empowerment are liberal 'feminazis', a term originally coined by Rush Limbaugh, the doyen of Neoconservative pundits.[35] Coulter's crusade is a twin-edged sword concurrently applied against liberals and Muslims. She cherishes the conservative dream of a colour-blind America as against the liberal espousal of ethnic and cultural pluralism. Even to talk of race and multiculturalism, to her, is a liberal sin.

Coulter accuses liberal Americans of being immoral, treacherous and monopolistic, who flourished under Clinton, when individuals such as Strobe Talbott, Richard Inderfurth and Sidney Blumenthal acquired higher positions in the Administration. Her verdict: 'Liberals are like the dog food company president who furiously demands to know why their dog food isn't selling.'[36] On the contrary, she defends George W. Bush for his religious convictions and allocates him a higher IQ than is generally assumed. However, it is the liberals who are responsible for whatever is wrong in America and the Neoconservatives are the redeemers: 'If you threw a glass of cold water on a liberal in the middle of a sound sleep, he'd jerk awake denouncing the religious right.'[37] Her kind of expression goes well with George Bush followers especially in Middle America and Deep South. Like a student politician, she defends conservatives as 'the most tolerant people in the world.'[38] From amongst Muslims, she is enamoured of two Pakistanis: General Pervez Musharraf for aligning himself with America and secondly, Anwar Iqbal, a journalist based in Washington. The journalist had broken the story about some Arabs in upstate New York having been to an Al-Qaeda camp in Afghanistan.[39]

In her recent book, *Treason,* she further unleashes her anger at liberals for misrepresenting history and for entertaining a soft corner for Osama bin Laden. She begins with the history of the post-Second World War anti-Americanism, presumably upheld by individuals like Alger Hiss, and then focuses on present-day critics of the Bush Administration including Professor Eric Foner. She has much praise for Senator Joe McCarthy whose role in stopping the communist intrigues was 'undisputable' yet he still remains a misunderstood hero in American history.[40] She believes that the liberals were wrong in their criticism of the US attack on North Korea and their objections to the US invasions of Afghanistan and Iraq will also prove exaggerated. She contends their criticism of the Bush Administration as 'modern McCarthyism' and rejects the charge levelled by some that the White House knew of the 9/11 attacks in advance.[41]

In her preoccupation with the liberals she takes them to task for not being vocal enough in denouncing terrorist attacks and instead being concerned about the civic rights of the perpetrators. She is definitely an unquestioned defender of the Attorney General, John Ashcroft and his censorial policies. Her unease with American liberals is due to their reluctance in accepting the fact 'that the perpetrators of those attacks were Muslims.' Her grudge with the American Muslims is that they had supported terrorist suspects, which is in fact, a blanket denunciation of a community that itself is disturbed over the misrepresentation of their faith.[42] Coulter, quite often and rather unhesitatingly, intermingles American liberals with Muslim activists and carelessly generalises about seven million American Muslims. She notes:

America was at war with Islamic fanatics, but liberals treated every new onslaught like a bolt out of the blue. If the 9-11 terrorists had been fundamentalist Christians, the shoelace strangler a fundamentalist Christian, the shoe-bomber and snipers fundamentalist Christians, the Los Angeles airport killer a fundamentalist Christian, sure the media would not censor the terrorists' religion. Liberals bar the most benign expression of religion by little America. Only a religion that is highly correlated with fascistic attacks on the US commands their respect and protection.

Aggregation and a cursory bundling together of Islam, terror, fundamentalism and liberalism are not so unique to Coulter and is an enduring aspect of the Orientalist discourse. Her antagonism towards liberals does not allow her to understand Islam and Muslims more judiciously and instead she ends up using extremely uncouth terms such as 'the psychopathology of Islamofascists'.[43] She does not forgive liberal writers like Eric Foner, Tom Paulin and Michael Moore for displaying sympathy for Palestinians while objecting to the unmitigated and one-sided American support for Israel. On the contrary, she reserves all epithets for Palestinians and does not hesitate from calling Yasser Arafat 'a despicable man'.[44] Islam and liberalism, according to Coulter and her Neoconservative ilk, are the most serious threat to the United States and Israel, as she sums up her views towards the end of *Treason*: 'Liberals promote the rights of Islamic fanatics for the same reason they promote the rights of adulterers, pornographers, abortionists, criminals, and Communists. They instinctively root for anarchy and against civilization. The inevitable logic of the liberal position is to be for treason.'[45] Her identification of the internal and external enemy has been posited forcefully; though it is a different question whether such a pontification, soaked in extreme intolerance and myopia, will ever reflect anything true about a plural society such as the United States'. Coulter's views cannot be taken in isolation nor can one overlook them as sheer ignorant rhetoric, since they reflect a wider malaise, and being a charismatic person, millions of her fellow citizens follow her.

Coulter has been more emphatic about her hatred for Muslims and liberals in a special interview for *Guardian*. Jonathan Freedland interviewed 'the darling of conservatives' and 'the undisputed star' of the Neoconservatives, who 'worships' Bush, Dick Cheney and Donald Rumsfeld and is anguished over the fact that only Afghanistan and Iraq had been targeted. America, to her, 'missed out all the other Muslim countries that should be on America's target list.' Her well-known statement on 13 September 2001 has been widely quoted in the media when she famously observed: 'We should invade their countries, kill their leaders and convert them to Christianity.' She was unforgiving to the East Coast elite, many of whom are her hated liberals and who would not care for the rest of America. In a column on 21 September 2001, she advised passport checks of suspicious people—'swarthy males'—even while on domestic travel. In her columns in the right-wing *National Review* and available on her web site, she advocated elimination of 10 per cent of all Muslims as they harbour terrorist ideas, even though this ratio may account for millions of people. She is also the architect of the nefarious idea of 'Muslim-free air travel' and is not bothered about how the Muslims may travel. Her solution: 'They could use flying carpets'.

Coulter is quite used to making wild statements without any compunction, like identifying Bobby Kennedy's assassin—Sirhan Sirhan—as an Islamic terrorist though he was a Christian. Despite the fact that Coulter had a Muslim boyfriend her Islamophobia knows no bounds. She has never been to the Middle East nor to any other Muslim region but continuously pontificates on Islam. Freedland calls her general ignorance of global affairs including American interventionism in Latin America as 'selective blindness'. Her support for US militarism is unbound as she observes: 'I just can't imagine anyone not seeing 9/11 as a really good reason for wiping out Islamic totalitarians'. (Her terminology on Islam often reminds one of Lewis and Pipes!) She is for the US exit from the UN and the UN's expulsion from New York—an opinion fervently shared by many ultra-right groups. She is nostalgic for the 1950s and blames all the socio-political ills on the 1960s when feminism and liberalism began to hold sway.[46]

Evangelists on Islam

Where colonialism afforded a golden opportunity to European and American missionaries to spread across the Afro-Asian world to reinvigorate a long-time dormant Christianity, 9/11 has reignited interest amongst a whole generation of missionaries, evangelists, charities and other Bible-carrying polemicists to energise their enterprise. The American military might and Israeli campaigns enjoy vital support from a wider array of Christian and Jewish lobbies in North America and elsewhere. The Second Coming of Christ through born-again Christian and Jewish leaders such as Bush, Blair, Sharon and Berlusconi has galvanised these elements in mounting their plans quite vocally. Notwithstanding their verbal attacks on Islam, Frank Graham, Jerry Falwell, Pat Robertson and such other evangelists fully supported Bush whose own references to the war on terror as a moral mission (crusade) embodied a special dimension. In his State of Union Address in 2004, President Bush invoked God, moral values and culture several times while he did not make a single reference to his European colleagues or anybody else, showing both his moral uprighteousness as well as a staunch belief in American self-sufficiency, probably ordained under some divine scheme.[47]

In the wake of the UK–American invasions of Afghanistan and Iraq, several missionary and evangelical groups rushed to convert Muslims in these countries to Christianity. With two born-again Christians of the two most powerful nations leading campaigns against two Muslim countries they felt as if their hour had come and crash courses on Islam were begun across the North Atlantic region:

> Not for a century has the idea of evangelizing Islam awakened such fervour in conservative Christians. Touched by Muslims' material and (supposed) spiritual needs, convinced that they are one of the 'unreached mega peoples' who must hear the Gospel before Christ's eventual return, Evangelicals from all over the world have been rushing to what has become the latest host missions field'.[48]

The age-old collaboration between the Western political authorities and missionary enterprises has been revived to its fullest, which may have its own serious ramifications. The missionary enterprise is still the junior partner in this Westernising mission—a major component of modernity—and will certainly lead to a significant discomfort among Muslims despite disavowals from Western politicians including Bush who, immediately after 9/11, had stated that he was to lead a 'crusade' against terrorism. But he quickly retracted the word when told of bitter memories of bloodshed perpetrated by the medieval Christians on Muslims and others. However, that did not stop many important military and civil officials from invoking the age-old rivalries and claims of Divine intercession for Jews and Christians. For instance, Lieutenant-General William G. 'Jerry' Boykin, deputed to hunt for Osama bin Laden and Saddam Hussein, often made denunciatory statements about Muslims. He declared the war on terror to be a clash between Judeo–Christian values and Satan. He had earlier clashed with Muslim groups in Somalia in 1993 and had been ratified as an assistant secretary of defence by the US Senate. As a veteran of the secret Delta Force, in June 2003, he declared in Oregon that the radical Islamists disliked the United States 'because we're a Christian nation, because our foundation and our roots are Judeo-Christian...

and the enemy is a guy named Satan'. Then, he told another audience reminiscing about his clash with a Somali warlord: 'I knew my God was bigger than his. I knew that my God was a real God and his was an idol.' In his Oregon speech he said of Bush: 'He's in the White House because God put him there'. Such views were widely acclaimed by his audience though several American Muslims were anguished by this evangelical zeal. [49]

In early February 2004, a pilot for the American Airlines, while en route to New York from Los Angeles, asked his Christian passengers to identify themselves by raising hands. For the non-Christian passengers he went on to say that 'everyone who doesn't have their hand raised is crazy', which certainly shocked his predominantly American passengers. [50]

Boykin was not the only known official to have cast the war on terror in religious terms, even in Britain ruled by the Labour Party, Denis McShane, a foreign affairs minister, incensed British Muslims and other critical groups by issuing insulting remarks about Muslims. In a speech to his constituents in Rotherham, including many Muslim voters, he exhorted them to choose between the British way and the way of terrorists. His clarification ran short of an apology especially when the minister had been quiet about the killings in Chechnya, Kashmir, Gujarat and Palestine. [51] This was not for the first time a senior politician had maligned Muslims, since Margaret Thatcher, the former Conservative Prime Minister, Robert Kilroy-Silk (a former Labour MP), Rabbi Meir Kahane, Jean-Marie Le Pen, India's Bal Thackery, a former NATO Secretary-General Willy Claes and several other prominent public figures have often delivered their derogatory verdicts on Muslims. While Pakistani-born Michael Nazir-Ali, the Bishop of Rochester, supported the attack on Iraq to get rid of Saddam Hussein, several Anglican bishops voiced their protests against the legality of the invasion. Bishop Desmond Tutu not only criticised the British–US invasion and occupation of Iraq, but continued to demand apologies from Bush and Blair for pursuing an 'immoral', illegal and ill-justified war. In his Langdon Lecture at King's College, London, Tutu questioned the rationale of the war, based on 'a dangerously flawed intelligence'. To him, Bush and Blair were weak since such people would not admit their fault though an open apology would have restored their credibility. The South African Bishop noted: 'It is large-hearted and courageous people who are not diminished by saying: 'I made a mistake'. President Bush and Prime Minister Blair would recover credibility and respect if they were able to say: 'Yes, we made a mistake'.[52]

The reaction to 9/11 has not only accompanied a strong evangelical sentiment, it has rendered it even further assertive. Amidst a host of self-righteous outpourings, Christopher Catherwood's work reaffirms a divine scheme and glory in pursuing Biblical work among Muslims. He noted:

> The fact that we can call God our Father and have that kind of relationship with him is one of the things that stands out most strongly in our Christian knowledge of God in comparison with the much more remote inscrutable god whom Muslims worship. Let us all pray in confidence that the lands that are populated by so many of God's people in the Middle East will, in his love and providence, hear the sound of the Gospel clearly again and turn to it as their ancestors did before them.[53]

This English academic from Cambridge, married to an American, and claiming to have taught in Cambridge and Virginia, is certainly being an Orientalist missionary and does not mince his words when it comes to Islam. His division of gods will certainly raise some eyebrows even at his Oxbridge colleges! Fond of Bernard Lewis and his characterisation of the clash of cultures, Catherwood is impatient with the Middle East that turned Muslim such a long time ago: 'What we are doing here is looking at a spiritual battle that has been going on now for over 1300 years...' and that has to be won for the cross.[54] To him, 'Al-Qaeda is a symptom of a much wider malaise' and there may be more to come as quoting from Thomas Friedman of the *New York Times*, he finds a mass-based Muslim support—'Muslim basement'—for the organisation.[55] Going back to early history, he absolves the Crusaders of any major crimes in the Near East, whose atrocities were not at par with those of the Mongols. Catherwood has special praise for Professor Akbar S. Ahmed, his former neighbour in Cambridge, for being a proponent of peace and love, and a kind of Muslim that Catherwood could presumably tolerate.

Catherwood reaffirms the faith of two allied leaders, as he says: 'Britain has a devout Anglo-Catholic prime minister (Tony Blair) and the United States the first evangelical president in over twenty years (George W. Bush).'[56] He deeply appreciates Christian influence at No. 10 Downing Street but comes back to his cherished theme of converting Muslims: 'We should want them not merely to reform but to repent and be saved.'[57] In view of a huge Muslim population, it must be a gigantic project! However, interestingly, he feels that, compared with Sunnis, Shia Muslims may be in a better place to bring about an Islamic reform. However, in a typical evangelical mode, he turns his attention to the 'stans' where, once again he fears danger due to the Great Game, though his strongest comments are reserved for Pakistan: 'Perhaps the most dangerous 'stan' is the one that has been independent since 1947…'.[58] But, claiming to be the God-chosen, Christians like Catherwood need not worry, as God is both in charge and on their side.

Academicians or Travelling Experts

Writing in the style of Orientalists, a whole generation of travellers and journalists have made name and money by writing about their travels and experiences in the developing countries. Muslim lands seem to have been an area of constant fascination all the way from the early colonisers to missionaries and spies. People like Richard Burton, Mary Kingsley, Rudyard Kipling, Charles Masson, Alexander Burnes, George Moorcroft, Auriel Stein, Younghusband, George Robertson, Wilfred Thesiger, T.E. Lawrence, Robert Byron and several others have written millions of words about these 'exotic' societies.[59] The Kiplingesque views of the empire, also depicted by Joseph Conrad, Rider Haggard, E.M. Forster, M.M.

Masters and M.M. Kaye, reflect a pervasive objectification of colonized peoples and their curious interaction with the colonizers. While the colonials receive laurels by assuming the core positions, the colonized are depicted both as childish or childlike species, whose modernization remains a noble aim. Control, conquest and civilizing the masses turn out to be the main and morally acceptable objectives of the colonial enterprise. In particular, the genre of more recent travelogues, despite a greater emphasis on political correctness, still exude exotica and dramatisation, though in several cases they also tend to respect the local cultures.[60] However pity, pathos and surprise provide the underlying themes to these generations of writers who still dwell on the strangeness and even otherness of these people and by focusing on corrupt officials, uncouth feudal and tribal chieftains and the pathetic state of the underprivileged, like women, they reveal their own patronizing attitudes.[61]

Other than the novelists, journalists and travel writers, one sees a steady interest of scholars streaming into Muslim lands often without a prior immersion into the Islamic ethos or local languages. Particularly, anthropologists, otherwise known for linguistic proficiency and more sensitivity to the local cultures, can also make serious mistakes while studying 'traditional' societies, but their jobs, networks and an available collegial security often allows them to get away with several serious academic and judgmental blunders.[62] In several cases they tend to hide their professional inefficiencies under a veneer of theoretical models, verbose jargon and so-called comparative analysis. As a consequence, the *objectified* societies either disappear from the discourse itself or turn into mute statistics as the verbose theorisation takes over. Selective samples, attributed quotes and historical surveys are garnished by high-sounding concepts simply adding to academic delicacies in the small seminar rooms, thousands of miles away from the *subject* itself. Power point and statistical tables take over the communities *per se* with individuals turning into mute numerals. Some anthropologists, like similar other specialists, have not been able to divest themselves of their colonial, racial and cultural baggage while studying 'atomised' communities. Western historians and political scientists, in several contemporary cases, also lack first-hand immersion into the languages and cultures, and despite an aura of so-called probity and neutrality, end up making several philological and empirical mistakes.[63]

It is quite common to see Western scholars, sponsored by the British Council, Ford Foundation, USAID, DFID, the State Department or similar European counterparts undertaking research on complicated societies while staying in posh hotels and meeting a few like-minded academics and journalists (stringers) from the 'host' countries. In recent years, developing nations have seen the emergence of NGOs whose own authenticity and integrity in several cases remain dubious due to their links with the Western donors. A whole generation of retired khaki and civil bureaucrats have opened up thousands of NGOs, while receiving money due to contacts with the foreign donors in metropolitan cities and are quite adept in offering often cooked-up reports on socio-political issues. This has become another arena of corruption where like-minded elites, working as surrogates for a number of shadowy agencies and think tanks, may collect information for several unexplained purposes. In the meantime, their nations keep on accumulating more debts whereas vital information, like the cultural artefacts, is routinely transferred abroad. Other than the corrupt state structures, many organs of civil society too have become tainted giving impetus to fundamentalist outrage.

Media Rules the Roost

When Nobel-Laureates like V.S. Naipaul or other influential writers come up with their periodic Islamopbohic tirades, many Muslims are not shocked given a long tradition of Orientalism. However, apart from the serious ideological and intellectual lacunae, such opinionated works prove immensely insidious in influencing common views of Islam and the developing world. Other than the print media, visual presentations on television and cinema screens have informed generations on politico-cultural affairs of the world all around us. Despite the presence of serious guidelines delineated by watchdogs, the visual media, as investigated by academics from universities in Glasgow, Cardiff and Maine, remains the most effective and often controversial instrument as well as the architect of images and misimages.[64] From news coverage by freelance journalists to embedded correspondents, and from documentaries to chat shows and regular feature films, one sees a powerful and permeating factor in international affairs. Its constructive as well as subversive role is beyond doubt, and though the emerging civil societies among Diaspora groups, liberal elite and even the internet networks all attempt to offer alternatives and often corrective views on crucial issues, one cannot underestimate the outreach of CNN or Fox News. In Britain, even the BBC has often been criticised for its slanted coverage of the Israeli–Palestinian conflict or while reporting on Iraqi groups arrayed against the occupation forces.[65] Palestinians and Iraqis are routinely defined as militants, insurgents and radicals, while Israeli and American troops have never been attributed any such partisan adjectives.[66] Channel Four or even Euronews may, on several occasions offer a more balanced and all-encompassing coverage, whereas Al-Jazeera has been occasionally considered offensive and irritating by many Western official and media establishments. Its coverage of the war on Afghanistan and Iraq—with on-the-spot reportage, often contrasted with reports by the embedded Western correspondents, has irritated the Anglo–American alliance and the Iraqi regime established under its tutelage.

In his seminal study, *Covering Islam*, Edward Said pioneered a critique of Western media portrayals of Islam, which often, both by intent and content, distort historical and cultural facts, feed into derogatory views of Muslims and deeply reflect as well as influence public policies and private perceptions. Media, in its audio, video and visual forms and further beefed up by electronic facilities, in most cases, has been the most effective instrument of public policy, even more than political institutions. Its role, especially in powerful languages, has far reaching consequences for underprivileged communities, including Muslims. The Western media, while depending upon 'a corps of experts' is routinely fed by an exaggerated scholarship, and is overwhelmingly reflective of 'formulaic ideas about Islam'.[67] Except for a few positive and recent exceptions, it may be safe to suggest that the Western media, especially the tabloid press, several television channels, magazines and talk programmes on radio often caricature Islam and refuse to see Muslims beyond their two favourite categories of aggressive bearded men and oppressed veiled women. Correspondents freely use collective and insidious terms like Islamic terror, Muslim violence or Islamic fundamentalism and even solitary criminals are purposefully identified as *Muslim*. Often, the media is linked with powerful vested interests other than its commercialism that purports an element of intentional dramatisation for the sake of newsworthiness and to appease certain ethno-ideological lobbies.[68]

Powerful languages like English, French, German, Italian or Dutch are not void of Darwinian modernity and imperial past, and thus in their reportage of former colonized societies they reflect power centricity by assuming a moral upper ground. Their linkages with specific ideological and geo-political groups, out of ideological or ethnic reasons and to overshadow guilt over some past events, certainly with a few exceptions, again filter into media portrayals and reportage. Thus, even a minor news item, apparently innocuous, may, in fact, turn out quite inimical. For instance, the project on fundamentalism, funded by the American Academy of Arts and Sciences and undertaken by Martin E. Marty and R. Scott Appleby, has devoted several volumes on a subject without even defining the very term. Islam has been the mainstay of the project, which the sponsors and authors were hesitant to declare openly. The interface between such specialists and journalists like Judith Miller, William Safire or Martin Perez, with openly pro-Israeli inclinations, only fortify anti-Muslim biases. Media pundits and academics constantly influence each other by reiterating similar views. For instance, even before Samuel Huntington's piece on the clash of civilisations in *Foreign Affairs,* Bernard Lewis had published a piece in *The Atlantic Monthly* coining the controversial term. Lewis, like Huntington, has painted Islam 'outside the known, familiar, acceptable world that 'we' inhabit...', a theme that has often reverberated in various political and journalistic commentaries. Lewis is known for 'snide observations, the fraudulent use of etymology to make huge cultural points about an entire set of peoples, and no less reprehensible, his total inability to grant that the Islamic peoples are entitled to their own cultural, political and historical practice...'. Lewis, according to Said, was 'at his worst' in his mentioned article, 'The Roots of Rage'.[69] Moreover, the September (1990) issue of *The Atlantic Monthly*, carrying this article, had an offensive cover of a turbaned head.[70]

Robert Kaplan, a long-time contributor for the same influential American magazine, had covered the Afghan resistance during the 1980s and returned to Pakistan and Afghanistan a decade later to write a series of articles. In a typical sensational way, he only discovers drugs and warlords in the Frontier province of Pakistan and in Afghanistan, and brimming with primitive loyalties and possessing modern weapons. He focuses on fierce tribalism, *madrassas* teaching Islamic militancy and countless war orphans and refugees left helpless from the forgotten wars, whereas in Peshawar and Karachi he only finds intriguers, militants and criminals. Though his sensationalist pieces appeared before 9/11 yet he claims to enjoy intimate information on the Taliban, Hamid Karzai, Osama bin Laden and many former Mujahideen, and in the process, offers his opinions on the capricious Pakistani generals and politicians. The overall impression one gets from his writings is of unruly, wild-tempered, immensely dangerous men who have destructive weapons at their disposal while enjoying support from all types of shadowy international characters.[71] In the same vein, numerous journalists and columnists like Oriana Fallaci,[72] David Selbourne,[73] Ian Buruma[74] and Harry Cummins[75] have routinely spewed their partisan and negative views about Muslims by attributing collective violence and barbarity to all of them.

Monolithicisation of Islam and the depiction of Muslims as irrational and violent peoples have been internalised by generations of writers and analysts and thus a few laudable exceptions, away from a total objectification, fail to make any significant difference. Islam-bashing is so widespread that even several non-Muslim Asians, such as Hindus and Sikhs, have ironically started asserting their separateness by unwittingly falling into the trap of the racist outfits, which are trying to divide and communalise the Muslim–Asian Diaspora.[76] Following the Salman Rushdie affair, Islamophobia became quite pronounced since communism had vanished and erstwhile respect for the valiant Afghans had already dissolved into the thin air. Opinion surveys across Europe showed widening reservations on sharing the neighbourhood with Muslims, and the common apathy over Bosnia further underwrote a pervasive indifference towards the world of Islam. Occasional news reports on the Chechen or Kashmiri predicament due to state-led repression were quickly neutralised by a host of hostile and sensational writings about some wild Muslim practices. The emergence of the ultra right banking on exclusive nationalism and spewing hatred against largely exaggerated figures of asylum seekers found Muslim visibility—because of colour, class and culture—a convenient alibi to vent their myopia.

Europe, especially after the dissolution of the Cold War and the unification of Germany, has persistently and negatively focused on Muslim immigrants, as was duly recorded in *Islamophobia* (1997), the pioneering report on the subject, sponsored by the Runneymede Trust. Support for Zionism either out of political correctness, sheer guilt, or owing to a persuasive propaganda, especially in the wake of post-9/11 vengeance, turned Muslims into the new-old enemies. Kilroy-Silk, despite his often-offensive remarks, still could count on a vast majority of public opinion that supported him against his dismissal by the BBC.[77] A few days earlier, when a British prison officer, Colin Rose, was sacked for using offensive language, the tabloids created a wave of protest across the nation. This happened soon after the diatribe by the Labour Minister, Denis McShane, and his mild clarification addressed to Muslims. An influential columnist and television presenter, in his column in the most widely read tabloid, blamed the British Left and Muslims for having 'poisoned the political debate in Britain'. Richard Littlejohn, while voicing his support for Denis McShane and Colin Rose, reminded Britain's Muslims: 'There is a legitimate body of opinion which holds that Muslim leaders should do more to condemn terrorism publicly and should co-operate more with the authorities in turning over al-Qa'ida sympathisers.'[78]

He should have paused to think about those numerous British Muslim internees at Belmarsh Jail—Britain's proverbial counterpart of Guantanamo Bay—who, even after years of incarceration, were still waiting for formal prosecution and indictment. Other than them, many more have been simply arrested on minor or mostly unfounded suspicions, and who happened to be either visitors or would-be immigrants whose cases were still undecided by the Home Office.[79]

NOTES

1. One can develop an entire bibliography of fiction and serious writings objectifying Arabs, all the way from Linda Blandford's *Oil Sheiks* to Philip Roth's *Coup* and more recent outpourings on Saddam Hussein and the Palestinians. Mostly written as exotica with a powerful mode of dramatisation, these writings appeared in the post-1973 years when the oil embargo and the Third Arab–Israeli war had generated anger among pro-Israeli sections in the West. Concurrently, one encounters a whole series of films and documentaries focusing on Arab-related themes. It is quite common to see abrasive opinions being expressed about Muslims and Islam without people having a deeper knowledge of the traditions and realities on the ground. Following 9/11, Islam-bashing became an all too familiar phenomenon. For instance, Martin Amis spoke of Islam and Muslims as if they suffered from some serious sexual problems. In an interview, he observed on his reading of a chapter from the Quran: 'The emphasis in that chapter was to do with male insecurity. It seems to me that the key to radical Islam is that it is quivering with male insecurity. It's an equation that never fully works out. There is a huge injection of sexuality—men's sexuality—in radical Islam'. It was viewed as a far-fetched and 'sensationalist' opinion and known British Muslims such as Zaki Badawi and Ghada Karmi wondered about the intellectual inadequacy of this British writer. See, *The Times*, 21 October 2002.

2. It is immaterial to reference those interviews he gave regarding his wife, Mrs Nadira Alvi, whom he had met at a party in Lahore. He, as he himself

confessed, had tormented his previous wife emotionally until she died of cancer. A known writer of international repute he met this Pakistani upper-middle-class admirer at a private residence and she announced her love for him at their first meeting. She had been an admirer of his writings and they soon fell in love and got married. These details are very important as she is the authenticator of several episodic details on his journey through Pakistan, though the trail was both hasty and equally annoying to some people who had personally entertained him. To them, he turned out to be a racist Orientalist.

3. Even until recently, Western scholars using the Weberian model of explaining Protestant ethics and capitalism, considered Roman Catholicism and Orthodoxy hindering economic growth. The economic development of Spain, Portugal, Italy, Ireland and Greece has displaced this culture-specific explanation of progress. If Muslims can achieve so admirably well in North America and still stay in close touch with their religion, the Naipaulesque simplification falls on its own feet.

4. Naipaul, p. 31.

5. Ibid., p. 53.

6. Ibid., p. 72.

7. Rob Nixon, 'Among the Mimics and the Parasites: V.S. Naipaul's Islam', in Emran Qureshi and Michael A. Sells, (eds.) *The New Crusades,* New York, 2003, pp. 152-5.

8. Ibid., p. 157.

9. *Indian Express,* 2 April 1995. Naipaul's endorsement of the demolition of the Ayodhya Mosque and the resultant communal riots in 1992–3 disappointed many of his readers. One commentator observed: 'It might seem unlikely that a Nobel Laureate would put himself in a position of apparently endorsing an act that spawned mass murder—or commend a party that has often been seen as virulently anti-intellectual.' In fact, the Nobel Committee, while honouring him with the award in 2001, had singled out his analysis of the Islamic world, and did not assess the extent and intensity of his anti-Muslim feelings: 'Naipaul's entirely negative understanding of India's Islamic history has its roots firmly in the mainstream imperial historiography of Victorian Britain'. William Dalrymple, 'Trapped in the ruins', *Guardian,* 20 March 2004.

10. http://www.nobel.se/literature/laureates/2001naipaul-bibl.html, quoted in Nixon, op. cit.

11. Eqbal Ahmad, *Confronting Empire,* London, 2000, p. 110. Ahmad takes him to task for spending more than sixty pages on Pakistani officials without suggesting that thousands of Pakistanis had been resisting the military regime and other oppressive systems in the country. To Ahmad, Naipaul was simply averse to resistance or counter-critique.

12. Naipaul, p. 272.

13. Ibid., p. 301.

14. Ibid., p. 329.
15. Ibid., p. 354. Naipaul, then, delves into the Nawab's harem, his armada of vintage cars and whole collection of curious toys. 'About six hundred, some made of clay, some bought in England and battery-operated. The (Pakistani) army dug a pit and buried these dildos. A lot of dirty magazines. He needed them, to use the dildos. He became impotent very early. His appetites were sated. Someone who went into the harem at the wrong time one day saw the Nawab using a dildo on a screaming woman' (p. 355). The Nawab, according to Naipaul, had more than 390 women, including local and foreign concubines and most of them had limited contacts with him: 'Some of these women developed a kind of hysteria; some became lesbians. Always in the harem he had sixteen or eighteen women on whom he could call'. Ibid.
16. In fact, the Victorian era and the early half of the twentieth century were all characterized by wars every few weeks in different parts of the empire, though one may only hear of some selective major events. For details, see Byron Farwell, *Queen Victoria's Little Wars*, London, 1973.
17. Even an otherwise sensational book on the CIA, Congressman Charles Wilson and the Afghan resistance, it allocates no responsibility to Afghans for 9/11. See, George Kreile, *My Enemy's Enemy*, London, 2003.
18. Hugh Tinker, *A New Kind of Slavery: The Export of Indian Labour Overseas, 1830–1920*, London, 1974. The author, in his work, has unearthed information on millions of Indians transported to Southern and Eastern Africa, Hong Kong, Malaya and the West Indies. As late as in the last quarter of the twentieth century, the British uprooted the original inhabitants of Diego Garcia—the island in the middle of the Indian Ocean—and scattered them elsewhere in Africa. The island, due to its strategic location, was leased to the Americans for their military campaigns.
19. Shabbir Akhtar, 'A grouse for Mr Biswas', *Times Higher Education Supplement*, 15 May 1998. For a laudatory review, see Geoffrey Wheatcroft, 'The sum of his books', *New Statesman*, 2 February 2004.
20. Patrick J. Buchanan, *The Death of the West: How Dying Population and Immigrant Invasion Imperil Our Country and Civilization?* New York, 2002, pp. 2-3.
21. See, Samuel P. Huntington, *Who Are We: America's Great Debate*, New York, 2004.
22. Buchanan, p. 22.
23. Ibid., p. 108.
24. Ibid., p. 118.
25. Patrick J. Buchanan, *Where the Right Went Wrong*, New York, 2004, p. 1. He then enumerates the global eagerness for Coca Cola, Levi's, Hollywood films, music and the number of Nobel Laureates in his country to show that it remains the most cherished place on earth.
26. Ibid., pp. 3 and 6.
27. Ibid., pp. 33-59.

28. Ibid., p. 80.
29. Ibid., p. 88.
30. Ibid., p. 241.
31. Her columns are accessible on: www.anncoulter.org
32. Ann Coulter, *Slander: Liberal Lies about the American Right,* New York, 2002, p. 1.
33. Ibid., p. 6.
34. Madeleine Albright, *Madam Secretary: A Memoirs,* London, 2003, p. 275.
35. Coulter, p. 28.
36. Ibid., p. 115.
37. Ibid., p. 213. At another place, she observes: 'Liberals hate religion because politics is a religion substitute for liberals and they can't stand the competition' (p. 247).
38. Ibid., p. 260.
39. She is mindful of Bush's error in confusing the name of the Pakistani military ruler in a quiz during the presidential campaign. Ibid., pp.186-8.
40. Ann Coulter, *Treason,* New York, 2003, pp. 6-7 and 55-71.
41. Ibid., p. 260.
42. Ibid., 272-8. It is here that she appreciates the reporting by Anwar Iqbal about eight Yemeni Americans who had visited Afghanistan, though one may not know the nature and extent of their culpability.
43. Ibid., pp. 282-5.
44. Ibid., pp. 287-92.
45. Ibid., p. 292.
46. For further details and quotes, see Jonathan Freedland, 'An appalling magic', *Guardian,* 17 May 2003.
47. Commenting on the presidential address, an analyst opined: 'I'm sure that by now Dubbya firmly believes God, too, is a Republican, someone who will guide him straight back into the White House when the nation goes to polls in November'. Andrew Stephen, 'America', *New Statesman,* 26 January 2004, p. 12. Tony Blair in his own speeches, especially in his constituency, would also apply Christian symbols so as to justify the invasion of Iraq.
48. David Van Biema, 'Missionaries under cover', *Time,* 4 August 2003. This is the most detailed report on secretive missionary work among Muslims to have been published in recent times. It offers a detailed exposé of the personnel, groups and funds involved all over the Muslim world.
49. Richard T. Cooper, 'General Casts War in Religious Terms', *Los Angles Times,* 16 October 2003.
50. 'Christian question alarms flight', http://news.bbc.co.uk/1/hi/world/americas/3472265.stm 9 February 2004, and, *Guardian,* 10 February 2004.
51. *Guardian,* 28 November 2003.
52. 'Apologise for your 'immoral' war, Tutu tells Blair', *Independent,* 16 February 2004. According to a senior British diplomat in Washington and a close

participant in Bush–Blair parleys on the invasion of Iraq, Blair usually avoided seeking out all the complex details on world affairs and Bush was able to convince the British Prime Minister of his own decision to invade Iraq. Sir Christopher Meyer, a supporter of the invasion, was the British Ambassador to the US from 1997 until 2003, and like Ambassador Jeremy Greenstock, posthumously showed his concern over the invasion. *Sunday Telegraph*, 6 November 2005.

53. Christopher Catherwood, *Christians, Muslims, and Islamic Rage: What is Going on and Why it Happened?* Grand Rapids, 2003, p. 12.

54. Ibid., p. 19.

55. Ibid., p. 28.

56. Ibid., p. 176.

57. Ibid., p. 186.

58. Ibid., pp. 220-2.

59. Just in the case of South-West Asia, there was a steady stream of visitors, travellers and certainly of spies going north and west from British India. For instance, see, John Keay, *Where Men and Mountains Meet*, London, 1981; and *Gilgit Game: The Explorer of Western Himalayas*, London, 1979.

60. There could be several exceptions. For instance, Geoffrey Moorehouse, *To the Frontier*, London, 1983.

61. There are dozens of such books appearing periodically and one cannot list them all. For instance, Emma Duncan, *Breaking the Curfew*, London, 1988. The journalistic book was based on a very short visit and interviews with a dozen powerful individuals in Pakistan from various walks of life. Earlier, another book by an American journalist, again based on a very short tour across the country, had shocked many people. See, Richard Reeves, *Journey to Peshawar*, New York, 1983. The book had been serialised in *New Yorker*. Another British journalist, Christina Lamb, invited to Benazir Bhutto's marriage in Karachi, launched herself as a journalist reporting on Afghanistan and over the years has produced several books. The books are mostly based on personal encounters often characterized by sweeping generalisations. See, Christina Lamb, *Pakistan: Waiting for Allah*, London, 1989; *The Sewing Circles of Herat*, London, 2003. William Dalrymple's early works such as *Delhi: The City of Jinns*, also often focused on exotica and the otherness. Robert Kaplan's whirlwind visits, true to a hasty journalistic tradition, caricatured socio-political facts in the Middle East and on the Pakistan-Afghan Frontier. The post-Soviet Central Asia has had its share of attracting such traveller-writers in recent years, some of them using their Western anthropologic models. For example, see Sheila Payne, *The Afghan Amulet: Travels from Hindu Kush to Razgrad*, London, 1994. (The author, a retired teacher from Oxford's Polytechnic now renamed the Oxford Brookes University, enjoyed the hospitality of ordinary Muslims all the way from Pakistan's Northern Areas to the Balkans and was showered with gifts from her hosts yet somehow remains preoccupied with a fear of being raped). After

the British and American invasion of Afghanistan, several journalists joined the bandwagon by decreeing on the Muslim cultures and societies such as Afghanistan. These 'new' subject specialists left no stone unturned in focusing on the exotic and brutal aspects of these communities, taking the age-old tradition of Orientalism to newer heights, even occasionally betraying the trust of their hosts. For instance in 2003, soon after publishing the reportage of her Afghan visits, a Scandinavian journalist attracted a significant amount of controversy. She had stayed with the family of a bookseller in Afghanistan and eventually published her book solely based on the inside secrets of her host family, though she changed the names in her account. The bookseller felt betrayed and eventually took her to court on defamation charges in her native country, but to no avail. See, Asne Sierestad, *The Bookseller of Kabul*, London, 2003. As noted earlier, such dramatized narratives about other African and Asian places abound.

62. There is a well-known case of a D.Phil dissertation at Oxford where the student built up a narrative on the Pushtun society and ended up confusing basic terms due to a lack of proper knowledge of Islam and Pushtu language. Interestingly, most of her respondents whose political careers must have started in the early twentieth century were still alive during the 1990s— almost a century later—to be interviewed on their political vision.

63. Two most prominent Oxbridge dons and known specialists on the history and cultures of South Asia, a region with the largest Muslim concentration, were found unaware of the basic five pillars of Islam. In a personally observed episode, they invited a Muslim postgraduate student to a lunch before his seminar. During Ramadan, while fasting, this student expressed his inability in joining them for lunch. Instead of understanding the principles governing a Muslim fast, they insisted on his having some juice or tea with them, to which he politely explained that Ramadan meant total prohibition. They both were taken aback as if they came to know of this for the first time. The present author personally witnessed this in 1993.

64. For details, see, John Lloyd, *What the Media are Doing to Our Politics*, London, 2004.

65. Cardiff University's empirical research has highlighted these serious anomalies in the media coverage of the War and West Asian politics. For a summary, see Justin Lewis, 'Biased Broadcasting Corporation', *Guardian*, 4 July 2004.

66. The researchers at Glasgow University have unearthed serious biases in the reportage of news and views on the Middle East, especially the Israeli–Palestinian discord. See, Greg Philo and Mike Barry, *Bad News from Israel*, London, 2004.

67. Edward Said, '*Covering Islam: How the Media and the Experts Determine how we see the Rest of the World*, London, 1997, p. xi.

68. For a well-informed recent expose, see David Domke, *God Willing? Political Fundamentalism in the White House, the 'War on Terror' and the Echoing Press*,

London, 2004.

69. Ibid., pp. xxix-xxxi.

70. When the *New Statesman*, a liberal British magazine, in early 2003, carried a Star of David on its cover, there was a serious backlash and the magazine eventually apologised while in the case of Muslims such misportrayals are daily occurrences. The same magazine published a veiled Muslim woman on its cover to highlight a piece on Islamophobia in its issue of 19 January 2004 and never bothered to apologise to the Muslims for stereotyping them.

71. Robert D. Kaplan, *Soldiers of God: With Islamic Warriors in Afghanistan and Pakistan,* London, 2001 (reissued).

72. Oriana Fallaci, the Italian journalist subsequently based in New York, published three books after 9/11 all focusing on the 'otherness' of Islam and a presumed Muslim threat to the West. Her books became bestsellers and were widely quoted in Europe and North America. A former left-leaning journalist, Fallaci made her name by interviewing Khomeini and other world leaders in the past. Her fictional-historical volume, *A Man*, gave her further global profile, which she used to its full by focusing on Islam. Her tirades against Islam only added to a pervasive racist discourse in her native Italy besides helping anti-Muslim lobbies elsewhere. For details, see Sophie Arie, 'Anti-Islamic books' success fuels fears of racism in Italy', and, 'Italy has a racist culture', says French editor', *Guardian,* 7 and 8 August 2004.

73. David Selbourne, a British writer based in Italy, has been often writing about Islam in the English papers such as the *Telegraph* and tried to show as if publishers were reluctant in carrying his work out of some fear of a Muslim backlash.

74. A former columnist for the *Guardian,* Buruma usually wrote on East Asia, but in the recent past he began to comment on Muslim politics and history. His sources have been usually biased besides which his own lack of disciplinary and philological immersion in the Muslim cultures only betrayed a superficial reading of a rather complex situation. Consequently, he would end up subscribing to the premise of an Islamic threat to the rest. For instance, see, Ian Buruma, 'Driven by history and hate: Islam's holy warriors', *The Times,* 3 August 2004.

75. Writing as 'Will' Cummins, this press officer for the British Council contributed four consecutive and derisory articles on Muslims in four issues of the *Sunday Telegraph* (London) during the summer of 2004. He found Muslims sharing characteristics with dogs; harbouring desires to conquer the entire world; and, subscribing to a false prophethood. To him, all the Muslim lands originally belonged to Christians, and instead of an inter-faith dialogue, Muslims have to be controlled and contained before they could achieve their shared objective of turning Europeans into *Palestinians* on their own soil. See his pieces in the *Sunday Telegraph,* 4, 11, 18 and 25 July 2004. After protests from Muslims, the British Council suspended him with a full salary and eventually, based on an internal inquiry, his services were terminated. Marina

Hyde, the diarist at *Guardian*, in fact, exposed his real identity.

76. Following the Robert Kilroy-Silk affair, several letters appeared even in the liberal press where the non-Muslim Asians appeared keen on distancing themselves from Muslims. Some of them seemed to imply that the caricatures only suited the Muslims otherwise the rest were different, hard working, rational and loyal citizens. One can well imagine the pressure on such minorities to distance themselves from fellow Muslim Asians. Scholars like Bernard Lewis have been emphatically portraying Muslims as *different* from the Judaeo–Christian peoples. Said, op. cit., pp. xxxiii, 137 and 149.

77. There were 22,000 callers to his paper, the *Express,* of whom 97 per cent showed their solidarity with him. In the same vein, he registered 93 per cent support in a vote on Sky TV. For details, see William Dalrymple, 'Islamophobia', *New Statesman,* 19 January 2004.

78. Richard Littlejohn, 'Heard one about Osama bin Laden…?' *Sun,* 5 December 2003.

79. Several British Muslims felt that the Labour Government was not fully supportive of demanding repatriation of nine British Muslims interned on Guantanamo Bay because that could create a strong precedent for the release of their own internees. Based on interviews with Dr Ghayasud Din Siddiqui, the head of the Muslim Institute in Oxford, 18 January 2004 and also with the families of the internees in 2003 in London.

5

ENCOUNTERING MODERNITY: MUSLIM REVIVALIST AND REFORMIST DISCOURSE

Want of accuracy, which easily degenerates into untruthfulness, is in fact the main characteristic of the Oriental mind... The mind of the Oriental...like his picturesque streets is eminently wanting in symmetry. His reasoning is of the most slipshod description.
— Lord Cromer, quoted in Edward Said, *Orientalism*, 1978, 38

The West is neither superior nor inferior to Islam.
— Rashid Ghannoushi, quoted in Emad Shahin, *Political Ascent: Contemporary Islamic Movements in North Africa*, 1997, 235

To put it slightly differently, being a progressive Muslim means not simply thinking more about the Qur'an and the life of the Prophet, but also thinking about the life we share on this planet with all human beings and living creatures.
— Omid Safi, 'Introduction', in Omid Safi (ed.) *Progressive Muslims*, 2003, 3

When Leonard Binder, the American academic, finished his research on Pakistani politics immediately after independence, he was sceptical of the uneasy intermingling of religion and politics. Half a century later, the combined religio-political parties governed two provinces besides a sizeable representation in the federal parliament. More than the mainstream politicians and parties like Benazir Bhutto's Pakistan People's Party (PPP) or Nawaz Sharif's

Muslim League (PML-N), they have assumed centre stage by cobbling a close relationship with General Pervez Musharraf on domestic and foreign issues. It was, in fact, their support that allowed him to amend the constitution drastically in his own favour—earlier ironically allowed by the Supreme Court—while simultaneously pontificating on Jinnah's ideal of an empowered, forward looking and progressive Pakistan. During 2003–4, both the army and the religio-political alliance, called the Muttahida Majlis-e-Amal (MMA), established a joint strategy to suit each other's interests, despite harping on two separate ideologies. A whole generation of Pakistani analysts have persistently underrated the electoral potentials of these religio-political groups, presuming that their occasional electoral performance was either too meagre or solely dependent upon the intelligence outfits such as Inter-Services Intelligence (ISI). Certainly, they have more often operated as a 'B' team for military dictators over the past several decades, yet denying them a constituency of their own would be equally fallacious. Pakistani political observers, who had essentialized a peripheral performance of these elements, often interpret the MMA's salience as just a one-off. Again, this misperception is no different from that of their Indian counterparts who, in the early 1990s, took the BJP and Ayodhya issue merely as an aberration with the polity soon settling back to its secular moorings.

One may differ with the dictum of the religio-political parties, but to write them off merely as the beneficiaries of anti-Americanism or the rehash of a military–mullah axis is fallacious. Religion, as witnessed in the former Eastern Europe, the United States, Israel, North Africa, Iran, Afghanistan, Turkey and now Iraq has refused to coexist as nationalism's junior partner, it is surely in the driving seat. The American Neoconservatives, Likud Zionists, Kar Sevaks and Jihadis are all imbued with a reinvigorated energy, and aim at filling the newfound power vacuum and ideological space within their respective societies where 'liberals' and modernists are deemed incorrigibly corrupt and hopelessly incompetent.[1] They aim at capturing power in the name of some ordained authenticity further backed up by a so-called majoritarianism. They express masculanized views of national identity, frown at pluralism and are eager not merely to obtain political power but also harbour several trans-regional agendas, and certainly benefit from external backing. They may all be invariably banking on traditions but, in fact, are largely the creations of modernity.[2] Whether the Muslim world is really unique because of some presumed reluctance to accept and implement democracy, inter-gender equality and a more receptive attitude towards modernist trajectories such as secularism, or is capable of reinventing itself through its ideological elite, makes the mainstay of the present section. Here we mainly dwell on some Muslim views as upheld by a few selected individuals besides visiting the contentious area of emerging interest—Muslim Secularism.

All the familiar trajectories—making vital components of modernity—are not consensual even in the Western heartland yet they certainly stipulate some crucial reinterpretation of Islamic knowledge and practices and thus become disputatious for Muslim intellectuals. The Muslim articulations on modernity may be roughly identified as reformist and revivalist, though these are immensely inadequate and contentious terms. Most Western scholars, publicists and politicians encountered in the preceding chapters, subscribe to some inherent reluctance and incompatibility among Muslims to adapt and change. Authors such as Eli Kedourie, Paul Johnson and William Lind, and populist preachers like Jerry Falwell, Frank Graham and Pat Robertson problematize Islam by positing it as a legacy of repression and backwardness. Such individuals have several followers from amongst the Muslims as well, to whom, in their uncritiqued emulation of modernity, Islam itself is the main hurdle, and it is only by ridding Muslims of its hold that a renaissance could come about.[3] Islam, to them, is a regimented dogma which through its various Shia and Sunni embodiments, is change–resistant; builds up on so-called divinely revealed unchallengeable truths, disallowing any human empowerment, and taxes its followers to commit even their lives towards some higher and sublime goals. Accordingly, Islam is not only coercive it equally promotes fatalism and otherworldliness, and by scoffing at critical analysis denies basic rights to women and minorities. In other words, Islam is perceived to be change-resistant and dismissive of democracy, logical critique, women's rights, and is an ideology that scoffs at secularism and pluralism. Islam, by dedicating sovereignty and primacy to a divine authority, refutes the basic concept of human sovereignty and like Medieval Christianity, is not only reactionary and irrational but also purports its followers to commit violence. Change, democracy and development, according to this view, will come about only by displacing Islam as a totalitarian force.[4] An extreme element within this group finds Islamists not only posing a challenge to their own societies but also to the rest and the West. To the alarmists within this group, Islam means unruly, shouting and chest beating mobs, sexist structures and suicide bombers, who retain international linkages and are mainly turbaned, bearded figures personified by Imam Khomeini, Osama bin Laden, Mullah Omar, Abu Hamza and Ayman Zawahiri.[5] While Muslim men are overwhelmingly caricatured in these familiar types—mostly as bleeding, Kalashnikov carrying multitudes—women are shown as all-black, veiled and scarved shadows of lifeless bodies. To deal with *this* Islam is not just a Muslim imperative but also invites a Western crusade.

Their ideological counterparts in the Muslim world harbour similar stereotypes of the West and its 'surrogates' in the Muslim countries. To them, West and likewise the Westernised Muslim elite, are inherently arrogant and ignorant, precluding the possibility of any dialogue and coexistence. Eradicating the West and its stooges is a sublime act of martyrdom, otherwise an effort to convert them as well as *misled* fellow believers, must continue. While the Western extremists justify the humbling of Islam as an obscurantist force, their Muslim radical counterparts are equally intent upon the demolition of *jahliya* (ignorance). To the former, Islam is the instigator whereas to the latter it is the redeemer. The Muslim literalists use terms such as *salafiya* (back to roots) or *tajdeed* (revival), and since the time of Muhammad Abdal Wahab (d. 1792), the theological precursor of the Saudi version of revivalist Islam, they have been shunning contacts with modernity. Al-

Afghani, Abduh, Rashid Rida and several others idealised the Salafi spirit but in consonance with modernity, though Qutb, Al-Banna, Mawdudi and the Taliban would have no professed interface with modernity, as it symbolised an immoral and deceptive West. Osama bin Laden is a literalist but not a total follower of Wahabiism as he finds it tainted with monarchical ills. However, his associate, Ayman al-Zawahiri and several other groups across the Sunni world have been deeply enthused by Wahabiism. The Ikhwan al-Muslimeen (Muslim Brotherhood) was founded as a party in 1925 by Hasan al-Banna to pursue an Islamist cause in Egypt but he was murdered apparently by the Egyptian secret services in 1950. Following the execution of Qutb by Nasser in 1966, the Ikhwan have more often followed a less radical course. Though, some radical elements undertook extreme activities such as the murder of President Anwar Sadaat in 1981, or attacks on foreign tourists, yet they have avoided a direct confrontation with the state.[6] While the Ikhwan or Salafi groups are present in almost every Arab state and have sympathisers in other Muslim regions, they have more often sought recruits by banking on Islamic revival, opposition to Israel and its Western backers, and have, in several cases like in Jordan, worked within the given political system. The Arab regimes have mostly tried to co-opt some of the religious elements for self-legitimisation and also to 'moderate' them. The states have not shirked from often using coercion against such elements, which has been a rather self-defeating exercise. For instance, in Egypt, hundreds of young Islamists are routinely apprehended by the police and secret agencies and are given physical and psychological punishment.[7] Many of them are poor, unemployed youths and given the elements of corruption and coercion in the police, they are pushed towards radicalisation.

9/11 has given the regimes everywhere a justification to use torture against their opponents by branding them as potential terrorists or fundamentalists. In North America, Europe, Russia, Australia and in the Muslim regions, the jails are full of thousands of internees who have been languishing for years while their civic rights remain suspended. For the most part there is no tangible evidence against them and they were picked up either due to some capricious intelligence or by happening to be at the wrong place at the wrong time. Other than the internees at Guantanamo Bay or Belmarsh Jail, many Muslim youths, especially those with the beards, have been rounded up merely for making sketches of aeroplanes or even for carrying the metropolitan maps. Other than this unprecedented and global witch-hunt, the racist attacks on Diaspora Muslim men and women wearing scarves, amidst ever-dwindling job opportunities for Muslim professionals due to enhanced institutional racism, has been taking a serious toll from among the Muslim minorities. Instead of speaking up for their human rights, several regimes in the North Atlantic region content themselves by blaming them for anti-Semitic incidents, which, in most cases, are carried out by neo-Nazis and not by Muslims. While European leaders have time and again shown concern on anti-Semitism, the official, institutional and group-based cases of Islamophobia register no significant attention. Such a legacy will not only further marginalise Muslims, it will certainly radicalise many elements amongst them. The issue of the scarf in 2004 became so contentious not because an overwhelmingly large number of Muslims wanted to impose it on their women, but because, in the wake of an undiminished multi-dimensional assault on Islam, they felt impelled to register their anger.[8]

In countries like Pakistan or Bangladesh, regimes usually co-opt religio-political elements as junior colleagues and even as buffers to forestall the mainstream political opposition. The situation is quite bleak in those Muslim countries where no political processes or civic institutions are available to allow even a modicum of participation to religio-political elements. It is here that, aggravated by politico-economic disempowerment, youths undergo radicalisation. The problem with most of these extreme Muslim elements is that, despite their emotional rhetoric, they are weak, disparate and self-defeating, as they do not have strong states and other such trans-regional instruments at their disposal. The post 9/11 vigilance, to a large extent, has apparently diminished the possibility of any new massive attacks in the West, yet the Anglo-American campaigns in

West Asia have duly added new cadres of sympathisers to their cause.[9] In their own countries, while excluded from electoral politics and dialogue, they have usually resorted to violence. They are fully aware that their Western and Israeli counterparts represent some of the most powerful institutions and regimes whereas they themselves are stragglers or mostly confined to some limited ideological and territorial space, and their acts of desperation often turn out to be self-immolative. However, with all the unease over their perceptions and strategies, one cannot be dismissive towards their ideological commitment to their causes and belief in an eventual triumph. 9/11 has offered them a unique precedent to hurt the West and shake its confidence through a selected act of terror, involving just a few dedicated individuals, astute planning and some uncanny mobility. The post-9/11 revengeful, illogical and even unlawful retaliation by the United States, Israel and such other countries has, by default, provided them with a vast reservoir of support and even more volunteers. That is why, even after years of massive bombing, large-scale arrests, and internment of thousands of people, the sense of insecurity in Israel and the North Atlantic regions remains quite unprecedented.

Other than these few radical and extreme elements, the vast majority of Muslims are keen on peaceful dialogue and seek an end to political conflict, which in most cases retain colonial antecedents. They are deeply disillusioned with Western interventionism for specific interests yet seek sovereign rights to decide their own problems through a wider empowerment. To them, the West and its surrogates have successively operated for partisan interests over and above societal prerogatives and redemption must come about where poverty, authoritarianism and humiliation give way to prosperity, empowerment and an honourable existence. This pervasive discourse may hold the future for Muslims involving dialogue, debate, democracy, development and reinterpretation of classical texts for an equitable, egalitarian and just order across the Muslim lands. The powerful West has to be aware and sensitive to this Muslim polarity and while taking sides must not aggravate the predicament by only strengthening the extremists and ignoring reconstructionists.

Muslim Discourses

An international and immensely diverse civilisation like Islam, despite its avowal and idealism for unity, remains plural and thus views on democracy, feminism and secularism remain variable. There are three main trajectories of Muslim discourse: the official policies of the states, the views held by religio-political parties, and the activism of societal groups consisting of *ulama*, intellectuals and activists. The vigorous rise of religio-political constellations is a global phenomenon and not essentially confined to the Muslim world, as the Neo-Orientalists and several media portrayals may like to suggest. In the case of the Muslim world, due to economic and political contradictions and official roadblocks towards full empowerment, religion turns out be not only a *communal* soothsayer, it also becomes a vehicle for political mobilization. All the way from the colonial era to the new Millennium, Islam has been a political actor at various levels, though defined in numerous ways. The global Muslim communities, other than the vital politico-economic determinants, are deeply impacted by a host of forces, which also continue to fashion views on Islam. In addition, the space of differential between the above three articulations is often blurred.

While autocratic regimes use Islam for legitimacy, many others try to co-opt Islamic groups such as in Pakistan, Bangladesh, Indonesia and elsewhere to sustain their hold on power. The secularists such as in Turkey may apparently veto Islam as a factor in politics yet the recent years have seen religio-political parties forming the government in Ankara. Even Iraq and Syria, the so-called secular authoritarian regimes, have often used Islam, whereas after Habib Bourguiba, Tunisia has gradually turned more towards Islam. In countries like Iran, elections allow Islamists to form a government under the strong thumb of a higher clerical authority whereas Jordan and other Gulf states may retain Islamic elements as junior members in the parliament while Algeria pursues a politics of crushing religious forces even if they have been elected through the ballot. The post-Soviet Central Asian republics have also moved between cooption to sheer suppression of Islamist elements though the contestation remains unresolved. Thus, in one form or the other, religio-political forces have remained a dominant feature among Muslims, who in some cases, have also enjoyed Western official support. As long as Islam—both at the state and societal levels—remains a means of preserving the status quo without undergoing some form of radicalisation, the United States and the EU would stay contented but the moment it becomes a slogan for mass empowerment and a critique of corruption by the Westernised or the surrogate forces, it poses a threat and has to be crushed. Such a strategy may suit the external powers and their intermediaries, in the wake of several outstanding political problems in the Middle East and elsewhere, yet it grievously takes its toll from ordinary Muslim masses who are stuck between the proverbial rock and the hard place.

There is a need to recognise Islam as a political force and to let it move within the mainstream democratic structures so as to make its proponents more at ease with all. Its suppression and selective military campaigns only add to pervasive fury and retaliation. Unfettered democratisation and not selective exploitation are the best *modus operandi* to let the energies of Muslims concentrate on eradication of poverty and underdevelopment. In that sense, instead of eradicating Islam as a political force, there is greater urgency to harness it through participatory institutions, even if it may beckon an eclipse of surrogacy, as that is the only way to fight extremism. The suppression of dissent, by decrying it as terrorist or the denigration of religio-political forces with an inherent fear of their anti-Westernism will only exacerbate violence, with the democratic and civic forces in the Muslim world turning into the main losers. Historically speaking, democracies are more prone to dialogue while regional cooperation can diminish inter-state and communal strife and this twin-pronged strategy could offer the best way forward towards global peace.[10]

Of course, the world of Islam has its enduring politico-economic problems besides the hackneyed views of a static *sharia*—formulated many centuries ago and several years after the Prophet—yet Islam is the rallying cry both for the societal and statist forces. The recourse to Islam—away from the East or West—is as much a retort to external highhandedness as it is an abysmal despondency. For instance, the dogmatic adherence to a rather stultified Kemalism maintained by an overpowering military synchronised with a greater sense of humiliation felt by all the Turks (and Kurds!) from scornful European pundits. Several Eastern European countries have been allowed to join the EU whereas Turkey, the largest contributor to NATO, has been endlessly sidelined. 'Turkey's values are different from ours', many Europeans including the former French President, Valery Giscard d'Estaing, unhesitatingly propound. In the meantime, the Turkish economy and nationhood remain tarnished thanks to uneven policies where the non-development sector and a unilateral Turkification have aggravated the despair. Like the Pakistani Supreme Court, the Turkish senior judges outlawed the Rifaah Party under the pretext of Kemalism, which has rebounded with more public support for religio-political elements. They elected these elements into power, which espoused a long overdue ideological consensus and autonomous foreign policies and has already valiantly resisted the US temptations and coercion over Iraq; not a minor decision given the bilateral relationship. The eventual reaction from Washington and the Turkish generals will be worth watching!

In the post-Second World War decades of optimism and polarised realism, religion was considered to be less of a unifying force and more of a nuisance in nation building. Nationalism, despite its racist and fascist undertones in Europe, was perceived by scholars such as Eli Kedourie and Hans Kohn to be a liberationist ideology with secular elite homogenising the emerging post-colonial states. 'Modernisation', not just to these Jewish liberals but also to the sociologists such as Ernest Gellner, Carl Deutsch, Benedict Anderson and Clifford Geertz, after all, was a mundane project where its Western prototypes could hold true for all. (Gellner was an exception in a sense, as he saw no clash between Islamic civil society and democracy.)[11] Jinnah, Nehru, Kenyatta, Fanon, Mao, Gandhi, Soekarno and Nkrumah were all modernists in their own ways though this generation was soon to give way—in several cases—to the 'men on horse-back' being welcomed as the new, post-national modernizers. Simultaneously, the embryonic mediatory discourse on Islam and modernity as spearheaded by Al-Afghani, Abduh, Syed Ahmed, Muhammad Iqbal, Maulana Azad, Fazlur Rahman and Allama Shariati was left asunder. The shining armour, inflated chests full of jingling medals and their associations with Sandhurst and West Point were sufficient credentials of these generals—adored by Samuel Huntington and others of his Harvard clan. Instead of scholar-activists and intellectuals interfacing across diverse traditions, Muslims were bequeathed to the simplistic and autocratic whims of uniformed harbingers of modernization and development. The role of feudal intermediaries of the colonial days now taken over by these khaki bureaucrats, submissive to their patrons yet regressive to their own peoples. However, by the 1980s and especially after the dissolution of the Cold War, these modernizers were found seriously lacking in proper representative, professional and accountable wherewithal. They were devoid of competence and conviction to run these plural societies and in the process invariably turned out to be unpopular tin-pot dictators, proving a liability to their Western backers. Despite their serious shortcomings, the Western powers, for their own partisan interests, steadily used them as allies—Ayub, Yahya, Amin, Pincohet, Manuel Noriega, Mobutu Sese Seko, the Shah of Iran, Numeiri, Saddam, Zia, Suharto, Ershad, Musharraf and the list goes on.

The current mantra, however, resounds with the desirability of empowerment of civil society, pre-eminence of liberal universalism and the reconstruction of a non-hegemonic modernity. Thus, the khaki leaders, like their other monarchical counterparts, largely stay exposed of their inherent weaknesses and inadequacies and if they are still in power it is largely due to external backing and internal divisions. This is not to suggest that the contemporary rise of religio-political outfits—using mish-mash ideologies such as Hindutva (Ram Raj) or Hukumat-i-Ilahiyya (Allah's kingdom)—are just temporary outbursts against the corruption and inability of the modernists. They have been present on the political spectrum for sometime but have only recently graduated from cultural paradigms into fully-fledged political movements. The pervasive Muslim disempowerment is mainly owed to their own leaders, and likewise their internal schisms are due to the vicious clericalization of this otherwise holistic civilisation, which, in its pristine form, had broken loose from such a bondage. This situation is not to undervalue the role of Islam as a mobilizer, aggregator and de-hegemoniser. Both the literalists and syncretists from amongst Muslim intellectuals and ideologues have been steadfast actors in the Afro-Asian decolonisation but this tradition of resistance and sacrifice predictably has often fallen victim to waywardness and schisms. Thus, like the modernists, if the Islamists of today are unable to radically improve the quality of life and fail to enthuse and lead their societies to a better, peaceful and prosperous future, their fate will not be different from the others. Ritualistic and selective implementation of rather coercive measures in the name of an uncritiqued *sharia* is only going to further divide the House of Islam. The proponents of Political Islam need to trust, protect and celebrate their masses and a radical redirection of energy and resources on the eradication of poverty away from militarization and violence deserves prioritisation. It is only through the people's power and prosperity that Political Islam may prove a balm instead of a taxing and perplexing ideology.

Muslim Revivalists and Reconstructionists

It will be ahistorical to suggest that the recent Muslim ideological debate is a home-grown development without any impact or input from the West-led modernity. Colonialism, Orientalism, post-colonial political economy, powerful Western institutions, print and visual capitalism and Diaspora all have played an important role in raising issues concurrent with the disillusionment with underdevelopment and autocratic structures. The political marginalization, often interspersed with foreign invasions and humiliations, have certainly reinvigorated the quest for a way-out from this multiple predicament and thus the West emerges both as a factor and as an ideal. Distrust as well selective idealisation of Western modernity, especially in technological and political fields, remains transcendent among Muslim opinion makers who may like to appropriate this modernity selectively without accepting its cultural baggage. Concurrently, it is pertinent to remember that over the last fourteen centuries, Islam has often, if not always, reinvented itself so as to meet different exigencies and thus if today, some Muslim revivalists idealize tradition as an emancipator, given their experience it cannot be simply brushed aside as an empty nostalgia. However, this back-to-roots, as well as selective adoption of modernity continues to underpin the ongoing debate between the Muslim revivalists and reformers. Simultaneously, they are unhappy with the current state of affair yet in their reconstructive discourse offer altogether different paradigms.

Opposed to reformist or modernist Muslims such as Al-Afghani, Sir Syed, Muhammad Abduh, Muhammad Iqbal, Ali Abdal Raziq, Asaf Fyzee, Muhammad Al-Ghazali, Fazlur Rahman, Ali Shariati and Abdul Wahid one comes across Muslim *ulama* such as Abul Ala Mawdudi, Sayyid Qutb, Hasan al-Banna, Syed Ali Nadwi, Imam Khomeini, Sheikh Ahmed Yasin, Allama Fazlullah, Maulana Samiul Haq, Mullah Omar and other known jurists belonging to parties such as the Jama'at-i-Islami, Ikhwan, Jamiat-i-Ulama-i-Hind, Jamiats (in Pakistan), Hamas, Hizbollah, or such other organizations across the Muslim world seeking a Salafi solution. They are, however, fully aware of the scientific, economic, political and military power of the West and while highly suspicious of the West, they are not entirely dismissive of its achievements though it is purely in the areas of culture and morality that they find it highly unacceptable. The current intellectual debate among Muslims has involved both Muslim and non-Muslim scholars and analysts where one comes across valuable works by Khurshid Ahmad, Rashid Ghannoushi, Abdolkarim Soroush, Tariq Ramadan, Hasan al-Turabi, Anwar Ibrahim, Ziauddin Sardar, Maryam Jameelah, Gai Eaton, Hasan Hanafi, Richard Bulliet, John Esposito,

Bruce Lawrence, Karen Armstrong and several others. In the same vein, one sees the emergence of a new generation of Muslim intellectuals, called progressive Muslims, who are steeped in the humanist traditions of Islam and are eager to acculturate positive attributes of modernity.

While the role of the Muslim *ulama*—both Shia and Sunni—remains disputatious among Muslim intellectuals, the sufis and *sajjada nishins* have also come under serious academic scrutiny. Anthropologists may attribute several meanings to sufi culture at the local levels, and while historians may seek in the sufi order a deeper political dissent to alien control, the critical Muslim intellectuals may flag their syncretic as well as fatalistic and feudal imprints.[12] However, it is the *ulama* who have caused a wider debate among Muslim thinkers and analysts. While some scholars highlight the oppositional role of the *ulama* in seeking an autonomous sphere within the community, others find a division amongst them in reference to their attitudes towards the Muslim ruling dynasties.[13] Whereas liberal and modernist Muslims have been critical of certain *ulama* for shunning inquiry and promoting unquestioned imitation, several religious scholars have been quite *political* in their views, and in several cases, along with Sufi partners such as Imam Shamil in the Caucuses they have been in the forefront of resistance. Even during the Soviet occupation of Afghanistan and the Israeli policy of dispossession, several religious leaders have constantly shown a progressive politics, though intellectually they may have been conformists.[14] It is in reference to their attitude to modernity that one enters an exciting area of interpretations. While many Muslim scholars may view the role of Muslim clergy as simply stubborn and even obscurantist—despite the outbreak of the Iranian Revolution, Afghan resistance or Hizbollah activism—a few scholars continue to believe that the Muslim clergy, in their own way, have often accepted and promulgated change.[15]

One of the most important Muslim modernists of the recent era has been Fazlur Rahman, who was groomed in the traditional as well as modern instruction.[16] Following a degree from Oxford and a teaching career at Durham University, Rahman went to Pakistan in the 1960s where he undertook to advise the regime of General Ayub Khan on Islamic reforms. He was a scholar-activist who was ultimately hunted out of the country due to some antagonistic religious groups enraged over his modernist views. He found himself a teaching position at the University of Chicago. Fazlur Rahman believed that both the past Sunni (Asha'ri) and Shia jurists usually banked upon *irja* or predestination so as to avoid any inter-community dissension.[17] Their reinterpretations for reforms were largely amenable to communitarian goals though the early Muslim groups such as the Kharijites and Mutazilas raised serious intellectual questions about prophecy, revelation and even Quranic knowledge. The renewal and reforms were further compromised by colonialism and Muslim fragmentation, which, according to Professor Rahman, could have been arrested through educational overhaul, political empowerment and a greater emphasis on rationalism. To him, Islamism or neo-fundamentalism was meant to benefit from innovation (*ijtiha'ad*) yet the *ulama* continued to cause the main roadblocks. Rahman was quite critical of these 'politics-mongering mullahs' and 'certain Islam-mongering politicians' for destroying institution-building in countries such as Pakistan. Mawdudi, to Rahman, was 'Islam-mongering' and, as early as the 1930s, had erroneously suggested that democracy 'was incompatible with Islam'.[18] Rahman died in 1988 in Chicago before several significant developments would engulf the world with new anxieties and uncertainties.

Whereas Rahman was an intellectual combining Islamic learning with modern philosophy, Mawdudi was both a scholar and an activist. His books, pamphlets, speeches, and most of all, the creation of the Jama'at-i-Islami in Lahore in 1941, followed by the formation of several other research institutes inside and outside Pakistan ensured the enduring influence of a prolific analyst. Until his death in 1979, Mawdudi carried on his publications, mainly in Urdu, besides grooming new generations of followers and activists. Professor Khurshid Ahmad is the intellectual heir to Mawdudi whose own work on Islamic economics and organization of several research bodies in the West has proffered him a vanguard role as a pre-eminent Muslim scholar. A whole generation of former students, trained and organised by several chapters of the Islami Jamiat-i-Tulaba (IJT), now hold important positions in these institutes and elsewhere in the West and reflect the permeating influence (generally referred to as *da'awa*) of Syed Mawdudi. While some Muslim intellectuals are gradually rediscovering Fazlur Rahman, still it is Mawdudi who remains the most powerful influence over Islamist movements across the Muslim world, including the Diaspora.

Mawdudi's vision of Islam was of an international federation of Muslim states with a holistic transformation on the patterns of the Pious Caliphs—the immediate four political successors to the Prophet. Mawdudi, of course, envisioned a kind of *shoora*—a government of Islamist advisors—and had his own reservations about fully-fledged democracy, territorial nationalism, feminism and certainly secularism. Women were to be organized separately, and to him, the West, despite its economic growth, largely meant cultural void—*jahliya*—that the Muslims must avoid. A separate domain for women and politics confined to qualified individuals— a kind of Islamic meritocracy—and a systemic overhaul were the major ingredients of Mawdudi's Islamist vision. Return to Islam was not only desirable for Muslims but was an ultimate human urgency given the psychological and moral chaos that he felt in the world around him. His mistrust of modernist leaders, feminists and secularists knew no bounds, as he undertook to establish a middleclass, small-town, urban party of activists, where membership was to be an earned privilege instead of a universal possibility. His influence on the new state of Pakistan, across the Middle East and elsewhere remained quite crucial though the rulers usually felt uncomfortable with his dissent. His puritanical views, scathing attack on Western materialism and immorality and a powerful critique of modernity won him many followers including Sayyid Qutb and even Imam Khomeini. His influence in North America and the United Kingdom spread through the arrival of Muslim professionals from the South Asian subcontinent, whereas in South-

East Asia, his teaching flourished through an active network of students, visitors and translated works. Organizations like the Muslim Students Association of America (MSA), established in 1963 and now called ISNA (Islamic Society of North America), and generations of Indonesian and Malaysian students were influenced by Mawdudi's regenerative thoughts, many of them seeing in him a *Mujaddid* (a de facto revivalist in the second Millennium). His influence in Malaysia has been stronger than in Indonesia and even reached the Moros in Southern Philippines.

Unlike the Western preoccupation with the Afghan Taliban and Osama bin Laden's Al-Qaeda, it is Mawdudi's school of thought that has been more crucial and far reaching among an emerging urban Muslim middle class. This middle class consists of literate professionals who seek systemic changes through sustained organizational and political effort. Mawdudi's influence has been quite crucial in inculcating a sense of common identity among the disparate Cambodian Muslims as well, of whom 250,000 to 750,000 had been killed by the Pol Pot regime.[19] W.C. Smith considered Mawdudi to be 'the most systematic of thinkers of modern Islam', whereas according to the *New Statesman* he has been one of the thirteen most influential thinkers of the twentieth century.[20] His 130-volume work problematizes modernity, idealizes the classical Muslim past and considers Islam to be the superior-most of all religions. He shuns the Western critique of human rights and women's inequality among Muslims by suggesting that Islam, in its pristine form, guarantees better rights to all and the contemporary Muslims societies are not proper barometers to judge Islam's primacy of human rights. On women, he is too concerned about the biological difference between men and women and in a rather polemical way, censures the West for destroying its moral values in the name of feminism. His Urdu book, *Purdah* (1939), based on rather sweeping statements on Western popular culture somehow reveals his confusion on seclusion and discrimination.[21]

The partition of the Subcontinent led to several complex developments including the bifurcation of pre-1947 religio-political parties like the Jamaat-i-Islami (JI) and the Jamiat. Despite migration of around ten million Indian Muslims into Pakistan, many more remained in India. The Indo-Pakistan disputes have continuously created serious challenges and tensions for Indian Muslims though breathing space was partly provided by Gandhi's struggle for communal peace and Nehruvian secularism. The political, socio-psychological and even economic cost of the events of 1947 has been manifold for Indian Muslims, whose lack of a united political platform, economic underdevelopment, serious ethno-regional divisions and the outflux of professional elite groups to Pakistan all led to a pervasive morass. The problems were further compounded by a series of periodic riots where Muslims turned out to be the main sufferers, especially in the Hindi-speaking areas. The rise of the BJP, Shiv Sena and Kar Sevak, all espousing Hindutva or majoritarian nationalism, has been inimical to secular traditions and especially to minorities like Muslims though comparatively more political freedom allowed some Muslims to build up alliances with the Congress or local low-caste parties.[22] However, given the fall-out from Ayodhya and the Gujarat massacres of 2002–3, Muslims in India are still far from secure, though an overdue Indo-Pakistani amity may help minorities in both the countries who have suffered the most for six decades.[23]

The political leadership of Indian Muslims after 1947 has been either under the clerical tutelage of people like Delhi's Shahi Imam, or has often been managed by regional parties such as the Muslim League in Kerala. Concurrently, the pre-1947 organisations such as the JI and Jamiat have attempted to carry on the debate on Muslim identity within the Indian and even modernist constructs. In this context, Darul Nadwa has been on the forefront unlike its age-old rival Aligarh where the debate has been diffused after 1947 due to prevailing circumstances. Aligarh Muslim University is no more the pioneering advocate of Muslim nationalism (separatism) unlike its role in pre-Partition days whereas Nadwa, especially under Maulana Nadwi, has assumed a more centre-stage position on Islamic discourse. Born in 1914 in the family of well-known Syeds of the UP, Syed Abul Hasan Ali Nadwi, a prominent scholar of Islam and a guiding force for Indian Muslims, represented an entire era in modern intellectual history. Until his death in 2001, Nadwi carried on the traditions of his predecessors and fellow scholars such as Shibli Nomani, Mahmood Hasan, Hussain Madani and Abul Kalam Azad. He was the Secretary of Nadwatul Ulama, Chairman of Darul Musannifin (Shibli Academy) and was awarded the King Faisal Award in 1980 for his services to Islam.[24] His multi-volume *Saviours of Islamic Spirit* offers detailed biographical and intellectual information of Muslim jurists and intellectuals of the past. He considered this project quite crucial towards the regeneration of *millat*, which he refused to call 'revival', and instead defined it as 'a spirit of reawakening among Muslims'.[25] The Academy of Islamic Research Publications in Lucknow published scores of volumes by Nadwi, mostly written in Urdu and Arabic, and it was at Nadwa that he taught while not travelling and lecturing abroad. He was an advisor to Rabita Alam-i-Islami, Rector of Nadwatul Ulama and on the trusteeship of several research institutes outside India.

While Mawdudi believed in governance-based Islamism, Nadwi urged for one that was guidance-based. In other words, Mawdudi advocated collective efforts towards the transformation of state and society including the acquisition of political power, while Nadwi felt that individual and small group-based programmes, not necessarily of the political kind, could guarantee the same results. Perhaps it had to do with the realities within a Muslim-majority Pakistan that Mawdudi saw the attainability of an Islamic state, whereas a holistic Islamic political order[26] in a largely Hindu India with a dispersed Muslim community, did not stand a chance. The first part of Nadwi's *From the Depth of the Heart in America* is devoted to a survey of Western civilisation and how it is reflected in American life. Here his analysis is neither polemical nor does it turn into a pedestrian harangue. In the second part, he focuses on the Muslim immigrants, whom he met during his lecture visits. America, to Nadwi, reflects 'supremacy of machines' and is awash with wealth and luxury though only for the privileged as the system lacks an egalitarian distributive system.[27] As a true disciple of Muhammad Iqbal, he finds the malaise accruing out of an overpowering materialism that marginalizes spiritual underpinnings. Nadwi feels that Europe, by accepting Christianity, likewise disallowed itself a moral debate on the unbound growth of materialism. Given the concept of original sin, Christianity, to Nadwi, itself circumscribes intellectual vistas:

> Today, America has enslaved the world, but it has, itself become the slave of machines... The properties of rock and iron have entered his (American/Western) soul. He has become narrow and selfish, cold, unfeeling and impervious. There is no warmth in his heart; no moisture in his eyes. This is the reality I have sadly observed during my stay in America.

He warns American Muslims against this unchecked materialism that poses the greatest challenge to human civilization.[28] His lecture at Harvard's Divinity College was captioned 'The History of the World would Have been Different, Had America been Blessed with Islam'. While criticizing an immense dependence on material well-being, Nadwi observed, 'The Western World, which stretches from Europe to the Americas is most fortunate yet is most unfortunate.' Its single-factor focus 'on material progress' and concentration on the physical world as 'the sole sphere of activity' have diminished the forces of heart and soul. He finds fault with Christianity for making serious compromises and likewise with the Muslim regimes for being apologetic on the virtues of Islam.[29] In another speech in Washington, he felt that the United States lacked in real and sincere friends, largely because of America's own tradition of insincerity. Its 'generosity is a cloak for the exploitation of the weaker and the poorer nations. It gives, but not to enable them to stand on their feet. Its magnanimity is aimed at the peripheralization of their dependence upon it.'[30] In his addresses to the MSAs convention in Chicago in 1977, he spoke on Iqbal, Muslim women, Indian Muslims and Western civilisation and also warned against a *European* or *American* Islam that may compromise its transterritoriality. Nadwi's influence will prove to be quite significant not only in the perspective of Indian Islam but also in reference to its position on modernity. Several of his students have

commented on him and espoused his views, some even accepting
the term, Islamic fundamentalism as an overdue resurgence.[31]

Convert scholars to Islam such as Muhammad Asad[32] and Gai
Eaton[33] have inspired generations of Muslims with their scholarship
and self-assurance whereas activists such as Yusuf Islam[34] and sufis
like Martin Lings[35] have also left their enduring imprints. The
Diaspora influence whether through conversion such as the Nation
of Islam or sufi followers, or through a vanguard debate with non-
Muslim counterparts is equally important in diffusing Islamic
precepts.[36] However, one has to be careful in subscribing big figures
on conversions to Islam since the Diaspora has its own problems
including institutional racism, and many Muslims are withdrawing
from professing Islam as well. However, it is always Islam which is
posited as the second largest growing religion in the West, and even
Muslims seek greater satisfaction in presuming a steady increase in
their numbers. The fact is that the numbers have increased largely
due to immigration and not essentially owing to some large-scale
conversions. For instance, in Italy there are only 10,000 Muslim
converts, compared to 50,000 converts to Buddhism but it is
always Islam which is presented as a threat of growing proportions
and the exaggerated numbers are cited to substantiate such claims.
In Britain and Germany the numbers of converts are again not that
high and one needs to take into account the ratio of reversion to
the previous religious identities of the converts though studies have
not focused on such issues.[37]

Most of the recent scholarship on the interpreters of Islam and
modernity still remains preoccupied with the well-known
modernists and revivalists such as Al-Afghani, Iqbal, Abduh, Rashid
Rida, Syed Mawdudi and Sayyid Qutb, while a new generation of
Islamists and modernists has already been quite vocal on several
academic fronts. It is a different thing that only the radicals and
extremists receive total attention whereas the intra-Muslim debate
remains largely unknown. In her book on Muslim scholarship on
Christianity, Kate Zebiri finds a pervasive indifference on the part
of Muslim intellectuals, though her tone is not as critical as that of
Bernard Lewis. She finds more Christians studying Islam than

Muslims showing serious interest in the former, which is in fact an erroneous concept. The survival of Christians among Muslim majority communities allowed a continuous interaction besides scholarship in local languages, if not in English. As a growing number of works reveal, Muslims have been discussing various Abrahamic traditions over the last several centuries, though authors like Zebiri may not be aware of them.[38] One of her own colleagues, in fact, has shown that even in nineteenth century India several *ulama* engaged in debates with European missionaries.[39] Some recent studies by John Cooper, John Esposito and John Voll have focused on two new generations of Muslim revivalists and modernists, while historians such as Allan Austin have unearthed the memories and archives of early African Muslim slaves.[40] One may endlessly go on recording an increasing list of names who have been engaged in the intra-Muslim debate—though often not so smooth and easy—while simultaneously pursuing an inter-cultural dialogue. Well-known scholars such as the Late Professor Ismail Faruki, Tariq Ramadan, Shabbir Akhtar and Ziauddin Sardar are a few from amongst many. While Marayam Jameela, Hasan Turabi and Khurshid Ahmad may assert Islamic self-sufficiency in the tradition of Syed Mawdudi and Sayyid Qutb, Hasan Hanafi, Rashid Ghannoushi, Zaki Badawi, Abdolkarim Soroush and Anwar Ibrahim urge for dialogue and acculturation.[41] Muslim scholars including Fatima Mernissi, Leila Ahmed, Riffat Hasan, Meliha Malik, Asma Barlas and several journalists, freelance writers and activists do not find any conflict between Islam and the positive attributes of modernity. Muslim feminism and even Muslim secularism are seen as actualities by some of these widely quoted analysts though one has to acknowledge that many Muslim women, like men, may also seek solace in a revival instead of reforms. Such a forward-looking intellectual position is being espoused by a number of Muslim intellectuals, sometimes known as progressive Muslims.

Progressive Muslims, a Fact or yet another Label?

Several Muslim intellectuals share reservations on the usage of terms such as fundamentalism, orthodoxy, Islamism, Islamicism, Islamic terrorism, Muslim reformism, Islamic renaissance, Islamic revivals, and some of them find terms like Muslim secularism or Muslim feminism oxymorons. Not only do these terms represent a Foucoultian or Derridian perspective, these also reflect Eurocentricity highlighting a uniformist cultural hegemony. On the one hand, some Muslims do not deny being fundamentalists as it denotes belief in the five fundamentals of Islam, but given the negative connotation they also feel offended by its application to them. *Orthodoxy* also assumes a pejorative reference whereas *Islamism* simplifies Islamic civilisation to a mere 'ism'. Simultaneously, *Islamists* will be those who are Muslim by conviction and would seek to implement Islam in its holistic sense, whereas *Islamicists* would be simply the scholars of Islam, irrespective of their own ideological background. They do not have to be Muslim as such. Some Muslims like Abdullah an-Naim have used the term Islamic reformism without any hesitation by suggesting that a host of socio-political and economic issues in the Muslim world need rectification. In the same manner, Muhammad Iqbal, Fazlur Rahman, Aziz Ahmad and several other Muslim writers have used the term, Islamic modernism, in a rather syncretic sense to benefit from both the trajectories. To them, Islam has its own humanist heritage and to draw from any area of human excellence is inherently Islamic. It is true that some Muslims do not like to be labelled or hyphenated with any other ideology or ism as it may compromise their ideational authenticity, yet there are several intellectuals who feel no qualms in defining themselves as progressive Muslims.[42] The term 'progressive' picked up some leftist connotations during the 1960s and 1970s, when political figures in several Muslim countries began to profess Islamic socialism.[43]

Progressive Muslims have no dispute with the classical sources of Islam, though they seek newer and dynamic interpretations in consonance with a wider, shared human experience. They focus on democracy, inter-gender equality, human rights and respect for pluralism and are prepared to co-opt Western and other non-Islamic experiences. They are vocally critical of obscurantism, feudalism, dictatorships and ideological nihilism while being abhorrent of violence against non-Muslims and women, nefariously ordained in the name of a narrowly defined Islam. To them, Islamic humanism, in its reincarnation, can reflect secularism, feminism and a fully participatory politico-economic order. These intellectuals are neither rejecting Islamic mores nor are absorbing modernist precedents uncritically, and instead have attempted to articulate with honesty and humility. They are aware of the concept of 'multiple critique' with its relevance for Muslim deconstructionists committed to social justice, pluralism, and gender justice. They may not be comfortable with terms such as *liberal* Muslims or Muslim *liberals* given the obfuscation as well as controversial nature of such terms. They are aghast at the hijacking of Islam by a few terrorist groups and likewise the partisan and often destructive vengeance wreaked both by the states and societal groups on Muslims in general. In their humanist view, even sufism, despite its ritualistic and often hierarchical aspects, could be redefined to strengthen Islamic humanism.[44]

In the progressive discourse, Saadi, Khayyam, Rumi, Bob Dylan and John Marley can all coexist without claiming separate and conflictive domains. Khaled Abou El-Fadl, one such progressive Muslim, locates terrorist groups like Al-Qaeda as 'a sociological and intellectual marginality in Islam,'[45] while Farid Esack, the South African Muslim, has no patience for obscurant as well as liberal hegemonies.[46] To these progressive thinkers of Islam, their religion reflects both unity and diversity, appropriate of any such civilisation. They focus on early intellectuals such as Iqbal or Ali Abd al-Raziq, who attempted to separate religion from law and politics without feeling humble about their Muslimness. Ebrahim Moosa is, in fact, inspired by this early debate in India and Egypt led by Syed Ahmad Khan, Muhammad Iqbal, and Asaf A.A. Fyzee, who tried to delineate separate domains for ecclesiasts, politicians, jurists and philosophers. They were deeply concerned about clerical authoritarianism in the name of ritualistic legitimacy and were equally uncomfortable with the imitation of an uncritiqued modernity. However, Moosa is aware of the fact that given the contemporary confrontational and often similar hegemonies on all sides, it may not be easy to be a progressive Muslim.[47] Such a position does not totally reject Tariq Ali's view of 'a clash of fundamentalisms' but refuses to look at the past with the contemporary condescending ideology of achievement. A progressive Muslim, without defining himself as a *moderate, a reformist* or *modern* is, in fact, seeking truth and inspiration from a variety of sources including Western. Such a gigantic task, as suggested by Sa'diayya Shaikh, the Indian African Muslim scholar, is no mean feat, since one has to be cognisant of pitfalls on all sides without pursuing outright imitation or sheer rejection. Obfuscation as well as contradiction is not confined to any single ideological group. She offers an axiomatic example 'of the British Consul General in Egypt, Lord Cromer, who in the late nineteenth century was the champion of Egyptian women's unveiling while in his homeland, England, he was the President of the men's league for opposing women's suffrage.'[48] A century later, following the invasions of Afghanistan and Iraq, both the United States and Britain were dithering not only in their promises for democracy but instead by supporting warlords and other non-representative forces, they were only regimenting anti-women policies. Women, both in Afghanistan and Iraq after 9/11, as admitted by their activists, turned out to be the main losers. While 'the rapists' from the Northern Alliance, and other hierarchies, were reinstated in Afghanistan,[49] some of the most liberal laws in the Arab world since 1959 were pushed aside by the coalition-based regime in Baghdad.[50]

Several forward-looking Muslims are engaged in reinterpreting laws governing property, evidence, personal and family affairs within the context of contemporary times by offering pragmatic and programmic discourse. Muslim feminists such as Leila Ahmed, Fatima Mernissi and numerous others are concurrently steeped in Islamic and Western traditions, and through their research, have been able to offer tangible alternatives on democracy, human rights and gender equity within the redefined and workable public and private spheres for Muslim women. While appreciative of some of the successes of feminists in the West, they are also aware of their stereotypes about Islam and a perceived notion of an eternal subjugation of women. To the Muslim feminists, empowerment of women has to come about through a reinterpretation of classical texts as well as of modernity avoiding a unilinear approach. Muslim intellectuals such as Amina Wadud have been trying to create a more dynamic interface between indigenous American Muslims and their immigrant coreligionists. Both need to interact and learn more from each other in the larger interest of intra-Muslim pluralism. For instance, while African-American Muslims allow more space to women on the religious committees and their *imams* are earning hands, the immigrants mostly depend upon *imported imams* and allow a very limited public role to women.[51] There is certainly an urgency to underpin this interface with the ideas put forth by Malcolm X and Warith Deen Muhammad.

Muslim Secularism: A Possibility or Wild Guess?

To some of the vocal 'dissidents', Islam and secularism—like Islam and feminism—have always represented not only two totally different (even antagonistic) traditions, but their conjoining is itself an oxymoron. In other words, while seeking an interface between the two opposite trajectories, either the proponents of Muslim secularism were being too irresponsible, or were mere apologists, to whom an uncritiqued and contentious modernity remained supreme over Islamic traditions. Certainly, modernity, despite its emphasis on human rights, democratization, reason, gender equality and other technological amenities, is itself problematic and has been largely responsible for major spirals in collective violence. Europeanization of the world since the fifteenth century is a mixed but significantly painful human experience and that is why there has been so much scepticism on the idea of progress. Concurrently, interpreting contemporary conflicts simply as a clash of cultures or contestation between modernity and tradition is also proving simplistic.[52] The contentious debate in India largely spearheaded by Saffron groups of the Hindutva while challenging Nehruvian secularism and Gandhian religious co-existence, is not that different from the pervasive Muslim suspicions of secularity. Gone are the days when it was thought that development and better economic standards will not only make people more tolerant but alike as well, and the uncouth poor whose fanaticism and superstitious beliefs were considered 'primitive', would become part of an enlightened global village. In fact, new ideologues and fundamentalists of all shades are curiously 'modern primitives', and in most cases, middle class professionals though their foot soldiers may come from the laity.

Within the context of this heated controversy, interestingly, some Muslim *ulama*, instead of an outright dismissal of secularism, have quietly begun to debate the possible interface between Islam and secularism rather than viewing them as eternal foes. However, even the progressive Muslim scholars accept that the reconstructive discourse is still in its embryonic stage, understandably due to often statist and societal rejectionism of secularism and of feminism. Their scepticism manifests a growing disgust with the hijacking of both religion and political authority by nefarious elements at the expense of societal prerogatives. While Islamists may seek the Muslim predicament, among other factors, in the absence of complete Islamization of the Muslim states, the fact remains that even the confessional states with professed Islamist orders such as Saudi Arabia, Iran, Pakistan or Taliban Afghanistan have consistently failed to induct participatory and accountable systems.[53] Islam in all these states has more often been used to serve specific interests, or is a mere whitewash leading to more communitarian schisms and feuds. As the history of the last half-century reveals, these so-called Islamic regimes have neither ameliorated the lot of the ordinary people nor have they augured any major uplift in socio-economic or intellectual areas. They have, in all these cases, encouraged fundamentalist groups with particularist agendas to further specific interests and now find themselves lost in an ideological maze. (Official) Islam, in many of these states, simply came to be used to legitimize sheer authoritarian oligarchies, anachronistic systems and discretionary policies.

Retrospectively, it will be safe to suggest that the selective and penal use of Islam by regimes has not only exacerbated public anguish but also worsened human rights in those societies. The contradictions—thanks to this partisan intermingling of religion and politics—are more obvious if one looks at the state of minorities in these states along with a clear deterioration in the status of women. The so-called Westernised elite in the post-independence decades have dangerously kow-towed to external backers while concurrently denying basic rights to their own people. Concurrently, the religio-political elements within the governments and outside have equally repressed civic rights, and their bombastic rhetoric has only exacerbated sectarian and inter-ethnic violence. Interestingly, both the Westernised and Islamist political elite have often used the West, neighbours and even modernity as convenient foes, not out of some genuine conviction but simply for selective expediency. While for the religio-political elite, the West is the given *other*, to the modernizing elite it is both a useful prop and a convenient scapegoat when the waters turn rough for themselves. In other words, other than the injudicious Western policies, it is the ruling and religious elite who have persistently famed anti-Western and even anti-modern sentiments among the laity.

Understandably, while there are problems within the respective trajectories such as Westernized modernity and politicized Islam, there is an urgency for promoting a reconstructive debate, which could steer Muslim peoples towards a better understanding, peace and progress. Lately, unlike their other counterparts elsewhere and more like progressive Muslims, some of the Iraqi and even Iranian *ulama* have begun to suggest a rethink on separation of religion from state. They are not advocating a complete banishment of religion from political discourse but are being increasingly critical of its routine exploitation by political authorities for personal or dynastic gains. They even use terms such as Muslim secularism more boldly, though such a discourse is ironically happening only after the Anglo-American occupation of vast West Asian regions. A similar debate is still not openly possible in any other Muslim state, though Muslims in India, Turkey and other countries often espouse a syncretic discourse, away from rejection of democracy, secularism and gender equality. Coming from the *ulama* in Najaf, Karbala, Baghdad or even Qum, such a quest is certainly nascent yet amazingly positive.[54] One may add that it is not just the political authority that has often misused and abused Islam as a legitimising force; the religious authorities with emotional rhetoric and half-baked ideas have been equally responsible for mayhem among ordinary believers. Millions of innocent Muslims have lost their lives in the past centuries owing to obscurantist *fatwas* and uncalled-for exhortation of *jihad*, of which many have been against fellow Muslims. The more recent examples are of General Zia's Pakistan where Muslim minorities paid a huge price to a growing Sunni majoritarianism.

According to common parlance in Pakistan, the mullah plus military axis causes most of the sectarian and anti-women violence. The promotion of *jihadi* elements in the 1980s and a nod from Washington and elsewhere resulted in a whole plethora of outfits pursuing several hazy ideas across the region. In neighbouring Afghanistan, Iran and Central Asia, Islam remains an instrument both for regimes and the mullahs to extract maximum blood from their own marooned populations. Denial of democracy and other human rights is a consensus point, for otherwise these often rival religious and political authorities. Algeria, where France in league with the army created chaos by disallowing the Islamists from forming an elected government during the 1990s, is yet another sad reminder of both religion and politics being hijacked by respective rent-seeking interests. Saudi Arabia and the Gulf regimes, while kow-towing to the Western elite, blatantly discriminate against workers from poor countries. They have altogether different policies and touchstones for Western convicts, while dozens of poor Bangladeshis, Sri Lankans, Pakistanis and Afghans are routinely executed by *muttawa* (religious police) outside the mosques. The Westerners, even after their convictions, are habitually pardoned for similar crimes by the Muslim kings and emirs. Not a single *alim* from this so-called Muslim heartland has ever raised his voice over this sheer discrimination that certainly smacks of racism and double standards.

Though the status quo or external hegemony are not acceptable options yet concurrently leading innocent and vulnerable Muslim citizens into kamikaze attacks is equally reprehensible. The humanist reinterpretation of Islam and likewise of secularism can surely deliver Muslims from this continued monopolist exploitation by the politico-religious authoritarianism, and may also augur an overdue Islamic renaissance. Simultaneously, it may offer a unique alternative to an abrasive modernity in the West—itself locked in collective violence perpetrated through institutional racism and unilateralist militarism.

Within the Muslim world, a pervasive dismissal of a precept originating in the West or from any other external source bespeaks of serious malaise, since Muslims were exhorted as early as almost fifteen centuries ago to seek knowledge from all over. Assuredly, the reconstruction of long overdue *ijtiha'ad* is the only way out from gnawing societal and statist oppression; it can offer a respite from suffocating conformity while halting foreign denigration of a human heritage like Islam. Certainly, the contemporary usage of secularism in Turkey and France as a tool for state-led superimposition also adds to common reservations towards it. By assuming immensely dogmatic and unassailable portents and by disallowing choice, which otherwise is seen to be the main attribute of secularism, there is a danger of its turning into a new tyranny.

The case of Turkey is especially difficult, as here Kemalism as a hegemonic force has not only displaced religion from the public sphere, it has equally put brakes on substantive democratization and equitable pluralism. Its imposition from above and then the statist insistence on its invincibility even at the expense of civic rights, only betray a partisan approach causing retaliation from various sections of Turkish and Kurdish societies. Secularism otherwise meant as a liberationist ideology has itself become regressive with serious ramifications for Turkish civic society, and it is only through universal, unfettered democratisation, greater recognition of plural rights, in league with the external persuasion and internal pulls, that the country can attain a balancing point. One can understand France's impatience with headgear or other distinct religious symbols, but such an annoyance is underpinned by a stated concept of assimilation, over and above plural prerogatives. It makes citizenship conditional upon a pre-established and almost sacrosanct assimilation in a majoritarian-led identity.

India's secularism, despite severe strains and some contradictions due to a rather erstwhile dismissive elitism and an aggressive Hindutva, is a possible *modus operandi* for similar plural societies and could offer a useful parallel for Muslim reconstructionists. Its Gandhian portents appear similar to Islamic sensitivities on religion, since here religion is accepted as a part of collective and individual life without being totally banished from the public domain. However, while Muslims in India have felt comparatively safer under a secular system and are certainly apprehensive of a majoritarian Hindutva, their own localism, dependence upon some clerics for political articulation and other socio-economic handicaps have not allowed them to fully benefit from the systemic dynamics in the country. But compared to any other Muslim state, India's democracy still affords the best hope for coexistence and its secular system a viable safety valve for minorities. It is a different thing that clerical versions of Islam abound in Muslim India, yet secularist polity is the best guarantee for collective survival and welfare of Indian Muslims and other such minorities. This is not to deny the fact that, to a great extent, India's own future and of its plural communities depends upon the policies of its majority population groups. If the Hindus, as egged on by the Kar Sevaks, Shiv Sena, RSSS and Vishwa Hindu Parishad, are intent upon turning the country into a Hinduist mould the minorities—both Hindu and others—may have fewer options at their disposal boding a major disaster for the most plural and equally populous country on earth. It is certainly difficult for practising and reconstructionist Indian intellectuals like Asghar Ali Engineer or Mushirul Hasan to be able to hoist the banner of a tolerant, accommodative and all-encompassing Muslim secularism when the opposition to them mainly comes from the Muslim clergy as well as from Hindu fanatics.

Empirically, secularism as seen in the West, despite a paucity of self-professing states, emerged through a gradual separation of church and state but in its original form secularism stood for the primacy of mundane knowledge away from the monopoly of ecclesiasts. From as far back as the classical Greek era, it has been a long march, though even now the Creationists and Neoconservatives would like to turn the clock back by using evolution as bait. But despite its three existing various models—France, Turkey and India, though the communist polities may also offer similar postulations as well—secularism is not culture-or region-specific. It needs to be seen as a human evolutionary heritage, with Islam as one of its contributory factors. Secularism, at one level, is anti-monopoly and dehegemonizing, whether the latter comes from sultans or religious scholars. Thus, it is uniquely akin to Political Islam in its struggle against colonialism. The development of the Umayyad literature and philosophy in Muslim Spain, promotion of learning and debate in Fatimid North Africa, Mughal India, pre-Safavid Persia, Central Asian and Turkish kingdoms—on several extended occasions—reflected a model where worldly knowledge and religious interaction coexisted without vetoing each other. The diffusion of Greek, Hindu and Chinese learning and a conscious synthesis with the African and European mores and customs energized Islamic civilisation at all times. Thus, irrespective of the heuristics of the term itself, the practice of a humanist secularism as an exploitation-free, egalitarian and forward looking system—both in politics and education—falls in line with the Islamic heritage spreading over centuries.[55] A hasty rejection of secularism due to its Turkish or such other embodiments, its various pitfalls as a Western construct or a modernist edifice, may not be a fair way to judge its merits. Muslim secularism is a possibility in the near future, as it has been a historic Muslim experience in the past and is not an alien proposition. It may prove a death knoll to the vast disempowerment and continued exploitation of Muslim masses both by the sultans and scholars and could also reinvigorate Muslim intellectual, literary and artistic efforts, which for so long had been the hallmark of Muslim humanism.

NOTES

1. There are an amazing number of commonalities in ideologies, strategies and actions of the religio-political groups, irrespective of their national and religious background. The Taliban, Khalistanis, Jihadis, Hindutva proponents and the followers of Pakistan as a Sunni state or Shias in Iran and Iraq, Kurdish clusters, or Likudists in Israel all use history, demography, religion, race, economy, nationalism, democracy and relationship with the outside world in their own ways. They espouse majoritarian nationalism, legalized by some religious fundamentalism. One could even see the groups in Northern Ireland, racist-Christian elements in the Balkans, Russia, the North Atlantic regions and in Australia also propounding similar creeds. They all seek power and would like to transform both the state structures and societies in their own ways. For the case of South Asia, I have discussed this in my other work, *Jihad, Hindutva and the Taliban: South Asia at the Crossroads,* Oxford, 2005.

2. The Khomeini-led revolution in Iran in 1979, the Taliban, proponents of a Sunni state in Pakistan, India's Hindutva proponents, Sinhalese nationalists in Sri Lanka or Nepal's Khas Hindu nationalists and Muslim Bengal radicals, like the Likuds, Neoconservatives and such other Ultra Right constellations have several commonalities, which have not been fully ascertained by scholars. In the same way, to write them off merely as *traditional* clusters at loggerheads with modernity is a superficial view. They are, in fact, the creations and consequences of modernity that has itself unleashed multiple forces in its wake. The selective use of contemporary issues intermingled with nostalgia underlie these ideological constructs. In their goals and strategies they fully apply all the available modernist instruments, symbols and technologies and promise a new interface between state and society. For a pertinent discussion, see John Gray, *Al-Qaeda and What It Means to be Modern,* London, 2003.

3. Such secularists, themselves the creation of Westernism, may include a wide variety of ideologues and activists such as Mustafa Kemal, Habib Bourguiba, Salman Rushdie, Ishtiaq Ahmed or Fouad Ajami.

4. For instance, Kedourie wrote: 'The idea of representation, of elections, of popular suffrage, of political institutions being regulated by laws laid down by a parliamentary assembly, of these laws being guarded and upheld by an

indepdent judiciary, the idea of the secularity of the state...all these are profoundly alien to the Muslim political tradition'. Eli Kedourie, *Democracy and Arab Political Culture*, Washington, 1992, p. 5.

5. The picture of a bearded and disheveled Saddam Hussein, following his capture in late 2003, was utilised fully to make him a prototype of Muslim militants. It was interesting and equally curious to notice his former uniformed pictures to have almost totally disappeared from the visual and print media.

6. Khaled Abou El Fadl, 'The Ugly Modern and the Modern Ugly: Reclaiming the Beautiful in Islam', in Omid Safi (ed.) *Progressive Muslims*, Oxford, 2003.

7. Based on interviews with some Egyptian exiles in the UK, in February 2004. Also, for a detailed investigative report on the global network of detention centres where torture is routinely administered see Adrian Levy and Cathy Scott-Clark, 'One Huge US Jail', *Guardian Magazine*, 19 March 2005.

8. Anti-Muslim sentiments and efforts by several Western leaders and groups are no more a secret, as they remain rooted in a strong religious evangelism and self-belief. Even some dons in Oxford at a College on 18 February 2004 were overheard by a Muslim employee saying that some people in and around the Bush Administration were intent upon 'obliterating' the Islamic factor from global politics. The dons were discussing Bush's daily worship of 60-90 minutes at the White House and were unaware of the presence of their Muslim colleague within hearing range.

9. Following 9/11, Mamoun el-Houdeiby (1921–2004), the leader of the Ikhwan, said: 'The United Sates has exploited the events to attack Islam as a creed and target Muslims and Islamic states. As a result, the Islamic movements will grow and will never be vanquished.' Quoted in Khalid Al Mubarak, 'Mamoun el-Hodeiby', *Guardian*, 18 February 2004. A former judge, he had succeeded his father to the leadership of the Ikhwan and from 1965–1971 was in jail. Earlier, in 1956, while posted in Gaza, the Israelis had arrested him. Hosni Mubarak tolerated the Ikhwan parliamentary presence under the banner of Wafd, though the regime had ensured a smaller number of seats for them in 1984 and only ten in 1987.

10. This argument can be challenged as since the French Revolution in particular, most of the global warfare and similar forms of collective violence have either been started by democracies or have at least involved them. The United States and West European countries, without any exception, have been the salient perpetrators of violence within Europe and elsewhere besides a regimentation of slavery and racism. After 9/11, the two leading exponents of democracy attacked two struggling and rather impoverished Third World countries. Israeli policies against Palestinians have continued undiminished under all the democratic regimes, and so has been the case with India in reference to its policies in Kashmir and the North-East. But that does not mean that dictatorship could be a better alternative to democracy as, unlike democracy,

it is itself based on violence and often imposes its verdict through non-democratic means.

11. There is a host of literature on nationalism and its primordial, modernist and instrumentalist explanations. Writers such as Anthony D. Smith, Benedict Anderson, Ernest Gellner, Eric Hobsbawm, Paul Brass and several others have added to an ongoing debate.

12. It is certainly impossible to list all the authors who have studied sufi *silsilahs* (orders) for doctrinal, political, historical and economic reasons. The works by Richard Eaton, Annmarie Schimmel, Michael Gilesenan, Pnina Werbner, Olivier Roy, Sarah Ansari, Bernard Heykal and David Gilmartin merit special attention.

13. Studies on the Sunni jurists, Shia hierarchies including the Ismailies, Seveners or Twelvers, and such other sects have received academic attention in almost every era. In recent times, scholars have looked at their role in reference to the issues of modernity especially during the period of Muslim political decline. Works by Annemarie Schimmel, Francis Robinson, Ishtiaq Husain Qureshi, Asghar Ali Engineer, Barbara Metcalf, David Lellyweld, Farzana Shaikh, S.A.A. Rizvi, W.C. Smith, Mushirul Hasan and V.R. Nasr have deeply added to our knowledge of Shah Wali Ullah Dehlvi, Deobandis, Brelvis, Syed Mawdudi, Abul Kalam Azad and other such luminaries.

14. As a matter of fact, the *ulama* led the resistance to the Soviets and displaced the regional landed aristocracy in Afghanistan. Thus the *Mullah* replaced the *Khan* as the Taliban became the ultimate exponents of this major shift in the power structure in rural Afghanistan. After 9/11 and the Western intervention in Afghanistan, the Khans reemerged in the country though the Taliban, now enthused by Jihad as well as a bruised Pushtun ethnicity, kept up the resistance to the Americans and their Afghan allies.

15. Fazlur Rahman, like Muhammad Iqbal, felt that obscurantism had dispirited Islam whereas Qasim Zaman may consider them 'the custodians of change'. To Rahman, Mawdudi was a rabble-rouser and not strictly a typical cleric but he failed to offer a new educational syllabus and built upon the stir created by a visionary like Iqbal. See, Fazlur Rahman, *Islam and Modernity: Transformation of an Intellectual Tradition,* Chicago, 1982. For a defense of *ulama* and the traditional *madrassa* traditions see, Muhammad Qasim Zaman, *The Ulama in Contemporary Islam: Custodian of Change,* Princeton, 2002.

16. For more details on him and other modernists, see Iftikhar H. Malik, *Islam, Globalisation and Modernity: The Tragedy of Bosnia,* Lahore, 2004, pp. 23-8.

17. Fazlur Rahman, *Revival and Reform in Islam: A Study of Islamic Fundamentalism,* Oxford, 2003. The work was largely edited by Ebrahim Moosa and was published posthumously.

18. Rahman was critical of Mawdudi for confining democracy to only a few advisory individuals (*shoora*) and for his rejection of parliamentary democracy. He was equally critical of Pakistani leaders for lagging behind and doing

'precious little'. See, Abdullah Ahsan, 'Pakistan since Independence: An Historical Analysis', *Muslim World*, 93, 3 and 4, July-October 2003, pp. 366-7. Mawdudi was also attacked by one of his former colleagues, Israr Ahmad, according to whom the former had confined the JI to Muslims and had 'nationalized' it to just Pakistan. Schism had taken place at a meeting in 1957 when Ahmad and Amin Islahi decided to leave the JI. Abdul Rashid Motem, 'Mawdudi and the Transformation of Jama'at-i-Islami in Pakistan', ibid., pp. 391-413.

19. M. Kamal Hassan, 'The Influence of Mawdudi's Thought on Muslims in Southeast Asia: A Brief History', ibid., pp. 429-64.
20. W. C. Smith, *Islam in Modern History*, Toronto, 1957, p. 236. See, Ziauddin Sardar, 'Maulana Sayyid Abul-Ala Maududi', *New Statesman*, 14 July 2003.
21. For further details, see, Sajjad Idris, 'Reflections on Mawdudi and Human Rights', *Muslim World*, 93, 2003, pp. 547-61.
22. For a comprehensive study, see Mushirul Hasan, *Legacy of a Divided Nation: India's Muslims since Independence*, London, 1997.
23. About five million Hindus in Pakistan have often been scapgoated by Muslim militants and, like some other minorities, have been under a negative searchlight. See, Iftikhar H. Malik, *Religious Minorities in Pakistan*, London, 2002.
24. For his views on Islam, the Prophet and Western civilisation see, Syed Abul Hasan Nadwi, *Inviting to the Way of Allah*, (eight lectures), Leicester, 1996. Here he considers *da'awa* (invitation to Islam) superior to *sharia* (law). He was well versed in Western scholarship—especially Orientalist—as is evident from his comments on Gibbon, Hitti, Muir, Arnold and others. See, his *Islam and the Earliest Muslims: Two Conflicting Portraits*, trans. by Mohiuddin Ahmad, Lucknow, 1985.
25. Syed Abul Hasan Ali Nadwi, *Saviours of Islamic Spirit*, vol. 1, transl. by Mohiuddin Ahmad, Lucknow, 1976, p. xi.
26. For a comparative study, see Ahmed Murkarram, 'Some aspects of Contemporary Islamic Thought: Guidance and Governance in the work of Mawlana Abul Hasan Nadwi and Mawlana Abul Ala Mawdudi', a D. Phil dissertation, Oxford, 1992.
27. Abul Hasan Nadwi, *From the Depth of the Heart in America*, translated by Mohammad Arif Kidwai, Lucknow, 1978, p. 10.
28. Ibid., p. 15. He further observes: 'This civilization has developed indigestion'. P. 17.
29. Ibid., pp. 24-31.
30. Ibid., p. 41.
31. Habibul Haq Nadwi, *Islamic Fundamentalism: A Theology of Liberation and Renaissance*, Durham, 1995. In this work, as endorsed by Rashid Ghannouchi, Nadwi is concerned about Muslims being vulnerable to another *jahliyya* in case of not being attuned to struggle against injustices and unjust rulers. This kind of fundamentalism, without being intolerant or terrorist, was seen by him as a theology of liberation and like in the past crisis could deliver

Muslims from recurring challenges. Thus, more than a mere religious rhetoric, fundamentalism—more like Rahman's neo-fundamentalism—this was to confront post-1991 social, political and spiritual challenges. Ghannouchi defines it as Mahdism while Habibul Haq Nadwi has no qualms in positing it as fundamentalism.

32. Muhammad Asad, *The Road to Mecca*, London, 1998. This best seller by a Hungarian Jewish convert was first published in 1954 and remains quite popular among Muslims.

33. This British Muslim served in the Middle East as a diplomat and accepted Islam. His works not only reveal a strong belief in Islam but also in its capacity to pursue interfaith issues. See, Guy Eaton, *Islam and the Destiny of Man*, Cambridge, 1994; and, *Remembering God: Reflections on Islam*, Cambridge, 2000.

34. Through his school, music and videos, Yusuf Islam (formerly Cat Stevens) has been a role model for many new and old Muslims. His sudden deportation from the United States in September 2004 was widely reviewed in the global media. The American officials not only ignored his charity work but also cast aspersions on his integrity, which made him seek legal advice on this dramatic action. See, *The Times*, 24 September 2004.

35. His works on Islamic mysticism and spirituality remain widely quoted other than the classics by Maulana Rumi, Faridud Din Attar, Omar Khayyam and Hafiz Shirazi. He accepted Islam in 1938 and changed his name to Al Hajj Abu Bakr Siraj ad Din. For one of his several oft-quoted works, see *Muhammad: His Life Based on the Earliest Sources*, London, 2003 (reprint).

36. The studies by Yvonne Haddad, Barbara Aswad, Karen Leonard, El-Kholy and classical works such as *The Autobiography of Malcolm X*, or research by historians such as Allan D. Austin on African Muslim slaves have offered a new exciting area of American historiography.

37. Privately, several Muslim intellectuals have been raising these issues. But any regular study on fluctuating numbers has not been undertaken so far. On these quoted figures, see Will Cummins, 'letter', *New Statesman*, 26 January 2004, p. 35.

38. See, Kate Zebiri, *Muslims and Christians Face to Face*, Oxford, 1997.

39. Avril Powell, *Muslims and Missionaries in Pre-Mutiny India*, London, 1993.

40. John Cooper, et al. (eds.) *Islam and Modernity: Muslim Intellectuals Respond*, London, 1998; John Esposito and John D. Voll, *Makers of Contemporary Islam*, Oxford, 2001. Also see, Aziz al-Azmeh, *Islams and Modernities*, London 1994; and, Allan D. Austin, *African Muslims in Antebellum America*, London, 1997.

41. For information on their biographies and views, see Esposito and Voll, op. cit. The institutional and intellectual influence of Syed Mawdudi has been quite crucial and is enduring, though his successors at the helm of Jama'at-i-Islami have been more of an activist mould and not of his intellectual calibre. Professor Khurshid Ahmad and his associates at the various research centres including Leicester's Islamic Foundation are carrying out most of the

intellectual work. For more on Mawdudi, see Seyyed Vali Reza Nasr, *Mawdudi and the Making of Islamic Revolution,* New York, 1996. Tariq Ramadan, a grandson of Hasan al-Banna and based in Geneva, does not find any conflict between Islam and Modernity. To, him, the division between the House of Islam and House of Unbelievers is incorrect and there is a greater need to reinterpret *Sharia* to formulate a Western/European Islam. See, Tariq Ramadan, *Western Muslims and the Future of Islam,* Oxford 2003; also, Turi Munthe, 'The 'Muslim Martin Luther' with faith in the hyphenated identity', *THES,* 23 April 2004.

42. A Pakistani scholar in his pioneering book on the Iranian Revolution first used the term in 1983. He defined Syed Ahmad Khan, Iqbal, Shariati and Mujahideen-i-Khalq as progressive Muslims. See Suroosh Irfani, *Revolutionary Islam in Iran: Popular Liberation or Religious Dictatorship?* London, 1983.

43. In contemporary times, it may be akin to Islamic social democracy, though several dictatorial regimes have used Islamic Shoora (advisory) system to legitimate their rule by skirting universal empowerment and democratic participation.

44. Omid Safi, 'Introduction', in Omid Safi (ed.) *Progressive Muslims on Justice, Gender, and Pluralism,* Oxford, 2003, pp. 1-29. In their agenda of rethinking Islam they do not mind mediating with Western science, popular culture and political systems.

45. Ibid., p. 61.

46. See, Farid Esack, 'In Search of Progressive Islam beyond 9/11', in ibid., pp. 78-97.

47. Ibrahim Moosa, 'The Debts and Burden of Critical Islam', in ibid., pp. 111-127.

48. Quoted from Leila Ahmed, *Women and Gender in Islam: Predicament and Promise,* New Haven, 1992, p. 153 in Sa'diyya Shaikh, 'Transforming Feminism', in ibid., p. 150.

49. Mariam Rawi, 'Rule of the rapists', *Guardian,* 12 February 2004.

50. Haifa Zangana, 'Why Iraqi women aren't complaining', ibid., 19 February 2004.

51. Amina Wadud, 'American Muslim Identity: Race and Ethnicity in Progressive Islam', in Omid, op. cit. The volume also includes valuable pieces by Ahmad Moussalli, Marcia Hermansen, Farish A. Noor, Scott Kugle, Kecia Ali, Amir Hussain, Tanzim Kassam and Gwendolyn Simmons, who have no qualms in identifying themselves as progressive Muslims.

52. For instance, as suggested by Edward Said and more recently by John Gray (op. cit.), Political Islam—or whatever one may call it—is, to a large extent, rooted in modernity and is not an entirely *traditional* assertion.

53. In all these cases, states have mostly superimposed their own specific version of Islam, either at the whim of individuals such as General Zia or the Saudi dynasty, or as seen in Iran, they were catapulted into a role of Islamizing the country. However, Iran is still different from such other Muslim states where efforts for Islamisation have often caused more chaos. In Iran, despite a

strong hold by the religious hierarchy and Ali Khamenei as the supreme leader, several reformers are still hopeful of reaching a workable synthesis. Shirin Ebadi, the Nobel-Laureate for peace in 2003, certainly spoke for many Muslims when she claimed that an ideal system is to come about along with Islam and not at the expense of Islam. Her speech in Sweden soon after accepting the honour, showed a keen confidence in Islam's capability to synthesise with changing exigencies.

54. In an interview in Baghdad, Sayyid Iyad Jamaleddine, an eminent Shia leader and the mentor of Sayyid Hussein Khomeini, the grandson of the late Imam Khomeini, candidly observed: 'We want a secular constitution. That is the most important point. If we write a secular constitution and separate religion from state, that would be the end of despotism and it would liberate religion as well as the human being. The Islamic religion has been hijacked for 14 centuries by the hands of the state'. *International Herald Tribune*, 11 August 2003.

55. It is certainly ironical to see even numerous educated Muslims taking secularism synonymous with atheism. Instead of seeking its roots in the separation of church and state and respect for pluralism, they tend to define it as a Godless ideology (*dehriyyat*). This is not merely confined to some orthodox Muslims as even liberal and rather critical Muslims see no interface between Islam and secularism. In their uncritiqued kowtowing to secularism as a given truth, they desire the undoing of several of Islam's early precepts. Such an approach cannot offer any reconstructive discourse and may only exacerbate the ongoing chasms. That is why several people were not persuaded by authors like Manji who, in her eagerness for a 'quick fix' sought to replace one form of essentialism with another of the same type. For her views, see Irshad Manji, *The Trouble with Islam: A Wake-up Call for Honesty and Change*, Toronto, 2004.

6

AFGHANISTAN AND IRAQ: FAILED MUSLIM STATES, OR DEMOCRACY ON HOLD?

Here (in Afghanistan) at last is Asia without an inferiority complex.
  – Robert Byron, *The Road to Oxiana*, London, 1937, 88

Because of our recent military gains in much of Afghanistan, women are no longer imprisoned in their homes. The fight against terrorism is also a fight for the rights and dignity of women.
  – Laura Bush, 14 October 2001

The neocons—a powerful group at the heart of the Bush Administration—wanted war against Iraq and pressed for it with great determination, overriding and intimidating all those who expressed doubts, advised caution, urged the need for allies and for UN legitimacy, or recommended sticking with the well-tried cold war instruments of containment and deterrence. War it had to be, the neocons said, to deal with the imminent threat from Saddam's fearsome weapons, which, as Tony Blair was rash enough to claim in his tragicomic role as Bush's 'poodle,' could be fired within forty-five minutes of a launch order. This flight of blood-curdling rhetoric has now come home to haunt him, earning him a headline (in *The Economist*, no less) of 'PRIME MINISTER BLIAR'.
  – Patrick Seale, 'A Costly Friendship', *Nation*, 21 July 2003

Because democracy is noble, it is always endangered. Nobility, indeed, is always in danger. Democracy is perishable. I think the natural government for most people, given the uglier depths of human nature, is fascism. Fascism is more of a natural state than democracy. To assume blithely that we can export democracy into any country we choose can serve paradoxically to encourage more fascism at home and abroad.

— Norman Mailer, *Why Are We at War?* 2003, 70-1

For Bush and Blair to go into Iraq together was like a bunch of white vigilantes going into Brixton to stop drug-dealing. This is not to deny there's a problem to be sorted, just that they are not credible people to deal with it.

— Tom Wright, Bishop of Durham, 'The Monday Interview', *Independent,* 29 December 2003

The US army came to Afghanistan as liberators and now are feared as governors, judges and jailors.

— Adrian Levy and Cathy Scott-Clark, 'One Huge US Jail: The Torture Network', *Guardian,* 19 March 2005

The Anglo–American attack on Afghanistan followed by a similar but more comprehensive yet disputatious and illegal invasion of Iraq may have come about due to several though quite flimsy reasons but the process shows some unique and variable features of global politics in a US-led unipolar world.[1] The dissolution of the Soviet block may have temporarily signalled 'the end of history' and an ebullient optimism for global peace, democracy and co-operation, yet the outburst of ethno-regional conflicts and increasing differences between the rich and poor continue to present a new spectre of instability. Contradictory and arbitrary intervention from outside, often in collaboration with unscrupulous native rulers, has only added to grave misgivings among major sections of the Afro-Asian and Latin American world. Instead of democratisation and establishment of equitable and just systems, many in the world remain poor, oppressed and unrepresented, sharing a serious dismay. Here, especially in the Muslim world, the rag-tag radicals, banking on selective use of history and religion, offer a back-to-roots solution and like the Maoists and Marxists, promise a deliverance in this world, and even hereafter. The Western powers, especially after 9/11, have been deeply suspicious of these ideologues and their followers who are imbued with a greater sense of sacrifice and grow on a widening anti-Western sentiment among the Muslim have-nots. Western draconian laws, discriminatory policies targeting Muslims citizens and visitors, and worst of all, thoughtless and equally ruthless military campaigns and further deterioration of the political situation in West Asia have allowed more support for fundamentalist groups. The constant absence of democratization in their own countries, often hand-in-glove with foreign forces, has by default strengthened these radicals who bank on tradition yet use modern means to obtain power. The Western powers, as seen in post-9/11 Afghanistan and post-Saddam Hussein Iraq, have been apprehensive of unfettered democratization, as it might bring into power several religio-political parties harbouring anti-American sentiments. Thus, despite a verbal espousal of democracy and women's empowerment, Western leaders, like their surrogates in the region, have not been enamoured of mass-based participatory systems. The Fukuyamian dream of liberal democracy never appeared so distant despite the Anglo-American control and unchallenged primacy in West Asia.

The UN, NATO, and the EU, while confronted with civil wars amidst fragmenting 'imperial' states such as Yugoslavia, Russia, Georgia, Somalia, Rwanda, Afghanistan and Iraq, have found themselves unprepared for these quagmires and incapacitated to undertake substantive measures amidst a systemic vacuum. The Iraqi invasion of Kuwait after an extended and equally taxing Iraq–Iran war, the harrowing Balkan imbroglio, increased tensions in a de facto nuclear subcontinent, volatile civil war in Afghanistan, and ethnic cleansing in Rwanda and Somalia, deflated the growing optimism engendered by the dissolution of the Cold War, overthrow of Apartheid and a temporary thaw in Israeli–Arab tensions. The eventual consolidation of the Taliban by co-opting most of the former Mujahideen now turned rent-seeking regional warlords, a defiant Saddam Hussein and an assertive trans-regional Islamic activism as embodied by groups such as Al-Qaeda seeking sustenance from historic and contemporary grudges against the United States, were initially perceived as mere local irritants. This low-priority image was dramatically jolted through the terrorist attacks on New York, Washington and Pennsylvania in September 2001. The newly established Bush Administration, still searching for viable policy measures amidst the signs of neo-isolationism and unilateralism on environmental and other global commitments, and not known for any lingual and political acumen, took upon itself the responsibility of seeking revenge as well as the 'reordering' of a turbulent world. To many observers, Bush was catapulted into a global role without adequate personal credentials in that domain, nor was he clear on the direction in which he planned to lead the fuming American juggernaut. However, to his supporters, the Republican President was candid, decisive and confident, unlike his pervasive notoriety of being an awkward communicator.[2] The daily exposures of the Bush Administration's preoccupation with Saddam Hussein to the extent of neglecting specific intelligence reports on possible airborne terrorist attacks in early 2001 have shown what the priorities of the Neoconservatives are.

The former treasury secretary, Paul O'Neill's critique of Bush's misplaced policies on West Asia was further underlined by Richard Clarke's detailed eyewitness account, as the former anti-terrorist chief in the White House censured the Bush Administration on its handling of the terrorist threat. Combined with the accounts by Hans Blix and American weapons experts deputed to Iraq, it is safe to suggest that Washington was solely intent upon an invasion of Iraq regardless of global public opinion.[3] The Bush Administration, in its single-mindedness, and pushed by the Neoconservative supporters of Israel, chose to ignore vital intelligence on an imminent terrorist threat. As was revealed before the US inquiry commission in April 2004 through the declassified intelligence memo of 6 August 2001, the White House had been aware of specific information on the probability of terrorism on American soil. The mentioned memo detailed Osama bin Laden's resolve to strike within the US as a retaliatory response to American missile attacks on Afghanistan and Khartoum in 1998.[4]

Following 9/11, the Neoconservative elements within the Bush administration pursuing their own plans for a new US-led order and an unchallenged Israel, over and above the UN or world opinion, were soon in action.[5] A hurt America with injured pride and no rival to challenge it except some disgruntled Muslim militants busied itself in building up global alliances for a multi-pronged campaign. However, it is a different matter that, in the process, Washington lost most of its global goodwill due to the overzealous and unilateral nature of its policies. In its so-called retaliatory ventures in West Asia, Tony Blair's support for President Bush remained persistent despite the unprecedented anti-war sentiment and a formidable peace movement in the country.[6] The invasions of Afghanistan and Iraq happened despite a powerful and vocal global peace movement, and seemed to substantiate Huntington's clash of civilisations theory. It was not merely overwhelming Muslim public opinion across the board and even in the Diaspora that decried further decimation of Muslim regions; the major global protestations equally displayed the resolute alliance of various ideological groups. Already in the Occupied Territories, Ariel Sharon's inflammatory visit to the Temple Mount on 28 September 2000 had wound up the remnants of the Oslo Peace Accords ushering in the bloodiest phase of the Israeli–Palestinian strife. Concurrently, seeking sustenance from Washington, Moscow, Delhi, Tel Aviv, the Philippines and several other governments across the globe began suppressing the dissenting voices of Chechens, Kashmiris, Palestinians and the Moros. Chechnya, Kashmir and Kurdistan bore the brunt of the state-led brutalization whereas the Diaspora Muslim communities and other intending immigrants and asylum seekers came under a negative spotlight. The North Atlantic region as well as Australia promptly raised invincible barriers against any possible refugees, especially from West Asia. Within this global milieu, the mild rebuttals of the cultural clash both by the Western governments and moderate Muslim leaders failed to assuage charged sentiments and instead inflamed a pervasive Muslim anger.

While the American military power, duly helped by Britain and largely challenged by most of the global public opinion, demolished the Taliban and Ba'athist regimes in those countries, followed by added pressure on Iran, Libya, Syria and Pakistan, it equally exacerbated anti-Americanism across the globe.[7] Following 9/11, a worldwide anti-Americanism, Political Islam and the weakening of post-colonial state-based order especially in the developing world— the three contemporary realities of an uneven global politics— entered a new phase and so has the debate on democracy. This chapter, after a brief theoretical overview, aims at seeking the convergence of internal and external forces in explaining the decline or even possible weakening of states such as Afghanistan and Iraq. It also looks at the inadequacies of the Western strategies as well as of Political Islam in meeting the challenges of nation building, peace and democracy in these countries.

Theoretical Maze: Neoconservatism, Zionism and Unilateralism

Contrasted with a rapid regionalization in the North Atlantic regions and South East Asia, the vast Afro-Asian territories have been experiencing fragmentation of states and polities, owing to internal schisms exacerbated by external interventions. The internal combustion accrues out of conflictive ethnic and ideological forces whereas border conflicts or sheer invasions account for external corrosive factors. Theoretically, these two variant trends in international politics can be interpreted in reference to economic, political and ideological factors.[8] In the case of the post-colonial world, economic stratification, contested nationhood, monopolist elitist control of the state simultaneous with a Western hegemonic as well as discretionary politico-economic dominance could explain the post-Second World War imbalances.[9] At another level, some analysts may seek a breakthrough in international deprivation and conflicts through allocating a centre stage role for civil society. Accordingly, the state is neither to be abolished nor to be totally left on its own, instead it has to be monitored and conducted through an alert, independent and vocal civil society. Such a democratic idealism seeks empowerment of civic groups, think tanks and a more active role for NGOs, away from official functionaries who may be either corrupt or simply inefficient. The concept of civil society has been in vogue since the German Renaissance of the eighteenth century but has obtained greater significance in the post-Cold war years. While to some, civil society may simply mean NGOs; to others it may be a holistic terrain reflective of universal democratisation.[10]

Scholars like Mary Kaldor see an ideal globalization to be properly anchored in the imperatives of a global civic society, away from the extremes of regression and total adulation.[11] To Monbiot, it should reflect global governance established through universal franchise and unhindered equality.[12] Political scientists from the Realist School following the Morgenthauan premises may translate the global proclivities in reference to conflictive interests, especially since the breakdown of the old bi-polar balance of power in the world. The current transitional stage, to them, may soon turn into a more stable neo-order once the world gets used to changed realities. However, the question of what should be the role of the United States and its 'junior' partners such as the EU and Britain, largely remains to them, a significant moot point.[13] The anti-Americanism and trans-Atlantic ambivalence has, by default, engendered two contrasting but equally vital articulations reflecting 'the deeply Europeanized anti-European and the deeply Americanized anti-American' characteristics. In the wake of a prevalent confusion, such a divide may suggest a new ideological polarity between the United States and a reinvigorated European Union, where Britain may often operate as a bridge between the two power blocks.[14] Such a debate has focused on the need for the redefinition and even reconstitution of global institutions such as the United Nations, IMF, the World Bank, the International Court of Justice and the newly formed International Criminal Court, and similar other instruments to combat terror, poverty, nuclear proliferation, wars and human rights violations.

In the same vein, the critics of US policies towards the Middle East in particular and the Muslim world in general, feel that Washington is being dangerously manipulated by a strong pro-

Israeli lobby at the expense of its interests and relationship with the world's 1.4 billion Muslims. Though Israel was delivered largely through Anglo-American assistance in 1948, yet the weakening of British imperial stature and its replacement with the United States especially after the Suez Crisis of 1956, coincided with the emergence of the latter as the leader and protector of the Western block. Concurrently, the Zionist lobbying efforts in America, cashing in on the traditional lack of proper information on Muslim affairs amidst pervasive Orientalist views of Islam, and duly helped by a common Western guilt over the Holocaust, have generated a new momentum. US-Israeli bilateralism at the expense of the Arab prerogatives was strengthened during the Kennedy era. The 1967 Arab-Israeli war happened at a time when President Johnson, faced with his travails in Vietnam and by choosing to ignore the Israeli nuclear programme at Dimona, offered generous assistance to Tel Aviv. The anti-Nasser feelings, a discomfort with assertive Arab nationalism and general Western obfuscation over the Ba'athist avowals of socialism helped Israeli lobbyists in maligning Arabs and Muslims. Accordingly, Islam was perceived as an ideology of bloodshed with its powerful trajectory of jihad. The Muslim hordes had to be contained only by force, since they were inherently anti-democratic and dangerously anti-Western. The patronage of corrupt monarchs, khaki dictators and other power elite—in the colonial tradition of the indigenous intermediaries—facilitated such control over and above the democratic aspirations of the Muslim masses, routinely depicted as ruthless mobs. Consequently, the American taxpayers ended up generously financing Israel's steady expansion and occupation at the expense of Palestinians, or even by ignoring vital interests across the Muslim world.

Stuck between these partisan policies and autocratic regimes propped up by the Western powers, the Muslim masses have been the real victims of malice and dictatorships. The vicious cycle seems never ending and, ironically, 9/11 has further consolidated it. Israel, since its inception in 1948, has remained the prime beneficiary of the cold war tensions with more Jews migrating to Palestine while Palestinians are maliciously branded as fanatical terrorists with an inherently anti-American disposition. Their expulsions, dispossession and selective killings, thus, remain justifiable. Such multi-pronged Zionist efforts bore real fruit after 9/11 when an angry and vengeful America, helped by Britain and a few other powers, undertook direct and extensive military campaigns in West Asia. In the meantime, not surprisingly, Sharon's Likud followers and the Israeli war machine ruthlessly engaged in cleansing Palestinian lands of its people.[15] As suggested by a leading Israeli intellectual, Sharon successfully 'dissolved the Jewish and the Palestinian public's belief in the possibility of achieving a genuine peaceful solution and any mutual trust.'[16] According to another Israeli analyst, Sharon was not only dividing Palestinian areas into Bantustans through a policy of a determined Apartheid, he has been successful in misleading many of his own liberal citizens.

According to Meron Benvenisti, in the partial withdrawal from Gaza while holding on to the West Bank in total defiance of world opinion, Sharon has plainly followed the supremacist South African precedent.[17] Even before President Bush announced the Roadmap for Peace serious doubts about Israel's real intentions, given its past record and flouting of several UN resolutions, foreclosed the possibility of any optimism. Soon, the Roadmap itself was abandoned as Sharon received unflinching support both from Washington and London for his policies of selective killings of Palestinian leaders, dislocation and starvation of the general Arab populace and the usurpation of more of their territories. The daily bombings of Gaza and assassination of the invalid Sheikh Ahmed Yassin and of Abdel-Aziz al-Rantissi under the pretext of eliminating Hamas-led terror has been carried out with Washington and London fully approving Sharon's ventures. The import of East Asian seasonal labour by Israel and total restrictions on the movement of Palestinian workers exacerbates the dire problems of millions in Gaza and the West Bank, already turned into refugees on their own soil. Whenever a few Muslim countries attempt even a mild reprimand of Israeli policies in the UN, Washington simply vetoes the draft resolutions. By 2005, Iraq and Palestine had been turned into lands of despair and destruction once again, confirming that London, Washington and Tel Aviv were totally insensitive to public opinion.[18] However, on this side of the Atlantic, other than a great majority of European public opinion, even some parliamentarians have been wary of the Zionist influence over the decision making processes exerted through powerful politicians, business and media. Yet they are unable to express this openly for fear of incurring a huge backlash.[19]

The growing pressure from the Muslim and Arab world for Palestinian self-determination and a right of return to their own land spawned anti-American and anti-Israeli sentiments where America was seen as the main supporter of an aggressive Israel over and above the legitimate Palestinian aspirations. Such a Muslim anger was also directed against surrogate Muslim regimes kow-towing to American dictates in the Middle East. Certainly, 9/11 happened at a time when the Neoconservative hold on the American political, military economic and other vital institutions was already complete. As the fact remains, most of the Neoconservatives share an unquestioned support for Israel and see only chaos, disorder and violence in the Muslim world. All these barren lands have to be fertilized by a Washington-ordained democratization and especially before the Second Coming of Jesus Christ. Islam, as seen in the previous chapters, is viewed by these Neoconservatives as a medieval and non-reformed repressive ideology whose proponents—both in the government and in the opposition—pose a most serious threat to Western (and Israeli) ideals, basically defined as superior Judaic-Christian values. Imam Khomeini, Osama bin Laden, Saddam Hussein, Yasser Arafat or turbaned Taliban look-alikes are the prototype Muslim terrorists who have to be struck down before they can threaten civilization's bastions. Bernard Lewis, Ann Coulter, Patrick Buchanan, David Blunkett, Oriana Fallaci, Daniel Pipes, Denis McShane, Robert Kilroy-Silk and a whole host of scare mongers keep reminding their Western followers of the impending multiple threat from the Muslim world that may eventually overrun Western civilization. To them, time is on the side of 'the Islamic threat' to the West as there are several Muslim terrorists within these countries waiting to strike.[20]

The Pentagon under Donald Rumsfeld certainly became the most powerful centre of pro-Israel and anti-Muslim strategists, that had been trying to capture key positions for a long time. The Pentagon's opposition to President Clinton also accrued from an ideological divide within the United States with Neoconservatives bandied together to see America rule supreme over the 'troubled lands'.[21] Led by the Deputy Secretary of State now President of the World Bank, Paul Wolfowitz, and advised by Richard Perle, the Pentagon gathered like-minded policy makers to steer American foreign and defence policies in a specific direction. Its cornerstone lay in defending Israel through the establishment of an unchallenged American primacy over the vital Muslim regions, irreverent of the UN, EU or a critical global public opinion. The precept was 'to get them before they get us' as the invincible US military might duly ensure a friendly world.

The Pentagon's Office of Special Plans (OSP) had been envisaging and implementing schemes for an active American military involvement in changing West Asian politico-strategic contours. Abram Schulsky, Douglas Feith, John Bolton and Elliot Abrams—known for their unequivocal Zionist views—led the OSP especially at a time when the US Department of Defense was ahead of a traditionally cautious State Department in the projection and implementation of the Neoconservative agenda. Within the powerful troika of Colin Powell, Donald Rumsfeld and Condoleezza Rice, Powell proved the weakest link, though Bush's apologists would like the world to believe that the President was a mature and responsible leader in his own right. Wolfowitz and Perle never minced words when it came to a new Middle East and in Rumsfeld they found an ambitious head, who for a long time, had sought the implementation of such a forward policy. All of them received further patronage and official protection from Dick Cheney, the Vice-President and an exponent of several major financial concerns. Other than Cheney and Rumsfeld the rest of the leading policy makers in Pentagon have been predominantly staunch pro-Israeli elements, duly supported by media pundits like William Kristol and Robert Kagan, and through organs such as *The Weekly Standard*, or think tanks including the Project for New American Century, the American Enterprise Institute, the Hudson Institute and the Centre for Middle East Policy. The last is the brainchild of the American-Israeli Public Affairs Committee (AIPAC), one of the most influential and vociferous pro-Israel pressure groups in the United States. Most of these facts have been unknown to ordinary Americans and the rest of the world,[22] who are usually warned of a looming threat to American national security from the Al-Qaeda or countries such as Iraq, Iran and Syria. Such tainted views when publicized through powerful obliging media channels like Fox and CNN, have always registered a ready approval, especially since 9/11. Unsuspecting Americans have traditionally been vulnerable to specific lobbies and partisan policies emanating from Washington. A global denunciation of Islam, combined with nationalist and xenophobic elements, has duly helped the Zionist assault on Arabs/Muslims while underwriting support for Neoconservatives in the most powerful country in the world.

Most ordinary Americans have limited access to analytical and unbiased information since a few power elite representing specific interest groups control the flow of information and also make vital decisions affecting millions. Thus, whereas the specific lobbies, through their negative agenda, have often precluded a wider participation in decision-making processes within their own countries, it may be equally right to suggest that their discretionary policies under the Bush Doctrine equally hindered a much-publicized democratisation of West Asia. Some including Fareed Zakaria and even Paul Bremer have often' warned against democratization for fear of anti-American forces ascending into power. Anglo-American forces, in the first place, have themselves decimated several political clusters while disallowing any alternatives, which only helped the sectarian clerics and regional warlords to assume centre stage. In other words, rash and retaliatory military campaigns with a high accent on intolerance and annihilation, created a power vacuum both in Afghanistan and

Iraq, offering a godsend to regional and sectarian vigilantism. As was feared, military unilateralism, despite its espousal for democracy and gender development, only exacerbated the problems of governance.[23] 9/11 put democracy and governance on hold in the entire Muslim world, as the authoritarian regimes were co-opted by the US for the war on terror. Consequently, the nascent civil societies became the main targets of societal and statist authoritarianism. Thus, despite moralization for empowerment and democratization, the military-led campaign only further marginalized civic forces in the Muslim world, allowing more space and following to the fundamentalists and dictators.

Afghanistan and Iraq: Democratisation or Fragmentation

In their single-minded pursuit to invade Iraq without any legal or moral justification, the Anglo-American leadership, by default and also to their deep consternation, has offered the religio-political elements a comeback. If Washington and London turn irreverent to the Shia majority and continue to eliminate Sunni elements in the central and northern regions, Iraq may become another Algeria where the military collaborated with France to thwart the elected religio-political parties. More than one hundred thousand dead and the country in shambles for an entire decade are the harrowing consequences of resisting the people's verdict. Instead of welcoming an electoral strategy adopted by such forces, their marginalization and suppression only accentuates their militarization.[24] Without pondering over the issues of a guaranteed federation in Afghanistan and a mutually acceptable role for religion and ethnicity in future set-ups through open dialogue and assurances from the outside, any effort to establish a new systemic order may unleash more instability. In the case of both Afghanistan and Iraq, the Anglo-American invasion has demolished two regimes, and in the process, has spawned regional and ethno-sectarian dissensions. If they allow full-fledged democracy in these countries, the Americans worry that these religio-political elements with strong anti-Americanism may gain ascendancy, and if they continue to occupy them, their own human losses and global criticism may escalate.

The remaining strategy is either to divide and rule or to establish a subservient façade of regimes before departing from these turbulent places. All these scenarios have serious security portents involving human costs underlining the hasty and partisan nature of military unilateralism. The ideal situation could have been a regional and global persuasion towards universal democratization based on decentralized systems allowing wider participation. Whether they are Islamic militants, Pushtun supporters of the Taliban, or Arab and Kurdish nationalists, they are all united in resisting foreign occupation and the absence of any accommodation from the Anglo-American forces will only intensify their resolve. Consequently, as has been witnessed, other than soldiers, it is the ordinary populace of Afghanistan and Iraq who have become casualties in the crossfire. The future of these plural and extremely unstable countries is in the hands of the occupiers, warlords, ethnic leaders and religious clerics and they abound in diversity and adversity.

There is no denying the fact that both Afghanistan and Iraq were being ruled by authoritarian regimes but still the regime change should have ideally come about through the people themselves like in Indonesia, Bangladesh and Argentina. Using terrorism as an excuse to invade Afghanistan, and weapons of mass destruction (WMDs) as a reason to invade Iraq have exposed the limitation of a unilateralist military strategy based on vengeance and the dictum of pre-emptive strike.

Afghanistan under Karzai has been restive and uncertain, and the situation in Iraq even after several promises of deliverance and changes in the top echelons has remained highly untenable. Moreover, it reaffirms the view that temporary interests rather than stipulated democratic imperatives had geared the Anglo-American decisions to attack these two countries. The Taliban, in the first place, had been the beneficiaries of indirect American support as most of them were the former Pushtun Mujahideen, whereas in Iraq, Saddam Hussein had been the recipient of generous assistance against Khomeini's Iran. In particular, the rekindling of the jihad ideology in Afghanistan during the Cold War is largely owed to Western support.[25] In the case of Iraq, opposition to the war waged without any legal and moral justification seemed to be quite vocal but Bush and Blair opted otherwise, much to the discomfort of a global public opinion. The promises about post-Saddam Iraq included the restoration of democracy and human rights, which, to many critics were already faltering in Afghanistan.[26] While Afghanistan seemed to have melted into warlordism, Iraq is witnessing the upsurge of ethno-religious defiance, both by the Shia and Sunni elements as was seen during 2004 in Baghdad, Falluja, Ramadi, Najaf, Karbala and Mosul where, despite massive bombing and large-scale raids, defiance by a number of groups continues. While the occupation forces remain wary of a 'Sunni Triangle', they are equally apprehensive of a Shia majority assuming full power in a schismatic state like Iraq, especially after the resistance mounted by the followers of Muqtada al-Sadr in 2004. A Shia majority gaining power through ballot or bullet and making assertive and autonomous decisions over and above the Sunnis has been traditionally perceived as a grave threat to US interests in West Asia besides hastening the end of Iraq as a multi-ethnic state. In April 2004 led by Muqtada al-Sadr, a Baghdad based Shia cleric, the Shias in Baghdad, Karbala and Najaf joined the ongoing rebellion in the so-called Sunni Triangle. The Mehdi Army of the youthful cleric even assumed control of several Southern cities and it appeared as if Iraq was slipping out of the coalition's control. The US response to this combined and unprecedented Shia-Sunni defiance was brutal and massive, resulting in 800 deaths in two days just in the town of Falluja owing to aerial bombing. Among the dead in Falluja, more than two hundred worshippers were killed while praying, which only added to Muslim anger both in Iraq and elsewhere.[27] As acknowledged by the State Department, the American forces routinely used shells containing depleted uranium and 'mark-77 firebombs, which have a similar effect to napalm' while phosphorus shells were exploded over towns.[28] Many residents fled to escape indiscriminate bombing. Despite reassurances to the Kurds, the Anglo-American planners hesitated to allocate fuller autonomy to the Kurds for fear of destabilizing the entire region. Thus, Iraq, even after the much hyped promises, occupation and the arrest of Saddam Hussein, remains ungovernable, defying post-9/11 postulations of creating a just West Asia.

The interim government under Iyad Allawi was created in June 2004 in a rather dramatic way to allow Paul Bremer a quick exit and mainly to show to the American voters that Iraq had been delivered back to the Iraqis. But the country suffered a few of the worst violence after this 'hand-over' when thousands of people—mostly Iraqis and a few Americans—got killed as both Shias and Sunnis demanded complete transfer of power and an end to occupation. The hostage taking and large-scale volatility across the country even prompted an otherwise cautious Kofi Annan to characterize the Anglo-American invasion as a contravention of the UN charter and thus an illegal venture. His statement in September 2004 on the eve of the General Assembly's session and a few weeks before the American presidential elections proved discomfiting for the Bush Administration. Even an otherwise non-charismatic Senator John Kerry—the Democrat presidential contender—vocally criticized the Bush policy on Iraq. The formation of the Iraqi parliament following the elections in 2004 and the installation of a transitional government under Ibrahim al-Jaafri—a Shia politician—did not help moderate the strong Sunni reservations, nor did it make Iraq secure from the daily bomb blasts and large-scale loss of innocent lives. The newly-agreed constitution accepted the plural imperatives of the society but with the continued dependence on military muscle and even the Iraqi regime's total dependence upon US protection—like Karzai in Kabul—many analysts remain uncertain of the future of the country as a single entity. Iraq in 2005, as is noted further below, remained volatile and ethnosectarian fissions kept multiplying without any mediating institutions and forces to bind its disparate and desperate inhabitants. A country otherwise endowed with natural resources, historical richness and a forward looking populace now miserably lay asunder. The erstwhile havoc caused by Saddam Hussein's authoritarianism had, following the unnecessary and brutal invasion, become an endless spectre of violence and bloodshed. Concurrently, worries about Syria and Iran as potential areas of armed interventionism do not augur hope for West Asia.

Apparently, or at least from the official Anglo-Western viewpoint, everything in post-Taliban Afghanistan appears stable and positive. The hated Taliban are scattered and defeated; the Al-Qaeda leadership has been either eliminated or is apparently in disarray; the women are assumed to have returned to schools in Kabul; the ISAF (International Stability Force for Afghanistan) and the NATO contingents are holding on to Kabul successfully and several thousand American and British troops helped the Karzai regime in holding the first-ever presidential elections in the country in early October 2004. But the country remains restive with several warlords still resisting control from Kabul; the Taliban have refused to wither away from the South-Eastern regions and the drug trade has reached its highest level yet in the country. The security situation has become so precarious that international humanitarian organizations have had to leave the country, and US and Pakistani troops continue their campaigns in the tribal belt amid alleged large-scale human rights violations.

The British Foreign Secretary Jack Straw's visit in June 2003 on the heels of a similar high-profile visit by Hamid Karzai to the West—one of several—was meant to reaffirm a continued Western commitment to Afghanistan. Reiterating Tony Blair's earlier pronouncement, Straw observed that Afghanistan would never be forgotten this time around.[29] Similar whirlwind visits by Colin Powell, Donald Rumsfeld, Laura Bush and Condoleezza Rice to Kabul were meant to reassure Karzai and his supporters of a steady American engagement in Afghanistan. Yet, the country's chronic problems of governance, economic disparities and volatile ethnicities refused to wither away. Astonishingly, anti-Western feelings remained very strong across the ethnic and ideological divides. For instance, the day Britain went to the polls on 5 May 2005 amidst a serious censure of Blair's invasion of Iraq across the country, Afghanistan was witnessing intense violence with the

Kabul regime and American troops claiming to have killed more than seventy Taliban fighters. A few days later, the entire country was astir with anti-American demonstrations over the desecration of the Quran in the Guantanamo detention centre, as the interrogators tried to coerce the internees into submission. Demonstrations against sacrilege of the holy book took place in several Muslim countries including the entire length and breadth of Afghanistan where nineteen protesters lost their lives. The American flag was torched at these protests and slogans were raised both against Karzai and Bush.[30]

In neighbouring Pakistan, General Pervez Musharraf's own pre-eminence in Pakistan's problematic power structure owed both to his khaki uniform and military constituency, duly solidified by backing from the Western governments, who, like their conservative predecessors in the 1980s, found in him a 'reborn' General Zia-ul-Haq with rather Kemalist assumptions. The disregard for Pakistan's democratic prerogatives and its constitutional proprieties both by Musharraf and his Western backers has disillusioned all those who want to see the restoration of unfettered democracy in a country that has suffered under military authoritarianism for so long. Pakistan, once again, became a front-line state vis-à-vis Afghanistan, though this time the enemy was not across the Khyber Pass but 'from within'. The age-old collaboration between the the military and the mullahs lost its support from Washington as Islamabad was now urged to roll back its jihadi elements, many of whom had been created during the 1980s by the intelligence agencies of Pakistan, the USA and Saudi Arabia.[31] Quite often Pakistani troops from across the Durand Line engage in extricating Al-Qaeda and pro-Taliban stragglers from their tribal hideouts in Waziristan though occasional tensions between Kabul and Islamabad over the rough and undefined tribal belt have often led to mutual denunciatory statements.[32]

Pakistan's own constitutional politics, its democratic and judicial institutions, despite a thin veneer of liberalism at the top, have once again become vulnerable to military-led authoritarianism, which enjoys unilateral support from the Western backers of General

Musharraf.[33] At the most, they are happy to nudge nuclearized India and Pakistan to stay peaceful and predictable if not totally committed to a resolution of their 60-year old imbroglio on Kashmir.[34] Eventually, following Musharraf's consolidation of power through unilateral constitutional amendments, a fraudulent referendum and by muzzling opposition, Islamabad hosted the South Asian summit in early 2004 where both India and Pakistan pledged to resolve their outstanding issues including dispute over Kashmir. Like on Afghanistan, Musharraf reversed age-old policies of his predecessors to keep India embroiled in a restive Valley and likewise, under US pressure, he restrained Pakistan's nuclear programme and even confessed the role of Pakistan scientists in illegal technology transfers.[35] In 2005, both India and Pakistan were cautiously establishing confidence-building steps. However, disputes over Kashmir, water resources and trade remained unresolved. Azad Kashmir and northern Pakistan suffered a major setback in human lives and resources when a powerful earthquake hit the region on 8 October 2005. It wiped out almost an entire generation of able bodied people besides destroying the entire infrastructure in the mountainous regions. Both India and Pakistan moved cautiously in their efforts to reach out to victims in the far-flung valleys, whereas Pakistani leaders and people complained of Western double standards in offering humanitarian assistance in their ordeal. While the Asian Tsunami and the hurricanes in the US had brought in generous sums in aid, Pakistani and Kashmir earthquake victims, despite UN appeals, did not receive any substantive assistance from otherwise richer countries.

A contrary view, not just shared by the wider Muslim world but also articulated by vocal pacifists and critics in the West, has been censurious of the Blair–Bush duo and their highhandedness in the post-9/11 years. To them, Afghanistan and its civilian populace have simply been made scapegoats to vent Washington's frustrations. Al-Qaeda and the Taliban were beneficiaries of American largesse when Zalmay Khalilzad—the Afghan-American arbiter on Afghanistan and Iraq—was hammering out agreements for Unocal and others. Like the late General Zia-ul-Haq (d. 1988), the Taliban, the Afghan Mujahideen and more recently the Iraqi Ba'athists all had gradually outlived their worth but not before justifying the greatest defence spending hike in US history. Afghanistan has been left to sort out its own intricacies and gradually the Western world has moved on except for a reduced military engagement to seek out Osama bin Laden and his close allies. Afghanistan is back to its pre-federation days of tribal demarcations with warlords ruling supreme and competing with one another in corruption, guns and opium. Karzai might stay in power as long as Afghan history does not repeat itself and his luck not run out. Certainly, his reception in Britain and the United States reminded one of King Amanullah's visit in the 1920s which eventually led to the latter's fall as well.[36]

Other than control of Kabul, socio-economic life in Afghanistan is far from settled though the emphasis, much like in a restive post-Saddam Iraq, has been on security related issues. Plainly, it is difficult to consider a country safe if its own president, despite his well-meaning disposition and natural affability, remains dependent on Western troops for his own personal security.[37] It is not merely the re-emergence of the Taliban that poses a serious threat but rather the recurrence of chaos and widespread socio-economic anarchy, much like Somalia, which needs serious, persistent and multi-dimensional global engagement in Afghanistan (and also in Iraq!). The paradigm of elimination and cooption pursued by the Western troops and a single-minded emphasis on security by eradicating the Pushtun-Taliban elements from the complex power equation in Kabul, does not allow for much optimism on this count.[38]

Karzai's visit in May 2003 and Jack Straw's subsequent foray into Kabul and Kandahar were partly to reassure new allies in the Afghan quagmire. But Straw's visit—especially to the battle-prone Kandahar and his session with an uneasy warlord, Gul Agha Sherazi was largely a pat on the back from Whitehall. It is interesting to note that Straw's visit did not follow any debate on Afghanistan nor did it elicit any major news coverage within Britain itself. This might have meant two assumptions: firstly, the Blair government, thanks to its hyped up propaganda on Iraq's WMDs and the subsequent embarrassment, was nervous with the dwindling Labour Party's lead over the Conservatives. Secondly, the confusion over economic integration into the Euro regime, a sustained criticism of the unrestrained relationship with Washington dominated by Neoconservatives and less inspiring news on economy and other social sectors kept the Blair regime on tenterhooks. The workers unions—the major component of the Labour party—had already characterized his Cabinet as a gang of 'criminals' who were 'putting the boot' on workers in Britain and abroad.[39] In the same manner, the top-up fees and foundation hospitals scheme turned out to be the proverbial last straw. The British populace was, however, showing signs of fatigue and disgust over mixed-up foreign policies, lack of direction on Europe, intermittent news of redundancies and an increased drift over Iraq, followed by a grave fear of terrorist attacks. The selective inquiries such as by Lord Hutton and Lord Butler over Iraq-related issues had very narrow remits and their findings only further disillusioned the Labour supporters. To serious observers like John Pilger, Robert Fisk and George Monbiot and many others, Afghanistan and Iraq have both been disastrous case studies in the foreign policy domain, which might continue to haunt Washington and London endlessly. Blair's controversial decision to join the US-led invasion of Iraq was re-ignited on the eve of elections and cost the Labour Party more than seventy seats besides frequent nervousness for an embattled prime minister at the hands of an inquisitive media and a critical civil society. Even in the United States, President Bush's following came down from 81 per cent in April to 58 per cent in early July 2003 though it was premature to read too much into this given the pervasive lack of analytical information available to the common American public. During the election campaign of 2004, the invasion of Iraq, non-discovery of WMDs and the continuous loss of human lives in that country became one of the major contentious issues with President Bush's popularity steadily diminishing. But the threat of terrorist attacks and a grassroots conservative support across the Midwest ensured President Bush's re-election. On 5 May 2005, when Britain went to the polls amidst serious reservations on the Bush–Blair invasion of Iraq, more than seventy Iraqis lost their lives in bomb blasts across the country, while mass graves of hastily buried and hand-bound Iraqi citizens were being broadcast on the television networks.

Iraq, in every sense, presents a major dilemma for London and Washington at a time when they had felt that the quick and less costly military conquest, over and above world opinion and the UN, would have its own dividends. Once again, the two allies are learning to their bitter realisation but without acknowledging it openly that demolishing weaker foes might have been easy but establishing a viable and acceptable political order is harder. Even the justification of war under the pretext of WMDs and Baghdad's connection with Al-Qaeda proved to be untrue and the demand for holistic inquiries refused to subside. The occupying Anglo-American troops in Iraq are confronted with an increasingly co-ordinated guerrilla resistance, with Shias demanding universal vote and with no Karzai-like personality available to ensconce in a highly uncertain Baghdad. Ahmed Chalabi is already too controversial and stupendously corrupt, and faced with the Ayatollahs al-Sistani, Muqtada al-Sadr and al-Hakim (the al-Khoeis had become tarnished due to the disclosures of their CIA connections), and the defiant Sunni Ba'athists, he is too uninspiring and peripheral. Chalabi's Iraqi National Congress, despite support from Dick Chenney and the Pentagon, has been tainted with scandals and shadowy deals with Western intelligence agencies. It was neither fully rooted among the Iraqis back home nor widely respected by critical Iraqi intelligentsia.

Eventually, in April 2004, the Shia followers of Al-Sadr took up arms against the occupation troops by joining hands with their Sunni counterparts. All the way from Mosul in the north to Nasiriya in the South, Iraqis fumed with anti-American sentiments which aerial bombardment only intensified. The Shia–Sunni alliance in Baghdad and elsewhere, for a while, proved unnerving to the occupation alliance amidst daily demonstrations, armed defiance and frequent incidents of hostage taking. Iraq, under Iyad

Allawi, following the transfer of some limited sovereignty in June 2004, turned more restive and ungovernable, though both Bush and Allawi often tried to reaffirm their commitment on electoral politics. The elections in early 2005 took place amidst secrecy and fear, and following prolonged negotiations, resulted in the formation of a regime led by Ibrahim al-Jaafari, an Iraqi Shia. Instead of returning to normalcy, the country has continued to suffer from recurring violence. Just in the month of April 2005, while the new regime was still in the offing, 67 incidents of suicide bombings were reported in the media costing 400 lives while injuring many more. In the same month, 35 car bombs had caused disarray and destruction in the country, while Washington continued to blame foreign insurgents, ignoring the pervasive dismay and desperation among the Iraqis.[40] For instance, in May 2005, several thousands Iraqis were fleeing from Qaem and other western regions because of the continuous US bombardment.[41] As noted by scientific research in Western scholarly journals and human rights groups, more than one hundred thousand Iraqis had already lost their lives immediately following the invasion in 2003. Other than such large-scale deaths, many more Iraqis suffered from grievous injuries and permeating effects of the latest weaponry, while the country's infra structure, archaeological sites, libraries, museums and galleries had been seriously damaged.

All this fitted the Neoconservative plan of destroying the Iraqi factor in Middle Eastern politics besides turning the juggernaut against Iran, so that all threats to Israel could be gradually neutralized. The American Enterprise Institute and individuals like Richard Perle, Bernard Lewis and Larry Diamond earnestly advocated a new front against Iran for allegedly supporting Iraqi Shia activists.[42] Thus, Iraq, even after its easy conquest, Saddam Hussein's downfall and the muted elections in early 2005 under the watchful occupation forces, remains restive and volatile unnerving the Anglo-American politicians more than Kabul.

Opium, drug trafficking and continued uncertainty due in part to the resurgence of warlords in Afghanistan have posed some serious concern to Western planners, but Iraq has been a bigger preoccupation. A solution to the age-old Palestinian–Israeli stalemate, according to them, might have neutralized anti-Western feelings in the Arab world, and Afghanistan like Somalia, could be gradually forgotten. After all, in terms of costs and benefits, the country's needs appeared bottomless! Karzai did not have to confront a similar critical intelligentsia and a powerful, anti-Western Arab nationalism, but a die-hard pessimism mingled with anti-Americanism and a pervasive sense of alienation among the Pushtun and Sunni tribes is proving to be his nemesis. Under the circumstances, Afghanistan deserves urgent global, regional and domestic initiatives, otherwise the prognosis appears negative. Even some Afghan women's groups such as the Revolutionary Association of Women of Afghanistan (RAWA) felt betrayed and let down by the West despite their early promises for rebuilding the country and its infrastructure. Women felt that they had been, once again, bequeathed to the warlords such as the Northern Alliance, and warlords such as General Abdul Rashid Dostum and Ismael Khan, who, before the Taliban, had turned the country into a patchwork of fiefdoms with thousands of women falling victim to frequent rape and violence: 'Those in power today—men such as Karim Khalili, Rabbani, Sayyaf, Fahim, Yunus Qanooni, Mohaqiq and Abdullah—were those who imposed anti-women restrictions as soon as they took control in 1992 and started a reign of terror throughout Afghanistan. Thousands of women and girls were systematically raped by armed thugs, and many committed suicide to avoid being sexually assaulted by them.'[43]

Internally, Karzai tried to herald an era of good feeling amongst his peoples through substantive efforts for re-establishing inter-tribal consensus on vital national issues and by holding a constitutional assembly (jirga). Instead of doling out money to buy individual loyalties, he needed to offer tangible development schemes to his people. He was expected to come out of his self-imposed security shell to establish a South Africa-style Truth and Reconciliation Commission aimed at re-engaging all Afghans in a cohesive nation-building project. As he observed at St. Antony's College in his lecture, Afghans were not factionalists by disposition and history, they were inherently nationalistic, but who would give them a chance to prove that?[44] His sole dependence on the Americans seriously compromised his own profile nor did his inability to fully restrain the Northern Alliance, General Rashid Dostam, Sherazi and Ismael Khan help him re-establish national prerogatives. However, by the summer of 2004, Karzai with full American backing, had been able to sideline General Fahim from the political equation and had resolutely replaced Ismael Khan with his own governor in Herat. These two major steps and the elections in early October, despite all the technical bottlenecks and Taliban defiance, certainly helped Karzai in gaining well-needed momentum. However, given the lack of a consensual politics and a long tradition of ethno-regional defiance, democracy, peace and development in Afghanistan remain chimerical.

Concurrently, in Iraq, given the chaos and the rise of sectarian vigilantes following the occupation, women have become more vulnerable to rape, kidnapping and other forms of violence. Some secular family laws have been overturned and placed under religious control though prominent Western women including Laura Bush, Cherie Blair, Condoleezza Rice and Patricia Hewitt promised a judicious environment for women. The short and unannounced visits to Kabul by Laura Bush and Condoleezza Rice were meant to reassure the world of continued Western interest in that tarnished country, yet socio-political and economic realities on the ground betray morass and gloom. The freedom from a brutal regime ironically spelt a newer menace for women outside their homes. Their pronounced public role since the 1980s due to the Iraq–Iran war seemed to have given way to fresher uncertainties and insecurity.[45]

Multitudes of impassioned yet totally orderly Shia pilgrims converged in late April 2003 in Karbala soon after the demise of Saddam Hussein's regime and their leaders resolved to implement Political Islam interspersed with democratic ingredients. The speakers also promised to induct a tolerant and non-theocratic version of Islam—mainly to reassure their foreign observers of their distance from the Iranian model of theocracy. While Muslims of

various sectarian and ethno-national backgrounds sought a greater
sense of pride from the spectacle of elderly and young men and
women defying heat and dust to celebrate the death anniversary of
Imam Hussein—the Prophet's grandson—the Anglo-American
alliance found itself in a quandary. It appeared as if the floodgates
of energy and pent-up feelings had been suddenly removed to usher
in a newfound solidarity among those who had experienced heinous
bombings and a total disappearance of civic authority. Instead of
fighting fellow Sunnis—the second major Muslim sect—or
garlanding the Arbram and Challenger tanks, these Iraqi masses
represented a new and equally crucial phase of Political Islam.

Notwithstanding the Anglo–American penchant for oil and easy
victory, the illegality of the invasion despite the non-discovery of
WMDs, marginalisation of the UN and a continuing humiliation
of the Arab–Muslim world, the fall of Saddam Hussein was
welcomed by these masses who wanted to find their own destiny.
The Anglo–American forces were understandably wary of such a
religio-political activity especially when it sought sustenance from
anti-Western sentiments. They could not allow a Khomeini-style
Iraq to raise its head in a crucial area where oil, economy and pro-
Israeli considerations reigned supreme. But this only further
aggravated the situation, intensifying the guerrilla warfare, while
Iraq descended into a Somalia–like anarchy. However, rather than
turning into a typical witch-hunt or a medievalist version of
Taliban-style theocracy, the educated Shia clerics such as Al-Sistani
were well-placed to offer a unique synthesis of democracy and
pluralism, away from violence, unilateralism and coercion. But
suspicions on all sides abounded which proved neither good for
peace nor for democracy. Eventually, in April and then in the
summer months of 2004, Iraqi Shias led by Muqtada al-Sadr took
up arms against American troops and the country experienced the
most tumultuous phase in its turbulent history. American tanks
and aircraft continuously pounded the historic and religious centres
of Najaf and Karbala with the entire Muslim world was aghast at
the bloodshed. The anger, dismay and helplessness led to more
chaos and disillusionment while Allawi's cabinet remained

barricaded inside the US-led security zone in Baghdad, away from the public ire.

The sight of the crowds—in the angry, devastated and marooned land of Mesopotamia—displaying a rare and peaceful consensus for a Muslim state, across the country and without rancour to anyone even after the grave tragedies of 2004, has been amazing. While the Anglo–American commanders and bureaucrats were still working out details on reconstruction and controlled democracy, the clerics had already assumed greater local civic responsibilities. The dictums of the failure of Political Islam by authorities and specialists stood rejected by the sea of humanity sharing grief and fraternity. Certainly, Islam has continued to enthuse, aggregate and mobilise masses even where food, water, medicines, shelter and electricity have been absent or even the basic civic amenities were non-existent. The spontaneity of people's power and their adherence to mutual respect and peaceful coexistence is not a minor feat, though it has remained peripheral in the news reports or has been cursorily seen as an overdue religious ritual with the usual anti-American undertones. Despite Western political and intellectual sceptics and critics, Iraq may still have a chance to establish participatory polity 'from below' where empowerment, education, economy and egalitarianism could run supreme in their universal connotations. It may also turn into a vast killing field with warring clerics, tribal chieftains and surrogates ruining the opportunity to rebuild Iraq as a role model for all. Neither a theocracy nor dictatorship will take Islamicists anywhere, it is only through democracy, peace and guarantees of pluralism, away from unilateralism and militarism, that Political Islam with its historic anti-colonial, anti-hegemonic, anti-racist and anti-violence traditions can come to the rescue of the have-nots. In the same vein, a prolonged occupation amidst irreverence to Iraq's plural and democratic prerogatives may further aggravate the situation. Iraq and Afghanistan need to stand on their own without any foreign interventions, and true democracy has to be based on universal empowerment, unchecked accountability and greater recognition for pluralism. Controlled elections, as seen in both the countries during 2004–5 under alien dictates, and similar other commandeered acts can only exacerbate the difficulties. It cannot whitewash the serious human rights violations perpetrated by the Western troops.

The discussion so far on historical, domestic and extra-regional factors in the case of the two unstable Muslim countries—Afghanistan and Iraq—highlights formidable challenges towards nation building. Whereas the issues of security and order need prioritisation, a greater global engagement, and substantive reassurances through an honest and unfettered politico-economic reconstruction may go a long way in establishing national cohesion, and most of all, allow democratization of these plural societies. Neither an intolerant and discretionary version of Political Islam nor an interest-centred and partisan approach by the Western powers towards the Muslim world may redeem democracy and regional security. Likewise, a rash and unilateral militarist interventionism, however justified through self-righteousness, cannot guarantee a stable West Asia. Pre-emptive and brutal military strikes, the usage of surrogates from amongst the developing world and subsequent abandonment to the forces of decay and disorder in an imperial tradition will make the march towards peace and democracy even more difficult. Like post-war Japan and Germany, Afghanistan and Iraq have been test cases for Western resolve and global community. Walking away after playing havoc with their human and natural resources might only intensify 'the clash of fundamentalisms,'[46] though prolonging the occupation through a brutal use of force is equally counterproductive.

The invasion of Iraq, a personal and ideological war for Bush and Blair, has already degenerated into a moral and political dilemma for them besides turning into a deep black hole for its traumatized populace. Reconstruction, followed by regional co-operation and integration into a just global order, could not only guarantee an enduring democracy in these countries but could have reversed the process of fragmentation so evident in nearly half of the world. A radical change of heart is needed not just in these countries but all around.

NOTES

1. Kofi Annan, the UN Secretary-General, in his well-publicised interviews and speeches during September 2004 declared the invasion of Iraq to be a contravention of the UN charter. He had no qualms in characterizing it as an illegal development. His critique came soon after the report submitted by the Iraq Survey Group, which despite an exhaustive search in occupied Iraq had not found any weapons of mass destruction. In addition, both Washington and London, even after their strenuous efforts, could not find any connection between Baghdad and Al-Qaeda. The rationale for regime change—another justification to attack Iraq— has also faltered following the manifold rise in the scale and diversity of violence across Iraq.

2. Despite the familiar jibes, mispronunciation or sheer confusion over names and places (Bushiism!) and no prior exposure to global complexities except for a single visit to nearby Mexico, during his gubernatorial career George W. Bush was, seen by several colleagues, as a leader in his own right. In fact, to some observers, 9/11 brought out the best in the American president. See, Bob Woodward, *Bush at War*, New York, 2002 and David Frum, *The Right Man*, London, 2003; also, Christopher Hitchens, *Regime Change*, London, 2003; James Moore and Wayne Slater, *Bush's Brain*, Hoboken, 2003. However, Bob Woodward's work on the US invasion of Iraq reveals several critical points including the hold of the Neoconservatives on the Bush Administration, which, even before 9/11 was determined to attack Iraq. See, Bob Woodward, *Plan of Attack*, New York, 2004. Works by other US whistle blowers like Paul O'Neill and Richard A. Clarke have also raised such contentious issues where Iraq, irrespective of its irrelevance with the war on terror, had been already singled out for a large-scale military operation. Such a single-minded pursuit, irreverent of just policies or serious ramifications, was hyped up by President Bush and his close aides. The Bush Administration was fully supported by Prime Minister Tony Blair in all the one-sided policies on Iraq and Palestine, much to the chagrin of Western critics and the Muslim opinion. The exposé of US and British brutalities on the Iraqi POWs reaching sinister and shameful proportions, despite their early concealment by Washington and London, further infuriated human rights activists and revealed the seamy side of the Anglo–American ventures in West Asia.

3. Douglas Hurd, the former British Conservative foreign secretary, while criticising American policy in Iraq also took Tony Blair to task for blindly following Bush in an unnecessary and equally dangerous venture. 'Hurd blasts US policy on Iraq', *Dawn*, 11 April 2004.

4. For details see, ibid., 12 April 2004; www.cnn.com; and the BBC World Service, monitored in Lahore, 11 April 2004.

5. For further details see, Angus Roxburgh, *Preaching of Hate: The Rise of the Far Right*, London, 2002, and, Naomi Klein, *Fences and Windows*, London, 2002; Norman Mailer, *Why Are We at War?* New York, 2003, and, Noam

Chomskly, *9/11,* London, 2002. For a rebuttal, see Ann Coulter, *Slander: Liberal Lies About the American Right,* New York, 2002.

6. While some observers may consider this support to be symptomatic of Britain's own weaker position in the world, especially after the Suez crisis of 1956, to others, it is in league with a rather insidious role that the United Kingdom has been playing over the recent past, mostly in league with the Americans. To such critics, Blair's unequivocal support for Bush despite a massive public uproar was nothing unique. For an interesting but powerful critique, see Mark Curtis, *Web of Deceit: Britain's Real Role in the World,* London, 2003. The critical view demolishes apparent British postulations on establishing democracies and human rights in the world. Blair himself was following a political strategy in close alliance with Washington whereas the threat from Baghdad of WMDs and its presumed linkage with terror were given out as the main justification for war. This comes out rather clearly in an otherwise chronological account of 10 Downing Street during the invasion of Iraq. See, Peter Stothard, *30 Days: A Month at the Heart of Blair's War,* London, 2003, p. 87.

7. Anti-Americanism is not merely confined to the Muslim regions, it is found all over the world. Curiously, the most anti-American country happens to be Canada, next-door neighbour and the largest trading partner of the United States. Even countries such as Britain, France, Europe, South Korea and Brazil have reflected long-term criticism of the American cultural 'assault'. The various surveys, BBC's documentaries and live programmes substantiate the view that since the installation of the Bush administration, anti-Americanism has multiplied. The sympathy for the Untied States found after 9/11 soon evaporated following the destruction of poor countries such as Afghanistan, amidst other factors. For interesting perspectives, see Ziauddin Sardar and Merryl Davies, *Why Do People Hate America?* London, 2002, and, Michael Moore, *Stupid White Men,* New York, 2002. For some other interesting works see, Ainslee T. Embree (ed.) *Anti-Americanism in the Third World,* New York, 1983, and, Eqbal Ahmad, *Confronting Empire,* London, 2000.

8. A very useful framework without any ideological straightjacket can be found in Ian Clarke, *Globalization and Fragmentation: International Relations in the Twentieth Century,* Oxford, 1999.

9. Of course, such a hypothesis is not a new one as the Marxist, Liberal and New Left have seen the global discrepancies in an exploitative relationship between a privileged North and an underprivileged South. Such an argument is being revisited following the unipolar nature of the world and more so after the inauguration of the Bush Administration and the rise of Neo-conservatives. All the way from Karl Marx to Antonio Gramsci, Eric Hobsbawm, Andre Frank, Noam Chomsky and several other influential analysts have seen the global 'disorder' within a class perspective. An increasingly powerful North, largely dictated by corporate interests and

beefed up by the military-industrial complex, seems to determine the class-based divisions across the globe. For a recent study see, John Pilger, *The New Rulers of the World,* London, 2003. Such critics are wary of globalisation but would seek a reorganisation of global institutions like the UN, IMF and the World Back through more egalitarian, democratic and consensual reforms. For instance, see George Monbiot, *The Age of Consent. A Manifesto for a New World Order,* London, 2003. (For the rebuttal of the latter by the editor of the *Economist,* see Bill Emmott, 'Democratic revolution', *New Statesman,* 23 June 2003.)

10. For several Muslim case studies, see Amyn B. Sajoo (ed.) *Civil Society in the Muslim World: Contemporary Perspectives,* London, 2002; and, Iftikhar H. Malik, *State and Civil Society in Pakistan: Politics of Authority, Ideology and Ethnicity,* Oxford, 1997.

11. Based on her lecture at the LSE on global inequalities on 12 June 2003. The lecture was a part of a special symposium in honour of Lord Desai. Also, Mary Kaldor, et al. (eds.) *Global Civil Society 2001,* Oxford, 2001.

12. George Monbiot, op. cit. For a polite critique of Monbiot's view, see Meghnad Desai, 'Utopia: Where pure politicians hand out free money', *Times Higher Education Supplement (THES),* 15 August 2003.

13. For these interesting perspectives, see Joseph Nye, *The Paradox of American Power,* Oxford, 2002; Fareed Zakaria, *The Future of Freedom,* New York, 2003; Robert Kagan, *Paradise and Power,* New York, 2003; and, John Keegan, *The Iraq War: The 21-Day Conflict and its Aftermath,* London, 2005. The last mentioned author is British and has worked in *The Daily Telegraph,* a newspaper that avowedly supported Zionism and the invasion of Iraq due to its ownership by the disgraced millionaire, Lord Conrad Black. His wife, Amiel Black, in her columns, vociferously supported Israel and routinely censured the Arabs. Under a pro-Israel editor, Dominic Lawson, this pro-Tory British newspaper often published Islamophobic articles. John Keegan had access to the highest echelons in the Pentagon besides frequent forays into Iraq to report back for his newspaper.

14. A pertinent perspective has been offered by Oxford-based Timothy Garton Ash, to whom strengthening of a more cohesive Europe (EU) should not aim at opposing the United States but rather play a moderating impact. Herein, the effort may also be directed towards the greater integration and incorporation of the United Kingdom within the EU as a moderator and an intermediary. See his 'The banality of the good', *New Statesman,* 16 June 2003.

15. Several Israeli groups such as Gush Shalom and other liberal elements have been opposed to ethnic cleansing and expulsions. Some pre-eminent British Jews such as Chief Rabbi Jonathan Sacks have been worried over the change in Jewish moral values with violence dominating the public consciousness, but under pressure he was made to withdraw his remarks. Also, see Baruch Kimmerling, *Politicide: Ariel Sharon's War Against Palestinians,* London, 2003.

His Zionist critics call him 'Quisling' out of hatred for his views. On the other hand, Norman Mailer while mildly sympathetic to Palestinians finds everything wrong with the Arab leaders and avoids criticising Israeli policies of expulsion and expansion. See, Mailer, op. cit. In March 2004, Max Hastings, the former editor of the *Daily Telegraph* alerted the Jews over unquestioned support for Israel and expansive Zionism, which was causing a rise in anti-Semitism. Max Hastings, 'A grotesque choice', *Guardian*, 11 March 2004.

16. Quoted in Chris Bunting, 'Seeds of the 'new Holocaust'?' *THES*, 4 July 2003.

17. Meron Benvenisti, 'Bantustan plan for an apartheid Israel', www.haarez.com in *Guardian*, 26 April 2004.

18. Some powerful voices alerted Tony Blair to the dangers and ramifications of partisan policies but London usually tended to ignore such advice in its single-minded support of the US. For a critique, see 'A letter from 52 former senior British diplomats to Tony Blair', *Guardian*, 27 April 2004.

19. In the United Kingdom, not only Muslims, but even veteran MPs, independent academics or individual writers cannot openly criticise Israel and its overpowering influence because they are soon denigrated as Holocaust deniers, or propounders of neo-semitism. Like the repressive fundamentalist view of Islam weary of any criticism, any reference to Zionism, Israel and the latter's manipulation of policies, institutions and sentiments, is strongly reacted to. Such a backlash and monopoly may backfire when the public finds more space to articulate a balanced and judicious view of Middle Eastern politics. The fact remains that denigrating Islam or turning Palestinians into American Indians on their own lands cannot compensate for the brutalities perpetrated against European Jewry, nor can Anglo–American governments continue with their highly dangerous policy of confrontation with the Muslim peoples. Even if it is called a clash of civilisations, it is ahistoric, irrational and dangerous. Muslims have not been historic Jew haters; rather more than anybody else they have protected Jews all over the Muslim world. It is only the dislocation of Palestinians—both Muslim and Christian—through the formation and expansion of Israel that the political divide has come about and its maligned depiction as a clash of civilizations is simply a misreading of political issues. Whereas Israel and Jewish minorities have equal and every right to prosper, the denial of the same to the Palestinians on their own lands, is not a cultural issue at all. (The present author is sensitive to the nuanced difference/similarities between anti-Jewish and anti-Zionist sentiments though it is itself a contentious point among Jewish writers.) See, Jonathan Freedland, 'Is anti-Zionism anti-semitism?' in Paul Iganski and Barry Kosmin (eds.) *A New Antisemitism: Debating Judeophobia in 21st Century Britain*, London, 2003.

20. Patrick J. Buchanan, *Death of the West*, New York, 2001; and for his columns see www.townhall.com/columnists/patbuchanan/pb20020327.shtml

21. Some very important recent studies have highlighted this 'extreme right wing conspiracy' to dislodge the Democratic administration while the Clinton–Lewinsky affair offered them a golden opportunity. See Hillary Clinton, *Living History*, New York, 2003; and, Sidney Blumenthal, *The Clinton Wars*, London, 2003. For a useful review highlighting an intense ideological rift among the American elite, see Will Hutton, 'America is a harsher place', *Observer*, 6 July 2003.

22. For further details, see Patrick Seale, 'A Costly Friendship', *Nation*, 21 July 2003.

23. Even the Middle East, North Africa, Central Asia and South Asian countries like Pakistan, once again, were bequeathed to dictatorship, and democracy turned out to be the main loser in the entire Muslim world.

24. Many reports on the rising guerrilla warfare in Iraq by correspondents such as Robert Fisk have already highlighted this trend where the Anglo–American troops are perceived as occupying forces and not liberators. Jonathan Steele, 'Iraqis wait for US troops to leave...'. *Guardian*, 5 July 2003. The new head of the Central Command of the US Army, General John Abizaid, in an interview characterized the resistance in Iraq as 'guerrilla warfare'. *Sky TV* News Report, 16 July 2003; also, see John Pilger, 'Bush's Vietnam', *New Statesman*, 23 June 2003.

25. For details, see Ahmed Rashid, *Jihad: The Rise of Militant Islam in Central Asia*, New Haven, 2003; and, *Taliban, Islam, Oil and the New Great Game in Central Asia*, London, 2000; and, Peter Marsden, *The Taliban, War, Religion and the New Order in Afghanistan*, London, 1998.

26. For various perspectives on Iraq, see, Milan Rai, *War Plan: The Reason against War in Iraq*, London, 2002; Michael Ratner, et al., *Against War in Iraq*, New York, 2003; Said K. Aburish, *Saddam Hussein: The Politics of Revenge*, London, 2000; Dilip Hiro, *Iraq: A Report from the Inside*, London, 2002; and, Andrew Cockburn and Patrick Cockburn, *Saddam Hussein: An American Obsession*, London, 2002.

27. In San Francisco, local Muslims signed a petition to express their resentment over the US bombing of towns and mosques. It was released to other cities for more signatures before being sent to the White House. For details, see *The News*, 12 April 2004.

28. For details see the official website: www.usinfo.state.gov/media/Archive_index/Illegal_weapons_in_Fallujah.html

29. See the text of his speech in the BBC online report, 2 July 2003, www.bbc.co.uk/southasia.

30. 'Karzai slams anti-US protests', BBC World Service, 14 May 2005, http://news.bbc.co.uk/1/hi/world/south_asia/4547413.stm

31. Iftikhar H. Malik, 'The Afghan Conflict: Islam, the West and the Identity Politics in South Asia', *Indo-British Review: A Journal of History*, XXIII, 2, 2002.

32. Such suspicions and cross-border forays raise tempers on both sides. On 8 July, an Afghan mob vandalized the Pakistan embassy in Kabul, for which Karzai had to apologize. Earlier, Karzai was annoyed by General Musharraf's criticism of the Kabul regime's lack of cross-ethnic support. See, www.bbc. co.uk/southasia. Pakistan, under US pressure sent its troops into the tribal belt in Waziristan in the teeth of opposition from its own civil society and Pushtun populace. Since 1947, this was the first-ever military operation of a massive magnitude in the tribal areas bordering Afghanistan and cost many lives on both sides though the Army was unable to catch any Al-Qaeda activists. Apparently, the operation was undertaken as a quid pro quo on the nuclear issue where Pakistan's alleged technology transfers to Iran, Libya and North Korea would not register any major American resentment.

33. For Pakistan's internal developments in post-9/11 months, see, Owen Bennett-Jones, *Pakistan: Eye of Storm*, London, 2002, and, Iftikhar H. Malik, 'The Afghanistan Crisis and the Rediscovery of a Frontline State', *Asian Survey*, 42, 1, 2002.

34. The balanced view of Pakistan-US relationship, especially after General Musharraf's visit to Washington in 2003 highlighted the need for re-evaluation of priorities and foreign policy trajectories in Islamabad's regional and global policies. See Zubeida Mustafa, 'Was the visit a success?' *Dawn*, 9 July 2003. (www.dawn.com/opinion)

35. Following the Libyan and Iranian disclosure of Pakistan's secret assistance to them in the nuclear area, Musharraf was pressurised by the US to weed out Islamabad's network, run by Abdul Qadeer Khan. The scientist went on television on 4 February 2004 and offered a national apology for his shadowy connections. Musharraf pardoned him the next day. For details see, *Guardian*, *New York Times* and *Times*, 4, 5 and 6 February 2004.

36. Ironically and rather interestingly, during 1928–9, T.E. Lawrence was apparently posted in Wana, South Waziristan Agency in Pakistan where ostensibly he had been translating Homer. To many, his presence like that of the CIA and other intelligence agents during the 1980s and then since 2001 in South-Western Asia, offers unique parallels on the Western involvement in this friendly and semi-independent region. In early 2004, it was in this area that the Pakistani military, helped by US and British special forces, were waging an operation against local tribesmen, who had allegedly given shelter to Al-Qaeda leaders. The military offensive caused many deaths on both sides and Pakistan was hailed by the US as the most favoured nation outside the NATO. For details, see *Guardian*, 19 March 2004 and www.bbc.co.uk/southasia. In May 2005, American authorities were jubilant over the arrest of Abu Farraj al-Libbi, allegedly a Libyan member of Al-Qaeda in Pakistan.

37. By the summer of 2003, it appeared as if Washington was simultaneously supporting Karzai and several regional warlords through hammering out deals with them. This added to Karzai's own untenable control over these

autonomous and rent-seeking warlords. All the actors in the country were seen as engaged in dangerously 'hedging their bets'. For a first-hand and detailed view on the American contradictory policies in Afghanistan, see Sarah Chayes, 'Dangerous liaisons', *New York Times* in *Guardian,* 7 July 2003.

38. For an interesting and well-informed reportage on Karzai, see Christina Lamb, 'Afghanistan', *Sunday Times Magazine,* 29 June 2003; also, *The Sewing Circles of Herat: A Memoir of Afghanistan,* London, 2003.

39. Kevin Maguire, 'Union goes to war with Labour. Cabinet branded 'criminal' on Iraq', *Guardian,* 2 July 2003. (www.guardian.co.uk)

40. Ibid., 12 and 13 May 2005. For an analytical perspective on suicide bombing, see Madeleine Bunting, 'Honour and martyrdom', ibid., 14 May 2005.

41. BBC24, teletext, 14 May 2005.

42. Jim Lobe, 'Neo-cons ask: who is behind Shia uprising?' *Dawn,* 11 April 2004.

43. Mariam Rawi, 'Rules of the rapists', *Guardian,* 12 February 2004.

44. For further details, see Iftikhar H. Malik, 'Karzai at Oxford', *Daily Times,* 8 July 2003. (www.dailytimes.com.pk)

45. Haifa Zangana, 'Why Iraqi women aren't complaining?' *Guardian,* 19 February 2004. An Iraqi novelist and painter, Zangana had been on a visit to her native country where once she had been a political prisoner. The exile found women's rights being pushed aside due to insecurity and societal pressures.

46. This is in reference to Tariq Ali's *The Clash of Fundamentalisms,* London, 2002.

7

JUDAISM, ISLAM AND XENOPHOBIA: POLITICS OF PARTICULARISM AND UNIVERSALISM

What is it with Islam in general and the Palestinians in particular? Is it some sort of cultural deficiency? Is it a genetic defect?
— Ze'ev Boim, Israeli Deputy Defence Minister, quoted in the *Guardian*, 18 March 2004

There is an Israeli price to the many concealed Palestinian dead.
— Gideon Levy, 'The Price of Ignorance', *Haaretz*, 28 December 2003

It is the refusers who have introduced a moral dimension into public discourse.
— Uri Avnery, 'The Categorical Imperative', 27 December 2003, http://www.gush-shalom.org/archives/article283.html

It is horrendous that two leaders of the Western world who profess to be of Christian faith are the two who are leading us towards war against an Islamic state. It is going to mean the whole of the Islam(ic) world will think this is a Christian-against-Islam war. America's notorious support for Israel only exacerbates that.
— Tom Wright, Bishop of Durham, *Independent*, 29 December 2003

Israel is free to choose. But America needs a Middle East policy made in the USA, not in Tel Aviv, or at AIPAC or AEI.
— Patrick Buchanan, *When the Right Went Wrong*, 2004, p. 241

This chapter looks at the complex issues of Jewish identity in reference to an unswerving commitment to Zionism and Israel, as upheld by an overwhelming majority of Jews in Diaspora, though the intertwining remains problematic and controversial. Building on the cases of the Muslim–Jewish relationship and its transformation in the modernist era, it seeks answers from a recent volume, *A New Antisemitism?*, edited by Paul Iganski and Barry Kosmin, which focuses on post-9/11 developments in reference to Jews in Britain.[1] The chapter also seeks an alternative discourse on Zionism, Israel and the Palestinian dilemma, as articulated by some eminent Jews, on both sides of the ideological divide. This axiomatic quest for identities is posited within the context of modernity, which has itself transmitted mixed results for all, and seeks tensions between particularism and universalism, articulated by Jews and Muslims respectively. As stated earlier, the stupendous loss of human lives in horrendous wars, the Holocaust, ethnic cleansing, communalism and ethno-sectarian violence during the twentieth century totalling several millions has led thinkers to question the entire domain of modernity. Essentialised as the bane to progress, development, democracy, human rights and greater technological advancement leading to a more comfortable life characterized by the leisure culture, alert media and greater awareness of the world and ecology collectively are no mean hall-marks of this post-Renaissance modernity. In the same vein, the struggle waged against slavery and discrimination accruing from colour, creed, class and gender, and colonialism is another enviable attribute of modernity. However, retrospectively, the institutionalization of racism—sometimes referred to as neo-racism or scientific racism—a continued exploitation of the poor and vulnerable by a few at the top, internecine wars in the name of nationalism or religious fundamentalism have certainly spawned scepticism towards modernity—often referred to as the Europeanization of the world.[2] Without feeling nostalgic for empires, such retrospection makes the hasty rejection of tradition *per se* equally questionable. Certainly, contemporary human beings, despite more awareness, mobility and greater amenities, are still as *violent* as were their imperial or tribal ancestors—in some cases even more callous and brutal. Maybe, the human nature with all its goodness is also prone to violent tendencies, and it is modernist demands such as weapons of mass destruction, more efficient gadgets and the outreach of monopolist and destructive trajectories that make our contemporary scale of killings massive and equally brutal.[3]

While there is no going back to the era of bows and arrows or of delivering prophets and gurus we are destined to make a better world of the mess we have created in the last two or three generations. Celebration of unquestioned modernity has its serious violent portents for the developing world where minorities, women and environment have become more vulnerable due to so-called majoritarianism—something one noticed in the West only recently. The developed world is itself not yet solely problem free when one looks at the changing trajectories and targets of newer forms of racism and the powerful avowals of Neo-conservatism. This form of unilateralism is underwritten by strong economies, xenophobic societal nationalist groups and unlimited resources with their sophisticated weaponry eliminating huge population groups. In the process, it is pluralism that often becomes the main casualty.[4] The Jews have been undoubtedly the worst sufferers of this process of modernity by virtue of being concurrently located in the very heart of a modernizing and globalizing Europe, and simultaneously akin to indigenous communities in the colonized world, who incessantly fell victim to an energized Europe. After the Second World War, the Jews in Europe and North America may have obtained more breathing space and political influence but the predicament of their other counterparts still remains unresolved. Within Europe and North America, their fellow monotheists—suffering from institutional racism and even outright discrimination—are the Muslim diasporas, who have never had smooth sailing and 9/11 has definitely turned them into the 'new Jews' of the West.[5] But why do both these groups not seem to realise this and instead keep on simmering in a mutually destructive cauldron of hatred and denigration? Is this due to the Middle East quagmire, or does it accrue from sheer ignorance, or does it stem from a mere internalization of attitudes bequeathed by 'manifest destiny'? These are some of the questions that Jews and Muslims should be raising. Sadly, in an atmosphere of mutual recrimination and suspicion, the desire or even avenues to 'confront' each other are missing. Both are positing themselves as the victims of each other's travesties whereas unstoppable events seem to be excruciatingly widening the gulf between them.

Politics of Identity: Particularism versus Universalism

Neither a sheer debunking of modernity nor a mere accusation of a New Europe/West will take us anywhere. However, one thing we have all lost is the enduring tradition of pluralism that, to an unprecedented degree, was characterized by an interdependent Muslim–Jewish relationship spanning several centuries. Such a delinking and its replacement by a unilateral particularism have created a wider chasm, which reverberates through several manifestations and not just in the troubled geo-politics of the Middle East. The definitional challenge of being a *Jew* or a *Muslim* has resurfaced with full force but that is not the end of it. When once somebody defines himself/herself as a Jew, where one draws the line in terms of hyphenation, specificity and loyalties is not a minor issue, the way defining oneself as a Muslim itself is opening a Pandora's box. Individualism may certainly allow personal choices—ethnic, cultural or ideological—yet it is the collective and plural domain where such individual choices are overrun by larger forces. To shrewd non-Jewish observers, being Jewish in a generic sense is non-problematic but when it becomes exclusive and particularistic, it certainly engenders problems. It assumes specific racial and religious features that make it distinct from others. Expecting uncritiqued support for Israeli policies also denies space for any alternative discourse.

On the other hand, Islam began as a universal message accepting and even submerging all types of racial, linguistic and sectarian diversities in order to establish an overarching universalism. Even beyond that, Islam, unlike any other religion, reaffirmed the earlier 'revealed truths', though while establishing its own profile, it equally espoused its own perfection. Not only has becoming a Muslim been the easiest act, at least historically, Islam has been the least conscious of ethnocentrism. However, over the years, the processes of feudalization and clericalisation of Islam have infected its otherwise all-encompassing and egalitarian characteristics. Presently, in the modernist era of states and competitive political loyalties, ethnocentrism and some form of religious particularism have evolved among Muslims though sufis and other cosmopolitans keep on espousing Muslim universalism. That is why classical Islam has been considerably popular among the underprivileged communities such as the African–Americans, Western women and the Indian Dalits (formerly 'Untouchables'). The Arabization of Islam, while originally meant to keep the sacred texts authentic and unified, led in some cases to a form of cultural travesty, though not as serious as V.S. Naipaul would like us to believe.[6] Historically, the so-called peripheries, such as Spain, the Indo-Persian, East Asian and Turkic regions, and Sub-Saharan Africa kept on replenishing Islam by operating as the new cores.[7] The global accent on particularism—mostly justified in the name of narrowly defined nationalism and religion—is invariably pushing all the communities and polities towards an often intolerant particularism, which may inadvertently substantiate the clash of cultures though Bernard Lewis and Samuel Huntington are not the pioneers to have predicted it. But the intensity of religio-national particularism remains behind several contemporary ethnic, sectarian and political conflicts and they are not merely confined to one region or ideology.

While Jewish identity, at one level, is consensual and co-opts any Jew as *Jewish,* at another level, it is consciously particularistic by emphasizing it as being a biological fact. On the contrary, Muslim fundamentalists have developed their own version of particularism by rendering adherence to Islam more taxing, especially in the realms of theocracy and gender. For instance, anybody can become a Muslim as an equal member of community and can even start rebuking others for not being *Islamic* enough. His/her entry into the *ummah* also misleadingly allows him to define Islamicity for others, which is a rather fundamentalist venture, since it is in conflict with the given concept of individual freedom, plus it contravenes the basic Islamic trait of disallowing imposition of religious strictures. Thus, to the Muslim fundamentalists or Islamists, simply being Muslim in a generic or general sense is not enough, one has to be *Islamic* in a specific manner. That is why critical and progressive Muslims, in their reconstructive discourse, desire the removal of clerical monopoly over the Islamic ethos and emphasize individual choices, inter-gender equity and the separation of public from private. In the same vein, these Muslim intellectuals feel that a minimalist consensus on 'Muslimness' could certainly steer the Muslims out of intra-Muslim violence.

Despite an overarching agreement over Jewishness, the dilemma of being Jewish without supporting Zionism or defending Israel on all counts, as a second-tier defence line for Jewishness, remains seriously unresolved within the community. The Zionists would like every Jew to be an unquestioning Zionist and an unrelenting supporter of Israel, whereas many groups or individuals may like to form their own opinions on the latter two without renouncing their Jewishness. If further pressed, some of them may even 'cop out' like those Muslims who may be uncomfortable with a similar ideological particularism. However, a Jew could be an atheist but still a Jew whereas, according to fundamentalists, a Muslim becoming anybody else—atheist, Christian or even secular—is rejecting his/her Muslimness. Certainly, Orthodox Jews both in Israel and elsewhere share a sense of betrayal with members leaving the flock either due to ideological shift or by marrying into the Gentiles. The smallness of the Jewish community understandably engenders its own anxieties to hold on to its withdrawing members, with such an attitude sometimes bordering on paranoia. That is where Jewishness is inclusive though Israel, as one can imagine, has its pulls and pushes much like in Pakistan, Turkey or any other Muslim polity, where societal and statist emphasis remains on particularism and not leaving the flock, which is construed as plain betrayal.

The minority nature of the Jewish Diaspora allowed Jews to assume such prefixes of atheist, communist, liberal, secular or even Orthodox, something that one sees gradually happening to Muslims, Hindus and other such diasporas as well. Some from amongst them are also turning into ardent supporters of Khilafat, Hindutva, Khalistan, and the Second Coming of Jesus Christ. These parallel processes of 'moving in' and 'copping out' are characteristics of many minority communities creating new forms of third cultures and unique cross-cultural niches, with their peers retaliating with a greater emphasis on stricter rules and a change-resistant particularism.[8] In other words, the ideological tensions have intra-community features where subalterns may be seeking their own space without rejecting the aggregate umbrella of an overarching identity. The Salman Rushdie affair highlighted such anxieties among the Muslims for the first time and has since been increasing with the Anglo-American campaign on terror, seen as an anti-Muslim 'crusade' by an 'immoral' and 'this worldly' West, justified by selective Judeo-Christian symbols. As seen earlier, to Bernard Lewis, Paul Berman, Oriana Fallaci, Silvio Berlusconi and a whole host of rightist and leftist ideologues, the fault lies totally with the Muslims—something the radical Zionists love to hear—and would like to see their hatchet men, Ariel Sharon and Benjamin Netanyahu, take it to its extreme limits. Like Fagin and the so-called baby killing and usury drawing, pernicious Medieval Jew, the contemporary Muslim is the new bogeyman. Many Muslims are bewildered at Jews generally not being sensitive enough to this 'repetition of history' and rather choosing a 'wrong enemy'.

History, A Co-optive or Conflictive Heritage?

Away from this confusing panoply of identities history offers a unique searchlight on plural interdependence, which is now being sadly retailored to suit particularist needs of the fundamentalists and nationalists. One can safely assume that very few people know that empires such as the Muslim sultanates, despite their occasionally unnecessary ventures, were the earliest epitomes of tolerance and pluralism. No wonder, until very recently, non-Muslim communities survived, and in some cases, prospered in the Muslim regions, though at present, selective nationalism and a twisted form of modernity are reversing these processes. Delhi, Constantinople, Salonika, Lahore and several other metropolitan centres of the Muslim empires were, until recently, Muslim minority cities where Hindus, Christians and Jews flourished at a time, when European Christian kings and Popes were not only killing one another but were engineering pogroms and events like that in Andalusia through ethnic cleansing of the Muslims, Jews and Gypsies. They were also killing fellow believers even while on the so-called divinely ordained Crusades. One may easily assume that it is not just the Muslim children who *en masse* are kept ignorant of this history, even their non-Muslim counterparts have forgotten it. The emphasis is on being different and on being the *other* rather than reconstruction of a past characterized by true pluralism and interdependent existence. No wonder, the unprecedented Hispanic Renaissance was a Christian, Jewish and Muslim experience of celebratory pluralism that has yet to be re-enacted; the Indo-Islamic culture has remained the most brilliant synthesis of its kind in South Asian history that is now being threatened by communalism, and certainly the Ottoman experience of inter-faith dependence was again quite unique.

In a moving episode in the last few days of the dying caliphate, while depicting the glum exile of the last Ottoman Caliph, Philip Mansell has beautifully narrated an encounter between the Sultan and the Turkish stationmaster on the expulsion of the former from his native lands. The deposed Sultan, in his worst misery and ignominy, was deeply moved and amazed by the protocol and respect given to him by this solitary Turk. On his query to being exceptionally hospitable, the stationmaster observed:

The Ottoman dynasty is the saviour of the Turkish Jews. When our ancestors were driven out of Spain, and looked for a country to take them in, it was the Ottomans who agreed to give us shelter and saved us from extinction. Through the generosity of their government, once again they received freedom of religion and language, protection for their women, their possessions and their lives. Therefore our conscience obliges us to serve you as much as we can in your darkest hour.[9]

Shifting Parameters of Judeophobia and Neo-Anti-Semitism

The book *A New Antisemitism?* highlights the inter-communal tensions but does not talk about the age-old mutualities that have also characterized this bi-communal experience for Jews and Muslims in Spain, North Africa, the Middle East, the Ottoman empire and South Asia. The chapters in this book, however, focus on Britain and more recent forms of racism—Judeophobia—that the Jews have encountered from various directions including religious, ideological and ethnic elements. Muslim fundamentalist groups, media organs especially espousing Leftist and Liberal views and several other clusters are perceived to accentuate the fault line by subscribing to neo-Anti-Semitism in Britain. It is only in the city and its financial cadres that professional Jews claim not to suffer any discrimination as they hold managerial positions, otherwise, subtle forms of victimization and denigration remain pervasive. One group of contributors find anti-Jewish, anti-Zionist and anti-Israeli sentiments aggregating together for all kinds of reasons—flimsy as they may be to the respective viewers—and Jews stay a focus of the same age-old hatred. Their influence over media, academia, global finances and politics through specific Jewish lobbies, on occasions, remains exaggerated. The other school feels that there are problems in defining a Jew—both ethnically and then religiously—and then there are difficulties in finding a holistic interface between the Jewish, Zionist and Israeli dispensations. To this latter opinion, being Jewish in post-1960 Britain may not be problematic, if it is simply an identity marker—one of several—but it becomes a dilemma once Zionism is essentialized into this Jewish identity. In other words, the view that both cannot be exclusive, is itself problematic.

A New Antisemitism? offers seventeen chapters under three sections—Manifestations, Media, and Politics and Religion—with foreword and epilogue through a professional summation seeking common strands in a wide variety of views and emphasis. Other than the two above-mentioned main opinion groups, the individual contributors represent various disciplines and pursuits in this collaborative effort. They are all prominent British Jews including the Chief Rabbi, Dr Jonathan Sacks, who himself has been on the receiving end for his views on the universality of truth, justice and compassion. Due to Israeli and Orthodox reaction, the first edition of his book had to be withdrawn with relevant pages expunged for equating Jewish 'specificity' with other creeds.[10] It shows that fundamentalism is not any one religious community's monopoly and may come from various directions. None of the contributors in this volume has any problem with their individual Jewish identity but beyond that, in issues of Zionism, attitudes towards Israel or the variable forms of Judeophobia, one encounters some minor differences. Based on a project sponsored by the London-based Institute for Jewish Policy Research (JPR), the volume could have certainly benefited from critical views on Zionism and Israel as well.

While discussing any community in a given plural setting, each study invariably begins by offering some statistics, and this compendium is no exception. Its introduction, while summarizing all the three mentioned domains of debate, posits the number of British Jews around 300,000, though the figures could vary slightly. However, one remains curious about general demographic trends within British Jewry in reference to smallness, gradual increase or decrease in numbers. For instance, while the aggregate Muslim statistics reveal a steady increase, the conceptual hypothesis like an eventual Andalusia syndrome or even Diaspora itself proving the vanguard of an Islamic Renaissance or that of European Islam, render demography into a hotly contested domain. Unlike a recent Muslim diaspora—still in its formative stage of settling down and focus of a negative spotlight unlike any other—the long-established Jewish communities mostly inhabit the Greater London area with smaller representations in other major British cities. British Jews are a totally professional community, well settled and economically secure unlike Muslims, who may be many times bigger as a community, yet are meagrely represented in professional cadres. Most of the Muslim immigrants are blue-collar workers who lack proper middle class institutions and effective networks, and are still trying to establish roots. Coming from the former colonies and being non-white further adds to their exclusion from a predominantly middle class, white society and thus they remain vulnerable to xenophobic attitudes.[11] The geo-political issues in the Middle East or in other Muslim regions add on to their challenges. That is why during the massive ethnic cleansing in the former Yugoslavia on the heels of the Rushdie affair, several Muslim intellectuals in Britain characterized their communities as 'the new Jews'. The Muslim Diaspora, statistics-wise, may seem impressive yet it lacks the proper wherewithal and some bonding and effective platforms, which renders it into a vastly under-represented, socially factionalized and politically marginalized community of mosque and kinship-based clusters.

The varying responses from second generation British Muslims, accounting for 70 per cent of the total, also present a mixed picture with apologia, anger and moderation characterizing various attitudes. Many Muslims, even in the second generation, remain self-employed due to paucity of job opportunities, which may be further exacerbated by the various forms of subterranean institutional racism. Thus, despite smaller numbers, British Jews, unlike their previous generations, enjoy certain advantages accruing from class, culture and other crucial denominators. Both the colour and class offer British Jews a useful 'invisibility' though the orthodox amongst them, like Muslims in general, may be vulnerable to racist remarks or rancour. Class, colour and creed—the three main denominators—are not in favour of Muslims, something that many Jewish intellectuals also privately accept.[12] In addition, as mentioned in this volume, the arrival of new immigrants from the former colonies has allowed more breathing space to Jews (and to the Irish!) as the racist outfits now focus on Muslims.

The Jewish–Muslim tensions are rooted largely in the Middle Eastern political imbroglio besides an unacknowledged internalization of the 'White Man's burden' on both sides. Many concerned Muslims and Jews believe that given a long history of mutual sharing, especially during the Muslim imperial era until well into the twentieth century, they can largely patch up their hostility if a credible solution is found to the Palestinian–Israeli conflict to the best collective interests. This is not to trivialize the fact that there are stubborn sections on both sides whose essentialization of Muslim–Jewish hostility goes beyond political parameters. Such antagonists have multiplied in recent times with selective killings, increasing Jewish settlements and Palestinian suicide bombings. But given the salience of the *political* factor, any tangible solution to the imbroglio may deflate polarity to a large extent. The issue is certainly not intractable if one looks at millions of rational and peace-loving Muslims and their counterparts, including open-minded Jews and groups like Gush Shalom. But again, it will be simplistic to overlook the volatile nature of this recent phase of the relationship besides the pernicious baggage from colonial times that has fed into the derogatory images of the Jews (and of Muslims) across the former colonies.[13]

The location of the Jewish groups in the former colonial countries—however peripheral it may have been—also adds to the problems of pervasive images and misperceptions. Jews, by history and even by their own choice and thanks to their proportionally larger numbers in the West, have been rightly perceived to be the torch bearers of Western civilization whose own experience in the colonized world has been problematic. The West as encountered by the East and South in the last five centuries and more effectively and rather unjustly in recent times with its multiple hold over the rest, is seen as hegemonic. It is a different story that while being part of the Western traditions, Jews, in several cases, were the 'poor cousins' or 'enemy within', but their contribution in the evolution of modern Western civilization is an established fact and that also underpins their alienation from the non-Western societies, including Muslims.[14] In this perspective, Zionist claims for a

Biblical Israel or Promised Land are plainly seen as history repeating itself. The non-Western world in general and the Arabs in particular do not perceive Zionism as a religious home-coming; to them, it is essentially a 'White Man's burden'—a merciless colonialism in a holy garb—which has been intermittently experienced beforehand. To them, Western domination stipulated sheer displacement of the natives, conquest and control of their lands and a holistic transformation of their socio-economic environment. To the peoples in the former colonies, Zionism is surely a late-nineteenth century construct and not at all a long-time utopia. There was no hindrance to Jewish migration to the Holy Land under the Muslim empires when they could have easily established their majority in some selected areas. That is why instead of soliciting sympathy, the project of Israel is widely seen as sheer aggression, abrasive land grab and a steady violence inducted through unmitigated expulsions of millions from their native lands, in league with the Western-led traditions of modern slavery and elimination of the indigenous communities.

The last half-century, as characterized by an absence of accommodation to the native factor in the Middle East, only strengthens this alien nature of the Zionist project though many recent immigrants to Israel are Asian and African Jews. But their expulsion materialised *only after* the Palestinian exodus.[15] The ambiguous status and a state-engineered alienation of Israeli Arabs in a confessional and self-avowed Jewish state further underwrite such views of Zionism and its propagation. A few centuries ago, the establishment of Israel with unbridled boundaries—much like the evolution of white-dominated *European/Western* polities of the United States, Canada, New Zealand, Australia and South America—would have been easier but not any more. A greater awareness of human rights, powerful media facilities and a growing aversion to continuation of such projects in recent times all make Israeli expansion highly visible and disputatious. When Palestinians refuse to become the new 'American Indians' on their own lands, people listen with care and concern. No wonder, Gandhi, Mandela, Tutu, Jinnah, Fanon, the Pope and several such international figures—and not merely the Left Liberals of the anti-Israeli variety—have openly questioned Israeli policies of expanding settlements in the wake of local displacements. The failure of Israel to establish itself as a Middle Eastern country, both by choice and by compulsion, plus its avowed identification and dependence on the West *per se* do not allow it sufficient *indigenous* credentials. The continued support from the Jews in the West only strengthens its image as a Western outpost in the heart of the Eastern, formerly colonized, underprivileged and denigrated world.

Since the 1990s, to Muslims at large, the Israeli project, with full support from Western Zionists has become an explicitly anti-Muslim campaign by its assertive policies in the Middle East, accompanied by anti-Muslim tirade through media and academia. The neoconservatives and entrepreneurs of American supremacy, joined by Likud supporters, Christian evangelists and their numerous colleagues are all intent upon further marginalizing the Muslim factor in the Middle East. Bernard Lewis, Daniel Pipes and several such scholars with long-held attitudes towards Islam readily find numerous problems with Islam and Muslims.[16] The events of 9/11 came as a welcome opportunity to implement American unilateralism by its strong evangelical and Zionist components before the Second Coming of the Christ. The invasions of Afghanistan and Iraq with some of the most horrendous weapons, when not a single Afghan or Iraqi had been involved in the terrorist attacks, and the resultant killings, destruction and instability are feared to be followed with similar ventures against Iran, Syria, Saudi Arabia, Yemen and Pakistan.[17]

Iran's nuclear programme, despite its adherence to the NPT has been made controversial whereas Israel's remain' untouchable, which raises serious eyebrows across the board as the Anglo-American alliance is accused of double standards.[18] In 2004, Pakistan's General Pervez Musharraf undertook another major shift on nuclear policy by exposing its leading scientists who had presumably been helping Iran, Libya and North Korea in their nuclear programmes. While the US had itself acquired its know-how from German scientists and had then shared it with Britain and other friendly countries for long. The spotlight on Muslim countries only strengthened the grudge against the West for pursuing anti-Muslim campaigns.

The close collaboration on a so-called war on terror tainted as it is with serious policies of revenge and vendetta, has certainly further consolidated serious concerns about this new Western onslaught, of which all the Zionists—but not all Western Jews—are a major component. The concurrent premises of victim-hood as well as of perpetration definitely do not convince non-Western people. While there is sympathy for Western Jewry over the pogroms and Holocaust, simultaneously there is confusion over its being a major component and instrument of the North Atlantic project of hegemony. One cannot ignore several of those Jews, both within Israel and elsewhere, who in the past and in recent times have stood for human rights, decolonization, abolitionism of slavery and racism, and have valiantly struggled for global justice. However, Israel's unequivocal credentials as a proto-Western state, its influence in the United States and willingness to operate as a trajectory for the neoconservatives do not raise its profile as a sovereign, native and peace-seeking actor in the region. Added to that, the triangular support for unpopular, unjustified and unilateral Israeli, American and British policies in the Muslim world equally obviate the residue of support for Israel. That is where Israel and Zionism become not a Muslim or Arab-specific issue, they turn into a larger-than-life tangle of intricate loyalties.[19]

Israel is a sovereign state yet its problematic relationship has only incurred hostility not just among Muslims but elsewhere as well. Here, Israel is not seen as a victim, rather it is perceived as a perpetrator with some of its critics even going beyond prevalent diplomatic politeness.[20] Such images will grow both in Europe and elsewhere especially when the peace movement gets stronger and people begin to vocally criticise unquestioned official support for Israeli expansionism at the expense of more than one billion Muslims.

Anti-Semitism in its Contemporary Forms

Basing his arguments on statistical information gathered on the cases of Judeophobia, Michael Whine's chapter finds a rising tide in racist incidents, especially in the recent past. He attributes its growth to the rise of the ultra right, and 'the left-liberal media obsession with Israel ..., and an increasingly blatantly anti-Semitic Arab and Muslim media help to create such an environment.' [21] Of course, the Israeli–Palestinian conflict remains a major topic in news reports and commentaries on Muslim and Arab channels but most such programmes do not preach any hatred towards Jews. Their criticism of Israel, as observed by this author closely, unlike the usual tabloid outpourings, remains focused on Sharon's policies and Washington's unflinching support for him. These newspapers, magazines and visual channels, except for a few hotheads like al-Muhajiroon disseminating hateful emails, are mostly responsible and cautious and one cannot issue a blanket verdict especially when Michael Whine may not know their languages.

The presence of Al-Jazeera in Israel and the Occupied Territories and of some other correspondents reveals that the news is not mere hearsay, otherwise Tel Aviv would have expelled them a long time back. The Muslim channels openly criticize double standards when it comes to Washington and London but avoid passing racist comments.[22] Certainly, the desecration of Jewish cemetaries or graffiti on the walls of synagogues do give cause for concern, but again given the long history of anti-Semitism in Europe, these cannot be solely attributed to angry Muslim youths. However, anti-Semitism, like Islamophobia, is a reality though the latter seems to have overshadowed every other form of racism, as has been documented and stipulated by the Runnymede Trust Report.[23] Concerned Muslims do not agree to the kind of diatribes dished out by Omar al-Bakri or Anjem Choudary. Certainly, the Muslims were deeply angered by Abu Hamza's rhetoric though he was also restrained in the last few years following his surveillance. His arrest in London involving a major police operation, however, did not go well with many Muslims who feared a persistent campaign against the Muslim community, their charities and clergy leading to further introversion of a predominantly marginalised ethnic section.

Chief Rabbi Jonathan Sacks also seems to subscribe to a view where anti-Americanism has rekindled anti-Semitism, though to him, 'it is wrong to see all criticism of the state of Israel as anti-Zionism, let alone as antisemitism.'[24] He seeks its roots in the age-old European and British traditions all the way from medieval times, when Jews were racially and culturally discriminated against. The nineteenth century further hyped up anti-Jewish sentiments when nationalist scholars reconstructed German identity on exclusionary lines and the malady eventually culminated into the Holocaust. Even in a comparatively tolerant England, as late as in 1930, the synagogue in Cambridge did not have windows opening on the street for fear of vandalism and abuse.

Antony Lerman seeks the roots of this new phase in anti-Semitism in the second Intifada in September 2000 followed by attacks on Jewish property, and like Jonathan Sacks, finds it on the rise. However, he is vocal enough to suggest, 'it is far easier and safer to be a Jew than a Muslim, a black person or an east European asylum seeker.'[25] But, subsequently, while dilating on the rise of anti-Semitism, he attributes it to three factors. Firstly, it hides behind the criticism of Israel; secondly, by portraying Israel as expansionist and oppressor, it allows Europeans to be relieved of their residual guilt, and thirdly, Muslim groups such as Hizbul Tahrir or even Arab newspapers feed into this European and Christian 'construct' by rehashing exaggerated accounts of Jewish customs and rituals. Lerman finds Europe to be the hotbed of antisemitism but his allusion to responsible media offering stories of Jews killing Muslim and Christian children for their ceremonies is not a tested fact. Anthony Julius also recognises the indigenization of British Jewry over the years based on mutual acceptance. Isaiah Berlin called himself an Anglophile Jew admiring English common sense, decency and fairness, though Muslim antisemitism as suggested by Julius, has had a longer history. While Fagin, Shylock and Svengali typified the English stereotypes of Jews in the past, Muslim traditions, as understood by Julius, aim at establishing a

Muslim International by subordinating everyone else, including Jews.[26] This is not totally true as the classical Islamic teachings value Jewish and Christian heritage, prophets and scriptures though are wary of their monopoly and tampering by clerical groups. Islam offers an honorific—*Ahal-i-Kitaab*—for Jews and Christians, meaning the 'People of the Book'. It is not a trivial designation when one thinks of the state of affairs prevailing in the world fifteen centuries ago. Julius and many of his fellow faithful may not know that other than a history of safeguarding Jews, ordinary Muslims in their daily five-time prayers, pray for the safety and welfare of the children of Abraham. In fact, if one calculates the frequency of these Muslim prayers each day, as uttered by Muslims across the world, they would reach several billions, something that one does not find in other religious traditions or sacred obligations. Islam establishes itself as a continuous message introduced by Adam and completed by Muhammad, neither alien nor overpowering, rather an evolutionary process in line with the universalistic teachings of the past prophets. Abraham, Noah, Jacob, Joseph, Isaac, David, Moses, Aaron, Solomon and Jesus are as much Muslim prophets as Ishmael and Muhammad. If Muslims ever overstepped these limits of respect and sanctity for the People of Book, contemporary jurists and other critics would be quick to reprimand them since Islam remains one of the most documented religious traditions without claiming any miraculous specificities.

Anti-Semitism, Israel and Zionism: Friendly Triumvirate or Troublesome Triangle?

In the second major section of *A New Antisemitism?* concerned with the media, several contributors express their unease with the Leftist–Liberal critique of Israel and Zionism as the new form of antisemitism. The intricate triangular relationship among the Jews, Israel and Zionism itself is slippery terrain and before forming any such opinion one has to contextualise such analysis. While criticism of Jews, both in the individual or collective context, in most cases, may be identified as anti-Semitism yet religious differences among the three Abrahamic religions and the related Muslim scholarly commentaries do not embody any hidden agenda. However, there is still a definitional problem: how would one define a Jew? Is it cultural/religious or ethnic, which, in the last case, would mean that one has to be of Jewish parentage? While some Jews accept conversions, still many traditional groups insist on Jewish lineage. The latter situation may be in line with the desire for the intactness of a rather smaller though well-knit community, but it could also mean that more like Zoroastrians, being Jewish denotes blood relationship and cannot be subscribed to. While to supporters of this premise, it may be a genuine fact but to its non-Jewish critics this may be a racial particularism itself vulnerable to misinterpretations. Despite being an intra-Jewish problem, it has its trans-communal dimensions and poses serious challenges for those who are liberal, or marry outside Jewish circles. In addition, the Jewish blood-based identity creates a sense of exclusion, making Jews vulnerable to attacks by non-Jews, as has been the case in Europe in the recent past. This further propels the conspiracy theories by xenophobes such as Henry Ford on the back of the *Protocols of the Elders of Zion,* who add pernicious meanings to it and continue to deride the dictum of a God-chosen people. Partly, due to this, several Jewish ideologues have been rebelling against a strict and ethnically defined Jewishness. Concurrently, it poses problems in reference to the stipulation of Zionism as the ultimate Jewish creed and the definition of Israel as a solely *Jewish* state.

The critics of Israel, even from amongst Israeli and Jewish groups, find this exclusive definition discriminatory both by intent and by practice. Since Israel is for Jews only, the rest are either non-citizens or are relegated to a second-class category. This kind of traditional 'segregation' continuously poses problems for Israel, and of course, for world Jewish communities when inter-marriages are becoming so common. It is interesting to note that in China, the Jewish community closely aligned itself with the Muslims (blue caps meeting up with the white caps) and eventually the Jewish identity was subsumed by the larger, Persian speaking, Turkic

Muslim identity. Thus, in a way, the emphasis on Jewish separateness, despite its problems both in the past and present, has to be approached in a sensitive way.

As seen in several other cases, minorities try to be self-contained and defensive, which is understandable and when European Jews are biologically prone to smaller families, their dwindling numbers, like the Zoroastrians, may further intensify their introversion. While on the one hand, in the desire to create a Zion it is important for Jews to stay together and to impart the Jewish heritage—both biological and cultural—to successive generations. Its focus on Jewish particularity despite its secular and democratic credentials, also compromises its profile. Of course, being predominantly a country of immigration, Israel is experiencing more cross-ethnic and strictly intra-Jewish pluralism yet its continued exclusion of the Israeli Arabs poses serious sociological and moral problems. Firstly, Israel came into being as a self-professed *Jewish* state but like the non-Israeli Jews, the undefined status of its Arab community offers a serious challenge and refutation to its Zionist credentials. Secondly, the expansion of settlements has further aggravated this identity crisis. Since 1967, Israel has established 143 settlements and scores of additional outposts for future settlements in the West Bank and Gaza Strip since capturing these territories in the war. Jerusalem is now solely held by Israel and virtually happens to be its capital. Following the Oslo Accords of 1993, the number of settlers on these territories including East Jerusalem has doubled to 400,000. Altogether between the Jordan River and the Mediterranean, there are 5.7 million Jews beside nearly 5 million Arabs. In the next decade or so, Arabs are predicted to be a majority thus unnerving Zionists with a serious dilemma for Israel on either to choose between a democracy, or a strictly *Jewish* entity based on force and exclusion. If it chooses to be a holistic democracy it has to allow equal rights to Arabs which means their majority, in the future will basically overwrite Israel's confessional status. Concurrently, if it goes on occupying territories along with denying citizenry to its Arab populace, its moral and political dilemma will compound beyond any resolution. Thirdly, if it agrees to a two-state

solution as laid down in the Oslo Accords or President George
Bush's Road Map, then its project of ghettoising Palestinians in
several Bantustans or keeping Gaza, the West Bank and Jerusalem
separated in the name of security or a Biblical justification, will
only aggravate tensions. Fourthly, Israel may agree to the formula
of one-state-two nations, or one state-two-equal/sovereign
communities, which may have its own ramification, though this
could also guarantee peace in the longer term. This is a kind of
viewpoint that many Palestinians and Israelis may be exploring
since Israeli expansion, accompanying the destruction of the
Palestinian Authority amidst growing settlements and selective
assassinations, is pushing everyone towards a point of no-return.[27]

Sharon or Netanyahu, like Golda Meir and other extremists,
cannot totally eliminate the Palestinians nor can Zionists keep on
postponing a resolution by misrepresenting the Palestinian struggle
for self-determination as sheer terrorism. Israel's emphatic campaign
to bring in more settlers is not only proving counter productive, it
is drying up the supply sources. Already there are stories of fake
Jews being imported from South America. In addition, as suggested
by William Burns, a senior American diplomat, the policy to
expand settlements pursued by the Likud to pre-empt and forestall
the road map for a Palestinian state, is seriously counterproductive.
This policy, to him, 'could threaten Israel as a Jewish
democracy.'[28]

As long as the Jews lived in the inner cities in Europe their
togetherness was guaranteed by their own efforts and because of
the so-called majoritarian backlash. Now they have a homeland
with a different set of problems, as the erstwhile minority has
become a majority—even though a minute one—yet dealing with
other minorities is itself not proving easy. It is just like the case of
Pakistan which the Muslims in India—indigenous though overall
a huge minority across a labyrinthine India—created in 1947 but
the very definition of being Pakistani first or a Muslim first, or the
inter-twining of these two identities, have posed formidable
challenges.[29] However, Zionism is an ideology, which despite its
nearness to many Jews (this volume claims 70 per cent Jews

subscribing to Zionism) is not sacrosanct. The Jewish aspiration for a homeland, either out of nostalgia, religious beliefs or even as an escape from European oppression, is not a divinely ordained article of faith that cannot be challenged both by the Jews and non-Jews. Making it something very Jewish and sacrosanct has itself spawned its critique.

The way Arab nationalism or the concept of the Khilafat has been disputatious among Muslims, Zionism is controversial among the Jews and 'Gentiles'. How would one characterize the Jewish critics of Zionism is a major moot point and a troublesome reality for the Jews themselves. Zionism, at different times, meant different things to different Jewish communities, though Theodore Herzl's reconstruction in the 1890s has been synonymous with Israel. If each nation or community starts demanding its own *Israel,* most of the countries, especially in the Western Hemisphere and Australasia will simply fall apart. Nazis used Zionism as a Jewish betrayal of a unilateral German patriotism and to the contemporary Neo-Nazis and other racist outfits, Jewish loyalties are for a homeland elsewhere and not to the country of their birth and hearth.

The dislocation of indigenous people and a continued denial to Palestinians of rights to their own land, while seeking the right to return for another community—the Zionists—raises serious ideological and moral questions that cannot be brushed aside under the panoply of anti-Semitism. To Peter Pulzer, the criticism of Israel in many cases stems from anti-semitism itself. It is a moot point. Criticism of any Muslim state such as Pakistan, Turkey or Iraq, which is always in vogue, is mostly seen as the critique of societies and polities that happen to be Muslim, but very few Muslim observers will perceive it as an anti-Islam ideology—though Islam remains a major critical point in such discourse.[30] However, viewing the Jews as an exceptional case or Israel as a victim state are equally contentious issues both for Jews and liberal-left media, as the reputed journalist, Jonathan Freedland, demands 'a clear ruling' on all the three trajectories.[31] However, Zionism, much like any other ideology including the contemporary Left, has its own varied shades and using it merely to justify the state of Israel and a policy of dispossession may not be entirely correct. For example, while one can be an atheist Jew, one can still be a non-Zionist Jew or even a Zionist without supporting Israel as a separate state. These differing ideological positions have been quite vocal both in Israel and in the Diaspora revealing that the creation of Israel, instead of resolving the problems of identity and ideology, has only accentuated them. The Israeli relationship with the Palestinians— irrespective of mutual accusations—has only added to Jewish criticism of both Zionism and Israel. Some of these critics are individuals of great international standing and may be Israeli citizens—first-generation immigrants or their descendants, to whom loyalty to Israel and Zionism should have been unquestionable. No wonder there is an increasing number of dissenting Israeli Jews who, as conscientious objectors, refuse to impose any embargo on Palestinians, much less kill them. Some groups such as Gush Shalom even acted as a shield around Yasser Arafat to protect him from any possible Israeli effort to snatch him or kill him in a staged encounter.

Politics and Religion, Uneasy Partners or Willing Rivals

The third section of *A New Antisemitism?* suitably ventures into tensions created by the intermingling of religion with politics, which to many contributors, is not the case due to a presumed Israeli/Jewish exceptionalism and strikes as a rather strange argument. However, the section also looks at the Muslim and Christian positions and their role in Judeophobia, especially in the light of post-9/11 instability in West Asia and a pervasive Muslim anger across the globe. The chapters do not challenge or even investigate Sharon's visit to the Mount—causing the second Intifada—followed by one of the most violent phases in Palestinian– Israeli history. In prevalent Zionist discourse, Islam, more than Christianity, emerges as the main culprit and one wonders if Jews are totally friendless people when presumably the left, liberal,

Christian and now Muslim clusters are all after their blood! Robert Wistrich, somehow, finds Britain to be the home of 'several dozen suspected al-Qaeda activists and hundreds of supporters, who may pose a threat, either in this country or as part of an international terror network.'[32] One wonders how come, despite Robert Wistrich's public knowledge of so many miscreants, Scotland Yard have been keeping them free and seem to have no evidence whatsoever against those they have arrested. One hopes the contributor does not take every observant British Muslim to be a potential al-Qaeda terrorist. He must visit the United States where Muslims citizens are being routinely profiled, finger printed and several thousand have already been extradited not to forget the undefined and equally painful status of the internees of Guantanamo Bay. One expects true humanists to raise their voice against these serious human rights violations instead of further maligning an already beleaguered community. Another of those wild statements made by him in the same chapter suggests that the Arabic editions of *Mein Kampf* are very popular in metropolitan cities.[33]

Melanie Philips, while unearthing the Christian myth of Judaism as 'an evil religion', sees its reverberations in reference to the whole ideology of replacement that the Christians and Muslims seem to subscribe to. Both these religions assert their own suitability by superseding the previous one(s) and thus inherently view Judaism as an 'outmoded' theology. Such hidden but enduring views among Christians allow a new kind of antisemitism where criticism of Israel becomes a useful excuse to ventilate anti-Jewish sentiments. But this is not unique to Israel as that happens all the time to each Muslim state and in greater numbers and more frequently, which, in fact, may make Jewish complaints of ant-Semitism rather untenable. Geoffrey Alderman's review of the Left's politics in reference to nationhood, colonialism, class and Israel is well informed and could have been further expanded. The British imperial project and the creation of Israel following the Balfour Declaration and subsequent partition and dispossession have been, according to the Left's view, a blunder and thus incurring critique of Israel and its policies. Certainly, many Jews, since their settlement in Britain, have been the vanguard Left and to their descendants Israel is definitely problematic in several ways. In her chapter, Kate Taylor investigates the political career of the British National Party (BNP) and its shifting positions on antisemitism. The BNP has both exaggerated as well as underplayed the Jewish influence in Britain, depending upon its expediency. However, Taylor accredits the serious media for fighting off racist outfits such as the BNP through exposing their xenophobia. Consequently, the typical BNP line has been simply to dramatize Jewish influence on the British media. Like the Left critics of Israel and Zionism, several Jewish academics in the UK have expressed their dissent and anger over Israeli policies by spearheading an academic boycott. In fact, Professor Stephen Rose of the Open University, on 6 April 2002, led a campaign for the academic boycott of Israel over its policies in the Occupied Territories through a petition in *The Guardian*. Himself a Jew, his other co-signatories included Jews, a few Muslim and several Christian academics. These conscientious objectors included Oxbridge dons and the Association of University Teachers (AUT) and the National Association for Teachers in Further and Higher Education (NAFTHE), the two main British organizations of college and university academics, which supported their argument. However, as highlighted by John Levy, it was Professor Mona Baker's expulsion of two Israeli academics from the editorial board of a journal in Manchester that made the issue highly contentious. Eventually, in April 2005, the AUT voted for the boycott of two Israeli universities on the plea that the staff at these institutions had failed to criticize and restrain the official brutalization of Palestinians.

The trade unions, as major supporters of the Labour and Left in Britain, have been vocally critical of Israeli policies and wary of an expansionist Zionism. However, one should not forget that it was Clement Attlee, the Labour Prime Minister, who readily recognized Israel in 1948. But traditionally, British Labour Unions including the mentioned lecturers' associations have been critical of Israeli policies and its flouting of UN resolutions. Ronnie Fraser, in his chapter, highlights this aspect yet stops short of accusing these unions and bodies of being anti-Semitic though definitely finds them anti-American, which, to him, also explains their discomfort with Israel. Towards the end, Richard Bolchover's piece on the absence of anti-Semitism from the city and business concerns may come as a pleasant surprise to readers who may, by now, be wary of finding anti-Semites in every echelon of British society. London, accounting for 58 per cent of global banking and related business, has a large number of Jewish professionals holding significant managerial positions. Such findings are correct, yet may also be interpreted as implying that racism is very class specific. Accordingly, if the community is economically strong the xenophobes will stay overawed and restrained; otherwise they remain on the prowl. The ascription of racism to the poor and working classes, fellow immigrants, media and academic professionals is not a tenable explanation of a rather complex phenomenon like neo-racism. In their summation, the editors, once again, try to find some common strands while agreeing upon most of the observations in the papers, simultaneously pinpointing the Muslim factor behind the rise of neo-Semitism.

Israel and Zionism: The Emerging Jewish Critique

As mentioned earlier, all the issues raised in the book *The New Antisemitism?* are both significant as well as contentious from a Jewish, Zionist and Israeli perspective without forgetting the fact that there are individuals and groups who do not feel comfortable with the 'perceived wisdom'. The inseparability of Jewish identity from an essentialised Zionism and from an ever-sacrosanct Israel is a dilemma and rather unacceptable tangle for many dissenting Jews and other analysts. Many critics of this imposition are lecturers, artists, writers and journalists, conscientious objectors of military draft, or even ordinary citizens whose being Jewish has not stopped them from establishing bridges with Palestinians, Muslims, Christians, leftists, anarchists and pacifists. In the wake of 9/11 and the Anglo-American vengeance wreaked on Afghanistan and Iraq in particular and Muslims in general, simultaneous with the hyper aggressive policy of the Likud Government, these Jewish activists have become vocal critics of the prevalent policies shared by London, Tel Aviv and Washington. Several Jews who left Israel for Britain and the United States have been vociferous critics of this recent yet emphatic intermixing of the Jewish, Zionist and Israeli. To them, extreme Zionism and Israeli policies are compromising Jewish moral scruples and dehumanizing a whole heritage. It is interesting to note that *Galoot*, a documentary made by a Moroccan Jewish expatriate in London, highlighted these issues by focusing on fellow expatriates from Israel. The film qualified for several prizes but has been banned in Israel and is not openly available elsewhere either.

The post-9/11 campaigns have created new moral dilemmas for concerned Israeli Jews and we may turn to two of them whose pieces are not included in the edited volume. Criticizing both Sharon and Arafat for their failings, especially after the resignation of Abu Mazan, Amos Oz has taken them to task though his strongest words are reserved for his own Prime Minister Ariel Sharon's plea of not being able to deal with Arafat or any of his associates This, to Oz, is an 'impossible position because it is not for Israelis to decide who represents Palestine, just as it is not for the Palestinians to choose which Israeli will be their partner. Arafat may be a nasty man with a record of violence and double-crossing. However, we Israelis cannot select Mother Teresa to become the leader of Palestinians.' He is critical of the Israeli policy of selective killings without sparing the perpetrators yet is desirous of a transparent and agenda-based solution.[34]

The most powerful critique of Zionism in the wake of Israeli coercive policies and a global unease and puzzlement over the general direction of Judaism under the flagship of Israeli-led Zionism comes from within Israel itself. Groups like Gush Shalom are spearheading a peaceful resistance to Israeli policies of dispossession, expulsion and assassination, while several military personnel are increasingly raising moral objections and expressing a pervasive disillusionment with their regime. These moral objectors and several other Jewish intellectuals are aghast not only at the sordid treatment of the original dwellers of the land but are resentful of the brutalization of women, children and intermittent socio-economic retaliatory policies pushing more Palestinians towards further acts of extremism. Many objective and equally patriotic persons have persistently found their own government responsible for exacerbating despair and helplessness among Palestinians.

Israel Shahak, in his classical works, critiqued Jewish fundamentalism for being antagonistic to democracy through sheer denial of equal citizenship to all. While contextualizing the assassination of Prime Minister Rabin, *Jewish Fundamentalism in Israel*, has avowedly censured punishment and killings of Jews who are perceived to be heretics.[35] Several Jewish academics in the West have been vocally critical of the entire Zionist movement. A British academic, John Rose, in his *The Myths of Zionism*, finds ancient, medieval and modern mythologies being used to justify a political movement which is aimed at the expulsion and persecution of the Palestinians. While sifting fact from fiction and dilating on recent and past archaeological findings, Rose challenges Zionism's biblical claims and offers a detailed perspective on Judaism's links with the Middle East. He reveals the falsehood of several Zionist claims on Jewish history besides debunking the rationale behind the assertion that Zionism was a response to European anti-Semitism, as he notes: 'Zionism is the problem; its removal is the precondition for peace in the Middle East. It is the precondition for Arab-Jewish reconciliation in Palestine.'[36] The idea of a Jewish homeland, according to Rose, falters on two counts: firstly it incorporates the denial of Palestinian rights, and secondly, 'homeland' is problematic for the Jewish majority living outside Israel. To him, Jews were flourishing among Muslims for centuries and despite the bloodshed caused by the Crusaders, they were invited to settle in Palestine by Saladin but still 'most had no intention of living in Jerusalem'. The co-existence with Muslims for so long would deter many Jews from emigrating and as late as 1949 several Baghdadi Jews were petitioning against moving to Israel. Despite the complexity of the

Jewish experience in Europe, Jews made immense contributions in the evolution of philosophy and culture besides putting up resistance to oppression. Presently, Jewish communities in the West are 'models of an enlightened assimilation' necessitating a similar cross-cultural fertilisation in Palestine instead of insisting on a solely *Jewish* statehood. Rose visualizes the possibility of such a post-Zionism scenario by observing: 'Imagine the great-great-grandchildren of European Jewish settlers in Palestine assimilating into Arab culture, absorbing it and contributing to its development, some time this century. A leap of faith? To be sure, but we Jews have always been rather good at that.'[37]

These objectors and pacifists enjoy support from several like-minded Jewish groups, who are uneasy with the hijacking of their humane traditions in the name of an exclusionist nationalism displaying extremism towards Palestinians and irreverence to international moral and legal institutions. To them, the radical version of the Zionist-Israeli dispensation is not only creating a wedge within world Jewry, it is going to rebound with vengeance for the community at large. While to them, Israel is certainly the homeland, but its control by extremists and intolerant elements, duly supported by similar Jewish elements from outside, is once again, rekindling the erstwhile reservations and criticism of the Herzl-led project. More than Palestinians and the Arabs, Israel, to them, is turning into a moral dilemma for its own adherents. For instance, Avraham Burg, the former speaker of Knesset (1999–2003) and one-time chairman of the Jewish Agency for Israel, offered the strongest criticism of Zionism in the Hebrew and English press. To him, the original two pillars of Zionism—just path and an ethical leadership—have been ironically lost in contemporary Israel, as he noted: 'The Israeli nation today rests on a scaffolding of corruption, and on foundations of oppression and injustice. As such, the end of the Zionist enterprise is already on our doorsteps. There is a real chance that ours will be the last Zionist generation. There may yet be a Jewish state here, but it will be a different sort, strange and ugly.' He feels that the entire Jewish tradition of peace, tolerance and kindness to all has been compromised in Israel by pursuing a ruthless policy towards the Palestinians. This has been a very powerful criticism, which did not go well with many of his fellow citizens and co-religionists, especially, when Burg observed: 'The Jewish people did not survive for millennia in order to pioneer new weaponry, computer security programmes or anti-missile missiles. We were supposed to be a light unto the nations. In this we have failed.' He reflected the thoughts of Jonathan Sacks and several others who might have felt the same privately but were compelled to withdraw such observations under pressure. He warned his fellow community: 'Note this moment well: Zionism's superstructure is already collapsing like a cheap Jerusalem wedding hall. Only madmen continue dancing on the top floor while the pillars below are collapsing.' This is, of course, a very serious indictment by a fellow Zionist and has nothing to do with the Gandhian pacifism or any special love for Muslims.

Burg tried to shake up the conscience of his colleagues by raising serious moral issues:

> We have grown accustomed to ignoring the suffering of the women at the roadblocks.... Israel, having ceased to care about the children of the Palestinians, should not be surprised when they come washed in hatred and blow themselves up in the centres of Israeli escapism. They consign themselves to Allah in our places of recreation, because their own lives are torture. They spill their own blood in our restaurants in order to ruin our appetites, because they have children and parents at home who are hungry and humiliated. We could kill a thousand ringleaders a day and nothing will be solved because the leaders come up from below—from the wells of hatred and anger, from the 'infrastructures' of injustice and moral corruption.

His comments cannot be brushed aside since they reflect those of a worried Jewish community; itself lost in a moral maze. To Burg, these 'Arabs, too, have dreams and needs... There cannot be democracy without equal rights for all who live here, Arab as well as Jew.'[38] Rather than feeling defensive or irritated about it, Zionists have to urgently redefine their mission and how it situates the Arabs—the natives—within its orbit. A continued denigration, expulsion, selective killings and the destruction of the Palestinian heritage as seen in Jenin, Nablus, Ramallah or the Gaza Strip, and the non-citizenship status for Israeli Arabs will definitely add to this serious ideological and moral dilemma, which has already been named political suicide by a prominent Israeli intellectual.[39]

Burg's censurious article elicited wider support from amongst many readers though there were a couple of letters expectedly putting the blame on Palestinians and Yasser Arafat. For instance, Syd Kaminsky defended Israeli policies since Zionism was meant to adapt for its survival. However, Judah Passow noted: 'What we have is a Zionist project that has been hijacked by a messianic agenda of a Greater Israel, using the army to make room for settlements on land that belongs to Palestinians, and by creating a climate of fear at home to fuel the emotional legitimacy of such a vision. This is not Zionism—this is colonialism.'[40] Instead of a two-state solution, a Toronto-based Arab correspondent suggested 'one state with two peoples, where everyone lives equally under the rule of law, just like Belgium, Switzerland and Canada.'[41] K. Mahmud, in his response, wondered: 'How could a nation of peace, justice and equality emerge when refugees are not allowed to return to their homes, but foreigners are paid to come and occupy their homes. This approach was, and is rooted in racist superiority. It can lead nowhere else.'

Several European Jews are not only critical of Israeli policies they are also offended by an unquestioned and always guaranteed US support. In a critical review of US–Israeli policies, Emmanuel Todd, in his best seller, has voiced a well-informed European criticism of the American anti-Arab and anti-Muslim extremism, which seriously lacks even-handedness on the Israel–Palestinian conflict. He feels that in a theatrical form of militarism, the US has targeted a military midget of 24 million people already exhausted by a decade-long sanctions. This, to him, is not an indicator of the American strength, but instead only affirms its increasing decline.[42] Following the Israeli cabinet's decision to expel or even eliminate Arafat, most UN members felt deeply concerned, and led by Syria, the Security Council heard a draft resolution, urging Israel to protect the life of the elected Palestinian president. The US vetoed it whereas Britain, Germany and Bulgaria abstained, and following several statements by Bush on singling out Arafat for all the violence in Palestine and failure of the peace accord, the American unconditional and perennially one-sided support for Sharon only further dismayed many people. It was felt that the 'veto will simply serve to ignite an already potentially explosive situation throughout the Middle East. I am tired of hearing the US champion Israel as the only democracy in the Middle East...The extra-judicial execution of a democratically elected leader would be a heinous and criminal act.'[43] Arafat still offered to pursue peace parleys with Israel, which were scuttled right away with Bush accusing Arafat of being a supporter of terrorism and not interested in the road map for peace.[44]

Max Hastings, a former editor of the *Daily Telegraph,* the British conservative newspaper, voicing the unease among numerous Europeans' cautioned against unquestioned Jewish support for Israeli policies. Otherwise an ardent supporter of the Jewish state, he expressed his unease with the intermingling of Jewish, Zionist and Israeli loyalties, which has caused a resurgence in anti-Semitism. He took issue with those who would deem any criticism of Israel as a betrayal of Judaism or even Zionism:

> They make the cardinal error of identifying the Jewish people with the Israeli government, wilfully confusing anti-Semitism and anti-Zionism. Often, they seem to demand that the behaviour of Israel should be judged by a special standard, that allows the likes of Sharon and Netanyahu a special quota of excesses, in compensation for past sufferings.

Without any regard for traditional Jewish humanism, the perpetration of violence while seeking justification in victim-hood, does not help Jews, Zionists or Israel:

> Attempts to equate anti-Zionism, or even criticism of Israeli policy, with anti-semitism reflect a pitiful intellectual sloth, an abandonment of reasoned attempts to justify Israeli actions in favour of moral

blackmail....If Israel persists with its current policies, and Jewish lobbies around the world continue to express solidarity with repression of the Palestinian, then genuine anti-semitism is bound to increase. Herein lies the lobbyists' recklessness. By insisting that those who denounce the Israeli state's behaviour are enemies of the Jewish people, they seek to impose a grotesque choice.

He warned against the increasing loneliness of Israel due to unbridled violence and its denial by Jewish groups.[45]

Such views reveal a growing sentiment across Europe, as erstwhile supporters feel disenchanted with mounting violence targeted against an already marooned community. Even within Israel, some diehard military strategists like Martin van Crefeld have recommended an end to occupation and settlements in the West Bank and Gaza, as these are militarily, psychologically, diplomatically and economically not sustainable. In addition to incurring billions in expenditure and global condemnation, the moral dilemma posed by such policies has been striking at least two soldiers per week. Just between October 2000 and June 2003, 360 cases were being investigated including 153 cases of homicide.[46] Sharon's unilateral support from London and Washington over his policies of occupation, expansion and selective killings of Palestinian leadership along with their impoverishment through a determined policy of divide and starve, created unease among several European sections including a large number of former diplomats and career officials.[47] The marginalization of world opinion in a unipolar world was more evident as the incapacitation of a global body like the UN in failing to reprimand Israel on its brutalization. The US, as per routine, would simply veto any such move while its approval and support from Tony Blair would simply result in further daring ventures by Tel Aviv. The erection of the boundary wall, assassination of a paralysed Sheikh Ahmed Yassin and that of Abdel-Aziz al-Rantissi, division of Gaza and the West Bank into several disparate bantustans while negating the Palestinian right to a sovereign state as laid down in the UN resolutions, occurred when its own architects had already abandoned the Roadmap for Peace.

Washington's unreserved and long-standing political and financial support for Israel ends up mostly blaming Palestinians and Muslims for violence in the Holy Land. Views such as a small, victimized yet the *only* democratic country surrounded by a vast sea of deadly antagonistic, authoritarian and vengeful Muslim and Palestinian leaders such as Yasser Arafat intent upon eliminating this Jewish state have clouded a balanced vision for a more peaceful region, as it existed for centuries in the past. The powerful Jewish lobbies within the United States and elsewhere would never allow a more balanced and holistic policy to be pursued by the president, Congress and media. Ordinary Americans, already vulnerable to specific influences, are now more attuned to such anti-Muslim and anti-Arab sentiments, especially after 9/11.

In recent decades both Clinton and Bush, in their own efforts to appease the pro-Israeli lobbies, came down hard on Yasser Arafat, the Palestinian Authority and religio-political groups such as Hamas. None of them has ever received any positive or sympathetic response from Washington; instead they were all routinely branded as terrorists out to destroy Israel. Israel's disregard for the UN, International Court of Justice and for wider global and European public opinion remains transcendent, making any move towards peace almost impossible. While Bush has been on the record as having demanded a new Palestinian leadership by sidelining Arafat, Clinton held Arafat responsible for his own failure in emerging as a global statesman. Clinton's *My Life* offers a detailed account of the Oslo Accords of 1993 and the Barak–Arafat talks at Camp David in July 2000, followed by several more such rounds, which failed to usher any breakthrough. Clinton held Arafat responsible for the failure of the peace talks by being stubborn and not being able to undertake vital decisions, as the former president notes: 'Perhaps he simply couldn't make the formal jump from revolutionary to statesman.' In a meeting before the end of his second term, Arafat called him a great man but Clinton's response was worth recalling: 'Mr Chairman', I replied. 'I am not a great man. I am a failure, and you have made me one.'[48] No American president would ever dare accuse an Israeli leader likewise to his face. Clinton accused Arafat for missing a golden opportunity for peace in late 2000 as 'Arafat's rejection of my proposal after Barak accepted it was an error of historic proportions.'[49] Clinton reiterated these statements in his interview with David Frost in 2004 and appeared to absolve Israel of any wrongdoing.[50]

As is evident from several recent studies, the Israeli government was totally disinterested in the principle of 'land for peace' and was not only reluctant to follow the UN resolutions of going back to prior 1967 borders but wanted to annex Al-Quds (Jerusalem), as well as deny the right of return to refugees. Even before the end of the parleys at Camp David, Israeli intelligence led by Amos Gilad orchestrated a campaign to malign Arafat and the Palestinian team and duly received a sympathetic hearing across the US establishments. Like in the build-up to Anglo-American invasion of Iraq in 2003, 'intelligence was politicised and corrupted to serve a preconceived agenda.' Accordingly, Arafat was caricatured as averse to peace and the wrecker of peace parleys. Clinton's partisan and equally inimical view of the Palestinian leadership reached its extreme under George Bush with neoconservatives and Likudists combining their efforts to present Arafat as antagonistic to reconciliation, thus allowing Sharon to play havoc with human rights in the Occupied Territories while putting the blame on suicide bombers. Now, Israelis were the victims whereas the desperate Palestinians were the perpetrators and Islamic terrorists, acting on cue from a Houdini-like Arafat. This inside information has been confirmed by Robert Malley, one of the insiders on Clinton's team during the negotiations and also by Amos Malka, the contemporary head of Israeli intelligence.[51]

Israel's role in exhorting the Bush Administration to invade Iraq has been substantially exposed by several recent publications including James Bamford's bestseller, *A Pretext for War*. He holds US intelligence agencies responsible for failing to pre-empt 9/11 and focuses on Israeli intrigues in leading America towards the invasion of Iraq.[52] According to David Hirst, the reputable and long-time correspondent on the Middle East, Israel's role in regional and US politics raises a number of critical moral and political issues, as he observes: 'It has long been clear that Israel played a big part in urging America to war in Iraq. Now it seems from Bamford's account that Israel was deeply involved, too, in supplying phoney intelligence to justify it.'[53] Israel is already deeply involved in the West Asian quagmire to ensure greater instability in the region. As recorded by Seymour Hersch, Israeli agents were already involved in Iraqi Kurdistan, training Iranian Kurds for future subversive activities in Iran. They were trying to establish sensors and other listening devices in the Kurdish regions under the excuse of eavesdropping on Tehran's allegedly military-oriented nuclear programme. Under this pretext they were hoodwinking the Americans, British, Turks and even the Iraqi interim rulers. According to the veteran American journalist, Israeli agents had even been interrogating Iraqi prisoners at the notorious Abu Ghraib Jail and were aiming their efforts at causing problems for Shia and Sunni Iraqis through Kurdish surrogates. An unstable Iraq offered them a golden opportunity to operate against Syria from its backyard, to the extent that the Turkish officials attempted to restrict their activities in their neighbourhood as any move towards a sovereign Kurdistan could stipulate instability in Turkey.[54]

The Jewish supporters of Zionism, Israel and the Sharon–Netanyahu duo must be generous enough to accept powerful objections from their own leading intellectuals rather than making scapegoats of Arabs, Muslims or even Western liberals.[55] The danger is that a situation may arise when after totally alienating the entire Muslim world and a sizeable public opinion elsewhere, the Americans and the British may one day come around to confront a bitter revisionism. A realization that for the sake of an illegal and immoral occupation enforced through brutal Israeli policies and anchored in a pervasive Western guilt over the Jewish agony in the West, they had, in fact, compromised their own ideals and interests, may spawn some negative retaliation. That will be a dangerous situation, as after decimating the fragile and already mostly impoverished Muslim states and economies, besides further marginalizing the disparate Muslim Diaspora, vengeful groups may turn against the Jews holding them responsible for all their maladies. Given the past history of Jewish–Christian relations in the West including the heinous tragedy of the Holocaust, and an ever-increasing fortress mentality, it may not be a mere wild prediction, though certainly grievous as well. Already, several powerful British public institutions like the BBC and other media channels are being criticized for lacking a comprehensive balance on contentious Middle Eastern issues with a clear bias for Israel and the official penchant for the invasion of Iraq.[56] Serious empirical studies by academics at the universities in Britain and the United States have disclosed serious imbalances in the public policy domains, which gravely add to existing plural chasms.[57] Even otherwise diehard strategists in the United States advocating Sherman-like annihilation through military campaigns against Muslim regions, are advising a revision of Israel-centred policies. 'Anonymous', a former CIA official generally guessed to be Mike Scheuer, wondered in his second book: 'Surely there can be no other historical example of a faraway, theocracy-in-all-but-name of only about six million people that ultimately controls the extent and even the occurrence of an important portion of political discourse and national security debate in a country of 270-plus million people that prides itself on religious toleration, separation of church and state and freedom of speech.'[58]

An Alternative Pathway

One has to accept that the erection of 12-metre high walls and growing settlements all ringing and isolating Palestinian villages while creating bantustans in the Occupied Territories, besides a totally militarist campaign against the Palestinian population and leadership and the ghettoization of Israeli Arabs are threatening the integrity and age-old pristine tradition of tolerance and humility shared by generations of Jews, even in adversity. They need to be immensely wary of falling in the category of perpetrators, and they should not allow Israel to get away with a false sense of victimhood. While maintaining their particularism, they must continue to reiterate their historic universalism by disallowing extremists and hate mongers amongst them from whitewashing their sublime traditions. For a generation or two, Westerners and others may tolerate Israeli extremism in the full glare of cameras and documented human rights reports, but eventually their guilt and soft corner for Israel may peter out. In the same way, Israel's continued dalliance with US foreign policies even at the expense of American interests vis-à-vis the Muslim world, their own moral dilemma and a bloody encounter in the tumultuous West Asia may eventually compel the Americans to review their unilateral support for Israel. A continued nonchalance towards world opinion, time and again defied by Israel through a simple shrug to numerous UN resolutions on the back of an unending supply of the American veto may, after all, prove fickle, especially in a world where interests remain salient but sometimes scruples also re-emerge. The serious contradictions in US policies in the Middle East underwritten by double standards, derision of the vast majorities and with a clear anti-Muslim animus especially after 9/11, cannot be taken for granted. The time may come sooner or later when the US will have to adopt balanced and more judicious policies for its own interests and it may even fall back upon its age-old, anti-Jewish, Christian unilateralism. This sort of extremism will be equally abominable to any sane citizen of the world.

The Jews in the West or elsewhere may be *en masse* defenders of Israel and as is obvious they may find sympathetic ears, especially in Washington and to some extent in London, yet world opinion is certainly discomfited over Israeli policies in the Holy Land.[59] Expulsions, assassinations, land grab and even vocal commitment to eliminate a popularly elected leader like Arafat do not stand well with the common image of world Jewry that has itself suffered in the West for so long. The transformation of the former victims into unbridled adventurers and purveyors of violence does not sit well with the simultaneous avowals of peace and victim-hood. Such world opinion is a moral censor that cannot be dismissed for too long by an unquestioned and solely partisan support for Israeli policies nor can it be justified in the name of the past oppression meted out to Jews in the Christian West. Moreover, Israel's security must define its limits and should not be left to an unbridled aggression, given the opportunities provided by 9/11. If the European Zionists can visualize a claim on a piece of land on the basis of their biblical traditions and largely due to the pogroms and the Holocaust in Europe, they cannot go on denying the same inalienable right to the actual inhabitants of that tragedy-stricken land. While to the Zionists, it may be a Promised Land rediscovered during the age of modernist nationalism, to Palestinians it is simply the right of self-determination on their own soil. Organizations like Hamas, PLO, PFLP, Hizbollah and Islamic Jihad are the results and reactions to Zionist enterprises in Palestine and not vice versa. The Jewish minority in the Holy Land, in general, never faced the wrath of their fellow Christian and Muslim Palestinians but the Balfour Declaration, migrations, European guilt, and Jewish militant organizations like Hagana catapulted Arab anger which, following the policy of denigration, continued expansion and expulsion, has spawned the present day suicide bombers. Europe-led modernity has been sad news for Palestine. Killing others may be easier but offering one's own life while leaving everyone behind with no support mechanism whatsoever is an act of real desperation and commitment and cannot be brushed aside as mere lunacy or some penchant for violence and terror.

The world and certainly the Muslims cannot understand why poor Palestinians had to pay the price for crimes that others committed against the Jews in Europe. Muslims protected the Jews from the Crusades, Inquisitors and other fanatics for countless centuries. They offered an environment conducive to Jewish scholars and artists which augured the Jewish Renaissance in Spain, North Africa and Ottoman Turkey. Even in so-called primitive societies like Afghanistan, Jews prospered and lived peacefully with their neighbours and fellow citizens. They had a visible and respectable presence in Baghdad, Istanbul, Salonika, Sarajevo, Fez and several such other citadels of Muslim power, but who destroyed the peace is a question that creates as much unease amongst Muslims as it does among critical Jews. To some maybe it is already too late while others may keep on trying to re-establish their mutuality and respect, though it may take many more bold and controversial initiatives including being branded as anti-Muslim or anti-Semite. But if history is to be a guide, Jews and Muslims, especially in Diaspora must rise to face common challenges of violence and racism rather than making scapegoats of each other. Just like Jews, Muslims need to rediscover the universalism and egalitarianism of their heritage in the true spirit of celebratory pluralism. While self-determination is an unalienable right deserving of fuller support, its achievement is possible through negotiations, persistent humanism and substantive dialogue. Racist typologies under any name or pretext are to be confronted by all, as that is the only way to fight the modernist monsters of Judeophobia and Islamophobia. The positive reality, however, is that there are plenty of sober, serene, kind and tolerant people across the board whose goodness and courage can steer the Holy Land away from the morass of desperation, bequeathed by the last century.

NOTES

1. Paul Iganski and Barry Kosmin, (eds.), *A New Antisemitism? Debating Judeophobia in 21st-Century Britain,* London, 2003.
2. There is a large amount of sociological and historical literature available on the history of different theories on racism in Europe. For a theoretical perspective, see Michael Banton, *Ethnic and Religious Consciousness,* London, 1997; and for an overview, Neil MacMaster, *Racism in Europe, 1870-2000,* Basingstoke, 2001. Institutional racism is a term which came into vogue following the murder of Stephen Lawrence in 1993 in London. White hooligans killed the Black youth and the police failed to undertake proper investigation and instead ended up protecting some of the culprits. The Macpherson Committee, in 1999, came up with revealing undercurrents of racism against ethnic minorities in the Metropolitan police and thus a larger picture of institutional racism was accepted across the board.
3. Paul Berman's analysis invites us to look at the recent tradition of totalitarianism and fascism prevalent in the West. It posits terrorism not merely as a clash of civilisations but rather as neo-fascism, which has found parallels and inspiration from certain Western typologies. However, the selective approach applied in reference to Political Islam by bundling it together with totalitarian fascism and absolute terrorism is immensely faulty.

Berman's own unequivocal pro-Israel and heavily pro-US biases compromise the quality of an otherwise needed comparative analysis of this kind. See, Paul Berman, *Terror and Liberalism*, New York, 2003.

4. Modernity has unleashed its own processes, which, in several cases, have engendered rather violent responses including the emergence of Muslim terrorist groups. Al-Qaeda and such elements are not totally alien or traditional *per se*, but rather are situated within the realm of a disputatious modernity. For details, see, John Gray, *Al-Qaeda and What it Means to be Modern*, London, 2003.

5. The term was initially used by Rana Kabbani, a British Muslim intellectual of Syrian background, in her article in the *Guardian* in 1992 during the ethnic cleansing and gang rapes of Muslims in Bosnia and the heightened Russian campaign in Chechnya. For further discussion in reference to the Balkan experience, see Iftikhar H. Malik, *Islam, Globalisation and Modernity, The Tragedy of Bosnia*, Lahore, 2004.

6. V.S. Naipaul, *Beyond Belief: Islamic Incursions among the Converted*, London, 1998.

7. An interesting case study has been offered in reference to Persia. See Richard Bulliet, *Islam: The View from the Edge*, New York, 1994. In case of the subcontinent, several intellectual commentaries such as by Syed Ahmed Khan, Syed Ameer Ali, Muhammad Iqbal, Fazlur Rahman and others have been offered in this regard, which an emerging field of intellectual history has tried to assess. The pioneering works by historians such as Aziz Ahmad, Farzana Shaikh, Francis Robinson and Rafiuddin Ahmed are worth mentioning though the rise of fundamentalism both amongst the Pakistani Muslims and India's Hindus, has come hard on this nascent discourse. The de-Indianisation of Pakistan (and Bangladesh) and de-Islamisation of India are very dangerous trends where particularism holds sway over a cherished historical consciousness.

8. Even the less vocal Chinese Diaspora in Europe is heading towards the same direction of establishing subaltern identities.

9. Philip Mansel, *Constantinople: City of the World's Desire, 1453–1924*, London, 1997, p. 414.

10. Jonathan Sacks, *The Dignity of Difference: How to Avoid the Clash of Civilisations?* London, 2003 (revised). The Chief Rabbi was again being rebuked in early 2004 for praising the BBC following the Hutton Inquiry report, which had cast serious aspersions on the Corporation's standards. Many pro-Israeli groups felt that the BBC had been critical of Israel and was not worthy of the Rabbi's praise in his comments on Radio 4. For details see, *Guardian*, 7 February 2004.

11. Studies by Jorgen Nielson, Tariq Modood, Philip Lewis, Gilles Kepel and Humayun Ansari are quite detailed on the subject. I have tried to look at the Muslim Diaspora in reference to the forces of history, modernity and hegemony. See, Iftikhar H. Malik, *Islam and Modernity: Muslims in Europe and the United States*, London, 2004.

12. This is based on informal discussion with some Jewish friends in Britain.

13. This could be a unique case of operating as Orientalists simultaneous with being *orientalized*. Undoubtedly, several Jewish scholars such as Ignaz Goldziher researched Islam outside the straitjacket of Orientalism.

14. I am borrowing this term from Any Manners, who studied the discriminatory and often-ambivalent attitudes of West European Jews settled in America towards their counterparts—the new, poor, Yiddish-speaking immigrants—from Eastern Europe. See Andy Manners, *Poor Cousins, New* York, 1976.

15. Understandably, Israel has become the home away from home for Jews all over the world. During Ariel Sharon's visit to India in September 2003, the 5,000-strong Indian Jews in Bombay eagerly awaited 'their leader'. They were deeply disappointed when he canceled his visit due to two bomb blasts in Jerusalem. In their interview to the BBC, these Jews, living rather comfortably in India, posited Israel as 'the homeland'. See, 'Sharon disappoints Bombay Jews', www.bbc.co.uk/south-asia

16. Their best sellers focus on the 'inadequacies' of Islam, which, as an ideology is lost between fundamentalism and terror. Muslims are not only centuries away from an overdue renaissance; they are the major-most threat to Western civilisation. See, Bernard Lewis, *Crisis of Islam,* London, 2003, and, *What Went Wrong?* London, 2002; and, Daniel Pipes, *Militant Islam Reaches America,* New York, 2001. The recent books by Pat Buchannan, Ann Coulter, Robert Kagan, Oriana Fallaci and Fareed Zakaria are already quite familiar on their simplification of issues and an aggressive attitude towards immigration, Islam, while being defensive about the US.

17. I have discussed this in greater detail in another study. See, *Jihad, Hindutva and the Taliban: South Asia at the Crossroads,* Oxford, 2005.

18. After the ultimatum to Iran by the UN watchdog on strictly confirming to the NPT requirements, a reader wrote to a paper: 'Why is that while the international community clamours to see Iran's nuclear facilities no such demand is made of Israel? Israel is thought to have hundreds of nuclear weapons. Why shouldn't the two countries be treated the same?', David Salter's letter in the *Guardian,* 9 September 2003. This happened at a time when Iran was already encircled by US troops in Afghanistan, the Gulf, Turkey and Iraq and had been characterized by President George W. Bush as one of the axis of evil. The Shia factor in post-Saddam Hussain Iraq was still being observed vigilantly after the murder of Ayatollah Al-Hakim and a former Iranian diplomat had been arrested in Britain on the charge of masterminding a bomb attack on a synagogue in Argentina several years ago.

19. For instance, during the 1940s, many non-Muslim Indians cheered Hitler over Nazi victories. Even now one comes across taxis with the swastika painted on them, but that is not out of any in-born hostility to Jews.

20. Daniel Bernard, the former French Ambassador to London, referred to Israel as that 'little shitty country' much to the consternation of many. Quoted in *A New Antisemitism?* p. 8.

21. Michael Whine, 'Antisemitism on the Streets' in ibid., p. 32.

22. This can be said safely about the four Pakistani and two Bangladeshi channels besides the Abu Dhabi satellite network that the present author has watched off and on.

23. The Runnymede Trust, *Islamophobia: an enemy for us all,* London, 1997.

24. Jonathan Sacks, 'A New Antisemitism?' in *A New Antisemitism?* p. 41.

25. Antony Lerman, 'Sense of Antisemitism', in ibid., p. 55.

26. Anthony Julius, ' Is there anything 'new' in the new Antisemitism?' in ibid.

27. For an interesting commentary on the Israeli dilemma of demography versus democracy, see Ahmad Sami Khalidi, 'A one-state solution', *Guardian,* 29 September 2003. The Palestinian author, a visiting fellow at St. Antony's College, Oxford, was involved in peace negotiations with Israel and offers some interesting foresight to move out of this triangular jam involving the Likud, the Palestinian Authority and societal peace groups.

28. David Blair, 'Settlers threaten Israel's future as Jewish state', *Daily Telegraph,* 1 October 2003.

29. I have discussed the similarities and differences between Pakistan and Israel in an article elsewhere. See, Iftikhar H. Malik, 'Israel and Pakistan: the Problem Twins', *Manna* (London), Summer 1998.

30. Peter Pulzer, 'When is a taboo not a taboo?', in *A New Antisemitism?* p. 94.

31. Jonathan Freedland, 'Is anti-Zionism antisemitism?' ibid., p. 115. To Freedland, Palestine already being a land populated by people with their own traditions, does pose problems for Zionists whose superimposition of their history and control necessitates serious self-questioning. Occupying an empty land might not have raised such moral issues even among the colonisers. Douglas Davis, Howard Jacobson and Winston Pickett, in their chapters, have lashed out at the BBC, specific print media journalists and Leftist papers like *The Guardian* and *New Statesman* for critiquing Israel and Zionism through a common bench-marking of antisemitism. The BBC may, however, suggest the concurrent criticism from the Arabs and Jews itself proved that the corporation was being objective enough.

32. Robert Wistrich, 'Muslims, Jews and September 11: The British Case', in ibid., p. 175.

33. Ibid., p. 186.

34. Amos Oz, 'There is no alternative to Arafat', *New Statesman,* 15 September 2003, p. 20.

35. See, Israel Shahak and Norton Mezvinsky, *Jewish Fundamentalism in Israel,* London, 2004.

36. John Rose, *The Myths of Zionism,* London, 2004, p. 201. The author is a London-based academic, who teaches at Southwark College and London Metropolitan University.

37. John Rose, 'We need a post-Zionist leap of faith', *Guardian,* 2 April 2005.

38. Avraham Burg, 'The end of Zionism', *Guardian,* 15 September 2003.

39. See, Baruch Kimmerling, *Politicide: Ariel Sharon's War against the Palestinians*, London, 2003.

40. 'Letters', *Guardian*, 16 September 2003.

41. Dr Sami Mahroun, in ibid., 18 September 2003. Alan Senitt from London, in his letter, urged the UN Security Council to focus on terrorism.

42. Emmanuel Todd, *After the Empire: the Breakdown of the American Order*, New York, 2003.

43. See F. Kermani in ibid. The Israeli newspapers such as *Ha'aretz* and *Jerusalem Post* called the Israeli attempts to eliminate Arafat 'as a scandal of historic dimensions', and questioned its rationale and long-term impact. Jimmy Carter has supervised Arafat's election and he symbolized the moral and political consensus among a vast majority of Palestinians and his expulsion and feared assassination by Israel were totally loathsome. Quoted in heller_adam@yahoo.com in gush-shalom-intl@mailman.gush-shalom.org (19 September 2003).

44. The BBC World Service monitored in Oxford on 18 September 2003. Colin Powell, in a statement in February 2004 at Princeton, accused Arafat of fanning violence. It appeared that both Tel Aviv and Washington were waiting for some new leadership to emerge so as to strike still another deal with the Palestinians.

45. Max Hastings, 'A grotesque choice', *Guardian*, 11 March 2004. For a Palestinian view, see Ghada Karmi, 'By any means necessary', ibid., 18 March 2004; also, In Search of Fatima, London, 2003. For an Israeli critique of Sharon's policy of separating Palestinians into Apartheid-style Bantustans, see Meron Benvenisti, 'Bantustan plan for an apartheid Israel', ibid., 26 April 2004. For a review, see Max Hastings, 'Their best defence', *Guardian*, 29 March 2005. In a discussion at Oxford in April 2005, the former editor of *The Daily Telegraph* reaffirmed his views on the Israeli defence strategies.

46. Martin van Crefeld, *Defending Israel*, cited in Max Hastings, 'The best defence', *Guardian*, 29 March 2005.

47. The British unquestioned support for the Neoconservative-led US policies both on Iraq and Palestine motivated British diplomats to flag their criticism. See, 'A letter from 52 former senior British diplomats to Tony Blair', ibid., 27 April 2004. Charles Wheeler, a seasoned BBC correspondent, called this letter 'undeniably a blockbuster' at a time when Tony Blair's policies in West Asia and on Europe appeared to confound even the Labour supporters. See, Charles Wheeler, 'Britain must lose its reluctance to question the special relationship', ibid., 28 April 2004. The unrestricted Israeli access to US powerful echelons like the Pentagon has often caused serious consternation off and on. In August 2004, it was reported that the FBI were investigating Douglas Feith's section in the Pentagon as a senior advisor working for him had been transmitting secret information to Tel Aviv, including the US policy options towards Iran. For details, see Paul Harris, 'FBI probes 'spy suspect deep inside' the Pentagon', *Observer*, 30 August 2004.

48. Bill Clinton, *My Life*, London, 2004, pp. 943-4.

49. Ibid., pp. 944-5.

50. Breakfast with Frost, BBC1, 18 July 2004, monitored in Oxford.

51. David Hirst, 'Don't blame Arafat', *Guardian*, 17 July 2004. Hirst, a well-known journalist, covered Middle Eastern affairs for this British paper from 1963 to 2001.

52. James Bamford, *A Pretext for War. 9/11, Iraq and the Abuse of America's Intelligence Agencies*, New York, 2004.

53. Hirst, op. cit.

54. Seymour Hersch, 'Plan B', *The New Yorker*, 28 June 2004.

55. The censuring of the Liberal-Left for critiquing Israel even after 9/11 has produced quite an interesting amount of literature. These arguments simply absolve the Western or Israeli hegemonic factors altogether and besides criticizing Muslims, they, quite tendentially, rebuke a presumably simple-heartedness or even mendacity of the Liberal Left in not being wary of Islamic terrorism. Such a commentary is a rather unconvincing defence of American unilateralism vis-à-vis complex problems in the developing world including Muslim regions and is a typical self-righteous reportage against an 'incompetent' Europe that needs America all the time to rectify the former's recurrent problems. See, Paul Berman, op. cit.

56. This was proven by a study at Cardiff University. For a summary, see Justin Lewis, 'Biased Broadcasting Corporation', *Guardian*, 4 July 2004.

57. For instance, Greg Philo and Mike Barry, *Bad News from Israel*, London, 2004; and, David Domke, *God Willing? Political Fundamentalism in the White House, the 'War on Terror', and the Echoing Press*, London, 2004.

58. 'Anonymous', *Imperial Hubris: Why the West is Losing the War on Terror?* Washington, 2004, p. 227.

59. On the eve of a trumped-up invasion of Iraq, Tony Blair made several promises for helping to resolve the Palestinian–Israeli conflict, but all through 2003 and further, the British Prime Minister never made any effort nor undertook any substantive measures to live up to his pronouncements. See, interview with the Palestinian Prime Minister, *Guardian*, 7 February 2004.

EPILOGUE: PAST AS THE FUTURE OR A WAY-OUT?

We live in scoundrel times. This is the dark age of Muslim history, the age of surrender and collaboration, punctuated by madness. The decline of our civilization began in the eighteenth century, when, in the intellectual embrace of orthodoxy, we skipped the age of enlightenment and the scientific revolution. In the second half of the twentieth century, it has fallen.

— Eqbal Ahmad, [after the Gulf war in 1993] in
Confronting Empire, 2000, p. xxvi

Immigrants may not all be Islamic, but Islam is the most visible and alarming threat from foreigners to hard-won secularism, tolerance, feminism or social democracy'.

— Polly Toynbee, 'The real reason why we should fear immigration', *Guardian*, 11 February 2004

Certainly, relations between the West and Muslims have considerably deteriorated following 9/11 and subsequent events. Mutual suspicions and denigration have received impetus from the respective and often similar intolerant and xenophobic groups on all sides. Ironically, the enduring discourse of essentialising a presumably change-resistant, inherently stubborn and solely anti-Western Islamic exceptionalism has become quite pervasive. Scholars, analysts, publicists, media pundits and evangelicists are united not only in monolithicising Islam but also in scare mongering, without reviewing the uneven politico-economic forces that have bedevilled this world for so long. While the Neoconservatives and their fundamentalist followers posit Islam as a civilizational foe, their Muslim counterparts also emphasise an unstilted reconversion of coreligionists in their own particular and often fractious ways. The nascent efforts for a synthesised

perspective, away from extremism and intolerance, have further
marginalized the reconstructive initiatives highlighting the serious
drawbacks of a Westernised modernity and a narrowly defined
Political Islam. It appears that the reaction is simply exacerbating
reaction with greater force and arrogance, vetoing sanity and
tolerance. The theological differences among the three Abrahamic
traditions and their respective symbols are being selectively and
irresponsibly quoted to substantiate a politics of hostility whereas,
in fact, the problems are overwhelmingly of historical, political and
economic types. The solution of long-time political problems in
West Asia through an honest consensus and willingness to
implement political and economic empowerment of the Muslim
masses away from discretionary surrogacy and interventionism will
certainly go a long way in auguring a long-awaited era of peace.
Whether the Western powers and their allies would be willing to
properly understand a wider Muslim predicament and instead of
using unilateral force and moral uprighteousness might be prepared
to resolve the regional conflicts, remain to be seen. After all, the
problems of the Muslim communities are not solely of their own
making and an intermixing of religion with politics is just not a
Muslim specialism.

Muslims, given the multiple pressure and often hostile war of
nerves, are either becoming further marginalised or are seeking
answers by transforming themselves into fundamentalists. Away
from these understandable extremes, several middle-of-the-road
clusters, both in the Muslim regions and Diaspora—are attempting
a reinterpretation of their classical heritage, as confronted by West-
led modernity. Avoiding both apologia and aggression, they are
seeking a synthesised paradigm for peace, co-existence, empowerment
and development. Such progressive and forward-looking traditions
deserve recognition as well as centre stage in any future Islam-West
equation. The world needs humanist, rational, tolerant, just and
democratic alternatives, anchored on the positive dictums of
modernity and tradition. In the true spirit of this humanist
globalisation, Islam needs the West (and the rest!) as much as the
West needs Islam, and 9/11 and 7/7 could, by default, be painful

reminders of an overdue and all-out commitment to higher noble objectives. Neither a state of siege nor a disproportionate outrage is going to be helpful as the world seeks better, justifiable and supportive structures instead of imagined enemies and discretionary policies.

Militarism is as dangerous as racism and the politics of exclusion. However, while we have focused on several powerful Western voices and echelons in their newfound critique and spotlight on Islam, one must not forget the diverse opinion groups and a wider well-meaning populace who have been valiantly striving for an equitable resolution of such crises. Like the Jewish and the Irish immigrants before, 'the war on terror has focused uncomfortable light' on Muslims in Western countries,[1] but concurrently several analysts and even ordinary citizens have tried to persuade Western leaders not to forget that the vast majority of Muslims—like other communities—seek peace and harmony and are not enamoured of fundamentalism. In the same vein, according to many Western scholars—and not just the Muslim analysts—the loyalty of Diaspora Muslims and those of Muslims worldwide towards peace has been irresponsibly problematised.[2] Jason Burke, a British journalist with first-hand experience in South and West Asia, alerted the West to the danger of an aggregate depiction of Muslims as fundamentalists: 'The greatest weapon in the war on terrorism is the courage, decency, humour and integrity of a vast proportion of the world's 1.2 billion Muslims...It is a battle for heart and minds. And it is a battle that we, and our allies in the Muslim world, are currently losing.'[3]

Away from the precedent of 'new Mongols',[4] the world does not deserve any new crusades and instead, as Edward Said suggested, a 'humanist understanding is now more urgently required than ever before.'[5] Simultaneously, quite a few bishops and church groups have been critical of the volume and frequency of Western and Israeli violence in West Asia.[6] The disastrous US–British venture in Iraq, apart from its short-sightedness and illegality, has led to greater insecurity and resentment among ordinary Iraqis who had been promised emancipation, democracy and prosperity. In the same vein, several powerful Western opinion groups have been persistently critical of illegal and extremely brutal policies in Iraq and Palestine. The use of cluster bombs, aerial bombardments and massacres of thousands of unaccounted civilians in Iraq seriously exposed the untenable rationale to attack yet another Muslim country. In the spring of 2004, the besieged cities of Falluja and Najaf and in 2005 the towns near the Syrian–Iraqi borders such as Qaem became killing fields, reminding observers of Vietnam and Afghanistan. Concurrently, the partisan British and American support for Ariel Sharon in splitting and even paralysing the Palestinian leadership and territories through a sustained policy of expansion and occupation and by creating Bantustans in Gaza and the West Bank deeply infuriated even the otherwise cautious and non-committed diplomats. On 26 April 2004, voicing their deep concern over a 'doomed' American policy in the Muslim world and its unquestioned and rather dangerous support by Tony Blair, fifty-two former British ambassadors sent a detailed letter to Downing Street. These envoys and area specialists warned Britain of dire consequences of abandoning a just policy on Iraq and Palestine: 'This abandonment of principles comes at a time when rightly or wrongly we are portrayed throughout the Arab and Muslim world as partners in an illegal and brutal occupation in Iraq.'[7] Even some of the supporters of invasion such as Ambassadors Christopher Meyer and Jeremy Greenstock—after their retirement from diplomatic service—kept linking terrorist blasts in Britain with the military intervention in Iraq. Greenstock's work was disallowed publication by the government whereas Meyer's *DC Confidential* was strongly rebuked by Jack Straw though its portrayal of Tony Blair overawed by the US military prowess and his sheer lack of comprehension of the ramifications of the invasion added to the prime minister's difficulties at an adverse time.[8]

Many scholars are certainly aware of diverse opinions on all sides though a dangerous monolithicisation of Islam remains the order of the day.[9] In that perspective, not only the war on terror but even the efforts to impose secularist uniformity in France over the headgear issue was considered to be reckless and a new kind of intolerance to a beleaguered minority.[10] It was felt that the regimes in the Western democracies were dangerously using Islam, the scarf, asylum, immigration, terror and such other issues not only to appease their extreme nationalist forces but were also attempting to gain more votes from among the intolerant sections.

Other than the voices of moderation and sanity on all sides, one has to take notice of opinion makers and media analysts on the issues of an Islam–West relationship. While a strong section such as the Neoconservatives and militarists may believe in coercion or 'empire lite',[11] others are urging for a significant 'rethink'. To such analysts, given the possibility that in the event of fully-fledged democracy, Muslims states would be overrun by anti-American forces the modus operandi should be to postpone universal empowerment and instead focus on gradual liberalisation of these societies. Fareed Zakaria, the editor of *Newsweek*, is the champion of this new strategy of postponement and redirection. He has warned the West that in view of the revolution in information technology during the 1990s, Muslim fundamentalists may conveniently use the ballot to capture power exactly like the Nazis did in Germany. Citing selective examples such as of India and criminalisation of some electoral processes, he feels that in the West both democracy and liberty have found a synthesis whereas in the developing world it is not yet attainable. He warns: 'Across the Arab world elections held tomorrow would probably bring to power regimes that are more intolerant, reactionary, anti-Western, and anti-Semitic than the dictatorships currently in place.'[12] Such a fear is simply myopic as it belittles the common sense, civility and humanity of these people. Democracy will not only empower these people it will engender tolerance and development in these vast regions. But, certainly, pro-Western autocrats will have to go and that may be a difficult choice for the West.

The above view ignores the fact that many political and ideological problems in these post-colonial societies, to a great extent, are the results of Western interventionism, which has engendered serious enduring imbalances. Already in regard to Iraq and Afghanistan, there have been various reservations on implementing universal franchise out of a staunch fear of Shia Muslims and Pushtun Afghans gaining the upper hand. Such continued ambivalence, indifference and a snide betrayal of democratic and judicious processes in West Asia will only exacerbate anti-Western sentiments. The discretionary policies based on opportunism and sheer militarism have not only seriously impacted the world's 1.5 billion Muslims, they have also engendered serious moral and ideological dilemmas elsewhere. Zakaria's precept is based on opportunism and reflects a misreading of democracy in places like India. In the name of a stalemated balance or simply to preclude the possibility of breaking the status quo one cannot keep democracy and universal empowerment on hold. He praises the East Asian model for West Asia and is understandably appreciative of a military-led Turkish model for inducting necessary systemic changes. He is happy with pro-West autocrats such as Zine el-Abdine Ben Ali of Tunisia and General Pervez Musharraf for reigning in militants and ushering economic progress, which again is a superficial view, as nationhood is not just a superimposed peace and mere economic statistics. Governance is a painstaking task and cannot be left to *ad hoc* measures or to the will of a few dependable autocrats, especially when they exclude or even openly contradict democratic norms.

Bourguiba's policies in Tunisia and army rule in Pakistan never allowed democracy to function properly as they have sought power mainly through force and by disregarding constitutionalism. As is well known, the contradictions within the Turkish model owe their existence to a pro-West military establishment which uses Kemalism to justify its own hegemony, and likewise the scores of other dictatorial regimes, whose only credential is their unflinching loyalty to Western interests. It is not judicious to bank on authoritarian rulers such as Hosni Mubarak or others as they may promise and pose a second-tier defence against fundamentalists or other anti-American elements. In the end, it is societal prerogatives and not American interests that should reflect governance in those countries. The Arab world is not totally trapped between autocrats and illiberal societies; it also includes emerging civil societies, humane groups and well-meaning clusters, who have never been taken on board. To deny the Arab world or other developing societies the benefits of overdue participatory systems is both malicious and dangerous. It does not help Zakaria's analysis at all, when he ironically posits: 'The Arab rulers of the Middle East are autocratic, corrupt, and heavy-handed. But they are still more liberal, tolerant, and pluralistic than what would likely replace them.'[13] This is what France did by blocking the Islamists from assuming power in Algeria after elections and the result has been continued and widespread violence. And if Washington and London repeat the same in Afghanistan, Iraq and elsewhere in West Asia, the consequences will not be totally different.

Zakaria's most crucial prescriptive chapter is titled, 'The Islamic Exception', which posits democracy, elections and an independent judiciary as inherently alien to Muslims, a view originally propounded by Eli Kedourie and the preceding generations of Orientalists.[14] Zakaria's generalising style offers a rather shoddy explanation: that Islam does not have an ingrained and overarching religious authority, and as a consequence, people like Osama bin Laden end up assuming the leadership. One wonders about his knowledge of the various traditions of Shia Islam or even Sufi orders! Hindus in India do not have any singular or linear hierarchy but along with Muslims and others, they have been practising democracy despite all the segmentary and factional pulls. His authorities on Islam and 'the Arab Mind'—a typical Orientalist term—are colonialists like Lord Cromer or T.E. Lawrence, whose lives were characterized by personal contradictions and imperial legacies of divide, denigrate and dominate. One wonders that as a Muslim himself, Zakaria might have shown a better grasp of such contentions. Instead of seeking a mundane explanation of politico-economic problems, exacerbated by external interventionism, he attributes all the maladies to the Muslim people and their 'sense of pride and fall', which is utterly simplistic.[15] It is like saying that the Indian Muslims are underprivileged because of some peculiar psychological make-up. He yearns for an Islamic Reformation but worries that Islam does not have a popedom to rebel against, which again is Eurocentric reductionism. The solution to the Muslim anguish, as laid out by Zakaria, is through installing economic, civil and religious liberties, which should precede democratisation, but the question is, why not simultaneously? Indirect democracy, as idealised by him, was not the solution as experienced in Pakistan under General Ayub Khan, since it shied away from real democratisation and was just a whitewash.

Zakaria is influential, articulate and is widely quoted, and his rather simplistic analysis is easier to accept without warranting any rigorous effort. In addition, it allocates a malady to the indigenous populace by extricating the rest from it. His formula sits well with US imperial imperatives but that is what is already in practice and has led the region to this precipice. The US has followed these policies in Latin America and other developing countries for so long by perpetuating tyrannies in the name of liberalism, and it is the local people who have paid the price. As opined by a reviewer, Zakaria 'imagines himself to be a hard-nosed neo-conservative US realist, but is in fact peddling a Utopian policy. Turbulent populations will not wait patiently to be fed democracy in judicious doses at the convenience of comfortable and condescending Anglo-Saxon elite.'[16]

Instead of prescriptive, restrictive and piecemeal solutions, the Muslim regions, and likewise the entire developing world, deserve urgent global ameliorative initiatives. A mutually reciprocal resolution of the Palestinian predicament in the true spirit of globalism, and most of all, in league with traditional Jewish humanism will have its dividends where security walls, selective extrajudicial killings, forced expulsions and suicide bombings will give way to substantive peace and mutual respect. The resolution of conflicts in Chechnya and Kashmir will allow a needed breathing space to Muslim minorities in Russia and India, removing the spectre of societal and state-led terrorism. A meaningful regional cooperation in Western and Southern Asia will redirect scarce resources towards human development and wider democratisation instead of wars and authoritarianism. The militant ideologies underwriting so-called majoritarianism can be tackled only through democratisation, dialogue, substantive regional cooperation and by a greater celebration of pluralism.

However, it is not merely the external interventionism and support for specific regimes that have continued to sap democratic experiences, the inter-state conflicts such as in South Asia, Central Asia and in the Middle East, have taken their toll from their plural societies. South Asia, home to the world's largest Muslim concentration and likewise for Hindus and Sikhs, has been characterized by decades of inter-state and inter-community turmoil nefariously feeding into each other. Frequent escalations of Indo–Pakistani tensions, characterized by undiminished hot and cold phases, have often thwarted well-meaning efforts for reconciliation. Both nuclearised nations, carved out of the dying days of the British Raj in 1947, have relentlessly pursued politics of vendetta irreverent to the magnitude of the cost to their premier socio-economic prerogatives. In the event of any major escalation, besides the spectre of a nuclear exchange, the Hindu–Muslim relationship will surely take a dangerous nosedive, pushing the most populous region into an irretrievable quagmire. The Indo–Pakistani imbroglio is not merely a state- or religion-centred issue, it has also spawned serious ideological divisions within these societies. According to optimists, the subcontinent will eventually steer its way out of this cycle of violence and mutually assured destruction, whereas to pessimists, if recent history is to be any guide, then one-fifth of humanity is perennially lost in a cul-de-sac.

The protagonists highlight enduring though overshadowed commonalties such as the brilliant Indo–Muslim culture, trans-national ethnic loyalties, shared history, undivided ecology, similar economies, cherished sufi-bhagat cultural moorings, and most of all, the sheer exhaustion with a half-century old and immensely taxing enmity. Shared denominators such as the socio-economic hardships of the masses and similar imprints of external developments over the region as a whole, besides a serious marginalisation from the global economic and geo-strategic core zones, further underpin a pervasive desire for regionalism. On the contrary, the antagonists—and they equally abound—posit Islam and Hinduism as two rival and even mutually exclusive civilisations, sharing nothing in common. They flag separate histories, life styles, names, heroes and villains, and can never imagine Rahman and Ram co-existing under the same sun. To them, India and Pakistan are the two logical manifestations of irreconcilable historical forces vetoing shared history, common cultures or a trans-regional amity. These unilateralists refuse to allow any meeting ground, nor do they acknowledge the inherent pluralism where de-Islamisation of India is as dangerous and ahistoric as is the de-Indianisation of Pakistan. The essentialisation of this permanent void and divide is further augmented through doctored textbooks, manipulated official media, alarmist popular culture and partisan official policies that collectively feed into mutual misperceptions bordering on total denigration. Such opinion groups do not recognise that the Indo–Pakistan dichotomous relationship is not simply confined to their borders; instead it squeezes multiple cost from their respective communities by turning into a systemic malady. The enemy is not across the border villages of Wagah or Attari where it may express itself through curiously orchestrated daily theatrics of the ludicrous flag (jhanda) ceremonies symbolising malfeasance of the cold war, but equally permeates the socio-political fabrics of these neighbours.

More recently, a third group of regionalists has started reviewing the issues of pluralism in both the countries within the context of this enmity. To such critical voices, the inter-state conflict has dangerously exacerbated—if not created—the Hindu–Muslim strife where Muslims in India and Hindus in Pakistan are routinely victimized by xenophobes. The lesser known plight of Hindus in Pakistan and steady massacre of Muslims in Gujarat have a powerful interface with this regional conflict in addition to underwriting intolerant forces of Hindutva and Sunni Islam. Thus, the Indo–Pakistan polarity reverberates powerfully across towns, communities and bazaars where minorities are constantly losing to the majoritarian onslaught, anchored on exclusive forms of religion and nationalism. The criminalisation of democracy in India at places like Gujarat and Maharashtra amidst an erosion of Nehruvian secularism and the decimation of democracy in Pakistan thanks to the military-*mullah* axis, is the most serious manifestation of this hostility, even if one ignores its accompanying economic costs. In particular, the volatile separation of East Pakistan in 1971, an embarrassing and wasteful Pakistani Kargil campaign in 1999, the stupendously costly Indian venture on the Siachin Glacier since 1984 and Delhi's scorched-earth punitive campaign in the disputed Kashmir Valley are just a few misdemeanours from amongst many others. Simultaneously, several concerned Indians are apprehensive that any dissolution/balkanisation of Pakistan due to internal combustion or external invasion may pose a serious threat to India itself with severe demographic, economic and security-related challenges enveloping Delhi. These people neither desire an annexation of a predominantly Muslim Pakistan nor its total decimation, rather, they seek a subservient state operating both as a buffer and an easy scapegoat for transferring all the problems. They are not eager to integrate another 160 million well-fed, independent-minded Muslims within their polyglot, even if that may stipulate an idealised *Akhand Bharat* (one united India). Such saffronists are not being solely faithful to a triumphant Ram; they are ardent descendants of the Raj, brandishing the Trishol (trident), which symbolises India's Monroe Doctrine for South Asia.

Amidst a vast plethora of diverse Indian public opinion, the secular, liberal and leftist elements genuinely desire peaceful coexistence, salience of human rights over monopolist pressure groups and espouse sovereign equality of all the states. On the contrary, within Pakistan, other than antagonists and protagonists, most of the ordinary people stay preoccupied with their basic daily needs and are on the receiving end of the endemic Indo-Pakistani discord. The costly wars have affected homes and hearths across the country especially in the recruiting areas of Punjab where Indo–Pakistan bickering and now a volatile Pak-Afghan Durand Line have caused hundreds of thousands of sad telegrams emanating from military headquarters (GHQ) in Rawalpindi. Destined for destitute peasant families they leave countless widows and orphaned children in their wake, whom *mullahs* and feudals will be only too happy to adopt for their ventures.

The ruling elites in Pakistan and India have been the main antagonists, refusing to attempt any alternative to the traditional but equally pernicious polices based on mutual denigration. The Pakistani 'steel-frame' sees in India a genuine and also a well-needed enemy both for escapism and also to continue with their own privileges and power. Other than a dozen think tanks in expensive neighbourhoods of Islamabad, the universities and some media sections faithfully parrot an elitist discourse on national security and identity, originally masterminded by the sleuths in the GHQ and ISI (Inter-Services Intelligence). In the same vein, the obliging and insecure politicians, whenever given a minor chance to be in the limelight, cry their loudest in denouncing India not just to please ordinary Pakistanis but mainly to appease the domineering khaki establishment that has misgoverned the country for most of its existence.

While a weak and turbulent Pakistan may serve as a useful alibi for Indian antagonists, the BJP chauvinists, the Shiv Sena activists and Kar Sevaks continue to draw a greater pound of flesh from Indian minorities and weaker neighbours. To them, Pakistan and Islam provide useful goalposts for transferring responsibility of their own failings. The obliging historians, Bollywood ideologues and a section in the biased media are loyal instruments of an irredentist and intolerant Hindutva, operating as holy warriors for Ram. However, one needs to acknowledge A. B. Vajpayee's two meaningful efforts aimed at a fresh start: firstly in 1999 at Lahore, and then more recently in 2003 from Srinagar. The first one was embarrassingly bamboozled by Pakistani military brass especially through their attack on the Kargil Heights and then by a coup, whereas his second offer led to some positive developments including a summit in Islamabad in 2004 amidst several confidence-building measures. Vajpayee's visit to Lahore in 1999 was historic and could have proven a threshold for a better relationship whereas General Musharraf's Agra *yatra* in 2001 proved inconsequential, as the reciprocity remained absent. However, their meeting in Islamabad in 2004, within the context of serious caution, care and guarded optimism, signalled fresh hope for some significant changes to come. Following the return of the Congress government in India in May 2004 after a landmark electoral victory, it took a while to re-establish linkages between the two neighbours. The meetings between Prime Minister Manmohan Singh and General Pervez Musharraf in New York in September 2004 and again in Delhi and New York in 2005 were viewed as confidence-building strides, though the observers on all sides remained cautiously optimistic.[17] Some progress in their commonalities was noticed during the severe earthquake that northern Pakistan and Kashmir suffered in October 2005 claiming more than 80,000 human lives besides large-scale destruction of homes, offices and other infra structure.

The next few decades are certainly crucial for auguring a compassionate discourse on Islam and modernity besides resolving several post-colonial conflicts through a multilateral and participatory system that neither smacks of double standards nor is tainted with hegemony. While there is an urgency to celebrate pluralism all around, the immigrants and their descendants have to be substantively offered an accommodative and receptive co-existence instead of positing them as economic spongers or the enemy within. After all, immigrants are not only needed for Western economies they are proven assets in many areas, who provide well-needed fresh blood in these otherwise ageing societies. In the same spirit, Muslim political leaders, whether motivated by partisan reasons or by their external backers for some unilateral interests, cannot go on denying democratic rights to their peoples. The prioritisation of empowerment, education, economy and related civic sectors—away from the inept security paradigms and militarization—have to assume centre stage, otherwise they will not be able to contain the massive rage that has been boiling over the last so many decades.

Democracy may have its chaotic phases but there is no other substitute to an overdue empowerment. Simultaneously, pre-emptive strikes and the Western preoccupation with the status quo must be replaced by an honest and all-encompassing engagement with these societies and their prerogatives. This is not to appease the terrorists, rather, it remains the only judicious way to isolate them through a proactive policy on all issues. Policies geared towards conflict resolution have to replace mechanisms for conflict management. Western Islamophobes may have their own problems with Islam yet their nefarious roles in poisoning their own plural societies need to be adroitly exposed by thoughtful and independent scholars and activists. It is not easy being a Muslim, especially when one seeks democratisation, urges tolerance and equal rights and criticises religious and political hierarchies that have sapped Muslim energies for so long. Yet, while there is a formidable challenge to confront, it is equally a test case of human vigour and valour. Sceptics on all sides must never forget that as long as there are millions of well-meaning people around, there is certainly a possibility of a better tomorrow.

NOTES

1. David Cesarani, 'Face has changed but fear remains', *Times Higher Educational Supplement (THES)*, 27 June 2003. Also, Jack O'Sullivan, 'British Muslims are the new Irish', *New Statesman*, 3 November 2003. The frenzied form of self-righteousness is leading people to all types of extreme behaviour. The BBC reported on 9 February 2004 a similar incident: 'An American Airlines pilot terrified passengers on his flight when he asked Christians to identify themselves and went on to call non-Christians 'crazy'. http://news.bbc.co.uk/1/hi/world/americas/3472265.stm

2. See, Richard Barltrop, *Muslims in Europe, post 9/11: Understanding and Responding to the Muslim World,* (a conference report from St. Antony's College), Oxford, 2003.

3. Jason Burke, *Al-Qaeda: Casting a Shadow of Terror*, London, 2003, p. 249. Also, William Dalrymple, 'Who is the real enemy?' (A review of Jason Burke's book), *Observer*, 20 July 2003.

4. Several Muslims have started using this term after the occupation of Iraq in 2003. See, Ziauddin Sardar, 'The new Mongols', a book review, *New Statesman*, 17 November 2003. Also, Tariq Ali, *Bush in Babylon: The Recolonisation of Iraq*, London, 2003

5. 'Today bookstores in the US are filled with shabby screeds bearing screaming headlines about Islam and terror, the Arab threat and the Muslim menace, all of them written by political polemicists pretending to knowledge imparted by experts who have supposedly penetrated to the heart of these strange

oriental people. CNN and Fox, plus myriad evangelical and rightwing radio hosts, innumerable tabloids and even middle-brow journals, have recycled the same unverifiable fictions and vast generalisations so as to stir up "America" against the foreign devil'. Edward Said, 'A window on the world', *Guardian Review*, 2 August 2003.

6. See interview with Dr Tom Wright, Bishop of Durham, *Independent*, 29 December 2003. Bishop Desmond Tutu has been vocally critical of Bush and Blair for pursuing an illegal and immoral war.

7. For full text see, 'A letter from 52 former senior British diplomats to Tony Blair', *Guardian*, 27 April 2004.

8. For selections from Ambassador Meyer's book and related comments, see *Guardian*, 4-12 November 2005; *Sunday Telegraph*, 6 November 2005, and *Independent*, 11 November 2005. Also, Christopher Meyer, *DC Confidential*, London, 2005.

9. Karen Armstrong, 'A question of faith', review of Richard Fletcher's *The Cross and the Crescent: Christianity and Islam from Muhammad to the Reformation*, London, 2002, in *Guardian Review*, 1 March 2003.

10. Madeleine Bunting, 'Secularism gone mad', *Guardian*, 18 December 2003.

11. Without suggesting an outright military conquest, Michael Ignatieff is recommending something almost similar to an occupation. The question is who has given the West a right to control and fashion non-Western societies in a particularistic way. Western intervention for the last several centuries, in fact, caused many of these abnormalities and contradictions in these polities. For his views see, *Empire Lite: Nation-building in Bosnia, Kosovo and Afghanistan*, London, 2003.

12. Fareed Zakaria, *The Future of Freedom: Liberal Democracy at Home and Abroad*, New York, 2003, p. 18.

13. Ibid., p. 120.

14. Elie Kedourie, *Democracy and Arab Political Culture*, Washington, D. C., 1992, p. 5, and Zakaria, p. 123.

15. Ibid., p. 139.

16. For an interesting critique, see Radhakrishanan Nayar, 'Fat fingers, juicy pies and Uncle Sam's sorely embarrassingly not-so-little problem', *THES*, 15 August 2003.

17. On 24 September 2004, the meeting took place on the sidelines of the UN General Assembly session in New York. The Indian Prime Minister called it 'historic' and General Musharraf felt that this would augur 'well for the future of Indo-Pakistan relations'. See, http://news.bbc.co.uk/1/hi/south_asia/3685418-stm, A similar meeting took place a year later in New York between the two leaders and they reaffirmed their commitment to peace. Accessed on 24 September 2004. The 'cricket diplomacy' in 2005 and contacts after the October earthquake strengthened people-to-people ties, which are, however, strictly controlled by watchful officials on both sides though the bus service across the Line of Control in Kashmir increased hopes

for regional peace. But the continued human rights abuses in the Valley, widespread anger over thousands of killings and lack of any substantive move on the dispute itself only allowed a guarded optimism.

GLOSSARY

Ahl-i-Kitab	People of the Book
Alim	Muslim religious scholar
Ayatollah	preeminent shia jurist/imam
Bhagat	a Hindu holy man
Chador	a loose wraparound for women
Chardiwari	four walls of the home
Da'awa/Dawah	invitation to Islam
Fatwa	a religious decree
Fiqh/Fiqah	jurisprudence
Hajj	annual pilgrimage to the Hejaz, Arabia
Ijtiha'ad	innovation
Imam	a religious leader
Jahliya	ignorance
Jihad	holy struggle
Jihadi	holy warrior
Madrassa	a Muslim seminary
Mahdi	promised revivalist (Messiah)
Mai bap	lit: parents
Maulvi/Mullah	Muslim religious leader
Muezzin	caller to prayers
Mujaddid	revivalist
Mujahid	one who undertakes *jihad*
Mujahideen	pl. of *mujahid*
Muhajir	Muslim migrant
Muhajireen	pl. of *muhajir*
Mujta'ahid	a senior shia Muslim theologian
Pir	sufi saint
Salafiya	back-to-roots
Sajjada nishin	successor to a sufi
Sharia/Shariat	Islamic law; jurisprudence

Shia/shi'ite	follower of the Caliph Ali, a doctrinal *Muslim sect*
Silsilah	a sufi order
Sufi	a mystic
Sunni	lit. a follower of the Prophetic traditions, a majority doctrinal sect
Tajdeed	revival
Taliban	plural of *taleb/talib*: students
Taqli'd	uncritiqued imitation
Tariqa	sufi way; order
Ulama	Muslim religious scholars (pl. of *alim*)
Ummah	transnational Muslimhood

BIBLIOGRAPHY

Selected Articles, Reports and Books

Abrahamian, E., *Iran Between Two Revolutions*, Princeton, 1982.

Abu Rabi, M. Ibrahim, *Intellectual Origins of Islamic Resurgence in the Modern Arab World*, Albany, 1996.

Aburish, Said K., *Saddam Hussein: The Politics of Revenge*, London, 2000.

Advani, L. K., et al., *Hindus Betrayed*, New Delhi, 1995.

Ahmad, Eqbal, *Confronting Empire*, London, 2000.

Akbar, M. J., *The Shadow of Swords*, Delhi, 2002.

Alagiah, George, *A Passage to Africa*, London, 2002.

Albright, Madeleine, *Madam Secretary: A Memoirs*, London, 2003.

Ali, Tariq, *Bush in Babylon: The Recolonisation of Iraq*, London, 2003.

Ali, Tariq, *The Clash of Fundamentalisms: Crusades, Jihads and Modernity*, London, 2002.

Anonymous (A former CIA Official), *Imperial Hubris: Why the West is losing War on Terror?* Washington, 2004.

Armstrong, Karen, *Islam: A Short History*, London, 2000.

Armstrong, Karen, *Muhammad: a Biography of the Prophet*, London, 1995.

Asad, Muhammad, *The Road to Mecca*, London, 1998.

Asher, Michael, *Lawrence: The Uncrowned King of Arabia*, London, 1998.

Austin, Allan D., *African Muslims in Antebellum America*, London, 1997.

Bacevich, Andrew J., *American Empire: The Realities and Consequences of US Diplomacy*, Cambridge, Mass., 2003

Bamford, James, *A Pretext for War. 9/11, Iraq and the Abuse of America's Intelligence Agencies*, New York, 2004.

Barber, Benjamin R., *Jihad Vs. McWorld*, London, 2003.

Barltrop, Richard, *Muslims in Europe, post-9/11: Understanding and Responding to the Muslim World* (a conference report), Oxford, 2003.

Bennett-Jones, Owen, *Pakistan: Eye of Storm*, London, 2002.

Bergen, Peter, *Holy War Inc.: Inside the Secret World of Osama bin Laden*, New York, 2002.

Berman, Paul, *Terror and Liberalism*, London, 2002.

Blix, Hans, *Disarming Iraq: The Search for Weapons of Mass Destruction*, London, 2004.

Blumenthal, Sidney, *The Clinton's Wars*, London, 2003.

Bodansky, Yossef, *Bin Laden: The Man Who Declared War on America*, New York, 1999.

Buchanan, Patrick J., *When the Right Went Wrong*, New York, 2004.

Buchanan, Patrick J., *The Death of the West: How Dying Populations and Immigrant Invasions Imperil our Country and Civilization?* New York, 2001.

Bulliet, Richard W., *Islam: The View from the Edge*, New York, 1994.

Burke, Jason, *Al-Qaeda: Casting a Shadow of Terror*, London, 2003.

Buruma, Ian, and Margalit, Avishai, *Occidentalism: A Short History of Anti-Westernism*, London, 2004.

Byron, Robert, *The Road to Oxiana*, London, 2004 (reprint).

Carew, Tom, *Jihad*, Edinburgh, 2001.

Catherwood, Christopher, *Christians, Muslims, and Islamic Rage: What is Going on and Why it Happened?* Grand Rapids, 2003.

Cheney, Lynne V., *Telling the Truth: Why Our Culture and Our Country Have Stopped Making Sense*, New York, 1996.

Chomsky, Noam, *Rogue States: The Rule of Force in World Affairs*, London, 2002.

Chomsky, Noam, *9/11*, New York, 2002.

Chua, Amy, *World on Fire: How Exporting Free Market Democracy Breeds Ethnic Hatred and Global Hostility*, London, 2003.

Clarke, Richard A., *Against All Enemies: Inside America's War on Terror*, New York, 2004.

Clinton, Hillary Rodham, *Living History*, New York, 2003.

Clinton, William, *My Life*, London, 2004.

Cockburn, Andrew, and Cockburn, Patrick, *Saddam Hussein: An American Obsession*, London, 2002.

Cooley, John K., *Unholy Wars: Afghanistan, America and International Terrorism*, London, 2000.

Cooper, Robert, *The Breaking of the Nations: Order and Chaos in the Twentieth-First Century*, London, *2003*.

Corbin, Jane, *The Base*, London, 2003.

Coughlin, Con, *Saddam: The Secret Life*, London, 2002.

Coulter, Ann, *Treason*, New York, 2003.

Coulter, Ann, *Slander: Liberal Lies About the American Right*, New York, 2002.

Crile, George, *My Enemy's Enemy: The Story of the Largest Covert Operation in History. The Arming of the Mujahideen by the CIA*, London, 2003.

Curtis, Mark, *Web of Deceit: Britain's Real Role in the World*, London, 2003.

Dalrymple, William, *The White Mughals*, London, 2003.

Daniel, Norman, *Islam and the West*, Oxford, 2000.

Domke, David, *God Willing? Political Fundamentalism in the White House, the 'War on Terror' and the Echoing Press*, London, 2004.

Dubashi, Jay, *The Road to Ayodhya*, New Delhi, 1992.

Eaton, Guy, *Remembering God: Reflections on Islam*, Cambridge, 2000.

Eaton, Guy, *Islam and the Destiny of Man*, Cambridge, 1994.

Eaton, Richard M., *Essays on Islamic and Indian History*, New Delhi, 2001.

Esposito, John L., *The Islamic Threat: Myth or Reality?* New York, 1993.

Esposito, John L., and Voll, John D., *Makers of Contemporary Islam*, New York, 2001.

Fallaci, Oriana, *The Rage and the Pride*, New York, 2003.

Fazlur Rahman, *Revival and Reform in Islam: A Study of Islamic Fundamentalism*, Oxford, 2003.

Fazlur Rahman, *Islam and Modernity: Transformation of an Intellectual Tradition*, Chicago, 1982.

Ferguson, Niall, *Colossus: The Rise and Fall of the American Power*, London, 2004.

Fisk, Robert, *The Great War for Civilisation: The Conquest of the Middle East*, London, 2005.

Fisher, Michael H., *The First Indian Author in English: Dean Mahomed (1759-1851) in India, Ireland, and England*, Delhi, 1996.

Fox, Jeremy, *Chomsky and Globalisation*, London, 2002.

Friedman, Thomas L., *Longitudes and Attitudes: Exploring the World Before and After September*, London, 2003.

Frum, David, *The Right Man*, London, 2003.

Frum, David, and, Perle, Richard, *An End to Evil: How to Win the War on Terror?* New York, 2003.

Grare, Frederic, *Political Islam in the Indian Subcontinent: The Jamaat-i-Islami*, Delhi, 2002.

Gray, John, *Al-Qaeda and What it Means to be Modern*, London, 2003.

Griffin, Michael, *Reaping the Whirlwind: The Taliban Movement in Afghanistan*, London, 2001.

Gunaratna, Rohan, *Inside Al-Qaeda: Global Network of Terror*, London, 2002.

Haddad, Yvonne Y., and Smith, Jane I., *Mission to America: Five Islamic Sectarian Communities in North America*, Gainesville, 1993.

Halliday, Fred, *Two Hours that Shook the World*, London, 2001.

Halliday, Fred, *Islam & the Myth of Confrontation*, London, 1996.

Halper, Stefan, & Clarke, Jonathan, *America Alone: The Neo-Conservatives and the Global Order*, Cambridge, 2004.

Hansen, G.H., *Militant Islam*, New York, 1979.

Harman, Chris, *Prophet and the Proletariat: Islamic Fundamentalism, Class and Revolution*, London, 2002.

Haykel, Bernard, *Revival and Reform in Islam: The Legacy of Muhammad al-Shawkani*, Cambridge, 2003.

Hersch, Seymour, *Chain of Command: The Road from 9/11 to Abu Ghraib*, New York, 2004.

Hertsgaard, Mark, *Eagle's Shadow: Why America Fascinates and Infuriates the World*, London, 2002.

Hillenbrand, Carole, *The Crusades: Islamic Perspectives*, Edinburgh, 1999.

Hitti, Philip K., *History of the Arabs*, London, 1961.

Howard, Roger, *Iran in Crisis: Nuclear Ambitions and the American Response*, London, 2004.

Hourani, Albert, *Islam in European Thought,* Cambridge, 1993.

Huntington, Samuel P., *Who Are We: America's Great Debate,* New York, 2004.

Huntington, Samuel P., *The Clash of Civilizations,* London, 1997.

Hutchinson, Robert, *Weapons of Mass Destruction,* London, 2003.

Iganski, Paul, and Kosmin, Barry (eds.) *A New Antisemitism? Debating Judeophobia in 21ˢᵗ Century Britain,* London, 2003.

Ignatieff, Michael, *Empire Lite: Nation-building in Bosnia, Kosovo and Afghanistan,* London, 2003.

Irfani, Suroosh, *Revolutionary Islam in Iran: Popular Liberation or Religious Dictatorship?* London, 1983.

Jamie, Kathleen, *Among Muslims: Meetings at the Frontiers of Pakistan,* London, 2002.

Jerichow, A., and Simonsen, J., *Islam in a Changing World,* London, 1997.

Jog, B. W., *Threat of Islam: Indian Dimension,* Mumbai, 1994.

Jurgensmeyer, Mark, *Terror in the Mind of God,* Berkeley, 2001.

Kabbani, Rana, *Imperial Fiction: Europe's Myths of Orient,* London, 1994.

Kaplan, Lawrence F., & Kristol, William, *The War over Iraq,* San Francisco, 2003.

Kaplan, Robert D., *Soldiers of God: With Islamic Warriors in Afghanistan and Pakistan,* London, 2001.

Kagan, Robert, *Paradise and Power: America and Europe in the New World Order,* New York, 2003.

Kaldor, Mary et al. (eds.) *Global Civil Society 2001,* Oxford, 2001.

Kedourie, Eli, *Democracy and Arab Political Culture,* Washington, 1992.

Keegan, John, *The Iraq War: The 21-Day Conflict and its Aftermath,* London, 2004.

Kelsey, John and Johnson, James T., (eds.) *Just War and Jihad: Historical and Theoretical Perspectives on War and Peace in Western and Islamic Traditions,* New York, 1991.

Kepel, Gilles, *The Roots of Radical Islam,* trans. by J. Rothschild, London, 2005.

Kepel, Gilles, *The War for Muslim Mind: Islam and the West,* trans. by Pascale Ghazaleh, London, 2004.

Kepel, Gilles, *Jihad: The Trail of Political Islam,* London, 2003.

Kepel, Gilles, *Bad Moon Rising: A Chronicle of the Middle East Today,* London, 2003.

Kepel, Gilles, *Allah in the West,* Oxford, 1997.

Khan, M. Asghar, (ed.) *Islam, Politics and the State. The Pakistan Experience,* London, 1985.

Kimmerling, Baruch, *Politicide: Ariel Sharon's War Against Palestinians,* London, 2003.

Klein, Naomi, *Fences and Windows,* London, 2002.

Kramer, Martin, *The Salience of Islamic Fundamentalism,* London, 1995.

Kristol, Irving, *Neoconservatism: The Autobiography of an Idea,* New York, 1995.

Lamb, Christina, *The Sewing Circles of Herat: My Afghan Years,* London, 2002.

Landau, Jacob, *The Politics of Pan-Islam*, London, 1994.

Lawrence, T. E., *Seven Pillars of Wisdom*, London, 1997.

Levy, Bernard-Henri, *Who Killed Daniel Pearl?* transl. by James X. Mitchell, London, 2004.

Levy, Bernard-Henri, *War, Evil and the End of History*, transl. by Charlotte Mandell, London, 2004.

Lewis, Bernard, *From Babel to Dragomans*, London, 2004.

Lewis, Bernard, *The Crisis of Islam: Holy War and Unholy Terror*, London, 2003.

Lewis, Bernard, *What Went Wrong? Western Impact and Middle Eastern Response*, London, 2003.

Lewis, Bernard, *The Assassins: A Radical Sect in Islam*, London, 2003.

Lewis, Bernard, *Islam and the West*, Oxford, 1994.

Lewis, Bernard, *The Arabs in History*, Oxford, 1993.

Lewis, Bernard, *The Muslim Discovery of Europe*, London, 1982.

Lewis, Bernard, *Race and Slavery in the Middle East*, London, 1974.

Lewis, Bernard, and Holt, P. M., (eds.) *Historians of the Middle East*, Oxford, 1962.

Lings, Martin, *Muhammad: His Life Based on the Earliest Sources*, London, 2003.

Mailer, Norman, *Why Are We At War?* New York, 2003.

Maley, William, (ed.) *Fundamentalism Reborn: Afghanistan and the Taliban*, London, 1998.

Malik, Aftab Ahmad, (ed.) *The Empire and the Crescent: Global Implications for the New American Century*, Bristol, 2003.

Malik, Iftikhar H., *Jihad, Hindutva and the Taliban: South Asia at the Crossroads*, Oxford, 2005.

Malik, Iftikhar H., *Islam and Modernity: Muslims in Europe and the United States*, London, 2004.

Malik, Iftikhar H., *Islam, Globalisation and Modernity: The Tragedy of Bosnia*, Lahore, 2004.

Malik, Iftikhar H., *Religious Minorities in Pakistan*, London, 2002.

Malik, Iftikhar H., *Islam, Nationalism and the West: Issues of Identity in Pakistan*, Oxford, 1999.

Malik, Iftikhar H., *State and Civil Society in Pakistan: Politics of Authority, Ideology and Ethnicity*, Oxford, 1997.

Malik, Iftikhar H., *U.S.-South Asian Relations, 1940-47: American Attitudes towards Pakistan Movement*, Oxford, 1991.

Malik, Iftikhar H., *U.S.-South Asia Relations, 1784-1940: A Historical Perspective*, Islamabad, 1988.

Malik, Iftikhar H., 'The Afghan Conflict: Islam, the West and Identity Politics in South Asia', *Indo-British Review*, XXIII, 2, 2002.

Malik, Iftikhar H., 'Pakistan in 2001: The Afghanistan Crisis and the Rediscovery of the Frontline State', *Asian Survey*, 42:1, 2002.

Malik, Iftikhar H., 'Turkey at the Crossroads: Encountering Modernity and

Tradition', *Journal of South Asian and Middle Eastern Studies*, XXIV, 2, 2001.

Malik, Iftikhar H., 'Military Coup in Pakistan: Business as Usual or Democracy on Hold!' *The Round Table*, 360, 2001.

Mamdani, Mahmood, *Good Muslim, Bad Muslim*, New York, 2003.

Manji, Irshad, *The Trouble with Islam: A Wake-up Call for Honesty and Change*, London, 2004.

Mann, James, *Rise of the Vulcans*, London, 2004.

Mann, Michael, *Incoherent Empire*, London, 2003.

Mansfield, Stephen, *The Faith of George W. Bush*, New York, 2003.

Marsden, Peter, *The Taliban: War, Religion and the New Order in Afghanistan*, London, 1998.

Matar, Nabil, *Islam in Britain, 1558-1685*, Cambridge, 1998.

Matinuddin, Kamal, *The Taliban Phenomenon*, Karachi, 1999.

Mawdudi, Abul Ala, *Tafheem Al-Quran: Towards Understanding Islam*, transl. by Zafar I. Ansari, Leicester, 1988-90.

Mawdudi, Abul Ala, *Al-Jihad fil Islam*, Lahore, 1947.

Mawdudi, Abul Ala, Banna, H., and Qutb, Sayyid, *Al-Jihad fi Sabil Allah*, Cairo, 1977.

Mazower, Mark, *Salonika, City of Ghosts: Christians, Muslims and Jews, 1430-1950*, London, 2004.

Meyer, Christopher, *DC Confidential*, London, 2005.

Milton-Edwards, Beverley, *Islam and Politics in the Contemporary World*, Cambridge, 2004.

Monbiot, George, *The Age of Consent: A Manifesto for a New World Order*, London, 2003.

Moore, James, and Slater, Wayne, *Bush's Brain*, Hoboken (New Jersey), 2003.

Moore, Michael, *Stupid White Men*, London, 2002.

Moore, Robin, *Task Force Dagger: The Hunt for Bin Laden*, London, 2003.

Muir, William, *The Life of Mahomet*, London, 1877.

Nadwi, Abul Hasan, *Inviting to the Way of Allah*, Leicester, 1996.

Nadwi, Abul Hasan, *From the Depth of the Heart in America*, trans. by M. Arif Kidwai, Lucknow, 1978.

Nadwi, Abul Hasan, *Saviours of Islamic Thought*, vol. 1, trans. by Mohiuddin Ahmad, Lucknow, 1976.

Naipaul, V.S., *Beyond Belief: Islamic Excursions Among the Converted*, London, 1999.

Nasr, Seyyed Vali Reza, *Mawdudi & The Making of Islamic Revolution*, Oxford, 1996.

National Commission on Terrorist Attacks Upon the United States (chaired by Thomas H. Kean), *The 9/11 Commission Report*, Washington, D.C. & London, 2004.

Naughtie, James, *The Accidental American: Tony Blair and the Presidency*, London, 2004.

Nye Jr., Joseph, *The Paradox of American Power*, Oxford, 2002.

Pearl, Marianne, *A Mighty Heart*, London, 2003.

Philo, Greg, & Barry, Mike, *Bad News from Israel*, London, 2004.

Pilger, John, *The New Rulers of the World*, London, 2003.

Pipes, Daniel, *Militant Islam Reaches America*, New York, 2001.

Pipes, Daniel, *Slave Soldiers and Islam: The Genesis of a Military System*, New Haven , 1981.

Piscatori, James, (ed.) *Islam and the Political Process*, New York, 1983.

Powell, Avril, *Muslims and Missionaries in Pre-Mutiny India*, London, 1993.

Powers, Samantha, *A Problem from Hell: America in the Age of Genocide*, London, 2003.

Rai, Baljit, *Is India Going Islamic?* Chandigarh, 1994.

Rai, Milan, *War Plan: The Reason against War on Iraq*, London, 2002.

Ramadan, Tariq, *Western Muslims and the Future of Islam*, Oxford, 2003.

Rashid, Ahmed, *Jihad: The Rise of Militant Islam in Central Asia*, New Haven, 2002.

Rashid, Ahmed, *Taliban: Islam, Oil and the New Great Game in Central Asia*, London, 2000.

Reeve, Simon, *The New Jackals: Ramzi Yousef, Osama bin Laden and the Future of Terrorism*, London, 2000.

Ridley, Yvonne, *In the Hands of the Taliban*, London, 2002.

Ritter, Scott, *Frontier Justice, Weapons of Mass Destruction and the Bushwhacking of America*, New York, 2003.

Robinson, Adam, *Bin Laden: Behind the Mask of Terrorism*, Edinburgh, 2001.

Rodinson, Maxime, *Islam and Capitalism*, trans. by Brian Pearce, London, 1974.

Rodinson, Maxime, *Mohammed*, London, 1993.

Rogerson, Barnaby, *The Prophet Muhammad: A Biography*, London, 2003.

Rose, John, *The Myths of Zionism*, London, 2004.

Roxburgh, Angus, *Preaching of Hate: The Rise of the Far Right*, London, 2002.

Roy, Arundhati, *The Ordinary Person's Guide to Empire*, London, 2004.

Roy, Arundhati, *War Talk*, London, 2003.

Roy, Olivier, *The Failure of Political Islam*, London, 1994.

Roy, Olivier, *Islam and Resistance in Afghanistan*, Cambridge, 1984.

Rubin, Barnett R., *The Fragmentation of Afghanistan: State Formation and Collapse in the International System*, New Haven, 1995.

Ruthven, Malise, *A Fury for God: The Islamist Attack on America*, London, 2002.

Sacks, Jonathan, *The Dignity of Difference: How to Avoid the Clash of Civilizations?* London, 2003 (revised).

Safi, Omid, (ed.) *Progressive Muslims on Justice, Gender, and Pluralism*, Oxford, 2003.

Said, Edward, *Covering Islam: How the Media and the Experts Determine how we see the Rest of the World*, London, 1997.

Said, Edward, *Orientalism*, London, 1978.

Sajoo, Amyn B., (ed.) *Civil Society in the Muslim World*, London, 2002.

Sardar, Ziauddin, *Desperately Seeking Paradise. Journeys of a Sceptical Muslim,* London, 2004.

Sardar, Ziauddin & Davies, Meryl W., *Why Do People Hate America?* London, 2002.

Sayeed, Khalid B., *Western Dominance and Political Islam: Challenge and Response,* Albany, 1995.

Schimmel, Annemarie, *Islam: An Introduction,* Albany, 1992.

Sells, Michael, & Qureshi, Emran (eds.) *The New Crusades,* New York, 2003.

Shahak, Israel and Mezvinsky, Norton, *Jewish Fundamentalism in Israel,* London, 2004.

Shahin, Emad, *Political Ascent: Contemporary Islamic Movements in North Africa,* London, 1997.

Sierstad, Asne, *The Bookseller of Kabul,* London, 2003.

Sikand, Yoginder, *Sacred Spaces: Exploring Traditions of Shared Faith in India,* New Delhi, 2003.

Simpson, John, *News From No Man's Land,* London, 2002.

Singh, Patwant, *The World According to Washington: An Asian View,* Cheltenham, 2004.

Soros, George, *The Bubble of American Supremacy,* New York, 2004.

Stern, Jessica, 'Pakistan's Jihad Culture', *Foreign Affairs,* November-December 2000.

Stothard, Peter, *30 Days: A Month at the Heart of Blair's War,* London, 2003.

Strauss, Leo, *Natural Right and History,* Chicago, 1965

The Runnymede Trust, *Islamophobia,* London, 1997.

Todd, Emmanuel, *After the Empire,* London, 2004.

Transparency International, *Global Corruption Report, 2004,* Pluto, 2004.

UNDP/Regional Bureau for Arab States, *The Arab Human Development Report 2002: Creating Opportunities for Future Generations,* New York, 2002.

Unger, Craig, *House of Bush, House of Saud: The Hidden Relationship Between the World's Two Most Powerful Dynasties,* London, 2004.

Vertovec, Steven and Peach, Ceri, (eds.) *Islam in Europe: The Politics of Religion and Community,* London, 1997.

Vidal, Gore, *Imperial America,* London, 2004.

Wadud, Amina, *Qur'an and Women: Rereading the Sacred Text from a Woman's Perspective,* Oxford, 1999.

Watt, W. Montgomery, *The Influence of Islam on Medieval Europe,* Edinburgh, 1982.

Watt, W. Montgomery, *The Majesty That was Islam,* London, 1974.

Watt, W. Montgomery, *Islamic Political Thought,* Edinburgh, 1968.

Wheen, Francis, *How Mumbo Jumbo Conquered the World?* London, 2003.

Weiner, Myron, 'Peoples and states in new order?' *Third World Quarterly,* 13, 2, 1992

Wheatcroft, Andrew, *Infidels: The Conflict between Christendom and Islam, 638-2002,* London, 2003.

Winchester, Simon, *Krakatoa: The Day the World Exploded*, London, 2002.

Woodward, Bob, *Plan of Attack*, New York, 2004.

Woodward, Bob, *Bush at War*, New York, 2002.

Zakaria, Fareed, *The Future of Freedom*, New York, 2003.

Zakaria, Rafique, *The Widening Divide: An Insight into Hindu-Muslim Relations*, New Delhi, 1995.

Zaman, Muhammad Qasim, *The Ulama in Contemporary Islam: Custodians of Change*, Princeton, 2002.

Zebiri, Kate, *Muslims and Christians Face to Face*, Oxford, 1997.

Newspapers, Magazines, Websites and Videos:

Al-Ahram
BBC
Channel 4
Cherwell
CNN
Commentary
Daily Times
Dawn
Express
Financial Times
Guardian
http://www.aiindex.mnet.fr
http://www.fas.org/irp/congress/1992_rpt/bcci/04crime.html
http://www.gush-shalom.org/archives/article283.html
http://www.hrw.org
http://www.opendemocracy.net
http://www.people-press.org
http://www.rediff.com/news/2003/aug/16pak.htm
http:// www.usinfo.state.gov/media/Archive_index/Illegal_weapons_in_Fallujah. html
Independent
International Herald Tribune
Los Angeles Times
Nation
New Internationalist
New Statesman
News
Newsweek
New Yorker
New York Times
Observer

Outlook
Sky
Sun
Sunday Times
Daily & Sunday Telegraph
Times
Times Higher Education Supplement
Washington Post

INDEX